MW01130049

To my wife

Merry

and our daughters

Eileen and Sue-Lynn

The material of Chapter One originated from my notes on how the late Mlle. Yvonne Combe taught our daughters. Mlle. Combe was Debussy's disciple and helped transcribe his new compositions as he played them out on the piano. She performed that incredible Second Piano Concerto by Saint Saens with the composer conducting. Every audience that attended recitals by her students, especially when they played Debussy and Saint Saens, was mesmerized. This book had to be written: without it, her passing would have deprived this world of a priceless art.

Chapter One: PIANO TECHNIQUE

Chapter Two: TUNING YOUR PIANO

References

March 6, 2009
Copyright © 2009, copy permitted if author's name,
Chuan C. Chang, and this copyright statement are included.
ISBN: 1-4196-7859-0
ISBN-13: 978-419678592
Library of Congress Control Number: 2007907498
Order this book at www.booksurge.com or Amazon.com

This entire book can be downloaded free at:
http://www.pianopractice.org/

Table of Contents

Request: to those who have found this material useful, please make an effort to let at least two people know about my web site, so that we can start a chain reaction of ever more people that will be informed of this site.

I am looking for volunteers to translate this book into any language. See "Notes for Translators" on P. 257. Please email me at cc88m@aol.com to discuss this matter. This book is presently being translated into German, Polish, Italian, Spanish, French, Simplified and Traditional Chinese, and Japanese.

Teachers can use this book as a textbook for teaching practice methods. It can save you a lot of time, allowing you to concentrate on teaching music. The Preface is a good overview of the book, and the book reviews in the Reference section contains detailed reviews of the most relevant books.

Students: If you don't have a teacher, pick any piece of music you want to learn (that is within your technical skill level) and start practicing it using the methods described here; the methods are arranged roughly in the order in which you will need them as you start learning a new piece. In either case (with or without a teacher), read the entire book quickly the first time. Skip any section that you think is not relevant or is too detailed; do not try to understand every concept or to remember anything – read it like a science fiction novel (but none of this is fiction) – you just want to get acquainted with the book and get some idea of where certain topics are discussed. Finally, read as much of the Testimonial section as you find interesting. Then re-start from where you think the book gives material that you need; most people will need to read all of Chapter One, sections I and II. Then you can skip around to specific topics that apply to the composition you are learning. If you don't have a clear idea of what compositions to learn, this book cites many examples, from beginner material (Chapter One, III.18) to intermediate; therefore, in your first reading, look for where these examples/suggestions are.

Testimonials

(Received prior to July, 2004)

These testimonials illustrate the hopes, trials, tribulations, and triumphs, of pianists and piano teachers. I am heartened by the number of teachers who provided testimonials and by their indication that they are having more success with their students by using these types of methods. It seems inescapable that teachers who conduct research and improve their teaching methods are more successful. Numerous pianists mentioned that they were taught all wrong by previous teachers. Many, who liked their teachers, noted that these teachers used methods similar to those in this book. There is almost uniform agreement on what is right and what is wrong; therefore, when you follow the scientific approach, you don't get into the situation in which people cannot agree on what is right. I was impressed by how quickly some people picked up these methods.

The excerpts have been edited minimally, but irrelevant details have been excised so as not to waste the readers' time. I want to thank everyone who wrote; they have helped me to improve the book. I can't get over the fact that readers keep writing the book for me (i.e., I could insert their remarks in my book, and they would fit perfectly!). In the following, I have not selected just the flattering remarks; I chose material that seemed significant (educational), whether positive or critical. Entries in [….] are my comments:

1. [From a Christian Minister]
This book is the Piano Bible. I have made such tremendous progress since purchasing it [1st edition book]. I continue to recommend it to others.

2. [In Jan., 2003, I received this email (with permission)]
My name is Marc, and I am 17 years old. I just started playing the piano about a month ago and have been reading your book, The Fundamentals of Piano Practice. . . . I do not have an instructor yet, but am in the process of looking for one . . . . [followed by a series of precocious questions for a young person with so little piano experience. I answered his questions as well as I could; then in May, 2004, I received this astounding email]

I don't quite expect you to remember me, but I sent you an email a little more than a year ago. . . I would like to let you know how piano has been coming along for me using your method. I began playing the piano about Christmas of 2002, using your method from the beginning. Mid-March of 2003, I entered my high school's concerto competition for fun and experience – not in the hopes of winning their $500 scholarship. I unexpectedly won first place, competing against more seasoned pianists of up to 10 yrs. It did shock the judges when I told them I had been playing for 3 months. A few days ago, I won this year's competition, as well. In other words, progress has come very quickly. Such progress is one of the greatest motivators (aside from the general love of music), so I can now see myself playing – and improving in – the piano for the rest of my life. And, though I must give my teachers credit as well, your method is my foundation upon which they build, and I believe it is the main reason for my progress. However, I still consider myself a beginner . . . . My website has all of the recordings which I have made to date (18). . . . recently, I have been re-recording Chopin's "Raindrop" prelude, Scarlatti's K.466, and Bach's Invention in F major. . . . My next recording will be Bach's Sinfonia in E minor, and I plan to have that done by the end of next week. Your book is far more than any lover of music and the piano could expect, and I cannot thank you enough for the help you have given to me and so many other aspiring pianists . . . . [Go to the website and listen to those amazing recordings!! You can even find him at the Music Download web site (search Marc McCarthy).]

3. [From a respected, experienced piano teacher.]
I just skimmed your new section [on parallel set exercises] and thought I'd share my initial reaction. As the Queen Regent of Exercise-Haters, I've lobbied loud and strong for the criminalization of Hanon et al, and was at first aghast to think you may have joined the downtrodden masses of the pseudo-voodoo-esque practitioners, hopelessly, helplessly, repeating, repeating, ... Anyway, to get to the point, I do see a point of merit in your approach, IF IF IF the student follows your COMPLETE directions and uses the described key combinations as a diagnostic tool – NOT to repeat each and every combination as a daily routine. As a diagnostic tool and subsequent remedy, you've succeeded marvelously! There was something familiar about your exercises, so I dug around at the studio today and found the Technische Studien by Louis Plaidy, Edition Peters, first printing ca 1850. Although Plaidy's philosophy concerning the use of his exercises is much different from yours, the actual notes printed on the page follow nearly to the letter (tee, hee, I should say to the note) what you have described in your exercise chapter. Plaidy's exercises were highly respected in Europe throughout the late 1800's and were used during that time at the Conservatory in Leipzig. Plaidy himself was quite a sought-after instructor, with several of his (students were) accepted into Liszt's inner circle and/or having some sort of success on the concert stage. You're in the company of greatness!

4. I am curious to know if you know of the work of Guy Maier. Does his approach with "impulse" practice of 5 finger patterns go along with the "parallel sets" you mention? Maier does use the principle of repeating one note with each finger as the others are held quietly at the key surface as one of the 5 finger exercises. Thinking Fingers was one of the books of exercises Maier wrote with Herbert Bradshaw in the early 1940s. One of his first 5 finger exercises that seems to mirror what

you have said about "quads" repetitions on one note using one finger is as follows:

a. Single fingers in repeated note impulses of 1, 2, 3, 4, 8, and 16.

b. Practice each finger separately, depress other keys lightly or hold fingers silently at key top position.

c. Using CDEFG in right hand, place 5 fingers on these notes one octave above middle C, right hand thumb on C.

d. Similarly with left hand, one octave below middle C, with fifth finger on C.

e. Exercise hands separately; starting with right hand thumb play one impulse C, then release, then two impulses, etc., up to 16. Repeat with each finger, then do the left hand.

[See my Exercise section III.7b; it is amazing how we independently arrived at groups of "quads" (four repetitions), up to 4 quads (16 repetitions) for this exercise which is almost identical to my Exercise #1.]

f. Beginners will have to do the impulses slowly, working up to full speed (and here I think your "quads" come into play – so many repetitions per second is the goal).

Maier mentions 16 as his limit. He gives a great many patterns for using this approach to 5 finger impulse exercises, in Book 1 and Book 2 of *Thinking Fingers* published by Belwin Mills Inc., NY, NY in 1948. I think Maier was striving to help students get the facility they needed without the endless repetitions of Hanon, Pischna, et al.

5. Please send me your book – I've been a piano teacher for over 50 years, still eager to learn.

6. [This testimonial is an eye opener: it teaches us about one of the most frequently misdiagnosed problems that stops us from playing fast.]

At a young age, I started, and then quit piano. Then as a teenager, I went to a [famous] conservatory and tried for years to acquire technique but failed miserably and ended up with an engineering career. Years later, I have returned to piano (Clavinova) and am trying to do what I failed to do years ago. One of the reasons I stopped practicing is that my wife and son would get irritated when they heard me repeat passages over and over; the Clavinova allows me to practice guiltlessly at any hour. I read your web page and was fascinated. Wish I had thought of some of your ideas years ago. I have a question and I can't seem to get an answer that makes any sense, yet it is such a basic question. I was taught that when you play piano, you support the weight of your arm on each finger that plays. Gravity. You never push down, you must be relaxed. So I asked my teachers how to play pianissimo. The answer was that you play closer to the keys. This does not work for me. [Long discussion of various methods of trying to play pianissimo with arm weight and why they don't work. Seems he can play pianissimo only by consciously lifting his hands off the keys. Also, since everything tends to come out forte, speed is a problem.] Would you kindly answer this question for me? What does one do with ones arm weight when one plays pianissimo? I have read many books about playing the piano and have spoken with many accomplished pianists. It is one thing to know how to play anything and it is quite another to be able to teach someone how to play. [I could not have said this any better!] Your writings are brilliant and in many ways revolutionary, I knew instinctively that if anyone could help me you could.

[After such a compliment, I had to do something, so I read the account of his difficulties carefully and came to the conclusion that he must, after so many years of trying, be unwittingly pushing down on the piano, almost as if he were hypnotized. I told him to find a way to see if he was actually pushing down – not an easy task. Then came this reply.]

Thank you for your response. Truth is best examined through extremes. Your suggestion gave me the idea that maybe I should ALWAYS play like I play MY pianissimo – by lifting my hands off the keys. I rushed to my Hanon, and YES! I can play much faster! I quickly rushed to the Bach Prelude II that I could never play to speed (144) and I always had troubles getting the fingers to land together when playing fast, and at speeds above 120 the fingers were landing like one note together. No fumbles, no strain. Not only that, I can play piano or forte as fast as I want. It feels so incredibly EASY! Just discovered it now! I can't believe this. [Long discussion of how, through the years, he had come to equate arm weight with pushing down, mainly caused by a fear of not understanding the teacher who was a strict, arm weight disciplinarian. This is actually something I have been very suspicious of, about the arm weight method: that so much emphasis on arm weight and overly strict discipline might cause some type of neurosis or misunderstanding – perhaps even some type of hypnosis.] A huge wall just crumbled and now after so many years of thought and hours of practice (I practiced up to 10 hours a day at the conservatory and still only memorized music without ever improving my technique) and now I can see beyond. I discovered that I have the ability to play faster than I ever dreamed I could (just tried the C major scale and I was shocked that this was me playing) with full range of sound that I want WITHOUT TENSION. [A long description of all the new things he is now doing and comparing them to his previous years of struggles and criticisms from others.] I have you to thank for this. Yours was the only book I have ever read that offered enough variation from the mainline to get me to finally free my mind from a huge misconception. I was pushing down, not letting go. My arms simply don't weigh a ton, but they are free. Because I was afraid of my teacher and was obsessed with the weight of my arms, I was subconsciously bearing down. I never dared play PPP for her. I knew how, but I was certain it was the wrong technique. [I am afraid this happens frequently with youngsters; they don't understand the teacher but are afraid to ask, and end up assuming the wrong thing.] What she should have told me was DON'T EVER PUSH DOWN; instead, I fixated on the weight of my arms as being key to everything. [A youngster must push down to put any "weight" on his arms! How are you going to explain that this is wrong to a child who hasn't studied physics?] She also never allowed me to play quickly. [This is another comment I have heard from students of strict arm weight teachers – speed is a no-no until certain milestones are achieved; although we must exercise caution when practicing for speed, slowing down is not the quickest way to speed.] Because I was tense, and she said I would never play quickly if I'm tense. In your book you say that we have to play fast to discover technique. I was never allowed to! Your book and your email freed the chains in my mind that held me captive for all these years. Thank you so very much. I cannot describe how grateful I am to you and your insight. [Although my comments seem to be directed against the arm weight school, that is not the case – similar difficulties apply to any teaching based on insufficient knowledge in the hands of strict disciplinarian teachers. Unfortunately, a large number of piano teachers has historically adopted inflexible teaching methods because of a lack of a theoretical understanding and rational explanations. For systematic treatments of speed, see sections II.13 and especially III.7.i]

7. I found your book on the internet and consider myself very lucky. Thank you very much for making such a great effort on describing the piano technique and practice habits that make sense. I am a piano teacher. I've only started to read the book and have already applied some practice techniques with my students. They liked it and I liked it too. The practice becomes so much more interesting. Do you know the book called "The Amateur Pianist's Companion" by James Ching, published by Keith Prowse Music Publishing Co., 1956, London. This book may be out of print, but I found it second hand at:
http://dogbert.abebooks.com/abe/BookSearch
You might be interested because "the detail of correct postures, movement and conditions as outlined in this book are the result of extensive researches into the physiological-mechanics of piano technique carried out by the author in conjunction with Professor H. Hartridge, Professor of Physiology, and H. T. Jessop, Lecturer in Mechanics and Applied Mathematics, at the University of London".

8. I am so grateful that I found your web site. I am an adult piano player, that was taught all wrong, when I was young. I am still trying to unlearn my bad techniques and habits. I now take lessons from a very good teacher.

9. A few weeks ago I downloaded your book from the Internet and have been trying it out. I'm about halfway through and a long way from fully applying everything, but I'm so pleased with the results up to now that I thought I'd give some spontaneous feedback.

Firstly some background. I studied piano up to an advanced level and started a music degree, which I dropped after a year to study math. After graduation I was an enthusiastic amateur, but over the last 20 years my playing has become less frequent, mainly due to my frustration at a lack of progress, convinced that I would never be able to find the hours of exercise needed to be able to play better.

I was looking for some hints for buying a piano and came across your site. After reading a couple of chapters I downloaded the whole thing and started trying it out. This is not the first time I have tried to improve with a book or advice from a teacher, but I'm a sucker for punishment. Here are my experiences after three weeks. [Note how quickly people can learn and immediately make use of these methods.]

I've been concentrating on studying 4 pieces which are very dear to me:
- Ravel's Prelude
- Chopin Prelude no. 26 in Ab major
- Poulenc Novelette no. 1
- Ravel Alborada del Graziosa from Miroirs

The Ravel Prelude is a small piece of no apparent technical difficulty. This is a piece that I had always played on sight, but never really well. There is a crossed hands section in the middle with some exquisite dissonance that poses some difficulties, but that's about it. I applied the practice methods in the book to this piece and it suddenly came alive with far more nuance than I had ever credited it. It's anything but the throwaway I thought it was, but without proper practice methods it will always seem that way.

The Poulenc Novelette is one of the pieces that I have played at least once a week for 20 years and am very fond of. I've never really played this fully to my satisfaction, but I'd always assumed that this was due to a lack of exercise time. Using your suggestions I started analyzing what was wrong. Aside from some obvious flubs that had never really been learnt correctly the most surprising result was that it was impossible for me to keep in time to the metronome!! Some more detailed analysis revealed the cause – a lot of Poulenc's writing requires rapid and awkward shifts of hand position with melodies that need to be sustained across these shifts. The bad habit that I had learnt was to "grab" at the keys during these shifts, hence destroying the melody line and gradually speeding up the piece. The revelation to me was that the problem could not be fixed by practicing with the metronome! It could only be fixed by analyzing this problem and working out a strategy for dealing with the shifts. Now I am very satisfied with the way I play and even have a lot of time left over to consider the music.

Alborada del Graziosa is a case apart. This is a fiendishly difficult piece which I had tried to learn in the past, but was unable to bring most of the passages up to the correct speed. My assumption had always been that more practice was necessary and that I could never find the time. Again – applied the methods in your book to learning this and, after three weeks, I'm not yet there but I can now play most of it up to speed and reasonably musically as well. I reckon I'll have it all in my fingers in a couple of weeks then I can concentrate on the music.

Last but not least, the Chopin prelude. I learnt this for an exam when I was 16 yrs. old, but have never really played it since. I started relearning it and made a couple of discoveries. Firstly I had never played it up to speed, even for the exam, so this was something I needed to fix. However this just didn't work – I discovered that for two reasons I couldn't speed up. Firstly I had learnt to fake the legato with the pedal – but once you speed up you just get a jumble of sound and if I try to pedal correctly I just couldn't get the legato. Secondly the middle section contains some highly stretched broken chords in the left hand that shift on each beat. Played slowly this is ok, but at speed it becomes fiendishly difficult and even painful to play. Basically I have had to relearn this piece – new fingerings, new hand positions, different pedaling etc. Now I can play this at any speed I like with no stress. I found this an interesting proof of what you say in the book – this is a very small piece that seems fairly easy, but at speed it completely changes character and will frustrate any student using the intuitive method, unless they are blessed with a span of over 1.5 octaves.

In closing I'd like to thank you for writing the book and even more for making it available on the Internet. I have in the past spent enormous amounts of money on highly recommended teachers and not one of them, although I have no doubt that they understood these techniques themselves, could teach me how to practice.

10. I think your book is worth my reading although many of the "rules" (such as hands separate practice, chord attack . . .) I have learned from our teachers. In my logic even if just one rule I learned from your book works, it is worth far more than the $15 I paid for the 1st Edition. I also like the section on how to prepare for recitals. I agree that practicing full speed before the recital is a "no no". I discussed this with my teacher and we see several reasons why [extended discussions on why playing full speed on day of recital can lead to problems, not excerpted here because I can't understand them]. Thus practice fast before the recital is a no-win situation. Finally, I would like to see more about how to gain speed and how to put hands together more efficiently. Some music (Bach's Inventions come to mind) is easy to play hands separate but difficult hands together. Overall, I enjoy reading your book.

11. I encourage everyone to try hands separate practice as stated in your book. While studying with Robert Palmieri at Kent State University, he had me do this as part of my practice. It helped me get past the amateur stage and on to much better technique and musical playing.

12. Based on what I was able to glean from your web site, I applied one of the principles – hands separate playing at full tempo -- on a couple of difficult passages in two completely different types of songs I was playing, one a church hymn, the other a jazz tune. Interestingly, I found that when I got to church yesterday and it came time to accompany the congregation, the difficult portions I had learned by the hands separate method were among the most solid and sure of the entire hymn. It seemed that each time I came to one of those difficult spots, a mental trigger went off that alerted my brain/nervous system to execute those parts with particular care and accuracy. Same goes for the difficult spot in the jazz tune, which is now no longer a problem at all.

13. About one and a half years ago I ordered the book Fundamentals of Piano Practice from you. I just wanted to personally thank you for your contribution. It has helped me a great deal! I never knew how to practice before your book because I was never taught. I took lessons, mind you, but my teachers never taught me how to practice. Isn't that amazing! I suspect that it is commonplace. The most beneficial piece of advice for me is your suggestion to play at a much slower speed on the last run-through of the piece you are practicing. I must admit developing this habit has been most difficult for me. But I am trying. I find that slow practice is a big help. Also, practicing just a measure or two at a time has been valuable! I wished that memorizing music came easier; if you have any new ideas on memorizing, please let me know. [I have added considerable material on memorizing since this correspondence.]

14. Thank you for answering my piano practice questions. I must tell you that there is one

particularly tricky Prelude of Chopin's – the one in C Sharp Minor. When I received your book, I mastered this Prelude more than up to its rapid speed in one day. Granted it is a short one, but many pianists wrestle with it. This experience has been very encouraging.

15. I have been playing piano for 8 years now and bought your book about a year ago. After reading this book, my 1 hour a day practice sessions are much more productive. I also learn new pieces much faster. You show insight on the following:
Correct methods of practice.
How to start a new piece.
Slow practice (when to do it and why).
When to play faster than normal.
How to get ready for a performance.
I don't agree with everything you write, but I read your book about every couple of months so I don't lose sight of the proper way to practice. [This is a common refrain: my book is such a dense compilation that you need to read it several times.]

16. After one week, I was very pleased with myself and the method since I thought that I had successfully MEMORIZED!!! A whole page HS. This was an absolutely unknown achievement as far as I was concerned. But problems arose when I tried to put the two hands together, which I then tried to do whilst learning the rest of the piece. I also found on trying to learn the rest of the piece that I had 'memorized' the first page wrongly, and I ended up writing notes to myself. [This probably happens more often than most of us would like to admit – when you have difficulty in getting up to speed HT, CHECK THE SCORE! The cause could be an error in reading the music. Errors in rhythm are particularly difficult to detect.] Your book HAS given me exactly what I was looking for – i.e. some basis for working out how to learn more quickly and efficiently. No teacher has ever been able to give me any clue as to how to go about learning a piece. The only suggestion I have ever had is, 'Have a look at this and see what you can make of it', and as for how to improve the accuracy and/or speed, 'Keep practicing, practicing, . . .' WHAT????? I've now got answers to these vital questions. Thanks.

17. I have been reading your book on your site and have been getting a lot out of it. You have inspired me to practice the way I have always known was the best way but never had the patience to do it. What you outline about even chords before trying to play fast lines sure has helped me a lot. I think my inability to play beyond a certain speed is due to a basic unevenness in my fingers that I have never really addressed. I always would just say, "I just can't play fast well". I have worked up a small portion of an etude using the chord attack approach and can actually play it fairly smoothly and evenly! I am curious about your theories on absolute pitch development. The camps seem very divided on that subject: genetics vs. environment. [Since this correspondence, I added the parallel set exercises for chord practice, and have written an expanded section on acquiring absolute pitch.]

18. I just wanted to let you know how much my family of musicians has been enjoying your book on piano playing. Without doubt, you set forth some innovative, unorthodox ideas in your book that really do work in spite of the fact they sound extreme by most practicing piano teachers' standards. [I agree!] The method of practicing hands separately seems to be working quite well as well as the method of not playing everything soooooo slowly! Also, putting less emphasis on the metronome has also been proving beneficial. Certainly, your methods have helped speed up the entire learning process on new pieces, and now I can't imagine how we ever managed before without knowing these "musical truths" of yours. Thank you again for writing such a marvelous JEWEL of a book!

19. I read the online sections and think every piano teacher should be required to have read this book. I'm one of the unfortunate who spent 7 years practicing scales/Hanon without any hints about relaxation or efficient practice methods. I started to pick good practice hints from internet discussion groups and various books, but your book is by far the most comprehensive and convincing source I have found yet.

20. I am a piano player at an intermediate level. A month ago I downloaded parts of your book and I must say in one word that it is fabulous! Being a scientist I appreciate the structural way the subject matter is presented and explained on a down to earth level. It changed my way of looking at piano practice. Especially the part on memorizing helped me already to reduce memorizing efforts considerably. My private teacher (a performing soloist) uses bits and pieces from your method. However this teacher is a Czerny addict and never heard of thumb over. You need to spend more attention to the thumb over, especially how to smoothly join parallel sets. I gave a copy of the book to my teacher and I recommend it to everybody.
[A year later]
I already wrote you once more than a year ago about your fantastic book on the internet. The methods really work. Using your methods I was able to learn and master some pieces much faster. Your methods really work for pieces that are notoriously difficult to memorize, like some Mozart sonatas, and pieces of which my piano teacher said are difficult to memorize like the Bach Inventions or some preludes of Chopin. Piece of cake using your method. I am now tackling the Fantaisie Impromptu and this seemingly impossible piece appears to be within my reach! I also like your contribution about the subconscious mind. I wonder whether you know the book of J. D. Sarno: The Mindbody Prescription. This book treats the subconscious exactly like you do. While working on my PhD thesis, I solved many seemingly unsolvable theoretical enigmas just like you did. I fed it to my brain and some days later the solution just popped out. So what you write is dead right!

21. Your suggestions on how to memorize music by creating associations (a story, for example) sounded silly to me. But when I was practicing, I couldn't help asking what I could associate with a certain musical phrase that had a problematic F chord. "Give yourself an F for failing" popped into my mind. I thought that was not very encouraging thinking! But now every time I come to that phrase I remember the F. I've got it. Sheesh! Thanks. Your book is very useful. It mirrors my teacher's suggestions, but with more detail. When I can't play the piano nothing is more fun than reading about playing the piano . . . . In the final weeks before my last recital, my teacher suggested playing through my mistakes during practice. Then going back and working on the problem measures, much as you suggest, though that was the only time that it came up. She says most people will not even know the mistake was made unless it interrupts the music. Her point is to not interrupt the music and to correct the problem at the source by going back to the measure. I find that I do correct myself (stutter) a lot; I'm going to focus on not doing it. This advice is not intuitive, you know. One corrects mistakes naturally when they happen. But I can see that constantly doing that is actually building the mistakes in.

22. I stumbled on your online book on piano practice when I was searching for articles on absolute pitch. When I read it, I was impressed by the scientific approach used. Especially the concept of "speed wall" and how to overcome it helped me a lot. I found your book at just the right time. Many problems I encounter in playing the piano are discussed in your book. Many piano teachers don't seem to have a clear scientific concept on how to handle specific problems of intermediate piano players. So I am working through the book, section by section with good success. There are several things I am missing in your book. In some chapters, pictures would be very helpful, such as correct hand position, thumb over, parallel set exercises. Something like a chronological table for the

practice routine might be useful. "Practicing cold" would be on position number one, for example. You always mention the importance of WHEN to do WHAT. Could you order the exercises you explain in a way that makes them most efficient? Anyway, I want to express my deep appreciation for your project!

23. All this winter, I continued my personal piano learning and I must say that every word in your book is true. I have been studying piano for several years and made only average progress. Because I love piano and romantic music, that makes me sometimes crazy and deeply frustrated. After application of your methods from about 1 year ago, I made tremendous progress. I am now working on several pieces at once, compositions I never thought before that I can play. It's wonderful. Today, I have a small repertoire that I can play with great satisfaction.

24. I have ordered and received your 1st Ed book and have read sections of your 2nd Ed. I have found your information to be extremely valuable. I am sending you this email because I was hoping to get some advice on my upcoming recital. I am extremely nervous but after reading your sections on recitals I understand their importance. I wish I had your notes on memorizing when I started because it has taken me an extremely long time to finally memorize it (the improper way). I am not sure how to perform the piece for the recital. On the few occasions that I played for others I would stumble on certain sections because I would forget where I was in the piece because of nerves. This is my first recital so I don't know what to expect. Any tips or advice on practice routines would be much appreciated.
[After a few exchanges about what he was playing, etc., I gave him a scenario of typical practice routines for recital preparation and what to expect during the recital. After the recital, I received the following email.]
I just wanted to let you know that my recital went extremely well considering it was my first time. The advice you gave me was very helpful. I was nervous starting the piece but then I became extremely focused (just like you said would happen). I was even able to concentrate musically rather than just going through the motions. The audience was impressed at my ability to do it from memory (just like you said they would). You were right in saying that a positive experience like this would help me with my confidence. I feel great about the experience! My teacher is from [a famous Conservatory], and teaches Hanon exercises and other technique material. That is why your book was and is a gold mine for me. I want to be able to play the pieces that I enjoy without having to spend 20 years to learn them. But I also feel that I need a teacher.

25. [Finally, hundreds of communications of the type:]
    I must say that you book is excellent . . . .
    Since reading C. C. Chang's Fundamentals of Piano Practice, I've been trying out his suggestions; thanks to those who recommended it and to Mr. Chang for taking the time to write it and make it available.
    Etc., etc.

26. Since July, 2004 (cut-off date of these testimonials) I have continued to receive similar emails, especially from students at music conservatories. Most gratifying are the increasing number of teachers who say that they are successfully using these methods to teach, and that their students are happier and making faster progress.

Abbreviations and Frequently Used Phrases
Sections (…) are in Chapter One unless otherwise noted

ABBREVIATIONS

AP = Absolute Pitch (III.12)
ET = Equal Temperament (Ch. Two, 2c & 6c)
FFP = Flat Finger Position (III.4b)
FI = Fantaisie Impromptu by Chopin (II.25, III.2&5)
FPD = Fast Play Degradation (II.25, near end)
HS = Hands Separate (II.7)
HT = Hands Together (II.25)
K-II = Kirnberger II Temperament (Ch. Two, 2c & 6b)
LH = Left Hand
MP = Mental Play (see Index)
NG = Nucleation Growth (III.15)
PPI = Post Practice Improvement (II.15)
PS = Parallel Sets (see below)
RH = Right Hand
SW = Speed Wall (III.7i)
TO = Thumb Over (III.5)
TU = Thumb Under (III.5)
WT = Well Temperament (Ch. Two, 2c)

Frequently Used Phrases

Cartwheel Method (III.5, in Arpeggios section)
Chord Attack (II.9)
Conjunction (II.8)
Curl Paralysis (III.4b)
Intuitive Method (II.1)
Mental Play (II.12, III.6j)

Parallel Sets (II.11, III.7b, see Index)
Pyramid Position = "flat finger" position (III.4b)
Quiet Hand (III.6l)
Segmental Practice (II.6)
Speed Wall (III.7i)
Spider position = "flat finger" position (III.4b)

Preface

This is the best book ever written on how to practice at the piano! The revelation of this book is that there are highly efficient practice methods that can accelerate your learning rate, by up to 1,000 times if you have not yet learned the most efficient practice methods (see IV.5). What is surprising is that, although these methods were known since the earliest days of piano, they were seldom taught because only a few teachers knew about them and these knowledgeable teachers never bothered to disseminate this knowledge.

I realized in the 1960s that there was no good book on how to practice at the piano. The best I could find was Whiteside's book, which was an utter disappointment; see my review of this book in References. As a graduate student at Cornell University, studying until 2 AM just to keep up with some of the brightest students from all over the world, I had little time to practice piano. I needed to know what the best practice methods were, especially because whatever I was using wasn't working although I had taken piano lessons diligently for 7 years in my youth. How concert pianists could play the way they did was an absolute mystery to me. Was it just a matter of sufficient effort, time, and talent, as most people seem to think? If the answer were "Yes", it would have been devastating for me because it meant that my musical talent level was so low that I was a hopeless case because I had put in sufficient effort and time, at least in my youth, practicing up to 8 hours a day on weekends.

The answers came to me gradually in the 1970's when I noticed that our two daughters' piano teacher was teaching some surprisingly efficient methods of practice that were different from methods taught by the majority of piano teachers. *Over a period of more than 10 years, I kept track of these efficient practice methods and came to the realization that the most important factor for learning to play the piano is the* <u>practice methods</u>. Effort, time, and talent were merely secondary factors! In fact, "talent" is difficult to define and impossible to measure; it had become a meaningless word we use to hide our ignorance of the true definition of effective talent. In fact, *proper practice methods can make practically anybody into a "talented" musician*! I saw this happen all the time at the hundreds of student recitals and piano competitions that I had witnessed.

There is now a growing realization that "talent", "prodigy", or "genius" is more created than born (see Olson) -- Mozart is possibly the most prominent example of the "<u>Mozart Effect</u>". Some have renamed this "The Beethoven Effect" which might be more appropriate because Mozart had some personality weaknesses, etc., that sometimes marred his otherwise glorious music, whereas psychologically, Beethoven composed the most enlightening music. Listening to music is only one component of the complex Mozart Effect. For pianists, *making music* has a larger effect on mental development. *Thus good practice methods will not only accelerate the learning rate but also help to develop the musical brain, as well as raise the intelligence level, especially for the young.* The learning rate is accelerated, compared to the slower methods (it's like the difference between an accelerating vehicle and one going at a constant speed). Therefore, in a matter of a few years, students without proper practice methods will fall hopelessly behind. This makes those students with good practice methods appear far more talented than they really are because they can learn in minutes or days what it takes the others months or years. *The most important aspect of learning piano is brain development and higher intelligence. Memory is a component of intelligence and we know how to improve memory (see III.6). This book also teaches how to play music in our minds – this is called Mental Play (II.12), which naturally leads to absolute pitch and the ability to compose music.* These are the skills that distinguished the greatest musicians and led us to label them as geniuses; yet we show here that they are not difficult to learn. Until now, the musician's world was restricted to the few "gifted" artists; we now know that it is a universe in which we can all participate.

Practice methods can make the difference between a lifetime of futility, and a concert pianist in less than 10 years for young, dedicated students. Using the right practice methods, it takes only a few years for a diligent student at any age to start playing meaningful pieces from famous composers. The saddest truth of the past two centuries has been that, although most of these practice methods were discovered and rediscovered thousands of times, they were never documented and students either had to rediscover them by themselves or, if lucky, learn them from teachers who knew some of them. The best example of this lack of documentation is the "teachings" of Franz Liszt. There are a dozen Franz Liszt societies and they have produced hundreds of publications. ***Numerous books have been written about Liszt (see Eigeldinger, etc., in References), and thousands of teachers have claimed to teach the "Franz Liszt method", complete with documented teaching lineages. <u>Yet there is not one publication that describes what that method is!</u>*** There are endless accounts of Liszt's accomplishments and technical prowess, yet there is not one reference on the details of how he got that way. Evidence in the literature indicates that even Liszt could not describe how he acquired technique; he could only demonstrate how he played. Since piano pedagogy has succeeded in losing track of how the greatest pianist acquired his technique, it is little wonder that we did not have a textbook on learning piano. Can you imagine learning math, economics, physics, history, biology, or anything else without a textbook, and (if you are lucky) only your teacher's memory as a guide? Without textbooks and documentation, our civilization would not have advanced beyond that of jungle tribes whose knowledge base had been passed on by word of mouth. That's basically where piano pedagogy has been for 200 years!

There are many books on learning piano (see References), but none of them qualify as textbooks for practice methods, which is what students need. These books tell you what skills you need (scales, arpeggios, trills, etc.) and the more advanced books describe the fingerings, hand positions, movements, etc., to play them, but none of them provide a reasonably complete, systematic set of instructions on how to practice. Most beginner music books provide a few such instructions, but *many* of those instructions are wrong -- a good example is the amateurish advertisement on how to become "The Virtuoso Pianist in 60 Exercises" in the title of the Hanon exercises (see section III.7.h of Chapter One). ***In piano pedagogy, the most essential tool for the teacher and the student – a reasonably complete set of instructions on how to practice, had been missing until this book was written.***

I did not realize how revolutionary the methods of this book were until after I finished my first draft of this book in 1994. These methods were better than what I had been using previously and, for years, I had been applying them with good, but not remarkable, results. I experienced my first awakening after finishing that book, when I really read my own book and followed the methods systematically -- and experienced their incredible efficiency. So, what was the difference between knowing parts of the method and reading a book? In writing the book, I had to take the various parts and arrange them into an organized structure that served a specific purpose and that had no missing essential components. As a scientist, I knew that organizing the material into a logical structure was the only way to write a useful manual. ***It is well known in science that most discoveries are made while writing the research reports, not when conducting the research.*** It was as if I had most the parts of a terrific car, but without a mechanic to assemble the car, find any missing parts, and tune it up, those parts weren't much good for transportation. I became convinced of this book's potential to revolutionize piano teaching and, in 1999, decided to provide it free to the world on the internet. In this way, it could be updated as my research progressed and whatever was written would be immediately available to the public. In retrospect, this book is the culmination of over 50 years of research that I had conducted on piano practice methods since my first piano lessons.

Why are these practice methods so revolutionary? For detailed answers, you will have to read this book. Here, I briefly present a few overviews of how these miraculous results are achieved and to explain why they work. ***I did not originate most of the basic ideas in this book.*** They were invented and re-invented umpteen times in the last 200 years by every successful pianist; otherwise, they would not have had such success. ***The basic framework for this book was constructed using the teachings of Mlle. Yvonne Combe***, the teacher of our two daughters who became accomplished pianists (they have won many first prizes in piano competitions and averaged over 10 recitals a year each for many years; both have absolute pitch, and now enjoy composing music). Other parts of this book were assembled from the literature and my research using the internet. ***My contributions are in gathering these ideas, organizing them into a structure, and providing some understanding of why they work. This understanding is critical for the success of the method.*** Piano has often been taught like religion: Faith, Hope, and Charity. Faith that, if you followed procedures suggested by a "master" teacher, you will succeed; Hope that, "practice, practice, practice" will lead you to the rainbow, and Charity that your sacrifices and paying your dues will perform miracles. This book is different – ***a method is not acceptable unless the students understand why it works so that they can adapt it to their specific needs***. Finding the correct understanding is not easy because you can't just pluck an explanation out of thin air (it will be wrong) -- you must have enough expertise in that field of knowledge in order to arrive at the correct explanation. Providing a correct explanation automatically filters out the wrong methods. This may explain why even experienced piano teachers, whose educations were narrowly concentrated in music, can have difficulty in providing the proper understanding and will frequently give wrong explanations for even correct procedures. In this regard, my career/educational background in industrial problem solving, materials science (metals, semiconductors, insulators), optics, acoustics, physics, electronics, chemistry, scientific reporting (I have published over 100 peer-reviewed articles in major scientific journals and have been granted 6 patents), etc., have been invaluable for producing this book. These diverse requirements might explain why nobody else was able to write this type of book. As a scientist, I have agonized over how to concisely define "science" and argued endlessly over this definition with other scientists and non-scientists. Because the scientific approach is so basic to this book, I have included a section on "Scientific Approach to Piano Practice", IV.2, Chapter One. ***Science is not just the theoretical world of the brightest geniuses; it is the most effective way to simplify our lives.*** We need geniuses to advance science; however, once developed, it is the masses that benefit from these advances.

What are some of these magical ideas that are supposed to revolutionize piano teaching? Let's start with the fact that, when you watch famous pianists perform, they may be playing incredibly difficult things, but they make them look easy. How do they do that? Fact is, they *are* easy for them! Therefore, many of the *learning tricks* discussed here are methods for making difficult things easy: not only easy, but often trivially simple. This is accomplished by practicing the two hands separately and by picking short sections to practice, sometimes down to only one or two notes. You can't make things any simpler than that! Accomplished pianists can also play incredibly fast -- how do *we* practice to be able to play fast? Simple! By using the "chord attack" (II.9). ***Thus one key to the success of the methods discussed here is the use of ingenious <u>learning tricks</u> that are needed to solve specific problems.***

Even with the methods described here, it may be necessary to practice difficult passages hundreds of times and, once in a while, up to 10,000 times before you can play the most difficult passages with ease. Now if you were to practice a Beethoven Sonata at, say, half speed (you are just learning it), it would take about an hour to play through. Therefore, repeating it 10,000 times would take 30 years, or almost half a lifetime, if you had, say, one hour per day to practice and practiced only this sonata 7 days a week. Clearly, this is not the way to learn the sonata, although many students use practice methods not too different from it. This book describes methods for identifying just the few notes that you need to practice and then playing them in a fraction of a second, so that you can repeat them 10,000 times in a few weeks (or even days for easier material), practicing them for only about 10 minutes per day, 5 days per week – we have reduced the practice time from half a lifetime to a few weeks.

This book discusses many more efficiency principles, such as practicing and memorizing at the same time. *During practice, each passage must be repeated many times and repetition is the best way to memorize; therefore, it doesn't make sense not to memorize while practicing, especially because this turns out to be the fastest way to learn.* Have you ever wondered how every concert pianist can memorize hours of repertoire? The answer is quite simple. *Studies with super memorizers (such a those who can memorize pages of phone numbers) have revealed that they are able to memorize because they have developed memory algorithms onto which they can quickly map the material to be memorized. For pianists, music is such an algorithm!* You can prove this by asking a pianist to memorize just one page of random notes, and to remember them for years. This is impossible (without an algorithm) although this pianist may have no trouble memorizing several 20 page Beethoven Sonatas, and still play them 10 years later. Thus what we thought was a special talent of concert pianists turns out to be something anyone can do. Students who use the methods of this book memorize and perform everything they learn, except when practicing sight reading. This is why this book does not recommend exercises such as Hanon and Czerny, that are not meant to be performed; by the same token, the Chopin Etudes are recommended. *Practicing something that wasn't meant to be performed is not only a waste of time but also destroys any sense of music you originally had.* We discuss all the major methods of memory, which empower the pianist to perform feats that most people would expect only from "gifted musicians", such as playing the composition in your head, away from the piano, or even writing the entire composition from memory. If you can play every note in the composition from memory, there is no reason why you can't write them all down! Such abilities are not for show or bragging rights, but are essential for performing without flubs or memory lapses and come almost as automatic byproducts of these methods, even for us ordinary folks with ordinary memory. Many students can play complete compositions but can't write them down or play them in their minds -- such students have only partially memorized the compositions in a manner that is insufficient for performances. Inadequate memory and lack of confidence are the main causes of nervousness. They wonder why they suffer stage fright and why performing flawlessly is such a daunting task while Mozart could just sit down and play.

Another example of helpful knowledge is relaxation and the use of gravity. The weight of the arm is important not only as a reference force for uniform and even playing (gravity is always constant), but also for testing the level of relaxation. *The piano was designed with gravity as the reference force because the human body evolved to match gravity exactly*, which means that the force needed to play the piano is about equal to the weight of the arm. When performing difficult tasks, such as playing a challenging piano passage, the natural tendency is to tense up so that the entire body becomes one contracted mass of muscle. Trying to move the fingers independently and rapidly under such conditions is like trying to run a sprint with rubber bands wrapped around both legs. If you can relax all unnecessary muscles, and use only the required muscles for just those instants at which they are needed, you can play extremely fast, effortlessly, for long periods of time without fatigue, and with more reserve strength than needed to produce the loudest sounds.

We will see that many "established teaching methods" are myths that can cause untold misery to the student. Such myths survive because of a lack of rigorous scientific scrutiny. These methods include: the curled finger position, thumb under method of playing scales, most finger exercises, sitting high on the chair, "no pain, no gain", slowly ramping up your speed, and liberal use of the metronome. We not only explain why they are harmful but also provide the correct alternatives, which are, respectively: flat finger positions, thumb over method, parallel sets (II.11, III.7b), sitting lower on the chair, relaxation, acquiring speed by understanding "speed walls" (III.7i) and identification of specific beneficial uses of the metronome. *Speed walls are encountered when you try to play a passage faster, but reach a maximum speed beyond which the speed will not increase no matter how hard you practice.* What causes speed walls, how many are there, and how do you avoid or eliminate them? Answers: *speed walls are the results of attempts to do the impossible (you erect speed walls yourself by using incorrect practice methods), there are effectively an infinite number of them, and you avoid them by using the correct practice methods.* One way of avoiding speed walls is not to build them in the first place, by knowing their causes (stress, incorrect fingering or rhythm, lack of technique, practicing too fast, practicing hands together [II.25] before you are ready, etc.). *Another way is to come down in speed from "infinite speed" by using the parallel sets (II.11), instead of increasing the speed gradually.* If you can start at speeds above the speed wall, there is no spced wall when you come down in speed.

This book frequently deals with one important point -- that *the best piano practice methods are surprisingly counter-intuitive.* This point is paramount in piano pedagogy because it is the main reason why the wrong practice methods tend to be used by students and teachers. If they weren't so counter-intuitive, this book may not have been necessary. Consequently, we deal not only with what you should do but also with what you should not do. These negative sections are not for criticizing those who use the wrong methods but are necessary components of the learning process. The reason why intuition fails is that the piano tasks are so complex, and there are so many ways to accomplish them, that the probability of hitting the right method is nearly zero if you picked the simplest, obvious ones. Here are four examples of counter-intuitive practice methods:

(1) Separating the hands for practice (II.7) is counter-intuitive because you need to practice each hand, then both together, so that it looks like you have to practice three times instead of just once hands together. Why practice hands separately, which you will never use in the end? Approximately 80% of this book deals with why you *need* to practice hands separately. *Hands separate practice is the only way to rapidly increase speed and control without getting into trouble.* It allows you to work hard 100% of the time at any speed without fatigue, stress, or injury because the method is based on switching hands as soon as the working hand begins to tire. *Hands separate practice is the only way in which you can experiment to find the correct hand motions for speed and expression and it is the fastest way to learn how to relax.* Trying to acquire technique hands together is the main cause of speed walls, bad habits, injury, and stress.

(2) Practicing slowly hands together and gradually ramping up the speed is what we tend to do intuitively, but it turns out to be one of the worst ways to practice because it wastes so much time and you are training the hands to execute slow motions that are different from what you need at the final speed. *Some students compound the problem by using the metronome as a constant guide to ramp up the speed or to keep the rhythm. This is one of the worst abuses of the metronome. Metronomes should be used only briefly to check the timing (speed and rhythm).* If over used, it can lead to loss of your internal rhythm, loss of musicality, and bio-physical difficulties from over-exposure to rigid repetition (the brain can actually start to counteract the metronome click and you may either not hear the click or hear it at the wrong time). *Technique for speed is acquired by discovering new hand motions, not by speeding up a slow motion;* i.e., the hand motions for playing slowly and fast are different. This is why trying to speed up a slow motion leads to speed walls -- because you are trying to do the impossible. Speeding up a slow play is like asking a horse to speed up a walk to the speed of a gallop -- it can't. A horse must change from walk to trot to canter and then to gallop. If you force a horse to walk at the speed of a canter, it will hit a speed wall and will most likely injure itself by kicking its own hoofs to shreds.

(3) In order to memorize well, and be able to perform well, you must practice slowly, even after the piece can be played easily at speed. This is counter-intuitive because you always perform at speed, so why practice slowly and waste so much time? Playing fast can be detrimental to performance as well as to memory. Playing fast can cause "fast play degradation", and the best way to test your memory is to play slowly. *Thus practicing the recital pieces at full speed on recital day will result in a poor performance.* This is one of the most counter-intuitive rules and is therefore difficult to follow. How often have you heard the refrain, "I played awfully during my lesson

although I played so well this morning."? Therefore, although much of this book is oriented towards learning to play at the correct speed, it is the proper use of slow play that is critical for accurate memorization and for performing without mistakes. However, practicing slowly is tricky because you should not practice slowly until you can play fast! Otherwise, you would have no idea if your slow play motion is right or wrong. This problem is solved by practicing hands separately and getting up to speed quickly. After you know the hand motions for fast play, you can practice slowly at any time.

(4) Most people feel uncomfortable trying to memorize something they can't play, so they instinctively learn a piece first, and *then* try to memorize it. It turns out that **you can save a lot of time by memorizing first and then practicing from memory** (we are talking about technically challenging music that is too difficult to sight read). Moreover, for reasons explained in this book, those who memorize after learning the piece never succeed in memorizing well. They will be haunted forever by memory problems. Therefore, good memorizing methods must be an integral part of any practice procedure; memorizing is a necessity, not a luxury.

These four examples should give the reader some idea of what I mean by counter-intuitive practice methods. What is surprising is that *the majority* of good practice methods is counter-intuitive to most people. Fortunately, the geniuses who came before us have found the better practice methods and you will see them here.

Why does the fact, that the correct methods are counter-intuitive, lead to disaster? Even students who learned the correct methods (but were never taught what not to do) can drift back into intuitive methods simply because their brains keep telling them that they should use the intuitive methods (that's the *definition* of intuitive methods). This of course happens to teachers as well. Parents fall for it every time! Thus mere parental involvement can sometimes be counterproductive, because the parents must also be *informed.* This is why this book makes every effort to identify, and to point out the follies of, the intuitive methods. Thus many teachers discourage parental involvement unless the parents can also attend the lessons. Left to their own devices, the majority of students, teachers, and parents will gravitate towards the intuitive (wrong) methods. This is the main reason why so many wrong methods are taught today, and why students need informed teachers and proper textbooks. **All piano teachers should use a textbook that explains practice methods; this will free them from having to teach the mechanics of practicing and allow them to concentrate on music where the teachers are most needed.** The parents should also read the textbook because parents are most susceptible to the pitfalls of intuitive methods.

Piano teachers generally fall into three categories: (A) private teachers who can't teach, (B) private teachers that are very good, and (C) teachers at universities and conservatories. The last group is usually fairly good because they are in an environment in which they must communicate with one another. They are able to quickly identify the worst teaching methods and eliminate them. Unfortunately, most students at conservatories are already quite advanced and so it is too late to teach them basic practice methods. The (A) group of teachers consists mainly of individuals that do not communicate well with other teachers and invariably use mostly intuitive methods; this explains why they can't teach. By choosing only teachers that have web sites, you can eliminate many of the poor teachers because these have at least learned to communicate. Groups (B) and (C) are fairly familiar with the correct practice methods, though few know all of them because there has not been a standardized textbook; on the other hand, most of them know a lot of useful details that aren't in this book. There are precious few group (B) type teachers and the group (C) teachers generally accept only advanced students. The problem with this situation is that most students start with the group (A) teachers and never progress beyond novice or intermediate level and therefore never qualify for the group (C) teachers. **Thus the majority of beginner students give up in frustration although practically all of them have the potential to become accomplished musicians.** Moreover, this lack of progress feeds the general misconception that learning piano is a lifetime of fruitless efforts, which discourages the majority of parents and youngsters from considering piano lessons.

There is an intimate relationship between music and mathematics. Music, in many respects, is a form of mathematics and the great composers explored and exploited this relationship. Most basic theories of music can be expressed using mathematical terms. Harmony is a series of ratios, and harmony gives rise to the chromatic scale, which is a logarithmic equation. Most music scales are subsets of the chromatic scale, and chord progressions are the simplest relationships among these subsets. I discuss some concrete examples of the use of mathematics in some of the most famous compositions (section IV.4) and include all the topics for future music research (mathematical or otherwise) in Section IV. It does not make sense to ask whether music is art or math; they are both properties of music. Math is simply a way of measuring something quantitatively; therefore, anything in music that can be quantified (such as time signature, thematic structure, etc.) can be treated mathematically. Thus, although math is not necessary to an artist, music and mathematics are inseparably intertwined and a knowledge of these relationships can often be useful (as demonstrated by every great composer), and will become more useful as mathematical understanding of music progressively catches up to music and as artists learn to take advantage of mathematics. Art is a shortcut way of using the human brain to achieve results not achievable in any other way. Scientific approaches to music only deal with the simpler levels of music that can be analytically treated: science supports art. It is wrong to assume that science will eventually replace art or, on the other extreme, that art is all you need for music; art should be free to incorporate anything that the artist desires, and science can provide invaluable help.

Too many pianists are ignorant of how the piano works and what it means to tune in the temperaments, or what it means to voice the piano. This is especially surprising because piano maintenance directly affects (1) the ability to make music and (2) technical development. There are many concert pianists who do not know the difference between Equal (P. 224) and Well temperaments (P. 226) while some of the compositions they are playing (e.g. Chopin, Bach) formally require the use of one or the other. When to use electronic pianos, when to change to a higher quality (grand) piano, and how to recognize quality in a piano are critical decisions in the career of any pianist. Therefore, this book contains a section on piano selection and a chapter on how to tune your own piano. Just as electronic pianos are already always in tune, acoustic pianos must soon become permanently in tune, for example, by using the thermal expansion coefficient of the strings to electronically tune the piano (see Gilmore, Self-Tuning Piano). Today, practically all home pianos are out of tune almost all the time because it starts to go out of tune the moment the tuner leaves your house or if the room temperature or humidity changes. That's an unacceptable situation. In future pianos, you will flick a switch and the piano will tune itself in seconds. When mass produced, the cost of self-tuning options will be small compared to the price of a quality piano. You might think that this would put piano tuners out of work but that will not be the case because the number of pianos will increase (because of this book), the self-tuning mechanism requires maintenance and, for pianos in such perfect tune, frequent hammer voicing and regulation (that are too often neglected today) will make a significant improvement in musical output. This higher level of maintenance will be demanded by the increasing number of advanced pianists. You might suddenly realize that it was the piano, not you, that limited technical development and musical output (worn hammers will do it every time!). Why do you think concert pianists are so fussy about their pianos?

In summary, this book represents an unique event in the history of piano pedagogy and is revolutionizing piano teaching. Surprisingly, there is little that is fundamentally new in this book. We owe most of the major concepts to Yvonne (Combe), Franz, Freddie, Ludwig, Wolfie, Johann, etc. Yvonne and Franz gave us hands separate practice, segmental practice and relaxation; Franz and Freddie gave us the "Thumb Over" method and freed us from Hanon and Czerny; Wolfie taught us memorization and mental play; Johann knew all about parallel sets, quiet hands (III.6.l), and the importance of musical practice, and they all showed us (especially Ludwig) the relationships between math and music. The enormous amounts of time and effort that were wasted in the past, re-inventing the wheel and futilely repeating finger exercises with every generation of pianist, staggers the imagination. By making the knowledge in this book available to the student from day one of piano lessons, we are ushering in a new era in learning to play the piano. This book is not the end of the road -- it is just a beginning. Future research into practice methods will undoubtedly uncover improvements; that's the nature of the scientific approach. It guarantees that we will never again lose useful information, that we will always make forward progress, and that every teacher will have access to the best available information. We still do not understand the biological changes that accompany the acquisition of technique and how the human (especially the infant) brain develops. Understanding these will allow us to directly address them instead of having to repeat something 10,000 times. Since the time of Bach, piano pedagogy had been in a state of arrested development; we can now hope to transform piano playing from a dream that seemed mostly out of reach to an art that everyone can now enjoy.

PS: This book is my gift to society. The translators have also contributed their precious time. Together, we are pioneering a web based approach for providing free education of the highest caliber, something that will hopefully become the wave of the future. There is no reason why education can't be free. Such a revolution might seem to put some teachers' jobs in jeopardy, but with improved learning methods, piano playing will become more popular, creating a greater demand for teachers who can teach, because students will always learn faster under a good teacher. The economic impact of this improved learning method can be significant. This book was first printed in 1994 and the web site was started in 1999. Since then, I estimate that over 10,000 students had learned this method by year 2002. Let's assume that 10,000 serious piano students save 5 hours/week using these methods, that they practice 40 weeks/year, and that their time is worth $5/hour; then the total yearly savings are:

(5hrs/wk, per student)(40wks/yr)($5/hr)(10,000 students) = $10,000,000/yr, in 2002, which will increase every year, or

$1,000 per year per student.

$10M/yr is only the savings of the students; we have not included the effects on teachers and the piano and music industries. Whenever adoption of scientific methods produced such leaps in efficiency, the field has historically flourished, seemingly without limit, and benefited everyone. With a world population over 6.6B today (2007), we can expect the pianist population to eventually exceed 1% or over 66M, so that the potential economic impact of this book could exceed several $B/year. Such huge economic benefits in any sector have historically been an unstoppable force, and this engine will drive the coming piano revolution. This book is the beginning of that revolution. More importantly, music and any gain in the development of a young child's mind, are priceless.

CHAPTER ONE: PIANO TECHNIQUE

I. INTRODUCTION

1.   Objective

The objective of this book is to present the best known methods for practicing piano. For students, knowing these methods means a reduction in learning time that is a significant fraction of a lifetime and an increase in the time available for making music instead of struggling with technique. Many students spend 100% of their time learning new compositions and, because this process takes so long, there is no time left to practice the art of making music. This sorry state is the greatest hindrance to acquiring technique because making music is necessary for technical development. ***The goal here is to make the learning process so fast that we aim to allocate 10% of practice time to technical work and 90% to making music.***

How do musicians "make music"? ***Whether we compose music or play an instrument, all music must originate in the artist's brain.*** We can certainly shut our brains off and play the piano from rote memory after enough practice. That is absolutely the wrong way to make music because the level of the resulting music will be low. Many pianists have the misconception that the expensive, huge, concert grand produces its own sound with its characteristic music and therefore we must train our fingers for learning to play the piano. But the human brain is far more complex than, and superior to, any mechanical contraption in terms of musicality. The brain doesn't have the limitations of wood, felt, and metal. Therefore, it is more important to train the brain than the finger muscles, especially because any finger movement must originate as a nerve impulse in the brain. The answer to the above question is what we shall call Mental Play (MP) in this book. MP is simply the process of imagining the music in your mind, or even actually playing it on an imaginary piano. We shall see that MP controls practically everything we do in music, from the learning process (technique) to memorization, absolute pitch, performance, composition, music theory, interpretation, controlling nervousness, etc. It is so all-encompassing that it is not possible to devote one section to explaining it; rather, it is discussed in practically every section of this book. A fairly extended discussion is given in Section III.6.j.

MP is what made Mozart (and all great musicians) what he was; he is considered to be one of the greatest geniuses partly because of his MP abilities. The wonderful news is that *it can be learned.* The sad historical fact is that too many students were never taught MP; in fact, this book may be the first place where MP has been given an official name (definition) although, if you are a "talented" musician, you somehow had to magically pick it up yourself. ***Mental Play should be taught from the first year of piano lessons and is especially effective for the youngest youngsters; the most obvious way to start teaching it is to teach memorization skills and absolute pitch.*** MP is the art of controlling the minds of the audience thru the music you play and therefore it works best when it originates in your mind. The audience views your MP ability as something extraordinary, belonging only to a select few gifted musicians with intelligence far above the average person. Mozart was almost certainly aware of this and used MP to greatly enhance his image. MP also helps you to learn piano in a myriad of ways, as demonstrated throughout this book. For example, because you can conduct MP away from the piano, you can effectively double or triple your practice time by using MP when a piano is not available. Beethoven and Einstein often seemed absent-minded because they were preoccupied with MP during most of their waking hours.

Thus MP is nothing new; not only the great musicians and artists, but practically any specialist today, such as athletes, trained soldiers, businessmen, etc., must cultivate their own MP in order to compete successfully. *In fact every one of us does it all the time!* When we get up in the morning and quickly go over the planned activities of the day, we are conducting MP, and the complexity of that MP probably exceeds that of a Chopin Mazurka. Yet we do it in an instant, without even thinking about it as MP, because we have been practicing it since early childhood. Can you imagine what disasters would happen if we never had a mental plan for the day? But that is basically what we do if we walk onto a stage and play a recital without MP training. No wonder performers get so nervous! As we shall see, MP is perhaps the single best antidote against stage fright – it certainly worked for Mozart.

2.   What is Piano Technique?

We must understand what technique is because not understanding technique leads to incorrect practice methods. More importantly, a proper understanding can help us to develop correct practice methods. The most common misunderstanding is that technique is some inherited finger dexterity. It is not. *The innate dexterity of accomplished pianists and ordinary folk are not that different.* This means that practically anyone can learn to play the piano well. There are numerous examples of mentally handicapped people with limited coordination that exhibit incredible musical talent (savants). Unfortunately, many of us are much more dexterous but can't manage the musical passages because of a lack of some simple but critical information. *Acquiring technique is mostly a process of brain/nerve development, not development of finger strength.*

Technique is the ability to execute a zillion different piano passages; therefore it is not dexterity, but an aggregate of many skills. The wondrous thing about piano technique, and *the most important message of this book, is that piano skills can be learned in a short time, if the correct learning procedures are applied*. These skills are acquired in two stages: (1) discovering how the fingers, hands, arms, etc., are to be moved, and (2) conditioning the brain, nerves, and muscles to execute these with ease and control. Many students think of piano practice as hours of finger calisthenics because they were never taught the proper definition of technique. *The reality is that you are improving your brain when learning piano!* You are actually making yourself smarter and improving your memory; this is why learning piano correctly has so many benefits, such as success in school, the ability to better cope with everyday problems, and the ability to retain memory longer as you age. This is why memorizing is an inseparable part of technique acquisition.

We must understand our own anatomy and learn how to discover and acquire the correct technique. This turns out to be an nearly impossible task for the average human brain unless you dedicate your entire life to it from childhood. Even then, most will not succeed. The reason is that, without proper instruction, the pianist must discover the correct motions, etc., by trial and error. You must depend on the small probability that, as you try to play that difficult passage faster, your hand accidentally stumbles onto a motion that works. If you are unlucky, your hand never discovers the motion and you are stuck forever, a phenomenon called "speed wall". Most beginning piano students haven't the foggiest idea about the complex motions that the fingers, hands, and arms can perform. Fortunately, the many geniuses who came before us have made most of the useful discoveries (otherwise, they wouldn't have been such great performers) leading to efficient practice methods.

Another misconception about technique is that once the fingers become sufficiently skillful, you can play anything. Almost every different passage is a new adventure; it must be learned anew. Experienced pianists *seem* to be able to play just about anything because (1) they have practiced all the things that you encounter frequently, and (2) they know how to learn new things very quickly. There are large classes of passages, such as scales, that appear frequently; knowledge of how to play these will cover significant portions of most compositions. But more importantly, there are general solutions for large classes of problems and specific solutions for specific problems.

3. Technique, Music, Mental Play

If we concentrate only on developing "finger technique" and neglect music during practice, we can pick up non-musical playing habits. ***Non-musical playing is an absolute no-no at all times because it is one form of mistake.*** One common symptom of this mistake is the inability to play the lesson pieces when the teacher (or anyone else!) is listening. When an audience is present, these students make strange errors that they didn't make during "practice". This happens because the students practiced without regard for music but suddenly realized that music must now be added because someone is listening. Unfortunately, until lesson time, they had never really practiced musically! Another symptom of non-musical practice is that the student feels uncomfortable practicing when others can hear them. ***Piano teachers know that students need to practice musically in order to acquire technique. What is right for the ears and the brain turns out to be right for the human playing mechanism.*** Both musicality and technique require accuracy and control. Practically any technical flaw can be detected in the music. At the very least, the music is the supreme test of whether the technique is right or wrong. As we shall see throughout this book, there are more reasons why music should never be separated from technique. Nonetheless, many students tend to practice neglecting the music and preferring to "work" when no one is around to listen. Such practice methods produce "closet pianists" who love to play but can't perform. ***If students are taught to practice musically all the time, this type of problem will not even exist; performing and practice are one and the same.*** We provide many suggestions in this book for practicing to perform, such as video recording your playing from the very beginning.

Many students make the mistake of thinking that the fingers control the music and they wait for the piano to produce that gorgeous sound. This will result in a flat performance and unpredictable results. The music must originate in the mind and the pianist must coax the piano to produce what s/he wants. This is mental play, introduced above; if you had never practiced mental play before, you will find that it requires a level of memorization that you had never achieved before – but that is *exactly* what is needed for flawless, authoritative performances. Fortunately, mental play is only a few steps beyond the memorization procedures in this book, but it accomplishes a giant leap in your musical capabilities, not only for technique and making music, but also for learning absolute pitch, composing, and every aspect of piano playing. Thus technique, music, and mental play are inseparably intertwined. Once you are deeply involved with mental play, you will discover that it doesn't really work without absolute pitch. These discussions provide a firm basis for identifying the skills we need to learn. This book provides the practice methods needed to learn them.

4. Basic Approach, Interpretation, Musical Training, Absolute Pitch

Teachers play a critical role in showing students how to play and practice musically. For example, most pieces of music begin and end with the same chord, a somewhat mysterious rule which is actually a result of basic chord progression rules. An understanding of chord progressions is very useful for memorizing. A musical phrase generally starts and ends with softer notes, with the louder ones in between; when in doubt, this is a good default principle. This may be one reason why so many compositions begin with a partial bar – the first beat usually carries the accent and is too loud. There are many books that discuss musical interpretation (Gieseking, Sandor), and we will encounter numerous pointers throughout this book.

Musical training is most rewarding for the very young. Most babies exposed frequently to perfectly tuned pianos will *automatically* develop absolute pitch -- this is nothing extra-ordinary. Nobody is born with absolute pitch, because it is a 100% learned skill (the exact frequencies of the musical scales are arbitrary human conventions -- there is no natural law that says that middle A should be 440 Hz; most orchestras tune to 442 Hz, and before it was standardized, there was a much larger range of allowable frequencies). If this absolute pitch is not maintained, it will be lost later in life. ***Piano training of young children can begin around the ages of three to four. Early exposure of youngsters (from birth) to classical music is beneficial because classical music has the highest musical content (complex logic) among all the different types of music***. Some forms of contemporary music, by over-emphasizing certain narrow aspects, such as loudness or simplistic music structures that do not stimulate the brain, can detract from musical development by interfering with brain development.

Although you need to be musically gifted to compose music, the ability to play the piano is not that dependent on the musical brain. In fact, most of us are more musical than we give ourselves credit for and it is the lack of technique that limits our musical expression at the piano. We have all had the experience of listening to famous pianists and noticing that one is different from the other -- that is more musical sensitivity than we will ever need to start playing the piano. There is no need to practice eight hours a day; some famous pianists have recommended practice times of less than an hour. You can make progress practicing three or four times a week, one hour each.

Finally, total music education (scales, time signatures, ear training [including absolute pitch], dictation, theory, etc.) should be an integral part of learning to play the piano because each different thing you learn helps all the others. In the final analysis, a total music education is the only way to learn piano. Unfortunately, the majority of aspiring pianists do not have the resources or the time to follow such a path. This book was designed to give the student a head start by learning how to acquire technique quickly so that they can consider studying all the other helpful subjects. ***Statistically, students who excel in playing the piano almost always end up composing music of their own.*** Studying music composition is not a prerequisite for composing. Some teachers frown on learning too much composition theory before starting to compose your own music because that can prevent you from developing your individual style.

What are some unique features of the methods of this book?
(i) These methods are not overly demanding, like older methods that require students to commit to a dedicated lifestyle to fit the piano instruction. Students are given the tools to pick a specific procedure that will achieve a defined objective within estimable time limits. If the methods *really* work, they shouldn't require a lifetime of blind faith in order to achieve proficiency!
(ii) Every procedure of these methods has a physical basis (if it works, it always has one; the past problems in piano pedagogy have been in identifying the correct explanations); it must further contain the following required elements: (A) **objective:** what techniques to acquire, i.e., if you can't play fast enough, you can't trill, you want to memorize, etc., (B) **then do:** i.e., practice hands separately, use chord attack, memorize as you practice, etc.,(C) **because:** the physiological, psychological, mechanical, etc., explanations for why these methods work

-- HS practice makes difficult passages easier and (D) **if not:** problems that arise if uninformed methods are used. Without this "if not", students can pick any other method -- why this one? We need to know what not to do because bad habits and wrong methods, not insufficient practice, are the main causes of a lack of progress.

(iii) This book presents a complete, structured set of learning tools that transports you with minimum effort into the Magical Kingdom of Mental Play. Bon Voyage!

II. BASIC PROCEDURES FOR PIANO PRACTICE

This section contains the minimum set of instructions that you need before starting practice.

1.   The Practice Routine

Many students use the following practice routine:

(a) First, practice scales or technical exercises until the fingers are limbered up. Continue this for 30 minutes or longer if you have time, to improve technique especially by using exercises such as the Hanon series.

(b) Then take a new piece of music and slowly read it for a page or two, carefully playing both hands together, starting from the beginning. This slow play is repeated until it can be performed reasonably well and then it is gradually speeded up until the final speed is attained. A metronome might be used for this gradual speed-up.

(c) At the end of a two hour practice, the fingers are flying, so the students can play as fast as they want and enjoy the experience before quitting. After all, they are tired of practicing so that they can relax, play their hearts out at full speed; this is the time to enjoy the music!

(d) Once the piece can be played satisfactorily, memorize it and practice "until the music is in the hands".

(e) On the day of the recital or lesson, practice the piece at correct speed (or faster!) as many times as possible in order to make sure that it is in top condition. This is the last chance; obviously, the more practice, the better.

EVERY STEP OF THIS PROCEDURE IS WRONG! The above will almost guarantee that the students will not progress beyond intermediate level even if they practice several hours daily. For example, this method tells the students nothing about what to do when they hit an impossible passage except to keep repeating, sometimes for a lifetime, with no clear idea of when or how the needed technique will be acquired. This method leaves the task of learning to play the piano completely to the student. Moreover, the music will come out flat during the recital and unexpected flubs will be almost unavoidable. You will understand all this as soon as you read about the more efficient methods described below.

Lack of progress is the main reason why so many students quit piano. Students, especially youngsters, are smart; why work like a slave and learn nothing? Reward the students and you will get more dedication than any teacher could want. You can be a doctor, scientist, lawyer, athlete, or anything you want, and still become a good pianist. This is because there are methods that let you acquire technique quickly, as we shall soon see.

Note that the above practice routine is an "intuitive" (or "instinctive") method. If a person of average intelligence were marooned on an island with a piano and decided to practice, that person would most likely devise a practice method like the one above. That is, a teacher teaching this type of practice routine isn't teaching anything -- the method is intuitive. *When I first started to compile the "correct learning procedures" of this book, I was struck most by how counter-intuitive many of them were.* I will explain later why they are so counter-intuitive but this offers the best explanation for why so many teachers use the intuitive approach. These teachers never learned the correct methods and therefore gravitated naturally to the intuitive methods. The trouble with counter-intuitive methods is that they are harder to adopt than intuitive ones; your brain is constantly telling you that they are not right and to get back to the intuitive ones. This message from the brain can become irresistible just before a lesson or recital -- try telling (uninformed) students not to enjoy playing their finished pieces before quitting practice, or not to over-practice on recital day! It is not only the students or teachers. It is also any parents or friends with good intentions that influence the practice routines of young students. *Parents who are not informed will always force their children to use the intuitive methods.* This is one reason why good teachers always ask parents to accompany their children to the lessons. If the parents are not informed, there is a virtual guarantee that they will force the students to use methods that are in direct contradiction to the teacher's instructions.

Students who started with the correct methods from the beginning are the "apparently lucky" ones. However, they must be careful later in life if they weren't taught what the wrong methods are. Once they leave the teacher, they can stumble into the intuitive methods and have no idea why everything is suddenly falling apart. It's like a bear that had never seen a bear trap -- it gets caught every time. These "lucky" ones often can't teach either, because they may not know that many intuitive methods can lead to disaster. On the other hand, the apparently "unlucky" students who first learned the intuitive methods and then changed over to the better ones have some unexpected advantages. They know both the right and wrong methods and often make much better teachers. *Therefore, although this book teaches the correct methods, it is equally important to know what NOT to do, and why.* This is why the most frequently used wrong methods are extensively discussed here.

We describe the components of a proper practice routine in the following sections. They are presented in approximately the order in which a student might use them from start to finish of a new piece of music. *Beginners please read section III.18 first.*

2.   Finger Positions

Relax the fingers and place your hand on a flat surface with all the fingertips resting on the surface and the wrist at the same height as the knuckles. *The hand and fingers should form a dome. All the fingers should be curved. The thumb should point slightly down and bend slightly towards the fingers so that the last (nail) phalange of the thumb is parallel to the other fingers (viewed from above).* This slight inward bend of the thumb is useful when playing chords with wide spans. It positions the tip of the thumb parallel to the keys making it less likely to hit adjacent keys. It also orients the thumb so that the correct muscles are used to raise and lower it. *The fingers are slightly curled, curving down and meeting the surface at angles near 45 degrees*. This curled configuration allows the fingers to play between the black keys. The tip of the thumb and the other fingertips should form an approximate semicircle on the flat surface. If you do this with both hands side by side, the two thumbnails should be facing each other. Use the part of the thumb directly below the thumbnails to play, not the joint between the nail phalange and the middle phalange. The thumb is already too short; therefore, play with its tip for maximum uniformity with all the fingers. For the other fingers, the bone comes close to the skin at the fingertips. At the front pad of the fingertip (opposite the fingernail), the flesh is thicker. This front pad should contact the keys, not the fingertip.

This is the starting position. Once you begin play, you may need to stretch the fingers almost straight, or curl them more, depending on what you are playing. *Therefore, although the beginner must learn the ideal curled position, strict adherence to a fixed curled configuration is not correct; this will be discussed in detail later on, especially because the curled position has significant disadvantages.*

3.   Bench Height and Distance from Piano

The right height of the bench and its distance from the piano is also a matter of personal taste. For a good starting point, sit at the bench with your elbows at your sides and forearms pointing straight towards the piano. *With your hands on the keys in playing position, the elbows should be slightly below the height of the hands, about level with the keys.* Now place your hands on the white keys -- the distance of the bench from the piano (and your sitting position) should be such that the elbows just miss your body as you move them in towards each other. Do not sit at the center of the bench, but sit closer to the front edge so that you can plant your feet firmly on the floor or pedals. The bench height and location are most critical when playing loud chords. Therefore, you can test this position by playing two black key chords simultaneously, as loudly as you can. The chords are C2#G2#C3# (5,2,1) for the left hand and C5#G5#C6# (1,2,5) for the right hand. Press down hard, leaning forwards a little, with the whole weight of your arms and shoulders, to make a thundering, authoritative sound. Make sure that the shoulders are totally involved. Loud, impressive sounds cannot be made using only the hands and forearms; the force must come from the shoulders and the body. If this is comfortable, the bench and sitting positions should be correct. Historically, there has been a tendency of teachers to sit their students too high; consequently, the standard bench height of fixed height benches tend to be one to two inches too high, thus forcing the students to play more with their fingertips than the front finger pads. It is therefore important to have a bench with variable height.

4.   Starting a Piece: Listening and Analysis (Fur Elise)

The best way to start the learning process is to listen to a performance (recording). The criticism that listening first is some sort of "cheating" has no defensible basis. The purported disadvantage is that students might end up imitating instead of using their creativity. *It is impossible to imitate someone else's playing because playing styles are so individualistic.* This fact can be reassuring to some students who might blame themselves for the inability to imitate some famous pianist. If possible, listen to several recordings. They can open up all sorts of new ideas and possibilities that are at least as important to learn as finger technique. Not listening is like saying that you shouldn't go to school because that will destroy your creativity. Some students think that listening is a waste of time because they will never play that well. In that case, think again. If the methods described here will not make people play "that well", I wouldn't be writing this book! What happens most frequently when students listen to many recordings is that they discover that the performances are not uniformly good; that they actually prefer *their own* playing to some of those in the recordings.

The next step is to analyze the structure of the composition. This structure will be used to determine the practice program and to estimate the time needed to learn this piece. *As any experienced piano teacher knows, the ability to estimate the time needed to completely learn a piece is critically important to the success of the practice routine.* Let's use Beethoven's Fur Elise as an example. *Analysis always starts by numbering the bars on your music score.* If the bars are not already marked, mark every 10th bar in pencil, above the center of the bar. I count any partial bar at the beginning as bar 1; others count only full bars, but this makes it awkward to identify the first partial bar. In Fur Elise, the first 4 full bars are essentially repeated 15 times, so by learning 4 bars you can play 50% of the piece (it has 124 full bars). Another 6 bars are repeated 4 times, so learning only 10 bars enables you to play 70% of it. Using the methods of this book, therefore, 70% of this piece can be memorized in less than 30 minutes, because these bars are quite easy. Among these repeated bars, there are two interruptions that are difficult. A student with one to two years of lessons should be able to learn the required 50 different bars of this piece in 2 to 5 days and be able to play the whole piece at speed and from memory in 1 to 2 weeks. After that, the teacher is ready to work with the student on the musical content of the composition; how long that will take depends on the musical level of the student. We will now address the technical issues in the difficult sections.

The secret for acquiring technique quickly lies in knowing certain tricks for reducing impossibly difficult passages to not only playable but often to trivially simple ones. We shall now embark upon that magical journey into the brains of geniuses who figured out incredibly efficient ways to practice the piano!

5.   Practice the Difficult Sections First

Returning to Fur Elise, there are two difficult sections with 16 and 23 bars. *Start by practicing the most difficult sections first.* These will take the longest time to learn, so they should be given the most practice time. Since the ending of most pieces is generally the most difficult, you will learn most pieces starting from the end. Therefore, we will start by tackling these two difficult sections.

6.   Shortening Difficult Passages: Segmental (Bar-by-Bar) Practice

A most important learning trick is to choose a short practice segment. This trick has perhaps the biggest effect on reducing the practice time because of many reasons.

(a) *Within a difficult passage of say, 10 bars, there are typically only a few note combinations that stymie you. There is no need to practice anything other than those notes.* Let's examine the two difficult sections in Fur Elise and find the most troublesome spots. This may be the first bar or the last five bars of the first interruption (bars 45 to 56), or the final arpeggio in the second interruption (bars 82 to 105). In all difficult segments, it is critically important to observe the finger markings. For the last five bars of the first interruption, the difficulty is in the RH where most of the action is in fingers 1 and 5. For bar 52 (the one with the turn), the fingering is 2321231, and for bar 53, it is 251515151525. For the arpeggio in the second interruption, use the fingering 1231354321.... Either thumb under or thumb over (see section III.5) will work because this passage is not overly fast, but I prefer thumb over because the thumb under will require some elbow motion and this extra movement can lead to flubs.

(b) *Practicing short segments allows you to practice it dozens, even hundreds of times, in a matter of minutes.* Use of these quick repetitions is the fastest way to teach your hand new motions. If the difficult notes are played as part of a longer segment, the longer interval between repeats and the playing of other notes in between can confuse the hand and cause it to learn more slowly. This faster learning speed is quantitatively calculated in section IV.5, and that calculation provides the basis for the claim in this book that these methods can be 1000 times faster than the intuitive methods.

(c) We all know that playing faster than your technique allows is detrimental. However, *the shorter a segment you choose, the faster you can practice it without ill effects* because they are so much easier to play. Therefore, you can practice most of the time *at or beyond final speed*, which is the ideal situation because it saves so much time. In the intuitive method, you are practicing most of the time at slow speed.

7.   Hands Separate Practice: Acquiring Technique

Essentially 100% of technique development is accomplished by practicing hands separately (HS). Do not try to develop finger/hand technique hands together (HT) as that is much more difficult, time consuming, and *dangerous*, as explained in detail later.

Choose two short passages, one each for the right hand (RH) and the left hand (LH). ***Practice the RH until it begins to tire, then switch to the LH. Switch every 5 to 15 seconds, before either the resting hand cools and becomes sluggish, or the working hand becomes tired.*** If you choose the rest interval wisely, you will find that the rested hand is eager to perform. ***Don't practice when the hand is tired, because that will lead to stress (unnecessary muscle contraction) and bad habits.*** Those unfamiliar with HS practice will generally have a weaker LH. In that case, give the LH more work. In this scheme, you can practice hard 100% of the time, but you never practice with fatigued hands!

For the two difficult sections of Fur Elise, practice them HS until each hand becomes comfortable, up to speeds faster than final speed, before putting the hands together. This may take from a few days to several weeks depending on your level of play. As soon as you can play HS reasonably well, try HT to check that the fingering works.

It should be emphasized that HS practice is only for difficult passages that you cannot play. If you can play the passage adequately HT, by all means, skip the HS part! The ultimate objective of this book is for you to be able to quickly play HT with practically no HS practice after you become proficient. The objective is not to cultivate a dependence on HS practice. Use HS only when necessary and try to reduce its use gradually as your technique advances. However, you will be able to play HT with little HS practice only after you have become pretty advanced -- most students will be dependent on HS practice for 5 to 10 years, and will never completely abandon its use. The reason for this is that all technique is most quickly acquired HS. There is one exception to this option of skipping HS practice. That is memorizing; you should memorize everything HS for several important reasons (see "Memorizing", section III.6). Therefore, although you may not need to practice HS, you may need to memorize HS unless you are an advanced pianist with good mental play. Such advanced topics will be discussed later on.

Beginning students should practice HS with everything they learn so as to master this critically important method as quickly as possible. With HS practice, you acquire finger/hand technique; then with HT practice you only need to learn how to coordinate the two hands. By separating these tasks, you learn them better and faster. Once the HS method is mastered, the student should start to experiment with playing HT without using HS. Most students should be able to master the HS methods in two to three years. ***The HS method is not just separating the hands. What we will learn below are the myriad of learning tricks you can use once the hands are separated.***

HS practice is valuable long after you have learned a piece. You can push your technique much further HS than HT. And it is a lot of fun! You can really exercise the fingers/hands/arms. It is superior to anything Hanon or other exercises can provide. This is when you can figure out "incredible ways" to play that piece. This is when you can *really* improve your technique. The initial learning of the composition only serves to familiarize your fingers with the music. The amount of time spent playing pieces you have completely mastered is what separates the accomplished pianist from the amateur. This is why accomplished pianists can perform but most amateurs can only play for themselves.

8.   Continuity Rule

When practicing one segment, always include the beginning of the following segment. This continuity rule ensures that when you have learned two adjacent segments, you can also play them together. It applies to any segment you isolate for practice, such as a bar, an entire movement, or even to segments smaller than a bar. *A generalization of the* *continuity rule is that any passage may be broken up into short segments for practice, but these segments must overlap. The overlapping note or group of notes is called the conjunction.* If you are practicing the end of the first movement, then include a few bars of the beginning of the second movement. During a recital, you will be glad that you had practiced in this way; otherwise, you might suddenly find yourself stumped on how to start the 2nd movement!

We can now apply the continuity rule to those difficult interruptions in Fur Elise. To practice bar 53, add the first note of bar 54 (E played with finger 1), which is the conjunction. Since all the difficult sections are for the RH, find some LH material to practice, even from a different piece of music, in order to give the RH periodic rests by switching hands.

9.   Chord Attack

Suppose that you want to play the (LH) "do-so-mi-so" quadruplet ("Alberti accompaniment") many times in succession, very fast (as in the 3rd movement of Beethoven's Moonlight Sonata). The sequence you practice is CGEGC, where the last C is the conjunction. Since the conjunction is the same as the first note, you can "cycle" this quadruplet indefinitely without stopping. If you practice the quadruplet slowly and gradually speed it up HS, you will hit a "speed wall", a speed beyond which everything breaks down and stress builds up. *The way to break this speed wall is to play the quadruplet as a single chord (CEG). You have gone from slow speed to infinite speed! This is called a chord attack.* Now you only have to learn to slow down, which is easier than speeding up because there is no speed wall when you are slowing down. The key is -- how do you slow down?

First play the chord and bounce the hand up and down at the frequency at which the quadruplet will be repeated (say, between one and two times a second); this teaches the hand, wrist, arms, shoulder, etc., what they need to do for fast repetitions, and to exercise the appropriate muscles. Note that the fingers are now positioned correctly for fast playing; they are resting comfortably on the keys and slightly curled. Slow down and speed up the bounce frequency (even beyond the required speed!), noting how to alter the wrist, arm, fingers, etc., positions and motions to maximize comfort and avoid fatigue. If you feel fatigue after a while, then you are either doing something wrong, or else you have not yet acquired the technique of playing repeated the chords. Practice it until you can play without tiring because if you can't do it for a chord, you will never do it for quadruplets.

Keep the fingers close to or on the keys as you increase speed. Get the whole body involved; shoulders, upper and lower arms, wrist. The sensation is to play from your shoulders and arms, not the fingertips. When you can play this softly, relaxed, fast, and without any feeling of fatigue, you have made progress. Make sure that the chords are perfect (all notes landing at the same time) because, without this kind of sensitivity, you will not have the accuracy to play fast. *It is important to practice slowly because that is when you can work on the accuracy and relaxation. Accuracy improves faster at the slower speeds.* However, it is absolutely essential that you get up to fast speeds (if only briefly) before slowing down. Then, when you slow down, try to maintain the same motions that were required at high speed, because *that* is what you need to ultimately practice.

10.   Gravity Drop, Chord Practice, and Relaxation

Learning to play accurate chords is the first step in applying the chord attack. Let's practice the above LH CEG chord. The arm weight method is the best way to achieve accuracy and relaxation; this approach has been adequately treated in the referenced books (Fink, Sandor) and therefore will be discussed only briefly here. Place your fingers on the keys to play CEG. Relax your arm (the whole body, actually), keep your wrist flexible, lift the hand from 5 to 20 cm above the keys (the shorter distance in the beginning), and let gravity drop your hand. Let the hand and fingers drop as a unit, do not move the fingers. Relax the hands completely during the drop, then "set" your fingers and wrist at the time of impact with the keys and let the wrist flex slightly to take the shock of landing and to depress the keys. *By letting gravity lower your hand, you are referencing your strength or sensitivity to a constant force.*

It may seem unbelievable at first, but an under-weight 6-year-old and a gargantuan sumo wrestler dropping their hands from the same height will produce sound of the same loudness, if they both perform the gravity drop correctly (which is not easy, especially for the sumo wrestler). This happens because the speed of gravitational fall is independent of mass and the hammer goes into free flight as soon as the knuckle leaves the jack. Physics students will recognize that in the elastic limit (billiard ball collision), kinetic energy is conserved and the above statements do not hold. In such an elastic collision, the piano key would fly off the fingertip at high velocity, like a golf ball bouncing off a concrete floor. But here, because the fingers are relaxed and the fingertips are soft (inelastic collision), kinetic energy is not conserved and the small mass (piano key) can stay with the large mass (finger-hand-arm), resulting in a controlled keydrop. Therefore, the above statements hold as long as the piano is properly regulated and the effective mass for the key drop is much smaller than the mass of the 6-year-old's hand. Stiffening the hand after impact ensures that the entire arm weight transfers to the key drop. Do not stiffen the hand before hitting the bottom of the keydrop because this will add force – we only want gravity to play the keys.

Strictly speaking, the sumo wrestler will make a slightly louder sound because of momentum conservation, but the difference will be small, in spite of the fact that his arm may be 20 times heavier. Another surprise is that, once properly taught, the gravity drop may produce the loudest sound that this youngster has ever played (for a high drop), and is an excellent way to teach youngsters how to play firmly. Start with short drops for small youngsters because, in the beginning, a truly free drop can be painful if the height is too high. For a successful gravity drop, especially for youngsters, it is important to teach them to make-believe that there is no piano and the hand should feel like it is falling through the keyboard (but is stopped by it). Otherwise, most youngsters will subconsciously lift the hand as it lands on the piano. In other words, the gravity drop is a constant acceleration and the hand is accelerating, even during the key drop. At the end, the hand is resting on the keys with its own weight -- this way of playing produces a pleasant, deep, tone. Note that it is important for the key drop to accelerate all the way down - see section III.1 on producing good tone.

The well-known Steinway "accelerated action" works because it adds acceleration to the hammer motion by use of a rounded support under the center key bushing. This causes the pivot point to move forward with the keydrop thus shortening the front side of the key and lengthening the back side and thereby causing the capstan to accelerate for a constant keydrop. This illustrates the importance piano designers place on accelerating the keydrop, and the arm weight method ensures that we take full advantage of gravitational acceleration to produce good tone. The effectiveness of the "accelerated action" is controversial because there are excellent pianos without this feature. Obviously, it is more important for the pianist to control this acceleration than to depend on the piano.

The fingers must be "set" after the keys reach the bottom of the keydrop in order to stop the hand's downward motion. This requires a brief application of force to the finger. As soon as the hand stops, remove this force and relax completely so that you can feel gravity pulling the arm down. Rest the hand on the key with only this gravitational force keeping the keys down. What you have just accomplished is to depress the key with the least possible effort; this is the essence of relaxation. *Note that an important element of relaxation is the immediate relaxation of all muscles once the gravity drop is over.*

Beginning students will play chords with too many unnecessary forces that can not be accurately controlled. *The use of gravity can eliminate all unnecessary forces or tenseness.* It might seem like a curious coincidence that the force of gravity is the right force for playing the piano. *This is no coincidence. Humans evolved under the influence of gravity. Our strengths for walking, lifting, etc., evolved to match gravity <u>exactly</u>.* The piano, of course, was *designed* to match those strengths. When you are truly relaxed, you can feel the effect of gravity on your hands as you are playing. Some teachers emphasize relaxation to the point of neglecting everything else until "total" relaxation is achieved; that may be going too far -- being able to feel gravity is a necessary and sufficient criterion for relaxation. *The gravity drop is a method for practicing relaxation. Once this relaxed state is achieved, it must become a permanent, integral part of your piano playing.* Total relaxation does not mean that you should always play the piano using only gravity. Most of the time, you will be applying your own force; "feeling gravity" is simply a way of measuring your level of relaxation.

11.   Parallel Sets

Now that the LH CEG chord is satisfactory, try to switch suddenly from the chord to the quadruplet. You will now have to move the fingers but keep the finger motions to a minimum. To successfully switch, incorporate the proper hand/arm motions (see Fink, Sandor) discussed later but, that's advanced stuff, so let's back-track and assume that you cannot switch, so that we can demonstrate a powerful method for solving this type of problem.

The most basic way to learn how to play a difficult passage is to build it up two notes at a time, using the chord attack. In our (LH) CGEG example, we start with the first two notes. A two-note chord attack (strictly speaking, an interval attack)! Play these two notes as a perfect interval, bouncing your hand and fingers (5 and 1) together up and down as you did previously with the CEG chord. In order to play these two notes rapidly one after the other, lower both fingers together, but keep the 1 finger slightly above the 5 so that the 5 lands first. It is a rapid two-note rolling interval. Since you are bringing both fingers down at once and only delaying one slightly, you can play them as closely as you wish by decreasing the delay. *This is how you slow down from infinite speed!*

Is it possible to play any combination of notes infinitely fast in this way? Of course not. How do we know which ones can be played infinitely fast and which ones can't? In order to answer that question, we need to introduce the concept of parallel play. The above method of lowering fingers together is called parallel play because the fingers are lowered together, i.e., in parallel. *A Parallel Set (PS) is a group of notes that can be played simultaneously with one hand. All PSs can be played infinitely fast – chord attacks use PSs. The delay between successive fingers is called the phase angle.* In a chord, the phase angle is zero for all the fingers; see Exercise #2 of III.7.b for a detailed treatment of PSs. This is a chord attack, but the "parallel set" terminology is needed to avoid the confusion arising from the fact that in music theory, "chord" and "interval" have specific meanings that are not always applicable to all PSs. The highest PS speed is attained by reducing the phase to the smallest controllable value. This value is approximately equal to the error in your chord playing. In other words, the more accurate your chords, the faster will be your maximum attainable speed. This is why so much space was devoted above to practicing perfect chords.

Once you have conquered the CG, you can proceed with the next GE (13), then EG and finally the GC to complete the quadruplet and conjunction. Then connect them in pairs,

CGE, etc., to complete the quadruplet. Note that CGE (513) is also a PS. Therefore the quadruplet plus conjunction can be constructed from two PSs, (513) and (315). In this scheme, 3 is the conjunction. This is faster than the use of 2-note PSs, but more difficult. The general rule for the use of PSs is: *construct the practice segment by using the largest PSs possible that are consistent with the fingering.* Break it up into smaller PSs only if the large PS is too difficult. Section III.7 discusses details of how to use PSs.

After you can play one quadruplet well, practice playing two in succession, then three, etc. Eventually, you will be able to play as many as you want indefinitely! When you initially bounced the chord, the hand moved up and down. But in the end, when playing the quadruplets in rapid succession, the hand is fairly stationary; you will also have to add hand motions, etc., -- more on these topics later.

The second difficult section in Fur Elise ends with an arpeggio containing three PSs: 123, 135, and 432. First practice each PS individually (e.g. 123), then add the conjunction (1231), then connect them in pairs, (123135) etc., to build up the arpeggio.

In order for any practice segment to sound smooth and musical, *we need to accomplish two things: (1) control the phase angles accurately (finger independence) and (2) connect the parallel sets smoothly.* Most of the finger/hand/arm motions described in the references are aimed at accomplishing these two tasks in ingenious ways. We shall discuss many of those topics in Section III. The references are useful companions to this book. In order to help you decide which reference to use, I have provided (brief) reviews for many of them in the Reference section.

You will need to read most of section III in order to know how to use PSs most effectively. The parallel play described above is called "phase locked" parallel play and is the easiest way to start, but that is not the ultimate goal. In order to acquire technique, you need complete finger independence, that comes with practice, not phase locked fingers. *PSs accomplish two things: teach your brain the concept of extremely fast play, and give the hands an idea of what rapid play feels like.* For those who have not played that fast, these are totally new and amazing experiences. Parallel play gets you up to speed, so that you can experiment with different motions to see which ones work. Because these methods allow hundreds of trials in minutes, this experimentation can be conducted quickly.

12.   Learning, Memorizing, and Mental Play
There is no faster way of memorizing than to memorize when you are first learning a piece and, for a difficult piece, there is no faster way of learning than memorizing it. Start memorizing by learning how the music should sound: melody, rhythm, etc. Then use the sheet music to find and memorize each key on the piano for each note on the sheet music; this is called keyboard memory – you memorize how you play this piece on the piano, complete with the fingering, hand motions, etc. Some pianists use photographic memory, in which they photographically memorize the sheet music. If one were to take a sheet of music and try to memorize it note for note, this task would be impossibly difficult even for concert pianists. However, once you know the music (melody, chord structure, etc.), it becomes easy for everyone! This is explained in Section III.6, where you will find more detailed discussions on how to memorize. I prefer keyboard memory to photographic memory because it helps you to find the notes on the piano without having to "read" the music in your head. Memorize each section that you are practicing for technique while you are repeating them so many times in small segments, HS. *The procedures for memorizing are basically the same as those for technique acquisition.* For example, memorization should be started HS, difficult sections first, etc. If you memorize later, you will have to repeat the same procedure again. It might appear that going through the same procedure a second time would

be simpler. It is not. Memorizing is a complex task (even after you can play the piece well); therefore, students who try to memorize after learning a piece will either give up or never memorize it completely. This is understandable; the effort required to memorize can quickly reach the point of diminishing returns if you can already play the piece.

Two important items to memorize are the time signature (see III.1.b) and key signature (see III.5.d). The time signature is easy to understand and will help you to play with the correct rhythm. The key signature (how many sharps or flats) is more complex because it does not tell you the precise key (scale) that it is in (C-major, etc.). If you know that the composition is in a major or minor scale, the key signature tells you the key; for example if the key signature has no sharps or flats (as in Fur Elise), it is in either C major or A minor (see III.5.d). Most students know the major scales; you will need to know more theory to figure out the minor keys; therefore, only those with enough theory knowledge should memorize the key. If you are not sure, memorize only the key signature. This key is the basic tonality of the music around which the composer uses chord progressions to change keys. *Most compositions start and end with the base tonality and the chords generally progress along the circle of fifths (see Ch. Two, 2.b).* So far, we know that Fur Elise is either in C major or A minor. Since it is somewhat melancholy, we suspect a minor. The first 2 bars are like a fanfare that introduces the first theme, so the main body of the theme begins on bar 3, which starts with A, the tonic of A minor! Moreover, the final chord is also on the tonic of A minor. So it is probably in A minor. The only accidental in A minor is G# (see Table 1.III.5b), which we find in bar 4; therefore we conclude that it is in A minor. When you understand these details, you can *really* memorize well.

Let's revisit the time signature, which is 3/8; three beats per measure (bar), an eighth per beat. Thus it is in the format of a waltz but musically, it should not be played like a dance but much more smoothly because it is melancholy and hauntingly romantic. The time signature tells us that bars like bar 3 must not be played as two triplets because there are 3 beats. However, there is no need to overly accent the first beat of every bar like a Viennese Waltz. The time signature is clearly useful for playing musically and correctly. Without the time signature, you can easily form incorrect rhythmic habits that will make your playing sound amateurish.

Once students develop memorizing-learning routines that are comfortable for them, most of them will find that learning and memorizing together takes less time than learning alone, for difficult passages. This happens because you eliminate the process of looking at the music, interpreting it, and passing the instructions from the eyes to the brain and then to the hands. Material memorized when young (before about age 20) is almost never forgotten. This is why it is so critical to learn fast methods of technique acquisition and to memorize as many pieces as possible before reaching the later teen years. It is easier to memorize something if you can play it fast; therefore, if you have difficulty memorizing it initially at slow speed, don't worry; it will become easier as you speed it up.

The only way to memorize well is to learn Mental Play (MP). In fact, MP is the logical and ultimate goal of all these practice methods that we are discussing because technique alone will not enable you to perform flawlessly, musically, and without getting nervous. Read III.6.j for more details on MP. With MP, you learn to play the piano in your mind, away from the piano, complete with accurate fingering and your concept of how you want the music to sound. You can use keyboard memory or photographic memory for MP, but I recommend keyboard memory for beginners because it is more efficient; for advanced players, keyboard memory and photographic memory are the same, since if you can do one, the other follows naturally. Whenever you memorize a small section, close your eyes and see if you can play it in your mind without playing it on the piano. Once you have memorized an entire piece HS), you should also be able to play the complete piece HS in your head. This is the time to analyze the structure of the music, how it is organized and how the themes develop as the music progresses. With practice, you will find that it requires only a small investment of time to acquire MP. Best of all, you will also discover that once solid MP is established, your memory is as good as it can get; you will have confidence that you will be able to play without mistakes, blackouts, etc., and will be able to concentrate on music. MP also helps technique; for example, it is much easier to play at a fast speed after you can mentally play it at that speed; very often, the inability to play fast originates in the brain. One benefit of MP is that you can practice it at any time, anywhere, and can greatly increase your effective practice time.

Memory is an associative process. Super memorizers (including some savants) and all concert pianists who can memorize hours of music depend on algorithms with which to associate their memory (whether they know it or not). Musicians are especially fortunate in this regard because music is precisely such an algorithm. Nonetheless, this "memory trick" of using music as an algorithm to memorize is seldom formally taught to music students; instead, they are often advised to keep repeating "until the music is in the hands", which is one of the worst methods of memory because, as we shall see in section III.6.d, repetition results in "hand memory" which is a false type of memory that can lead to many problems, such as blackouts. With MP, you associate the music in your mind with how you produce it at the piano. It is important to practice MP without playing the piano because you can acquire "sound memory" (just as you can acquire "hand memory") and use the sound of the piano as a crutch for recall, and sound memory can cause the same problems associated with hand memory.

Why are memory and MP so important? They not only solve the practical problems of technique and performance but also advance your musicianship and increase intelligence. You can speed up a computer by adding memory; similarly, you can increase your effective intelligence by improving your memory. In fact, one of the first signs of mental deterioration, such as Alzheimer's, is loss of memory. *It is now clear that many of those "amazing feats" of great musicians such as Mozart were simple byproducts of strong MP, and that such skills can be learned.* More on MP in III.6j.

13.   Velocity, Choice of Practice Speed

Get up to speed as quickly as possible. Remember, we are still practicing HS. Playing so fast that you start to feel stress and make mistakes will not improve technique because you are mainly practicing mistakes and acquiring bad habits. Forcing the fingers to play the same way faster is not the way to increase speed. As demonstrated with parallel play, you need new ways that automatically increase speed and reduce stress. In fact, with parallel play, it is often easier to play fast than slowly. Devise hand positions and motions that automatically increase speed; this topic is one of the major contributions of this book, and will be treated topic by topic later on as it is too big to be covered here; it involves such specific skills such as thumb over method, glissando motion, relaxation, flat finger positions, arm and wrist motions, etc., and the use of "post practice improvement". If you do not make significant progress in a few minutes, you are probably doing something wrong -- think of something new. Students who use the intuitive method are resigned to repeating the same thing for hours with little visible improvement. That mentality must be avoided in order to learn faster. There are two types of situations you will encounter when increasing speed. One involves technical skills you already have; you should be able to bring these up to speed in minutes. The other involves new skills; these will take longer and will be discussed in section 15 below.

Technique improves most rapidly when playing at a speed at which you can play accurately. This is especially true when playing HT (please be patient -- I promise we will eventually get to HT practice). Since you have more control HS, you can get away with much faster play HS than HT without increasing stress or forming bad habits. Thus it is erroneous to think that you can improve faster by playing as fast as possible (after all, if you play twice as fast, you can practice the same passage twice as often!). Since one major objective of HS practice is to gain speed, the need to attain speed quickly and to practice accurately become contradictory. The solution is to constantly change the speed of practice; do not stay at any one speed for too long. For very difficult passages that require skills you don't already have, there is no alternative but to bring the speed up in stages. For this, use speeds that are too fast as exploratory excursions to determine what needs to be changed in order to play at such speeds. Then slow down and practice those new motions.

To vary the speed, first get up to some manageable "maximum speed" at which you can play accurately. Then go faster (using parallel sets, etc., if necessary), and take note of how the playing needs to be changed (don't worry if you are not playing accurately at this point because you are not repeating it many times). Then use that motion and play at the previous "maximum accurate speed". It should now be noticeably easier. Practice at this speed for a while, then try slower speeds to make sure that you are completely relaxed and absolutely accurate. Then repeat the whole procedure. In this way, you ratchet up the speed in manageable jumps and work on each needed skill separately. In most cases, you should be able to play most of the new piece, at least in small segments, HS, at the final speed during the first sitting. In the beginning, getting up to speed at the first sitting may seem unattainable but, with practice, every student can reach this objective surprisingly quickly.

14.   How to Relax

The most important thing to do as you get up to speed is to relax. Relaxing means that you use only those muscles that are needed to play. Thus you can be working as hard as you want, and be relaxed. The relaxed state is especially easy to attain when practicing HS. There are two schools of thought on relaxation. One school maintains that, in the long run, it is better not to practice at all than to practice with even the slightest amount of tension. This school teaches by showing you how to relax and play a single note, and then advancing carefully, giving you only those easy material that you can play relaxed. The other school argues that relaxation is certainly a necessary aspect of technique, but that subjugating the entire practice philosophy to relaxation is not the optimum approach. The second approach should be better, provided that you are aware of the pitfalls.

The human brain can be quite wasteful. For even the simplest tasks, the untrained brain uses most of the muscles in the body. And if the task is difficult, the brain tends to lock the entire body in a mass of tensed muscles. In order to relax, you must make a conscious effort to shut down all unnecessary muscles. This is not easy because it goes against the natural tendencies of the brain. You need to practice relaxation just as much as moving the fingers to play the keys. Relaxing does not mean to "let go of all muscles"; it means that the unnecessary ones are relaxed even when the necessary ones are working full tilt, which is a coordination skill that requires a lot of practice.

For those who are new to relaxation, you can start with easier pieces you have learned, and practice adding relaxation. The parallel set exercises of III.7 can help you to practice relaxation. One way to feel relaxation is to practice one parallel set and accelerate it until stress builds up and then try to relax. You will need to find motions and positions of arms, wrists, etc., that allow this; when you find them, you will feel the stress draining out from the hand as you play.

Relax and maintain all the various functions of the body, such as breathing and periodic swallowing. Some students stop breathing when playing demanding passages in order to concentrate on the playing. When relaxed, you should be able to conduct all of the normal body functions and still be able to concentrate on playing. Section 21 below explains how to use the diaphragm to breathe properly. If the throat is dry after a hard practice, it means that you had stopped swallowing. These are all indications of stress.

Many students who were not taught relaxation think that long repetitive practices somehow transform the hand so it can play. In reality, what often happens is that the hand accidentally stumbles onto the right motion for relaxation. This is why some skills are acquired quickly while others take forever and why some students acquire certain skills quickly while other students struggle with the same skills. Thus relaxation is a state of unstable equilibrium: as you learn to relax, it becomes easier to play, which makes it easier to relax, etc. This explains why relaxation is a major problem for some while it is completely natural for others. But that is a most wonderful piece of information -- it means that anyone can learn to relax, if properly taught.

Relaxation is energy conservation. There are at least 2 ways to conserve: (1) don't use unnecessary muscles – especially the opposing muscles and (2) turn off the working muscles as soon as their jobs are done. Let's demonstrate these with the one-finger gravity drop. (1) is the easiest; simply allow gravity to completely control the drop, while the entire body is resting comfortably on the bench. A tense person will contract both opposing muscles: those for raising and for lowering the hand. For (2) you will need to learn a new habit if you don't already have it (few do, initially). That is the habit of relaxing all muscles as soon as you reach the bottom of the key drop. During a gravity drop, you let gravity pull the arm down, but at the end of the key drop, you need to tense the finger for an instant in order to stop the hand. Then you must quickly relax all muscles. Don't lift the hand, but rest the hand comfortably on the piano with just enough force at the finger to support the weight of the arm. Make sure that you are not pressing down. This is more difficult than you would think at first because the elbow is floating in mid air and the same bundles of muscles used to tense the finger in order to support the arm weight are also used to press down.

Tensing opposing muscles is a major cause of tension. If the pianist is not aware of it, it can grow out of control can cause injury. Just as we must learn to control each finger or hand independently, we must also learn to control each opposing muscle, such as flexor and extensor, independently. The worst consequence of stress is that it gets you into a fight you can't win because you are fighting an opponent who is exactly as strong as you are -- namely, yourself. It is your own muscles working against your body. And the more you practice, the worse the problem. If it gets bad enough, it can cause injury because the muscles become stronger than the material strength of the body.

Without training, few people will bother to turn off muscles explicitly; normally, you simply forget about them when their work is done. However, in fast finger work, you need to relax rapidly; otherwise, the fingers will never get any rest, or be prepared for the next note. A good exercise for practicing rapid relaxation is to start with one key down and to play a quick, moderately loud note with that same finger. Now you have to apply an up and down force *and* turn it off. When you turn it off, you must return to the feeling you had at the end of a gravity drop. You will find that the harder you play the note, the longer it takes to relax. Practice shortening this relaxation time.

What is so wonderful about these relaxation methods is that after practicing them for a short time (perhaps a few weeks), they tend to be automatically incorporated into your playing, even into pieces that you have already learned, as long as you pay attention to relaxation. ***Relaxation (involving the whole body), arm weight (gravity drop), and*** *avoidance of mindless repetitive exercises were key elements in Chopin's teachings.* Relaxation is useless unless it is accompanied by musical playing; in fact, Chopin insisted on musical playing before acquiring technique because he knew that relaxation, music and technique are inseparable. This may be why most of Chopin's compositions (unlike Beethoven's) can be played within a wide range of speeds.

15.   Post Practice Improvement (PPI)

There is only a specific amount of improvement you can expect during practice at one sitting, because there are two major ways in which you improve. The first one is the obvious improvement that comes from learning the notes and motions, resulting in immediate improvement. This occurs for passages for which you already have the technique to play. *The second one is called post practice improvement (PPI) that results from physiological changes as you acquire new technique.* This is a slow process of change that occurs over weeks or months because it requires the growth of nerve and muscle cells.

Therefore, as you practice, try to gauge your progress so that you can quit and go to something else as soon as a point of diminishing returns is reached, usually in less than 10 minutes. *Like magic, your technique will keep improving by itself for at least several days after a good practice.* Therefore, *if you had done everything right,* then, the next day, you should discover that you can now play better. If this happens for just one day, the effect is not that big. However, the cumulative effect of this occurring over months or years can be huge.

It is usually more profitable to practice several things at one sitting and let them all improve simultaneously (while you are not practicing!), than working too hard on one thing. Over-practicing can actually hurt your technique if it leads to stress, bad habits or injury. You do have to practice a certain minimum amount, about a hundred repetitions, for PPI to take effect. But because we are talking about a few bars played at speed, practicing dozens or hundreds of times should take only a few minutes. Therefore, don't fret if you practice hard but don't see much immediate improvement. This might be normal for that particular passage. If you can't find anything wrong with what you are doing, it is time to stop and let PPI take over, after making sure that you made enough repetitions for PPI. Also, be sure to practice relaxed because you don't want PPI of a stressed motion.

There are many types of PPI depending on what is holding you back. One of the ways in which these different types manifest themselves is in the length of time over which PPI is effective, which varies from one day to many months. The shortest times may be associated with conditioning, such as the use of motions or muscles you had not used before, or memory issues. Intermediate times of several weeks may be associated with new nerve connections, such as HT play. Longer times may be associated with actual growth of brain/nerve/muscle cells, and conversion of slow to fast muscle cell types (see III.7.a).

You must do everything right to maximize PPI. Many students do not know the rules and can *negate* the PPI with the result that, when they play the next day, it comes out *worse.* Most of these mistakes originate from incorrect use of fast and slow practice; therefore, we will discuss the rules for choosing the right practice speeds in the following sections. Any stress or unnecessary motion during practice will also undergo PPI and can become a bad habit. The most common mistake students make to negate PPI is to play fast before quitting practice. The last thing you do before quitting should be the most correct and best example of what you want to achieve, which usually a moderate to slow speed. *Your last run-through seems to have an inordinately strong PPI effect.* The methods of this book are ideal for PPI, mainly because they emphasize practicing only those segments that you cannot play. If you play HT slowly and ramp up the speed for a long section, PPI is insufficiently conditioned because you don't have enough time to make the necessary number of repetitions. In addition, the PPI process becomes confused because you mix a large proportion of easy material with the small amount of difficult ones and the speed, motions, etc., are also incorrect.

PPI is nothing new; let's look at three well-known examples: the body builder, marathoner, and golfer. While lifting weights, the body builder's muscles don't grow; he will in fact lose weight. But during the following weeks, the body will react to the stimulus and add muscle. All the muscle growth occurs *after* the exercise. Thus the body builder does not measure how much muscle he gained or how much more weight he can lift at the end of the exercise, but instead concentrates on whether the exercise produces the appropriate conditioning. The difference here is that for piano, we are developing coordination and speed instead of strength and bulk muscle. Thus, whereas the bodybuilder wants to grow the slow muscles, the pianist wants to convert the slow muscles into fast ones. Another example is the marathon runner. If you had never run a mile in your life, and tried it for the first time, you might be able to jog for a quarter mile before you need to slow down for a rest. After some rest, if you tried to run again, you will still tire out in a quarter mile or less. Thus the first run resulted in no discernible improvement. However, the next day, you may be able to run a third of a mile before tiring -- you have just experienced PPI. This is how marathoners condition themselves to be able to eventually run 26 miles. Golfers are familiar with the phenomenon in which they can hit the ball well one day, but terribly the next because they picked up a bad habit. Thus hitting the driver (the most difficult club) too many times tends to ruin your swing, whereas practicing with the #5 wood (a much easier club) can restore it; therefore it is important to practice with a easier club before quitting practice. The analogy in piano is that playing fast, full tilt, tends to ruin the PPI whereas practicing simpler material (short sections HS) tends to improve it.

PPI occurs mainly during sleep. You can not repair your car while driving it on a highway; likewise, most of the growth and maintenance of the body cannot occur during the waking hours. Sleep is not only for resting, but also for growth and maintenance of the body. This sleep must be the normal, over-night type with all of its major components, especially REM sleep. Babies need so much sleep because they are growing rapidly. You may not get good PPI if you did not sleep well that night. The best routine for using PPI may be to practice in the evening for conditioning and then reviewing it the next morning. PPI is triggered by cell death; hard practice causes premature cell death, and the body over-compensates for this when there are excess cell deaths. You might think that 100 repetitions can't possibly cause cell death, but cells are always being replaced, and any extra work will increase this replacement rate.

16.   Dangers of Slow Play - Pitfalls of the Intuitive Method

Why is repetitive slow play (intuitive method) harmful when starting a new piece? When you start, there is no way of knowing whether the slow play motion you are using is right or wrong. The probability of playing incorrectly is nearly 100%, because there is almost an infinity of ways to play incorrectly but only one best way. When this wrong motion is speeded up, the student will hit a speed wall. Assuming that this student succeeded in overcoming the speed wall by finding a new way to play, s/he will then need to unlearn the old way and relearn this new play, and keep repeating these cycles for each incremental increase in speed until s/he reaches the final speed. Thus the method of slowly ramping up the speed can waste a lot of time.

Let's look at an example of how different speeds require different motions. Consider the horse's gait. As the speed is increased, the gait goes through walk, trot, canter, and gallop. Each of these four gaits usually has at least a slow and fast mode. Also, a left turn is different from a right turn (the leading hoof is different). That's a minimum of 16 motions. These are the so-called natural gaits; most horses automatically have them; they can also be taught 3 more gaits: pace, foxtrot, and rack, which likewise have slow, fast, left, and right: all this, with only four legs of relatively simple structure and a comparatively limited brain. We have 10 complex fingers, more versatile shoulders, arms, and hands, and a much more capable brain! Our hands are therefore capable of performing many more "gaits" than a horse. Most students have little idea of how many motions are possible unless the teacher points these out to them. Two students, left to their own devices and asked to play the same piece, will be guaranteed to end up with different hand motions. This is another reason why it is so important to take lessons from a good teacher when starting piano; such a teacher can quickly weed out the bad motions.

Ramping up a slow play in piano is like forcing a horse run as fast as a gallop by simply speeding up the walk -- it can't be done because as the speed increases, the momenta of the legs, body, etc., change, requiring the different gaits. Therefore, if the music requires a "gallop", the student ends up having to learn all the intervening "gaits" if you ramp up the speed. Forcing a horse to walk as fast as a gallop would erect speed walls, produce stress, and cause injury.

A common slow-play mistake is the habit of supporting or lifting the hand. In slow play, the hand can be lifted between notes when the downward pressure is not necessary. When speeded up, this "lift" habit coincides with the next keydrop; these actions cancel, resulting in a missed note. Another common error is the waving of the free fingers -- while playing fingers 1 and 2, the student might be waving fingers 4 and 5 in the air several times. This presents no difficulties until the motion is speeded up so fast that there is no time to wave the fingers. In this situation, the free fingers will not automatically stop waving at faster speeds because the motion has been ingrained by hundreds or even thousands of repetitions. Instead, the fingers are asked to wave several times at speeds they cannot attain -- this creates the speed wall. The trouble here is that most students who use slow practice are unaware of these bad habits. *If you know how to play fast, it is safe to play slowly, but if you don't know how to play fast, you must be careful not to learn the wrong slow playing habits or to end up wasting tremendous amounts of time.* Slow play can waste huge chunks of time because each run-through takes so long. As you speed up, you will need to increase the downward pressure because you are pressing more keys in the same interval of time. *Thus "feeling gravity" doesn't work most of the time because different downward pressures are needed as you play.*

Another problem associated with the intuitive slow practice approach is unnecessary body motions. These motions create more difficulties at higher speeds. *Unless they video record their playing and watch carefully for strange body motions, most pianists are unaware of all the motions they make. These can cause unpredictable mistakes at unpredictable times, creating psychological problems with insecurity and nervousness.* Cultivating an awareness of body motions can eliminate this problem. We see that intuition can lead to a myriad of difficulties; instead of intuition, we need a knowledge based system.

17. Importance of Slow Play

Having pointed out the dangers of slow play, we now discuss why slow play is *indispensable*. *Always end a practice session by playing slowly at least once. This is the most important rule for good PPI.* You should also cultivate a habit of doing this when switching hands during HS practice; before switching, play slowly at least once. *This may be one of the most important rules of this chapter because it has such an inordinately large effect on technique improvement.* It is beneficial to both the immediate improvement and to

PPI. One reason why it works may be that you can completely relax (see section II.14). Another reason may be that you tend to pick up more bad habits than you realize while playing fast, and you can "erase" these habits with slow play. Contrary to intuition, playing slowly without mistakes is difficult (until you have completely mastered the passage). Thus slow play is a good way to test whether you have really learned this piece of music.

The effect of a final slow play on PPI is so dramatic that you can easily demonstrate it for yourself. Try one practice session in which you only play fast and see what happens the next day. Then try one in which you play slowly before quitting, and see what happens on the next day. Or you can practice a passage fast only and another passage (of the same difficulty) slowly at the end and compare them the next day. This effect is cumulative, so that if you were to repeat this experiment with the same two passages for a long time, you will eventually find a huge difference in the way you can play them.

How slow is slow? That is a judgment call, and depends on your skill level. Below a certain speed, the slow play will lose its beneficial effects. It is important, when playing slowly, to maintain the same motion as when playing fast. If you play too slowly, this may become impossible. Also, playing too slowly will take too long, wasting time. The best speed to try first is one at which you can play as accurately as you want, around 1/2 to 3/4 speed. Slow play is also needed for memorizing (see III.6.h). The optimum slow speed for memorizing, below about 1/2 speed, is slower than that needed for PPI conditioning. As technique improves, this slow speed can become faster. Some famous pianists have been observed to practice *very slowly*! Some accounts document practice at one note per second, which sounds almost irrational, but may benefit memory and musicality.

An important skill to practice when playing slowly is to think ahead of the music. When practicing a new piece fast, there is a tendency to mentally fall behind the music and this can become a habit. This is bad because that is how you lose control. Think ahead when playing slowly and then try to maintain that lead when you get back up to speed. By thinking ahead, you can usually foresee flubs or difficulties coming and have the time to take appropriate action.

18.   Fingering

Except in beginners' books, the basic fingerings are not indicated in music scores. For those basic fingerings, go to the scales (III.5.d and III.5.h) and arpeggio (III.5.e) sections; *note that it is the scales that determine the fingerings for practically all runs. Therefore it is important to memorize the fingerings for all the scales*; this is not difficult because most scales follow a standard fingering and the exceptions follow simple rules, such as avoiding the thumb on black keys. Playing a black key with the thumb positions the hand too close to the fallboard, which makes it difficult to play the white keys with the other fingers. Most scores show fingerings for unusual situations where special fingerings are needed. Follow these fingerings unless you have a better one; if you don't follow the indicated fingering, you will probably get into trouble. An indicated fingering may feel awkward at first but it is there for good reasons. These reasons often do not become apparent until you get up to speed and/or you play HT. *It is most important to fix your fingering and not change it unless there is a good reason.* Not having a fixed fingering will slow down the learning process and give you trouble later, especially during a performance, when a fingering indecision can cause a mistake. If you do change the fingering, make sure that you always stick to the new one. Mark the change on the music so that you don't inadvertently change it during practice; also, it can be very annoying to come back to this music months later and not remember that nice fingering you had previously worked out.

Not all suggested fingerings on the music score are appropriate for everyone. You may have large or small hands. You may have gotten used to a different fingering because of the way you learned. You might have a different skill set; e.g., you might be a better triller using 1,3 than 2,3. Music from different publishers may have different fingerings. For advanced players, the fingering can have a profound influence on the musical effect you want to project. Fortunately, the methods of this book are well suited to quickly changing fingerings. Once you have become familiar with the methods of this book, you will be able to change fingering very quickly. Make all the changes before you start HT practice because once fingerings are incorporated into HT play, they become very difficult to change. On the other hand, some fingerings are easy HS but become difficult HT, so it pays to check them HT before permanently accepting any changes.

In summary, fingering is critically important. ***Beginners should not start practicing without knowing the proper fingerings.*** If you are uncertain about fingering, try to find sheet music with plenty of fingering indications or go to an internet piano forum and ask for help. If you look at how the scales and arpeggios are fingered, you will find some simple "common sense" rules of fingering; these should be enough to get you started.

19.   Accurate Tempo and the Metronome

Start all pieces by counting carefully, especially for beginners and youngsters. Children should be taught to count out loud because that is the only way to find out what *their* idea of counting is. It can be totally different from the intended one! You should understand the time signature at the beginning of each composition. It looks like a fraction, consisting of a numerator and a denominator. The numerator indicates the number of beats per measure and the denominator indicates the note per beat. For example, 3/4 means that there are three beats per measure and that each beat is a quarter note. Typically, each bar contains one measure. Knowing the time signature is essential when accompanying, because the moment that the accompanist starts is determined by the starting beat which the conductor indicates with the baton.

An advantage of HS practice is that you tend to count more accurately than HT. Students who start HT can end up with undetected mistakes in counting. Interestingly, these mistakes usually make it impossible to bring the music up to speed. There is something about wrong counting that creates its own speed wall. It probably messes up the rhythm. Therefore, if you run into problems with bringing it up to speed, check the counting. A metronome is very useful for this.

Use the metronome to check your speed and beat accuracy. I have been repeatedly surprised by the errors I discover when checked in this way. For example, I tend to slow down at difficult sections and speed up at easy ones, although I think it is actually the opposite when playing without the metronome. Most teachers will check their students' tempi with it. As soon as the student gets the timing, it should be shut off. The metronome is one of your most reliable teachers -- once you start using it, you will be glad you did. Develop a habit of using the metronome and your playing will undoubtedly improve. All serious students must have a metronome.

Metronomes should not be over used. ***Long practice sessions with the metronome accompanying you are harmful to technique acquisition and leads to non-musical playing.*** When the metronome is used for more than about 10 minutes continually, your mind will start to play mental tricks on you so that you may lose the timing accuracy. For example, if the metronome emits clicks, after some time, your brain will create anti-clicks in your head that can cancel the metronome click so that you will either not hear the metronome anymore, or will hear it at the wrong time. This is why most modern electronic metronomes have a light pulse mode. The visual cue is less prone to mental tricks and also does not interfere acoustically with the music. The most frequent abuse of the metronome is to use it to ramp up speed; this abuses the metronome, the student, the music, and the technique. If you must ramp up the speed gradually, use the metronome to set the tempo, then turn it off and then keep on practicing; then use it again briefly when you increase the speed. ***The metronome is for setting the tempo and for checking your accuracy. It is not a substitute for your own internal timing.***

The process of speeding up is a process of finding the appropriate new motions. When you find the correct new motion, you can make a quantum jump to a higher speed at which the hand plays comfortably; in fact, at intermediate speeds, neither the slow nor the fast motion applies and is often more difficult to play than the faster speed. If you happen to set the metronome at this intermediate speed, you might struggle at it for long periods of time and build up a speed wall. One of the reasons why the new motion works is that the human hand is a mechanical device and has resonances at which certain combinations of motions naturally work well. There is little doubt that some music was composed to be played at certain speeds because the composer found this resonance speed. On the other hand, each individual has a different hand with different resonance speeds, and this partly explains why different pianists choose different speeds. Without the metronome, you can jump from resonance to the next resonance because the hand feels comfortable at those speeds, whereas the chances of your setting the metronome at exactly those speeds are very low. Therefore, with the metronome, you are almost always practicing at the wrong speed, unless you know about the resonances (nobody does) and set the metronome accordingly.

Electronic metronomes are superior to the mechanical ones in every respect although some people prefer the appearance of the old models. Electronics are more accurate, can make different sounds or flash lights, have variable volume, are less expensive, are less bulky, have memory functions, etc., while the mechanicals always seem to need rewinding at the worst possible times.

20.   Weak Left Hand; Using One Hand to Teach the Other

Students who do not practice HS will always have a stronger RH than LH. This happens because the RH passages are generally more difficult, technically. The LH tends to get passages that require more strength, but it often lags behind in speed and technique. Thus "weaker" here means technically weaker, not strength-wise. ***The HS method will balance the hands because you will automatically give the weaker hand more work.*** For passages that one hand can play better than the other, the better hand is often your best teacher. To let one hand teach the other, select a short segment and play it rapidly with the better hand, then repeat immediately with the weaker hand, one octave apart to prevent collisions. You will discover that the weaker hand can often "catch on" or "get the idea" of how the better hand is doing it. The fingering should be similar but does not need to be identical. Once the weaker hand "gets the idea", gradually wean it off by playing the weaker hand twice and the stronger hand once, then three against one, etc.

This ability of one hand to teach the other is more important than most people realize. The above example of solving one specific technical difficulty is just one example -- more importantly, this concept applies to practically every practice session. The basic reason for this broad applicability is that one hand *always* plays something better than the other, such as relaxation, speed, quiet hands, and the innumerable finger/hand motions (Thumb Over, Flat Finger, etc., see following sections) -- anything new that you are trying to learn. Therefore, once you learn this principle of using one hand to teach the other, you will be using it all the time.

21.   Building Endurance, Breathing

"Endurance" is a controversial term in piano practice. This controversy originates from the fact that *piano playing requires control, not muscle power,* and many students have the wrong impression that they will not acquire technique until they grow enough muscles. On the other hand, a certain amount of endurance is necessary. This apparent contradiction can be resolved by understanding exactly what is needed and how to get it. Obviously, you can't play loud, grandiose passages without expending energy. Big, strong, pianists can certainly produce more sound than small, weak, pianists if they are equally skillful. And the stronger pianists can more easily play "demanding" pieces. Every pianist has enough physical stamina to play pieces at her/is level, simply because of the amount of practice that was required to get there. Yet we know that endurance *is* a problem. The answer lies in relaxation. When stamina becomes an issue, it is almost always caused by excess tension.

One example of this is the LH octave tremolo in the first movement of Beethoven's Pathetique. The *only* thing over 90% of the students need to do is to eliminate stress; yet many students practice it for months with little progress. The first mistake they make is to practice it too loud. This adds extra stress and fatigue when you can least afford it. Practice it softly, concentrating on eliminating stress, as explained in section III.3.b. In a week or two, you will be playing as many tremolos as fast as you want. Now start adding loudness and expression. Done! At this point, your physical strength and endurance is not much different from what it was when you started a few weeks ago -- the main thing you did was to find the best way to eliminate stress.

Playing demanding pieces requires about as much energy as a slow jog, at about 4 miles per hour, with the brain requiring almost half the total energy. Many youngsters cannot jog continuously for over one mile. Therefore, asking youngsters to practice difficult passages continually for 20 minutes would really strain their stamina because it would be about equivalent to jogging a mile. Teachers and parents must be careful when youngsters start their piano lessons, to limit practice times to under 15 minutes in the beginning until the students gain sufficient stamina. Marathon runners have stamina, but they are not muscular. You need to condition the body for stamina for piano, but you don't need extra muscles.

Now there *is* a difference between piano playing and running a marathon because of the need to condition the brain for stamina in addition to the muscular conditioning. Therefore mindless practicing of exercises for stamina does not work. The most efficient ways to gain stamina are to either play finished pieces and make music, or practice difficult sections HS continuously. Again using the jogging comparison, it would be hard for most students to practice difficult material continuously for more than a few hours because 2 hours of practice would be equivalent to jogging 6 miles, which is a terrific workout. Therefore, you will have to play some easy pieces between the hard practice sessions. Concentrated practice sessions longer than a few hours may not be that helpful until you are at an advanced level, when you have developed sufficient "piano stamina". It is probably better to take a break and restart practice after some rest. *Clearly, hard piano practice is strenuous work and serious practicing can put the student in good physical shape.* HS practice is most valuable in this regard because it allows one hand to rest while the other works hard, allowing the pianist to work as hard as s/he wants, 100% of the time, without injury or fatigue. Of course, in terms of stamina, it is not difficult (if you have the time) to put in 6 or 8 hours of practice a day by including a lot of mindless finger exercises. This is a process of self-delusion in which the student thinks that just putting in the time will get you there -- it will not. If anything, conditioning the brain is more important than conditioning the muscles because, for most students, it is the brain that needs more conditioning. Brain conditioning is especially important for performing. Strenuous conditioning of the muscles will cause the body to convert fast muscles to slow muscles (they have more endurance) -- this is exactly what you do not want. Therefore, contrary to common belief, pianists do not need more muscle; they need more nerve control and conversion of slow to fast muscles – see III.7.a.

What is stamina? It is something that enables us to keep on playing without getting tired. For long practice sessions of over several hours, pianists get their second wind just as athletes do (especially marathoners). Therefore, if you feel general fatigue, look for the second wind to kick in – this conscious knowledge of the second wind can make it kick in more reliably, especially after you have experienced it several times so that you know what it feels like. Therefore do not get into the habit of resting every time you feel tired if there is a chance that you might be able to catch the second wind.

Can we identify any biological factors that control stamina? Knowing the biological basis is the best way to understand stamina. In the absence of specific bio-physical studies for pianists, we can only speculate. ***Clearly, we need sufficient oxygen intake and adequate blood flow to the muscles, certain organs, and the brain.*** The biggest factor influencing oxygen intake is lung efficiency, and important components of that are breathing and posture. This may be one reason why meditation, with emphasis on proper breathing using the diaphragm, is so helpful. ***Use of only the rib muscles to breathe over-utilizes one breathing apparatus and under-utilizes the diaphragm.*** The resulting rapid pumping of the chest or exaggerated chest expansion can interfere with piano playing because all of the piano playing muscles eventually anchor near the center of the chest. Use of the diaphragm interferes less with the playing motions. In addition, those who do not use the diaphragm consciously can tense it when stress builds up during play, and they will not even notice that the diaphragm is tense. By using both the ribs and the diaphragm, and maintaining good posture, the lungs can be expanded to their maximum volume with least effort and thereby take in the maximum amount of oxygen.

The following breathing exercise can be extremely helpful, not only for piano, but also for general well-being. Expand your chest, push your diaphragm down (this will make your lower abdomen bulge out), raise the shoulders up and towards your back, and take a deep breath; then exhale completely by reversing the process. When taking a deep breath, complete exhalation is more important than a full intake. Breathe through your throat, not through the nose (the mouth can be open or closed). Most people will constrict the nasal air passage if they try to suck air through the nose. Instead, relax your nose muscles and suck air through the throat region close to the vocal chords -- even with the mouth closed, this procedure will relax the nose muscles, allowing more air to pass through the nose. If you had not taken deep breaths for a long time, this breathing should cause hyper-ventilation -- you will feel dizzy -- after one or two such exercises. Stop if you hyper-ventilate. Then repeat this exercise at a later time; you should find that you can take more breaths without hyper-ventilating. Repeat this exercise until you can take at least 5 full breaths in succession without hyper-ventilating. Now, if you go to the doctor's office and he checks you out with his stethoscope and asks you to take a deep breath, you can do it without feeling dizzy! Breathing normally, while playing something difficult, is an important element of relaxation. Perform this exercise at least once every several months and incorporate it into your normal breathing habit at and away from the piano.

Piano practice can be healthy or unhealthy depending on how you practice. Many students forget to breathe while practicing difficult material; this bad habit is unhealthy. It reduces oxygen flow to the brain when it needs it most, resulting in apoxia and symptoms similar to sleep apnea (organ damage, high blood pressure, etc.). The lack of oxygen will make musical and mental play difficult, and make it impossible to increase mental stamina.

Other methods of increasing stamina are to increase the blood flow and to increase the amount of blood in the body. In piano playing, extra blood flow is needed in the brain as well as the playing mechanism; ***therefore, you should fully and simultaneously exercise the muscles and the brain during practice. This will cause the body to manufacture more blood, in response to the higher demand for blood.*** Mindless repetitions of exercises, etc., are not helpful in this respect because you can shut off the brain, thus reducing the need for more blood. Practicing after a large meal also increases the blood supply and conversely, resting after every meal will reduce stamina – there is a well-known Japanese saying that claims that you will turn into a cow if you sleep after a meal. Since most people do not have enough blood to engage in strenuous activity with a full stomach, the body will rebel initially by making you feel terrible, but this is an expected reaction. Such activity must be conducted within safe medical limits; for example you may temporarily experience digestive problems or dizziness (which is probably the rationale behind the misguided belief that you should not exercise after a large meal). Once the body manufactures the necessary extra blood, these problems will disappear. Therefore, you should stay as active as you can after a meal, in order to prevent anemia. Practicing immediately after a meal will require blood for digestion, for the playing muscles, and for the brain, thus placing the greatest demand on blood supply. Clearly, participation in sports, proper health, and physical exercise are helpful for gaining stamina in piano playing.

In summary, beginners who have never touched a piano previously will need to develop their stamina gradually because piano practice *is* strenuous work. Parents must be careful about the practice time of very young beginners and allow them to quit or take a rest when they get tired (about 10-15 min.). ***Never allow a sick child to practice piano, even easy pieces, because of the risk of aggravating the illness and of brain damage.*** At any skill level, we all have more muscle than we need to play the piano pieces at our level. Even professional pianists who practice over 6 hours every day don't end up looking like Popeye. Franz Liszt was thin, not muscular. Thus acquiring technique and stamina is not a matter of building muscle, but of learning how to relax and to use our energy properly.

22.   Bad Habits: A Pianist's Worst Enemy

Bad habits are the worst time-wasters in piano practice. Most bad habits are caused by stress from practicing pieces HT, that are too difficult. Many of the bad habits from HT practice are difficult to diagnose, which makes them that much more dangerous. Clearly, the best defense against bad habits is HS practice. Non-musical play is one type of bad habit; therefore, don't forget that musical play starts with HS practice.

Another bad habit is the over-use of the damper or soft pedal as discussed below. This is the surest sign of an amateur student taking lessons with an unqualified teacher. Overuse of these pedals can only "help" a severely technically deficient student.

Another bad habit is to bang away at the piano without regard to musicality. The student equates loudness to excitement. This often results because the student is so engrossed with the practice that s/he forgets to listen to the sounds coming out of the piano. This can be prevented by cultivating the habit of always listening to yourself play. Listening to yourself is much harder than many people realize because many students (especially those who play with stress) expend all their effort playing, with nothing left for listening. One way to reduce this problem is to record your playing so that you can listen to it in a mentally detached way. Exciting passages are often loud, but they are most exciting when the rest of the music is soft. Too much loud practice can preclude you from gaining speed and technique, and ruin your sense of music. Those who play loud tend to end up with a harsh tone.

Then there are those with weak fingers. This is most common among beginners and is more easily corrected than those who bang too loud. Weak fingers is caused by not releasing your arms and letting gravity take over. The student subconsciously lifts the arms, and this habit is a form of stress. These students must be taught the full dynamic range of the piano and how to make use of this range.

Still another bad habit is playing at the wrong speed, either too fast or too slow, especially during a performance when you get too excited and lose your sense of tempo. The right speed is determined by many factors, including the difficulty of the piece with respect to your technical ability, what the audience might be expecting, the condition of the piano, what piece preceded or will follow this piece, etc. Some students might tend to perform pieces too fast for their skill level and end up with many mistakes, while others are timid and play too slowly, thus not taking full advantage of the music. Playing slowly can be more difficult than playing at the correct speed, which compounds a timid player's problems. Those who perform too fast can become very discouraged because they make too many mistakes and become convinced that they are poor pianists. These problems apply not only to performances but also to practices; those who practice too fast can end up thinking that they are poor pianists because they make so many errors. Slowing down just a little may enable them to play accurately and beautifully and, in the long run, master the technique for playing fast.

Poor tone quality is another common problem. Most of the time, during practice, no one is listening, so tone doesn't seem to matter. As a result, if the tone degrades slightly, it does not bother the student, with the result that the tone is ignored. Students must always strive for tone, because it is the most important part of the music. Good tone cannot be produced on a lousy or unregulated piano; this is the main reason why you want a decent grand instead of a poor quality upright and why tuning, regulation, and hammer voicing are more important than most students realize. Listening to good recordings is the best way to wake up the student to the existence of good tone. If they only listen to their play, they may have no idea what good tone means. On the other hand, once you pay attention to tone and start getting results, it will feed on itself and you can readily learn the art of producing sounds that can attract an audience. More importantly, without good tone, advanced technical improvement is impossible because good tone requires control, and technical development depends on control.

Stuttering is caused by stop-and-go practice in which a student stops and replays a section every time there is a mistake. ***If you make a mistake, always play through it; don't stop to correct it.*** Make a mental note of where the mistake was and play that section again later to see if the mistake repeats. If it does, fish out a small segment containing that mistake and work on it. Once you cultivate the habit of playing through mistakes you can graduate to the next level in which you anticipate mistakes (feel their approach before they occur) and take evasive action, such as slowing down, simplifying the section, or maintaining the rhythm. Most audiences don't mind, and often don't even hear, mistakes unless the rhythm is broken.

The worst thing about bad habits is that they take so long to eliminate, especially if they are HT habits. Therefore nothing accelerates your learning rate like knowing all the bad habits and preventing them before they become ingrained. For example, ***the time to prevent stuttering is when a student first begins piano lessons. In the beginning, most students don't stutter; however, they must be immediately taught to play through mistakes.*** If playing through mistakes is taught at this stage, it becomes second nature and is easy; no effort is needed to learn this "trick". To teach a stutterer to play through mistakes is a very difficult task.

The number of possible bad habits is so large that they cannot all be discussed here. Suffice it so say that a rigorous anti-virus attitude towards bad habits is a requisite to rapid improvement.

23. Damper Pedal

Practice any new piece without the pedal HS, then HT, until you can play it comfortably HT at final speed. This is a critically important method of practice that all good teachers use with all their students. It may seem difficult, at first, to practice musically without the pedal where it is needed; however, this is the best way to learn precise control so that you can play more musically when the pedal is eventually added. Students who practice with the pedal from the beginning will become sloppy players, develop numerous bad habits, and will not even learn the concept of precise control or the real meaning of musicality.

Rank amateurs often over-use the damper pedal. *The obvious rule is, if the music doesn't indicate a pedal, don't use it.* Some pieces might seem easier to play with the pedal (especially if you start slowly HT!) but this is one of the worst traps a beginner can fall into that will hold back development. The action feels lighter with the damper pedal down because the foot is holding the dampers off the strings instead of the fingers. Thus the action feels heavier when the pedal is released, especially for fast sections. Some students do not realize that where pedals are not indicated, it is usually impossible to play the music correctly at speed if you use the pedal.

For Fur Elise, use the pedal only for the large LH broken chord accompaniments (bar 3 & similar), bars 83-96 and the RH arpeggio passage (bars 100-104). Practically all of the first difficult interruption should be played without the pedal. Of course, everything should initially be practiced without the pedal until you have basically finished the piece. This will encourage the good habit of keeping the fingers close to the keys and discourage the bad habit of playing with too much jumping and lifting of the hands, and not pressing firmly into the keys. An important reason for not using the pedal initially is that technique improves fastest without the pedal because you can hear exactly what you play without interference from previously played notes. You should be actively controlling the tone.

Coordinating the pedal and hands accurately is not an easy task. Therefore, students who start learning a piece HT with the pedal will invariably end up with inconsistent and terrible pedal habits. The correct procedure is to practice HS first without pedal, then HS with pedal, then HT without pedal, and finally HT with pedal. In this way, you can concentrate on each new skill as you introduce it into your playing.

Inattention to the pedal can slow down technical development much more than many students realize; conversely, attention to the pedal can help technical development by increasing your accuracy and adding another dimension to musicality. When you do one thing wrong, it becomes difficult to do all the other things right. When the pedal is wrong, you can't even practice the correct finger technique because the music comes out wrong even when the fingers are technically correct.

The pedal was practically non-existent before Mozart's time; for example, no pedal is used in any of J. S. Bach's music. Mozart did not indicate any pedaling although, today, some pedaling is considered optional in some of his compositions and many editors have added pedal markings in his music. The pedal was basically fully developed by Beethoven's time, although it was not yet totally accepted as a serious musical tool. Beethoven used it with great success as a special effect (third movement of Waldstein Sonata); therefore, he tended to use it a lot (entire first movement of his Moonlight Sonata) or non at all (entire Pathetique Sonata, first and second movements of the Waldstein). Chopin used the pedal extensively to inject an additional level of logic into his music and fully exploited all the different ways of pedaling. Therefore, Chopin (and many later composers) cannot be played correctly without adequate training in pedaling.

See the references for all the different ways to pedal, when to use them, and how to practice those moves (Gieseking and Leimer, Fink, Sandor, *Pedaling the Modern Pianoforte* by Bowen, and *The Pianist's Guide to Pedaling* by Banowetz). Try to master all these moves before using the pedal with an actual piece of music. There are some very helpful exercises in the references for practicing proper pedaling. When you do use the pedal, know exactly which move you are using and why. For example, if you want as many sympathetic strings to vibrate as possible, depress the pedal before playing the note. If, on the other hand, you want one clear note to sustain, press the pedal after playing the note; the longer you delay the pedal, the fewer sympathetic vibrations you will get. In general, you should get into the habit of depressing the pedal a split second after playing the note. You can get a legato effect without too much blurring by rapidly lifting and depressing the pedal every time the chord changes. As with the keys, it is just as important to know when to lift the pedal as when to press it down. ***Clearly, the pedal must be "played" as carefully as you play the keys.***

24.   Soft Pedal: Hammer Voicing, Physics of the Piano Sound

Grand pianos: The soft pedal is used to change the mood of the sound from percussive to more serene and gentle when the soft pedal is depressed. It should not be used solely for producing a softer sound because it will also change the timbre. In order to play pianissimo, you must simply learn how to play more softly. You can produce very loud sounds with the soft pedal depressed. One difficulty with the soft pedal is that it (una corda, or more correctly due corda for the modern grand) is often not indicated, so the decision to use it is often left to the pianist. ***For uprights, it mostly decreases the volume of the sound.*** The soft pedal on most uprights has a negligible effect on timbre. Unlike the grands, the uprights cannot produce loud sounds with the soft pedal depressed.

Many pianists do not understand the importance of proper hammer voicing for the soft pedal to be effective. If you tend to need the soft pedal to play softly, or if it is distinctly easier to play pianissimo with the grand lid closed, the hammer almost certainly needs voicing. See "Voicing" in Chapter Two, Section 7. With properly voiced hammers, you should be able to control soft playing to any desired degree without the soft pedal. With worn, compacted, hammers, playing softly is impossible and the soft pedal has less effect in changing the tone. In most cases, the original properties of the hammer can be restored by voicing (re-shaping, needling, etc.). The action must also be well regulated, with the let-off properly minimized, in order to enable PPP.

The use of the soft pedal is controversial because too many pianists are unfamiliar with how it works. For example, many use it to play pianissimo, which is incorrect usage. As shown in Ch. Two, section 7, energy transfer from the hammer to the string is most efficient at impact, before the string starts to move. A compacted hammer transfers its energy during an extremely short time interval at impact and the hammer immediately bounces off the strings. This high efficiency of energy transfer gives the impression of a very light action. That is why there are old grands that feel feather light. Soft hammers on the same piano (with nothing else changed), would make the action feel heavier. This is because, with the softer impact point of the hammer, it stays on the string much longer, and the string is pushed out of its original position before all the hammer energy is transferred to the string. In this position, the energy transfer is less efficient (see Ch. Two, section 7) and the pianist must push harder to produce the same volume of sound. ***Thus voicing can be more effective in changing the apparent key weight than lead weights.*** Clearly, the *effective* key weight is only partly controlled by the force required to depress the key, since it also depends on the force required to produce a given amount of sound. The pianist does not know which factor (lead weights or soft hammer) is affecting the effective key weight. The piano technician must strike a compromise between voicing a hammer sufficiently soft so as to produce a pleasant tone but sufficiently hard so as to produce adequate sound. For all except the highest quality pianos, the hammer needs to be on the hard side in order to produce enough sound and to make the action feel nimble, which makes such pianos difficult to play softly. This in turn can "justify" use of the soft pedal where it should not be used. Piano owners who neglect voicing can make the piano tuner's job difficult because, after the hammers are properly voiced, the owner will complain that the action is too heavy to play. In reality, the owner had gotten used to playing a feather light action and never learned how to play with real power to generate that gorgeous piano sound.

In most uprights, the soft pedal causes all the hammers to move closer to the strings, thus restricting hammer motion and decreasing the volume. Unlike the grands, loud sounds cannot be produced in an upright when the soft pedal is depressed. One advantage of uprights is that a partial soft pedal works; partial soft pedaling is a complex subject for grands and will be treated in detail below. There are a few upscale uprights in which the soft pedal works similarly to that of the grands.

In modern grands, the soft pedal causes the entire action (including the hammers) to shift to the right so that the hammers miss one string in the 3-string section. Thus the hammers hit only two strings, causing a serendipitous transformation in the character of the sound, as explained below. The shift is exactly half the distance between adjacent strings in the 3-string section; thus the two active strings will hit the less used portions of the hammer between string grooves, creating an even gentler sound. The horizontal motion must not shift one string distance because then the strings will fall into the grooves made by adjacent strings. Since string distances and the amount of shift cannot be controlled sufficiently accurately, this would cause some strings to fall exactly into the grooves while others will miss, creating uneven sound.

Why does timbre change when two strings are struck instead of three? Here, timbre is controlled by at least four factors: (1) existence of the unstruck string, (2) the prompt-/after-sound ratio, (3) the harmonic content, and (4) vibrational polarization of the strings. Let's examine these in more detail.

The unstruck string acts as a reservoir into which the other two strings can dump their energy and produces many new effects. Since the vibration of the 3rd string is in anti-phase with the struck strings (a driven string is always in anti-phase with the driver), it takes the edge off the initial prompt sound (see below) and at the same time, excites vibrational modes that are different from those that result when all three are struck in unison. This is why the soft pedals in uprights don't work as well -- all the strings are struck even when the soft pedal is depressed, and the timbre cannot change.

The piano produces an initial prompt-sound and a sustaining after-sound; see the "Scientific American" and "Five Lectures" articles reviewed in the Reference section for more details on topics discussed in this paragraph. Unlike the simplified picture of fundamental and harmonic frequencies that we use when tuning a piano, the actual string vibrations consist of a complex time dependent series of events that are still incompletely understood. In such situations, the actual data from existing pianos are of more practical value, but those data are closely held trade secrets of piano manufacturers. Therefore, I summarize here some general knowledge based on the physics of the piano sound. The string vibrations can be polarized, either parallel to the soundboard, or perpendicular to it. When the strings are struck, vertically polarized traveling waves are generated that move away from the hammer in both directions, towards the agraffes (capo bar) and towards the bridge. These waves travel so rapidly that they reflect back from both ends of the strings and pass the hammer several hundred times before the hammer bounces off the strings; in fact it is these waves that throw the hammer back. Horizontally polarized waves are generated from the vertical waves because the piano is not symmetric. These traveling waves decay into standing waves consisting of harmonics (including the fundamental) because the standing waves are "normal vibration modes" (see a mechanics text book) that transfer energy slowly to the soundboards and are therefore long-lived. However, from the very beginning, the concept of fundamentals and harmonics remains valid because the Fourier coefficients (see a math or physics textbook) of the fundamental and harmonic frequencies are always large, even for the traveling waves. This is easily understood because the ends of the strings do not move, especially for well-constructed, large, heavy pianos. In other words, mostly wavelengths that have nodes (points of zero motion) at both ends are generated when the ends are fixed. This explains why, in spite of the traveling waves, tuners can tune accurately using only the fundamental and harmonic frequencies. The vertically polarized waves transfer energy more efficiently to the soundboard than the horizontally polarized waves and therefore produce a louder sound but decay faster, and create the prompt sound. The horizontally polarized standing waves produce the after-sound which gives the piano its long sustain. When the soft pedal is depressed, only 2 strings can produce the prompt sound but eventually, all 3 strings contribute to the after-sound. Therefore, the prompt-/after-sound ratio is smaller than for 3 strings and the sound is less percussive with the soft pedal.

The harmonic content is also different because the energy of the hammer is transferred to only 2 strings instead of 3, which is like hitting the string with a heavier hammer, and it is known that heavier hammers produce stronger fundamentals. The polarizations of the strings also change with the soft pedal because the third string will be polarized more horizontally, which contributes to the gentler sound.

This type of understanding helps us to use the soft pedal correctly. If the pedal is depressed *before* a note is played, the initial time dependent traveling waves will excite all strings, creating a soft background roar. That is, in the prompt sound, the non-harmonic Fourier coefficients are not zero. If you place your finger on any string, you can feel it vibrate. However, octave and harmonic strings will vibrate with higher amplitudes than the dissonant strings, which is a consequence of the larger Fourier coefficients for the harmonics. Thus the piano not only selectively traps the harmonics, but also selectively generates them. Now if the pedal is depressed *after* the note is struck, there will be sympathetic vibration in octave and harmonic strings, but all the other strings will be almost totally quiet because the standing waves contain only pure harmonics. This produces a clear sustained note. The lesson here is that, in general, the pedal should be depressed immediately after striking the note, not before, in order to avoid dissonances. This is a good habit to cultivate.

A partial soft pedal works on an upright; but can you use a half soft pedal on a grand? This should not be controversial but is, because even some advanced pianists think that if a full soft pedal gives a certain effect, a partial soft pedal will give a partial effect, which is false. If you use a partial soft pedal, you will of course get a new sound. There is no reason why a pianist shouldn't be allowed to do that, and if it produces an interesting new effect that the pianist likes, there is nothing wrong with that. However, this mode of play was not intentionally designed into the piano and I know of no composer who composed for partial soft pedal on a grand, especially because it is not reproducible from piano to piano, and from note to note on the same piano. Extensive use of partial soft pedals on the grand will cause some strings to shave off one side of the hammer, thus throwing the system out of regulation. Also, it is impossible for the piano technician to align all hammers and strings so accurately that the third string will miss the hammer at the same pedal travel for all 3-string notes. Thus the partial soft pedal effect will be uneven, and different from piano to piano. ***Therefore, unless you have experimented and are trying to produce some strange and irreproducible*** *new effect, half-pedaling is not recommended for the soft pedal on a grand. Nonetheless, anecdotal accounts indicate that use of partial soft pedal on a grand does occur, almost always because of ignorance on the part of the pianist about how it works.* The only way to use a partial soft pedal with reproducible results is a very slight soft pedal, in which case all the strings will hit the sides of the grooves in the hammer. Even this scheme will not really work, because it will affect only the 3-string section, resulting in a jarring transition from 2-string to 3-string sections.

In the double and single string sections, the strings have much larger diameters, so when the action moves sideways, the strings hit the side walls of the grooves, thus giving them a horizontal motion and increasing the after-sound by increasing the horizontally polarized string vibrations. Thus the change in timbre is similar to that in the 3 string section. This mechanism is fiendishly ingenious!

In summary, the name soft pedal is a misnomer for a grand. Its main effect is to change the timbre of the sound. If you play a loud sound with the soft pedal depressed, it will be almost as loud as without the soft pedal. This is because you have put roughly the same amount of energy into making the sound. On the other hand, it is easier to play softly using the soft pedal on most grands because the strings hit the less used, softer parts of the hammers. Provided that the piano is well regulated and the hammers are properly voiced, you should be able to play just as softly without the soft pedal. *A partial soft pedal will produce unpredictable, uneven effects and should not be used for an acoustic grand.* A partial soft pedal works on most uprights and all electronic pianos.

25.   Hands Together and Mental Play

We can finally start putting the hands together (HT)! Some students encounter the most difficulties here, especially in the first few years of piano lessons. Although the methods presented here should immediately help you to acquire technique faster, it will take about two years to be able to really take advantage of everything that the methods of this book have to offer.

Playing HT is almost like trying to think about two different things at the same time. There is no known, pre-programmed coordination between the two hands like we have between our two eyes (for judging distance), our ears (for determining the direction of oncoming sound) or our legs/arms (for walking). Therefore, learning to coordinate the fingers of the two hands accurately is going to take some work. The preceding HS work makes this coordination much easier to learn because we now only have to concentrate on coordinating, and not coordinating AND developing finger/hand technique at the same time.

The good news is that there is only one primary "secret" for learning HT quickly. That "secret" is adequate HS work, so you already know it! *All technique must be acquired HS; don't try to acquire technique HT that you can acquire HS.* By now, the reasons should be obvious. If you try to acquire technique HT, you will run into problems such as (1) developing stress, (2) unbalancing the hands (the RH tends to get stronger), (3) acquiring bad habits, (4) creating speed walls, etc. Note that all speed walls are *created*; they result from incorrect play or stress. Premature HT practice can create any number of speed walls. Incorrect motions are another major problem; some motions present no problems when played slowly HT but become impossible when speeded up. The best example of this is "thumb under" play (section III.5).

First, you will need some criterion for deciding when you have done adequate HS practice. A good criterion is HS speed. Typically, the maximum HT speed you can play is 50% to 90% of the slower HS speed, either the RH or the LH. Suppose that you can play the RH at speed 10 and the LH at speed 9. Then your maximum HT speed may be 7. The quickest way to raise this HT speed to 9 would be to raise the RH speed to 12 and the LH speed to 11. As a general rule, get the HS speed well above final speed. Therefore, the criterion we were seeking is: if you can play HS at 110% to 150% of final speed, relaxed, and in control, then you are ready for HT practice.

If you still have trouble, use the method of "outlining". Let's assume that you can play HS satisfactorily. Now simplify one or both hands so that you can play them HT easily, then gradually add the deleted material. There are many ways to do this, and you can develop really powerful methods depending on how much music theory you know, so outlining will be discussed in more detail in III.8. However, you don't need theory to use outlining; one example is the method of "adding notes": take a short segment of the difficult section, then play the more difficult hand HS, repeating the section continuously (this is called cycling, see section III.2); now start adding the easier hand note by note. First add one note and practice until you can play it satisfactorily. Then add another, etc., until the segment is complete. Make sure that, as you add notes, you keep the same fingering as used during HS practice. Very often, the reason why you cannot play HT although you can play HS is that there is an error somewhere. Frequently, this error is in the rhythm. Therefore, as you add notes, try to find out if there is an error in one hand; this is best accomplished by referring back to the music score.

There is a world of difference in how the brain handles tasks in one hand and tasks that require two-hand coordination, which is why it pays to learn them one at a time. HS practice does not tend to form habits not directly controlled by the brain because the brain controls each hand directly. HT motions, on the other hand, can be cultivated only by repetition, creating a reflex habit, which may involve nerve cells outside the brain. One indication of this is the fact that HT motions take longer to learn. ***Therefore, bad HT habits are the worst because, once formed, they take forever to eliminate. To acquire technique quickly, you must avoid this category of bad habits.***

Mental play (MP) is necessary for HT play exactly as for HS play but HT MP is, of course, more difficult for beginners. Once you become good at MP, HS and HT MP will be equally easy. Since you already know HS mental play (section 12 above), the main remaining job is to learn it HT. When memorizing MP HS, you should have encountered places in every composition where you had to go back and check it at the piano – you can play it at the piano but not in your mind – those places weren't entirely in your head yet. Those are the places where you could have had blackouts during performances. As a test that you have solid MP, there are 3 things that you should be able to do in your mind: (1) can you start from anywhere in the piece and start playing HT? (2) given any section that you are playing one hand, can you add the other hand? and (3) can you play both hands simultaneously in your head? You should find that if you can do these in your mind, you can easily do them at the piano.

Let us now proceed with real life examples of how to practice HT. I have chosen 3 examples to illustrate HT methods, starting with the easiest, the 1st movement of Beethoven's Moonlight Sonata, then Mozart's Rondo Alla Turca, and finally, the challenging Fantaisie-Impromptu (FI) by Chopin. You should choose the one best suited to your skill level. You might also try the Bach Inventions that are covered in detail in sections III.6.1 and III.19. I will leave the Fur Elise, discussed above, for you to try by yourself, as it is fairly short and relatively straightforward. For many pianists, Fur Elise is "too familiar" and often difficult to play; in that case, play it in a subdued way, concentrating on accuracy instead of emotion (no rubato), and let the music speak for itself. It can be quite effective with the right audience. This "detached" play can be useful for popular, familiar music.

The three compositions chosen here present certain challenges. The moonlight requires legato, PP, and the music of Beethoven. The Alla Turca must sound like Mozart, is fairly fast and requires accurate, independent hand control as well as solid octave play. The FI requires the ability to play 4-against-3 and 2-against-3 in the 2 hands, extremely fast RH fingering, the romanticism of Chopin, and accurate pedaling. All three are relatively easy to play HT in the mind because the LH is mostly an accompaniment to the RH; in the Bach Inventions, both hands play major roles and HT MP is more difficult. This demonstrates that Bach probably taught MP and purposely composed challenging pieces for his students. This increased difficulty also explains why, without proper guidance (such as this book), some students find the Inventions extremely difficult to memorize and play at speed.

Beethoven's Moonlight, 1st Movement, Op. 27, No. 2

The most notable controversy about this movement is the pedaling. Beethoven's instruction "senza sordini" translates to "without dampers" which means that the pedal should be down from the beginning to the end. Most pianists *have not* followed this instruction because on modern concert grands the sustain is so long (much longer than on Beethoven's piano) that the mixture of all those notes creates a background roar that is considered crude in conventional piano pedagogy. Certainly, no piano teacher will allow the student to do that! However, Beethoven was not only an extremist, but loved to break the rules. The Moonlight is built on contrast. The first movement is slow, legato, pedaled, and soft. The 3rd movement is the extreme opposite; it is simply a variation on the first movement played very fast and agitato – this is confirmed by the observation that the top double octave of bar 2 in the 3rd movement is an abbreviated form of the 3-note theme prominent in the 1st movement, discussed below (see section III.5 for discussions of the 3rd movement). There is also a glaring contrast between the dissonances and the clear harmonies that give this first movement its famous quality. The background dissonance is created by the pedal, as well as the ninths, etc. Thus the dissonances are there in order to make the harmonies stand out, like a sparkling diamond on a dark velvet background. Being the extremist that he is, he chose the most harmonious theme possible: one note repeated three times (bar 5)! Therefore, my interpretation is that the pedal should be down throughout the piece just as Beethoven instructed. With most pianos, this should present no problems; however, with concert grands, it gets difficult because the background din becomes louder as you play and you still have to play PP ("sempre pianissimo"); in that case you might reduce the background slightly, but never cut it out completely, as it is part of the music. This is not the way you will hear it in recordings, where the emphasis is usually on the clear harmonies, eliminating the background – the "standard" convention for "correct" pedaling. However, Beethoven may have decided to break that rule here. This is why he did not put any pedal markings in the whole movement – because you never have to lift it. ***Having decided to fully engage the damper pedal throughout, the first rule in learning this piece is not to use the pedal at all until you can play it comfortably HT.*** This will enable you to learn how to play legato, which can only be practiced without the pedal. Although it is played very softly, there is no need for the soft pedal in this piece; moreover, with most practice pianos, the action is not sufficiently smooth, with the soft pedal depressed, to enable the desired control at PP.

Start by memorizing HS, say bars 1-5, and immediately commit it to mental play. Pay attention to all the expression markings. It is in cut time, but the 2 first bars are like an introduction and have only one LH octave note each; the rest are played more strictly cut time. Beethoven tells us immediately, in bar 2, that dissonance is going to be a major component of this movement by inserting the octave B in the LH, jarring the audience with a dissonance. Continue memorizing in segments until the end.

The LH octaves must be *held*. For example, play the LH C# octave of bar 1 using fingers 51, but immediately slip the 4, then 3 finger onto the lower C#, replacing the 5, holding this lower C# down. You will end up holding the octave 35 before you reach bar 2. Now hold the 3 as you play the B octave of bar 2 with 51. In this way, you maintain complete legato in the LH *going down*. Using this procedure, you cannot maintain complete legato with the 1 finger, but hold that as long as you can. In the transition from bar 3 to 4, the LH octave must *come up*. In that case, play the F# of bar 3 with 51, then hold the 5 and play the next G# octave with 41. Similarly, for bars 4 to 5, play the 2nd G# octave of bar 4 with 51, then replace finger 1 with 2 while holding it down (you may have to lift the 5) so that you can play the following chord of bar 5, fingers 521, and maintain the legato. The general idea is to hold as many notes as you can, especially the lower note for the LH and the upper note for the RH. There are usually several ways to do these "holds", so you should experiment to see which is best for you in a particular situation. The choice of a specific hold procedure depends mostly on the size of your hand. For example, the LH octave of bar 1 could have been played 41 or 31 so that you do not have to replace any fingers; this has the advantage of simplicity, but has the disadvantage that you need to remember that when you start the piece. Throughout this piece, use the "finger replacement" method to hold as much legato as possible. ***You must decide on a specific replacement procedure when you first memorize the piece and always use that same one.***

Why hold the note legato when you are eventually going to hold all the notes with the pedal anyway? Firstly, how you depress the key depends on how you hold it; therefore, you can play a more consistent and authoritative legato by holding. Secondly, if you lift the key but hold the note with the pedal, the backcheck releases the hammer, allowing it to flop around, and this "looseness" of the action is audible – the nature of the sound changes. Moreover, as commander of the piano, you always want the backcheck to hold the hammer so that you have complete control over the entire piano action. This degree of control is extremely important when playing PP – you can't control the PP if the hammer is flopping around. Another reason for holding is that it provides absolute accuracy because your hand never leaves the keyboard and the held note acts as a reference for finding the following notes.

Music – how to make music? Bar 1 is not just a series of 4 triplets. They must be logically *connected*; therefore, pay attention to the connection between the top note of each triplet and the bottom note of the next triplet. This connection is especially important when transitioning from one bar to the next, and the lowest note often has melodic value, as in bars 4-5, 9-10, etc. The RH of bar 5 starts with the lowest note, E, and the music rises all the way to the G# of the 3-note theme. This theme should not be played "alone" but is the culmination of the arpeggic rise of the preceding triplet. If you have difficulty reaching the RH ninth of bar 8, play the lower note with the LH; similarly, at bar 16. In these instances, you cannot completely hold the legato in the LH, but the legato in the RH is more important, and the lifting of the LH can be made less audible when you use the pedal later. However, if you can reach it easily, you should try to play the ninth with the RH alone because that will allow you to hold more notes in the LH. Although the first note of the 3-note theme is an octave G#, the top note should be distinct from, and firmer than, the lower note. Bars 32-35 is a series of rising triplets of increasing tension. Bars 36-37 should be connected, because is it one smooth release of that tension.

The beginning is PP to bar 25 where there is a crescendo, decreasing to P in bar 28, and returning to PP in bar 42. In most cresc. and decresc., most of the increase or decrease should come near the end, not near the beginning. There is an unexpected crescendo in bar 48, and an abrupt jump to P at the first note of bar 49. This is the clearest indication that Beethoven wanted a clear harmony superposed on a dissonant din created by the pedal.

The "ending" starts near bar 55. Be careful to observe the cut time; in particular, emphasize the first and third beats of bar 57. What appears to be a normal ending is indicated by the (wrong) accents on the 4th beat of bar 58 and the 3rd beat of bar 59. The first chord of bar 60 is a false ending. Most composers would have ended the music here; it is the same chord as the first chord of this movement - a characteristic of standard endings. However, Beethoven often used double endings, which makes the real ending more "final". He immediately picks up the beat and leads you to the true ending, using a nostalgic recapitulation of the 3-note theme played by the LH, all played PP. The final two chords should be the softest notes of the entire movement, which is difficult because they contain so many notes.

For HT play, this movement presents no problems. The only new element is the holding of notes for legato which requires extra control over both hands simultaneously.

Once you have memorized the whole movement and can play it HT satisfactorily, add the pedal. If you choose to keep the pedal down all the time, the melody of the top notes in bars 5-9 can be played as an ethereal apparition superposed on a background dissonance created by the chord progressions. Beethoven probably chose this construction to demonstrate the sonority of the new pianos of that time and to explore their capabilities. This observation supports the idea that the dissonant background should not be completely eliminated by judiciously lifting the pedal.

Mozart's Rondo Alla Turca, from Sonata K300 (K331).

I am going to assume that you have already done the HS homework, and begin with the HT part especially because HS play is relatively simple with most of Mozart's music. The discussions will center on the issues of technical difficulties and "how to make it sound like Mozart". Before starting on the details, let's discuss the structure of the entire sonata because, if you learn its final section, you may decide to learn the whole thing -- there is not a single page of this sonata that is not fascinating.

The term sonata has been applied to so many types of music that it does not have a unique definition; it evolved and changed with time. In the earliest times, it simply meant music or song. ***Prior to, and including, Mozart's time, "sonata" meant instrumental music with one to four parts, consisting of Sonata, Minuet, Trio, Rondo, etc. A sonatina is a small sonata. There is also a sonata allegro, initially developed as the first part of a sonata, symphony, concerto, etc.; it generally contained an exposition, a development, and a recapitulation.*** The sonata allegro is important historically because this basic structure was gradually incorporated into most compositions. Curiously, no part of this Mozart sonata (No. 16, K300) is in sonata allegro format (Hinson, P. 552). It starts with a theme and 6 variations. Variation V is Adagio and should not be rushed. Then comes a break, which corresponds to the middle or slow movement of a Beethoven sonata. This break takes the form of a minuet-trio, a form of dance. The minuet originated as a French court dance with 3 beats and was the predecessor of the waltz. The waltz format also includes mazurkas; these originated as Polish dances, which is why Chopin composed so many mazurkas. They differ from the (Viennese) waltzes that have the accent on the first beat, in that their accent can be on the second or third beat. Waltzes started independently in Germany as a slower dance with 3 strong beats; it then evolved into the popular dances that we now refer to as "Viennese". Trios gradually went extinct as quartets gained popularity. Both the minuet and trio in our sonata have the time signature 3/4. Thus every first beat carries the accent; knowing that it is in a dance (waltz) format makes it easier to play the minuet-trio correctly. The trio should have a totally different air from the minuet (a convention in Mozart's time); this change in air gives the transition a refreshing feel. "Trio" generally refers to music played with 3 instruments; therefore, you will see three voices in this trio, which you can assign to a violin, viola, and cello. Don't forget the "Menuetto D. C." (De Capo, which means return to the beginning) at the end of the Trio; thus you must play minuet-trio-minuet. The final section is the Rondo. Rondos have the general structure ABACADA. . . , which makes good use of a catchy melody, A.

Our Rondo has the structure (BB')A(CC')A(BB')A'-Coda, a very symmetric structure. The time signature is a lively cut time; can you figure out the key of BB'? The rest of this Rondo is all in A, as is the formal key of this sonata. The entire sonata is sometimes referred to as a variation on a single theme, which is probably wrong, although the Rondo resembles Variation III, and the Trio resembles Variation IV. It starts with the "B" structure, constructed from a short unit of only 5 notes, repeated twice with a rest between them in bars 1-3; it is repeated at double speed in bar 4; he cleverly uses the same unit as a conjunction between these repetitions at the end of bar 3. It is again repeated at half speed in bars 7 and 8 and the last 2 bars provide the ending. Bar 9 is the same as bar 8 except that the last note is lowered instead of raised; this abrupt change in the repeating pattern is an easy way to signal an ending. The half speed units are disguised by adding two grace notes in the beginning, so that, when the entire B is played at speed, we only hear the melody without recognizing the individual repeat units. The efficiency of his composing process is astounding – he repeated the same unit 7 times in 9 bars using 3 speeds to compose one of his famous melodies. In fact, the entire sonata consists of these repeated sections that are 8 to 10 bars long. There are several sections that are 16 or 32 bars long, but these are multiples of the basic 8 bar sections. More examples of this type of micro-structural analysis are discussed in section IV.4 for Mozart and Beethoven. This type of analysis can be helpful for memorization and mental play – after all, mental play is how he composed them!

The technically challenging parts are (1) the fast RH trill of bar 25, (2) the fast RH runs from bar 36-60 - make sure you have good fingering, (3) the fast broken RH octaves of bars 97-104, and (4) the fast LH Alberti accompaniment of bars 119-125. Examine these elements to see which is the hardest for you, and start by practicing that element first. The broken octave sequence of bars 97-104 is not just a series of broken octaves, but two melodies, an octave and a half-step apart, chasing each other. Practice everything HS, without pedal, until they are comfortable before starting HT. Parallel set exercises are the key to developing the technique to play these elements and parallel set exercise #1 (quad repetitions, III.7b) is the most important, especially for learning relaxation. For fast trills, go to III.3.a. The broken chords in the LH (bar 28, etc., and in the Coda) should be played very fast, almost like a single note, and match the RH notes. The HT practice should initially be without pedal until you are comfortable HT.

How do you make music that sounds like Mozart? There is no secret -- the instructions have been there all the time! They are the expression markings on the music; for Mozart, each marking has a precise meaning, and if you follow *every* one of them, including the time signature, etc., the music becomes an intimate, intricate conversation. The "only" thing you need to do is to suppress the urge to insert expressions of your own. There is no better example of this than the last 3 chords at the end. It is so simple, that it is almost unbelievable (a hallmark of Mozart): the first chord is a staccato and the remaining two are legato. This simple device creates a convincing ending; play it any other way, and the ending becomes a flop. Therefore, these last 3 chords should not be pedaled although some scores (Schirmer) have pedal markings on them. Better pianists tend to play the entire Rondo without pedal.

Let's examine the first 8 bars in more detail.

RH: The first 4 note theme (bar 1) is played legato followed by an eighth note and exact 8th rest. The note and rest are needed for the audience to "digest" the introduction of the unit. This construct is repeated, then the 4-note theme is repeated at double speed (2 per bar) in bar 4, and climaxes at the C6 played firmly and connecting to the two following staccato notes. This doubling of speed is a device used by composers all the time. In bars 5-7, the RH plays staccato, maintaining the level of excitement. The series of falling notes in bars 8-9 brings this section to a close, like someone stepping on the brakes of a car.

LH: *The simple LH accompaniment provides a rigid skeleton; without it, the whole 9 bars would flop around like a wet noodle.* The clever placement of the ties (between the 1st and 2nd notes of bar 2, etc.) not only emphasizes the cut time nature of each bar, but brings out the rhythmic idea within this exposition; *it sounds like a fox trot dance step – slow, slow, quick-quick-slow in bars 2-5, repeated in bars 6-9*. Because every note must be staccato in bars 6-8, the only way to emphasize the rhythm is to accent the first note of each bar.

Both notes of bar 9 (both hands) are legato and slightly softer in order to provide an ending, and both hands lift at the same instant. It is clear that we must not only know what the markings are, but also *why* they are there. Of course, there is no time to think about these complicated explanations; the music should take care of that - the artist simply *feels* the effects of these markings. The strategic placing of legato, staccato, ties, and accents is the key to playing this piece, while accurately maintaining the rhythm. Hopefully, you should now be able to continue the analysis for the rest of this piece and reproduce music that is uniquely Mozart.

HT play is slightly more difficult than the previous Moonlight because this piece is faster and requires higher accuracy. Perhaps the most difficult part is the coordination of the trill in the RH with the LH in bar 25. Don't try to learn this by slowing it down. Simply make sure that the HS work is completely done using bars 25 and 26 as a single practice segment, then combine the 2 hands at speed. ***Always try to combine things HT at speed (or close to it) first, and use slower speeds only as a last resort because if you succeed, you will save lots of time and avoid forming bad habits.*** Advanced pianists almost never have to combine hands by slowing down.

After you are comfortable HT without the pedal, add the pedal. In the section starting at bar 27, the combination of broken LH chords, RH octaves, and pedal creates a sense of grandeur that is representative of how Mozart could create grandeur from relatively simple constructs. Hold the last note of this section a little longer than required by the rhythm (tenuto, bar 35), especially after the repetition, before launching into the next section. As stated earlier, Mozart wrote no pedal markings; therefore, after practicing HT without pedal, add pedal *only* where you think it will elevate the music. Especially with difficult material such as Rachmaninoff's, less pedal is looked upon by the pianist community as indicating superior technique.

Chopin's Fantaisie-Impromptu, Op. 66, Fast Play Degradation (FPD)

This example was selected because (1) everyone likes this composition, (2) without good learning methods it can seem impossible to learn, (3) the exhilaration of suddenly being able to play it is unmatched, (4) the challenges of the piece are ideal for illustration purposes, and (5) this is the kind of piece that you will be working on all your life in order to do "incredible things" with it, so you might as well start *now*! Most students who have difficulty do so because they can't get started and the initial hurdle produces a mental block that makes them doubt their ability to play this piece. There is no better demonstration of the efficacy of the methods of this book than demonstrating how to learn this composition. However, because this piece is reasonably difficult, you should read section III before learning it.

You will need about 2 yrs of piano lessons before you can start learning this piece.

For easier pieces, try the above Moonlight and Rondo, or section III.6.l, Bach's Inventions. Make sure you figure out the key before you start. Hint: after the G# "announcement", it starts with C# in bar 3 and the composition ends with C#, and the Largo starts with Db (same note as C#!); but is each in a major or minor key? *The large number of sharps and flats, as in this composition, often worries beginners; however, the black keys are easier to play than the white keys once you know the flat finger positions (see III.4.b) and the Thumb Over method (see III.5). Chopin may have chosen these "far out" keys for this reason, because the scale does not matter in the Equal Temperament that he probably used (see Ch. Two, 2.c,).*

We start by reviewing the preliminary work with HS practice and mental play. Therefore you should practice HT with the objective of attaining very accurate synchronization of the two hands. Although the last page might be most difficult, we will break the rule about starting at the end and start at the beginning because this piece is difficult to start correctly but, once started, it takes care of itself. You need a strong, confident beginning. So we will start with the first two pages, up to the slow cantabile part. The LH stretch and continuous workout makes endurance (ie, relaxation) a major issue. Those without sufficient experience and especially those with smaller hands, may need to work on the LH for weeks before it becomes satisfactory. Fortunately, the LH is not that fast, so speed is not a limiting factor and most students should be able to play the LH faster HS than final speed in less than two weeks, completely relaxed, without fatigue.

For bar 5 where the RH first comes in, the suggested LH fingering is 532124542123. You might start by practicing bar 5, LH, by cycling it continually until you can play it well. You should stretch the *palm*, not the *fingers*, which can lead to stress and injury. See section III.7e for palm stretching exercises.

Practice without the pedal. Practice in small segments. Suggested segments are: bars 1-4, 5-6, 1st half of 7, 2nd half of 7, 8, 10 (skip 9 which is the same as 5), 11, 12, 13-14, 15-16, 19-20, 21-22, 30-32, 33-34, then 2 chords in 35. If you cannot reach the 2nd chord, play it as a very fast ascending broken chord, with emphasis on the top note. After each segment is memorized and satisfactory, connect them in pairs. Then play the whole LH from memory by starting from the beginning and adding segments. Bring it up to final speed and check your mental play.

When you can play this entire section (LH only) twice in succession, relaxed, without feeling tired, you have the necessary endurance. At this point, it is a lot of fun to go much faster than final speed. In preparation for HT work, get up to about 1.5 times final speed. Raise the wrist slightly when playing the pinky and lower it as you approach the thumb. By raising the wrist, you will find that you can put more power into the pinky, and by lowering the wrist you avoid missing the thumb note. *In Chopin's music, the pinky and thumb (but especially the pinky) notes are most important,* so practice playing these two fingers with authority. The Cartwheel Method, explained in section III.5, may be useful here.

When you are satisfied with it, insert the pedal; basically, the pedal should be cut with every chord change which generally occurs either once every bar or twice every bar. The pedal is a rapid up and down ("cutting the sound") motion at the first beat, but you can lift the pedal earlier for special effects. For the wide LH stretch in the second half of bar 14 (starting with E2), the fingering is 532124 if you can reach it comfortably. If not, use 521214.

At the same time, you should have been practicing the RH, switching hands as soon as the working hand feels slightly tired. *The routines are almost identical to those for the LH, including practicing without the pedal.* Start by splitting bar 5 into two halves and learn each half separately up to speed, and then join them. For the rising arpeggio in bar 7, use the thumb over method because it is too fast to be played thumb under. The fingering should be such that both hands tend to play the pinky or thumb at the same time; this makes it easier to play HT. This is why it is not a good idea to fool around with the fingerings of the LH -- use the fingerings as marked on the score.

Now practice HT. You can start with either the first or second half of bar 5 where the RH comes in for the first time. The second half is probably easier because of the smaller stretch of the LH and there is no timing problem with the missing first note in the RH (for the first half), so let's start with the second half. *The easiest way to learn the 3,4 timing is to do it at speed from the beginning. Don't try to slow down and figure out where each note should go, because too much of that will introduce an unevenness in your playing that may become impossible to correct later on.* Here we use the "cycling" method -- see "Cycling" in section III.2. First, cycle the six notes of the LH continually, without stopping. Then switch hands and do the same for the eight notes of the RH, at the same (final) tempo as you did for the LH. Next cycle only the LH several times, and then let the RH join in. Initially, you only need to match the first notes accurately; don't worry if the others aren't quite right. In a few tries, you should be able to play HT fairly well. If not, stop and start all over again, cycling HS. Since almost the whole composition is made up of things like the segment you just practiced, it pays to practice this well, until you are very comfortable. To accomplish this, change the speed. Go very fast, then very slowly. As you slow down, you will be able to take notice of where all the notes fit with respect to each other. You will find that fast is not necessarily difficult, and slower is not always easier. *The 3,4 timing is a mathematical device Chopin used to produce the illusion of hyper-speed in this piece.* The mathematical explanations and additional salient points of this composition are further discussed under "Cycling" in Section III.2. You will probably practice this composition HS for years after you initially complete the piece because it is so much fun to experiment with this fascinating composition. Now add the pedal. This is when you should develop the habit of accurately pumping the pedal.

If you are satisfied with the second half of bar 5, repeat the same procedure for the first half. Then assemble the two halves together. One disadvantage of the HS-HT approach is that practically all technique acquisition is accomplished HS, possibly resulting in poorly synchronized HT play. You now have most the tools to learn the rest of this composition by yourself!

The cantabile section is the same thing repeated four times with increasing complexity. Therefore, learn (and memorize) the first repetition first because it is the easiest, then learn the 4th repetition because it is the most difficult. Normally, we should learn the most difficult part first but, in this case, starting with the 4th repetition may take too long for some students, and learning the easiest repetition first can make it much easier to learn the 4th repetition because they are similar. As with many Chopin pieces, memorizing the LH well is the quickest way to build a firm foundation for memorizing because the LH usually has a simpler structure that is easier to analyze, memorize and play. Moreover, Chopin often created different versions of the RH for each repetition while using essentially the same notes in the LH as he did in this case (same chord progressions); therefore, after you learn the first repetition, you already know most of the LH part of the 4th repetition, enabling you to learn this last repetition quickly.

The trill in the 1st bar of the 4th repetition, combined with the 2,3 timing, makes the 2nd half of this bar difficult. Since there are 4 repetitions, you might play it without the trill in the first repetition, then an inverted mordent the 2nd, a short trill the 3rd, and a longer trill the last time around.

The third section (Presto!) is similar to the first section, so if you managed to learn the first section, you are almost home free. However, this time, it is faster than the first time

(Allegro) – Chopin apparently wants you to play this at two different speeds, possibly because he saw that they can sound quite different when you change the speed; why should it sound different, and in what way? -- the physics and psychology of this speed change is discussed in III.2. Note that in the final 20 bars or so, the RH pinky and thumb carry notes of major thematic value, all the way to the end. This section may require a lot of HS practice with the RH.

If you play any composition at full speed (or faster) too often, you may suffer what I call "fast play degradation" (FPD). The following day, you might find that you can't play it as well any more, or during practice, you can't make any progress. This happens mostly with HT play. HS play is more immune to FPD and can in fact be used to correct it. FPD occurs probably because the human playing mechanism (hands, brain, etc) gets confused at such speeds, and therefore occurs only for complex procedures such as HT play of conceptually or technically difficult pieces. Easy pieces do not suffer FPD. FPD can create enormous problems with complex music like Bach's or Mozart's compositions. Students who try to speed them up HT can run into all sorts of problems and the standard solution had been to simply keep practicing slowly. However, there is a neat solution to this problem -- use HS practice! And remember that whenever you play fast, you will generally suffer FPD if you do not play slowly at least once before quitting. Also, FPD can be an indication that your mental play may not be solid or up to speed.

26.   Summary

This concludes the basic section. You have the essentials to devise routines for learning practically any new piece. This is the minimum set of instructions you need to get started. In section III, we shall explore more uses for these basic steps, as well as introduce more ideas on how to solve some common problems.

III. SELECTED TOPICS IN PIANO PRACTICE

1. Tone, Rhythm, Legato, staccato
a.   What is "Good Tone"?
The Basic Keystroke. The basic keystroke must be learned by every pianist. Without it, nothing else will make a meaningful difference – you can't build a Taj Mahal out of mud-bricks and straw. *The keystroke consists of 3 main components, the downstroke, the hold, and the lift.* This might sound like a trivially simple thing to learn, but it is not, and most piano teachers struggle to teach their students the correct keystroke. The difficulties arise mostly because the mechanics of the keystroke have not been adequately explained anywhere; therefore, those explanations will be the major topics of these paragraphs.

The downstroke is what creates the piano sound initially; in the correct motion, it must be as quick as possible, yet with control of the volume. This control is not easy because we found out in the gravity drop section that faster downstroke generally means louder sound. The quickness gives the note its precise timing; without this quickness, the timing of the note start becomes a sloppy affair. Therefore, whether the music is slow or fast, the downstroke must be basically fast. *These requirements of fast stroke, control of volume, and many others we will shortly encounter, bring us to a most important principle of learning piano – finger sensitivity. The finger must be able to sense and execute many requirements before you can master the basic keystroke.* In order to control volume, the downstroke should consist of 2 parts; an initial strong component to break the friction/inertia of the key and start its motion, and a second component with the appropriate strength for the desired volume. The suggestion to "play deeply into the keys" is a good one in the sense that the downstroke must not slow down; it must accelerate as you reach the bottom so that you never lose control over the hammer.

This 2-part motion is especially important when playing pianissimo. In a well regulated concert grand, friction is nearly zero and the inertia of the system is low. In all other pianos (which comprises 99% of all pianos) there is friction that must be overcome, especially when you first start the downstroke (friction is highest when the motion is zero), and there are numerous imbalances in the system that produce inertia. Assuming that the piano is properly voiced, you can play very soft pianissimo by first breaking the friction/inertia and then making the soft stroke. These 2 components must join seamlessly so that to an observer, it looks like a single motion, with the flesh of the fingers acting like shock absorbers. The required fast downstroke means that the finger muscle must have a high proportion of fast muscles (see section 7.a below). This is achieved by fast motion practice over extended periods of time (about a year) and avoiding strength exercises; therefore, the statement that piano technique requires finger strength is absolutely wrong. We need to cultivate finger speed and sensitivity.

The hold component of the keystroke is necessary to hold the hammer using the backcheck and to accurately control the note duration. Without the hold, the hammer can flop around, producing extraneous sounds, cause problems with repeated notes, trills, etc. Beginners will have difficulty with making a smooth transition between the downstroke and hold. *Do not push down on the key during the hold in an attempt to "push deeply into the piano"; gravity is sufficient to hold the key down.* The length of the hold is what controls color and expression; therefore it is an important part of the music.

The lift causes the damper to fall onto the strings and terminate the sound. Together with the hold, it determines the note duration. Similarly to the downstroke, the lift must be fast in order to control the note duration accurately. Therefore, the pianist must make a conscious effort to grow fast muscles in the extensor muscles, just as we did with the flexor muscles for the downstroke. Especially when playing fast, many students will forget about the lift entirely, resulting in sloppy play. A run may end up consisting of staccato, legato, and overlapping notes. Fast parallel sets may end up sounding as if they were being played with the pedal.

By controlling all 3 components of the basic key stroke accurately, you maintain complete control over the piano; specifically, over the hammer and the damper, and this control is needed for authoritative play. These components determine the nature of each note. You can now see why a fast downstroke and equally fast lift is so important, especially during slow play. In normal play, the lift of the previous note coincides with the downstroke of the following note. In staccato and legato (section c) and fast play (7.i), we need to modify all these components, and they will be discussed separately. If you had never practiced these components before, start practice with all 5 fingers, C to G, as you do when playing a scale and apply the components to each finger, HS. If you want to exercise the extensor muscles, you can exaggerate the quick lift stroke. Try to keep all the non-playing fingers on the keys, lightly. As you try to speed up the down and lift strokes, playing about one note per second, you may start to build stress; in that case, practice until you can eliminate the stress. The most important thing to remember about the hold component is that you must instantly relax during the hold after the quick downstroke. In other words, *you need to practice both stroke speed and relaxation speed*. Then gradually speed up the play; there is no need to play fast at this time. Just get up to some comfortable speed. Now do the same with any slow music you can play, such as the 1st movement of Beethoven's Moonlight, HS. If you had never done this before, HT will be initially very awkward because you now need to coordinate so many components in both hands. However, with practice, the music will come out better, you will gain much more control over the expression, and should get the feeling that you can now play more musically. There should be no missed or wrong notes, all the notes should be more even, and you can execute all the expression marks with greater precision. The performances will be consistent from day to day, and technique will progress more rapidly. Without a good basic keystroke, you can get into trouble when you play different pianos, or pianos that are not in good regulation, and the music can often come out worse as you practice more because you can acquire bad habits such as inaccurate timing. Of course, the whole process described in this one paragraph may take weeks or even months to complete.

Tone: Single versus Multiple Notes, Pianissimo, Fortissimo. *Tone is the quality of the sound; whether the sum total of all the properties of the sound is appropriate for the music*. There is controversy over whether a pianist can control the "tone" of a single note on the piano. If you were to sit at the piano and play one note, it seems nearly impossible to alter the tone except for things like staccato, legato, loud, soft, etc. On the other hand, there is no question that different pianists produce differing tones. Two pianists can play the same composition on the same piano and produce music with very different tonal quality. Most of this apparent contradiction can be resolved by carefully defining what "tone" means. For example, a large part of the tonal differences among pianists can be attributed to the particular pianos they use, and the way those pianos are regulated or tuned. Controlling the tone of a single note is probably just one aspect of a multi-faceted, complex issue. Therefore, the most important distinction we must make initially is whether we are talking about a single note or a group of notes. Most of the time, when we hear different tones, we are listening to a group of notes. In that case, tone differences are easier to explain. Tone is mostly produced by the control of the notes relative to each other. This almost always comes down to precision, control and musical content. ***Therefore, tone is mainly a property of a group of notes and depends on the musical sensitivity of the pianist.***

However, it is also clear that we can control the tone of a single note in several ways. We can control it by use of the soft and damper pedals. We can also change the harmonic content (the number of overtones) by playing louder or softer. The soft pedal changes the tone, or timbre, by reducing the prompt sound relative to the after-sound. When a string is struck with a greater force, more harmonics are generated. Thus when we play softly, we produce sound containing stronger fundamentals. However, below a certain loudness, there is insufficient energy to excite the fundamental and you mostly excite some higher frequency traveling waves, somewhat similar to the flautando in the violin (the inertia of the piano string acts like the finger in the flautando). Therefore, somewhere between PP and FF, there is an optimum strike force that maximizes the fundamental. The damper pedal also changes the timbre by allowing vibrations at the non-struck strings.

The tone or timbre can be controlled by the tuner by voicing the hammer or by tuning differently. A harder hammer produces a more brilliant tone (larger harmonic content) and a hammer with a flat striking area produces a harsher tone (more high frequency harmonics). The tuner can change the stretch or control the amount of detuning among the unisons. Up to a point, larger stretch tends to produce brighter music and insufficient stretch can produce a piano with unexciting sound. When detuned within the sympathetic vibration frequency range, all strings of a note will be in perfect tune (vibrate at the same frequency), but will interact differently with each other. For example, the note can be made to "sing" which is an after-sound whose volume wavers. No two strings are ever identical, so that the option of tuning identically simply does not exist.

Finally, we come to the difficult question: ***can you vary the tone of a single note by*** *controlling the downstroke?* Most of the arguments over tone control center on the free flight property of the hammer before it strikes the strings. Opponents (of single note tone control) argue that, because the hammer is in free flight, only its velocity matters and therefore tone is not controllable for a note played at a specified loudness. But the assumption of free flight has never been proven, as we shall now see. ***One factor affecting tone is the flex of the hammer shank.*** For a loud note, the shank may be significantly flexed as the hammer is launched into free flight. In that case, the hammer can have a larger effective mass than its original mass when it hits the strings. This is because the force, F, of the hammer on the strings, is given by $F = -M\mathbf{a}$ where M is the mass of the hammer and $\mathbf{a}$ is its deceleration upon impact with the strings. Positive flex adds an extra force because, as the flex recovers after the jack is released, it pushes the hammer forwards; when F increases, it doesn't matter if M or $\mathbf{a}$ increases, the effect is the same. However, $\mathbf{a}$ is more difficult to measure than M (for example you can easily simulate a larger M by using a heavier hammer) so we usually say, in this case, that the "effective mass" has increased, to make it easier to visualize the effect of the larger F on how the strings respond. In reality, however, positive flex increases $\mathbf{a}$. For a note played staccato, the flex may be negative by the time the hammer strikes the strings, so that the tone difference between "deep" playing and staccato may be considerable. These changes in effective mass will certainly change the distribution of overtones and affect the tone we hear. ***Since the shank is not 100% rigid, we know that there is always a finite flex. The only question is whether it is sufficient to affect tone as we hear it.*** It almost certainly is because the hammer shank is a relatively flexible piece of wood. If this is true, then the tone of the lower notes, with the heavier hammers, should be more controllable because the heavier hammers will cause a larger flex. Although one might expect the flex to be negligible because the hammer is so light, the knuckle is very close to the hammer flange bushing, creating a tremendous leverage. The argument that the hammer is too light to induce flex is not valid because the hammer is sufficiently massive to hold all of the kinetic energy required to make even the loudest sounds. That is a lot of energy!

Note that the hammer let-off is only several millimeters and this distance is extremely critical for tone. Such a small let-off suggests that the hammer is designed to be in acceleration when it hits the string. The hammer is not in free flight after the jack releases because for the first few millimeters after release the hammer is being accelerated by the recovery of the shank flex. ***The let-off is the smallest controllable distance that can maintain the acceleration without any chance of locking the hammer onto the strings because the jack could not release.*** This flex explains four otherwise mysterious facts: (i) the tremendous energy that such a light hammer can transfer to the strings, (ii) the decrease in tone quality (or control) when the let-off is too large, (iii) the critical dependence of the sound output and tone control on hammer weight and size, and (iv) the clicking sound that the piano makes when the hammer shank bushing deteriorates (a classic example is the clicking Teflon bushing). The clicking is the sound of the bushing snapping back when the jack releases and the shank flex takes over -- without the flex unwinding, there is no force to snap the busing back; therefore, without flex, there will be no click. ***Since the clicking can be heard even for moderately soft sounds, the shank is flexed for all except the softest sounds.***

This scenario also has important implications for the pianist (not only for the piano tuner). It means that the tone of a single note can be controlled. It also tells us how to control it. First of all, for PPP sounds, there is negligible flex and we are dealing with a different tone from louder sounds. Pianists know that, to play PP, you press down with a constant velocity -- note that this minimizes flex because there is no acceleration at release. When playing pianissimo, you want to minimize flex in order to minimize the effective mass of the hammer. Secondly, for maximum flex, the downstroke should accelerate at the bottom. This makes a lot of sense: "deep tone" is produced by leaning into the piano and pressing firmly, even with soft sounds. That is exactly how you maximize flex, which is equivalent to using a larger hammer. This information is also critical for the piano technician. It means that the optimum hammer size is one which is sufficiently small so that flex is zero somewhere around PP, but sufficiently large so that flex is significant starting around mf. This is a very clever mechanical arrangement that allows the use of relatively small hammers that enable rapid repetitions and can still transmit a maximum amount of energy to the strings. It means that it is a mistake to go to larger hammers to produce more sound because you will lose repetition speed and tone control. The existence of hammer shank flex is now well known ("Five Lectures on the Acoustics of the Piano").

Can the difference in tone of a single note be heard on the piano by playing only one note? Usually not; most people are not sensitive enough to hear this difference with most pianos. You will need a Steinway B or better piano, and you may start to hear this difference (if you test this with several pianos of progressively higher quality) with the lower notes. However, when actual music is played, the human ear is amazingly sensitive to how the hammer impacts the strings, and the difference in tone can be easily heard. This is similar to tuning: most people (including most pianists) will be hard pressed to hear the difference between a super tuning and an ordinary tuning by playing single notes or even testing intervals. However, practically any pianist can hear the difference in tuning quality by playing a piece of their favorite music. You can demonstrate this yourself. Play an easy piece twice, in an identical way except for touch. First, play with arm weight and "pressing deeply" into the piano, making sure that the key drop accelerates all the way down (correct basic keystroke). Then compare this to the music when you press shallowly so that there is complete key drop, but there is no acceleration at the bottom. You may need to practice a little to make sure that the first time is not louder than the second. You should hear an inferior tone quality for the second mode of play. In the hands of great pianists, this difference can be quite large. Of course, we discussed above that tone is controlled most strongly by how you play successive notes, so that playing music to test the effect of single notes is clearly not the best way. However, it is the most sensitive test.

Pianissimo: We saw that for PPP, you need an accurate basic key stroke, and rapid relaxation. Feeling the keys with the pads of the fingers is important. In general, you should always practice with a soft touch until the passage is mastered, then add mf or FF or whatever is needed, because playing with a soft touch is the most difficult skill to develop. There is no acceleration of the downstroke and no hammer shank flex, but the backcheck must be controlled (key down and held). ***The most important factors for PPP are proper regulation (especially minimum let-off, hammer voicing, and correct hammer weight). Trying to cultivate PPP technique without proper piano maintenance is futile.*** In an emergency (during a performance with unsatisfactory piano) you might try the soft pedal with an upright or a very slight partial soft pedal with a grand. PPP is difficult on most digitals because the key action is inferior and deteriorates quickly after about 5 years of use. But an acoustic that was not maintained can be much worse.

Fortissimo is a matter of transferring weight into the piano. This means body leaning forward so that the center of gravity is closer to the keyboard and ***playing from the shoulders***. Do not use only hands or arms for FF. Again, relaxation is important so that you do not waste energy, you enable maximum downstroke speed, and the proper force can be directed only where it is needed. ***For a passage to be played FF, practice without the FF until the passage is mastered, then add FF.***

In summary, tone is primarily a result of uniformity and control of playing and depends on the musical sensitivity of the player. *Tone control is a complex issue involving every factor that changes the nature of the sound and we have seen that there are many ways to change the piano sound.* It all starts with how the piano is regulated. Each pianist can control the tone by numerous means, such as by playing loudly or softly, or by varying the speed. For example, by playing louder and faster, we can produce music consisting mainly of the prompt sound; conversely, a slower and softer play will produce a subdued effect, using more after-sound. And there are innumerable ways in which to incorporate the pedal into your playing. We saw that the tone of a single note can be controlled because the hammer shank has flex. The large number of variables ensures that every pianist will produce a different tone.

   b.   **What is Rhythm?** (Beethoven's Tempest, Op. 31, #2, Appassionata, Op. 57)
   Rhythm is the (repetitive) timing framework of music. When you read about rhythm (see Whiteside), it often seems like a mysterious aspect of music that only "inborn talent" can express. Or perhaps you need to practice it all your life, like drummers. Most frequently, however, *correct rhythm is simply a matter of accurate counting, of correctly reading the music, especially the time signatures. This is not as easy as it sounds; difficulties often arise because most indications for rhythm are not explicitly spelled out everywhere on the music score since it is part of things like the time signature that appears only once at the beginning* (there are too many such "things" to be listed here, such as the difference between a waltz and a mazurka. Another example: without looking at the music, some would think that the beat in the "happy birthday" song is on "happy", but it is actually on "birth"; this song is a waltz). In many instances, the music is created mainly by manipulating these rhythmic variations so that rhythm is one of the most important elements of music. In short, most rhythmic difficulties arise from not reading the music correctly. This often happens when you try to read the music HT; there is too much information for the brain to process and it can't be bothered with rhythm, especially if the music involves new technical skills. That initial reading mistake then becomes incorporated into the final music from repeated practice.

   Definition of Rhythm: Rhythm consists of 2 parts: timing and accents, and they come in 2 forms, formal and logical. The mysteries surrounding rhythm and the difficulties encountered in defining rhythm arise from the "logical" part, which is at once the key element and the most elusive. So let's tackle the simpler formal rhythms first. They are simpler but they aren't less important; too many students make mistakes with these elements which can render the music unrecognizable.

   Formal Timing: *The formal timing rhythm is given by the Time Signature*, and is indicated at the very beginning of the music score. The major time signatures are waltz (3/4), common time (4/4), "cut time" (2/2, also alla breve), and 2/4. The waltz has 3 beats per bar (measure), etc.; the number of beats per bar is indicated by the numerator. 4/4 is the most common and is often not even indicated, although it should be indicated by a "C" at the beginning (you can remember it as "C stands for common"). Cut time is indicated by the same "C", but with a vertical line down the center (cuts the "C" in half). The reference note is indicated by the denominator, so that the 3/4 waltz has 3 quarter-notes per bar, and 2/4 is, in principle, twice as fast as 2/2 cut time. The meter is the number of beats in a measure, and almost every meter is constructed from duples or triples, although exceptions have been used for special effects (5, 7, or 9 beats).

   Formal Accents: Each time signature has its own formal accent (louder or softer beats). If we use the convention that 1 is the loudest, 2 is softer, etc., then the (Viennese) waltz has the formal accent 133 (the famous **oom**-pha-pha); the first beat gets the accent; the Mazurka can be 313 or 331. Common time has the formal accent 1323, and cut time and 2/4 have the accent 1212. A syncopation is a rhythm in which the accent is placed at a location different from the formal accent; for example a syncopated 4/4 might be 2313 or 2331. Note that the 2331 rhythm is fixed throughout the composition, but the 1 is at an unconventional location.

Logical Timing and Accents: This is where the composer injects his music. It is a change in timing and loudness from the formal rhythm. Although rhythmic logic is not necessary, it is almost always there. Common examples of timing rhythmic logic are accel. (to make things more exciting), decel. (perhaps to indicate an ending) or rubato. Examples of dynamic rhythmic logic are increasing or decreasing loudness, forte, PP, etc.

Beethoven's Tempest Sonata (Op. 31, #2), illustrates the formal and logical rhythms. For example, in the 3rd movement, the first 3 bars are 3 repetitions of the same structure, and they simply follow the formal rhythm. However, in bars 43-46, there are 6 repetitions of the same structure in the RH, but they must be squeezed into 4 formal rhythmic bars! If you make 6 identical repetitions in the RH, you are wrong! In addition, in bar 47, there is an unexpected "sf" that has nothing to do with the formal rhythm, but is an absolutely essential logical rhythm.

If rhythm is so important, what guidance can one use, in order to cultivate it? Obviously, ***you must treat rhythm as a separate subject of practice for which you need a specific program of attack***. Therefore, during the initial learning of a new piece, set aside some time for working on the rhythm. A metronome, especially one with advanced features, can be helpful here. First, you must double check that your rhythm is consistent with the time signature. This can't be done in your mind even after you can play the piece -- you must revisit the sheet music and check every note. ***Too many students play a piece a certain way "because it sounds right"; you can't do that.*** You must check with the score to see if the correct notes carry the correct accent strictly according to the time signature. Only then, can you decide which rhythmic interpretation is the best way to play and where the composer has inserted violations of the basic rules (very rare); more often the rhythm indicated by the time signature is strictly correct but sounds counter-intuitive. An example of this is the mysterious "arpeggio" at the beginning of **Beethoven's Appassionata** (Op. 57). A normal arpeggio (such as CEG) would start with the first note (C), which should carry the accent (downbeat). However, Beethoven starts each bar at the third note of the arpeggio (the first bar is incomplete and carries the first two notes of the "arpeggio"); this forces you to accent the third note (G), not the first note, if you follow the time signature correctly. We find out the reason for this odd "arpeggio" when the main theme is introduced in bar 35. Note that this "arpeggio" is an inverted, schematized (simplified) form of the main theme. Beethoven had psychologically prepared us for the main theme by giving us only its rhythm! This is why he repeats it, after raising it by a curious interval -- he wanted to make sure that we recognized the unusual rhythm (he used the same device at the beginning of his 5th symphony, where he repeated the 4-note motif at a lower pitch). Another example is Chopin's Fantaisie-Impromptu. The first note of the RH (bar 5) must be softer than the second. Can you find at least one reason why? Although this piece is in double time, it may be instructive to practice the RH as 4/4 to make sure that the wrong notes are not emphasized.

Check the rhythm carefully when you start HS. Then check again when you start HT. When the rhythm is wrong, the music usually becomes impossible to play at speed. Thus, if you have unusual difficulty in getting up to speed, it is a good idea to check the rhythm. In fact, incorrect rhythmic interpretation is one of the most common causes of speed walls and why you have trouble HT. When you make an rhythmic error, no amount of practice will enable you to get up to speed! This is one of the reasons why outlining works: it can simplify the job of correctly reading the rhythm. Therefore, when outlining, concentrate on rhythm. Also, when you first start HT, you may have more success by exaggerating the rhythm. Rhythm is another reason why you should not attempt pieces that are too difficult for you. If you don't have sufficient technique, you will not be able to control the rhythm. What can happen is that the lack of technique will impose an incorrect rhythm into your playing, thus creating a speed wall.

Next, look for the special rhythmic markings, such as "sf" or accent marks. Finally, there are situations in which there are no indications on the music and you simply have to know what to do, or listen to a recording in order to pick up special rhythmic variations. Therefore, as part of the practice routine, you should experiment with rhythm, accenting unexpected notes, etc., to see what might happen.

Rhythm is also intimately associated with speed. This is why you need to play most Beethoven compositions above certain speeds; otherwise, the emotions associated with the rhythm and even the melodic lines can be lost. Beethoven was a master of rhythm; thus you cannot play Beethoven successfully without paying special attention to rhythm. He usually gives you at least two things simultaneously: (i) an easy-to-follow melody that the audience hears, and (ii) a rhythmic/harmonic device that controls what the audience *feels*. Thus in the first movement of his Pathetique (Op. 13), the agitated LH tremolo controls the emotions while the audience is preoccupied with listening to the curious RH. Therefore a mere technical ability to handle the fast LH tremolo is insufficient -- you must be able to control the emotional content with this tremolo. Once you understand and can execute the rhythmic concept, it becomes much easier to bring out the musical content of the entire movement, and the stark contrast with the Grave section becomes obvious.

There is one class of rhythmic difficulties that can be solved using a simple trick. This is the class of complex rhythms with missing notes. A good example of this can be found in the 2nd movement of Beethoven's Pathetique. The 2/4 time signature is easy to play in bars 17 to 21 because of the repeated chords of the LH that maintain the rhythm. However, in bar 22, the most important accented notes of the LH are missing, making it difficult to pick up the somewhat complex play in the RH. The solution to this problem is to simply fill in the missing notes of the LH! In this way, you can easily practice the correct rhythm in the RH.

In summary, the "secret" of great rhythm is no secret -- it must start with correct counting (which, I must re-emphasize, is not easy). For advanced pianists, it is of course much more; it is magic. It is what distinguishes the great from the ordinary. It is not just counting the accents in each bar but how the bars connect to create the developing musical idea – the logical component of rhythm. For example, in Beethoven's Moonlight (Op. 27), the beginning of the 3rd movement is basically the 1st movement played at a crazy speed. This knowledge tells us how to play the 1st movement, because it means that the series of triplets in the 1st movement must be connected in such a way that they lead to the culmination with the three repeated notes. If you simply played the repeated notes independently of the preceding triplets, all these notes will lose their meaning/impact. Rhythm is also that odd or unexpected accent that our brains somehow recognize as special. Clearly, rhythm is a critical element of music to which we must pay special attention.

c. Legato, Staccato

Legato is smooth play. This is accomplished by connecting successive notes – do not lift the first note until the second one is played. Fraser recommends considerable overlap of the two notes. The first moments of a note contain a lot of "noise" so that overlapping notes are not that noticeable. Because legato is a habit that you must build into your playing, experiment with different amounts of overlap to see how much overlap gives the best legato *for you*. Then practice this until it becomes a habit so that you can always reproduce the same effect. Chopin considered legato as the most important skill to develop for a beginner. Chopin's music requires special types of legato and staccato (Ballade Op. 23), so it is important to pay attention to these elements when playing his music. ***If you want to practice legato, play some Chopin.*** The basic keystroke is absolutely necessary for legato.

In staccato, the finger is bounced off the key so as to produce a brief sound with no sustain. It is somewhat astonishing that most books on learning piano discuss staccato, but never define what it is! The backcheck is not engaged for staccato and the damper cuts off the sound immediately after the note is played. Therefore, the "hold" component of the basic keystroke is absent. There are two notations for staccato, the normal (dot) and hard (filled triangle). In both, the jack is not released; in hard staccato, the finger moves down and up much more rapidly. Thus in normal staccato, the key drop may be about half way down, but in hard staccato, it can be less than half way. In this way, the damper is returned to the strings faster, resulting in a shorter note duration. Because the backcheck is not engaged, the hammer can "bounce around", making repetitions tricky at certain speeds. Thus if you have trouble with rapidly repeated staccatos, don't immediately blame yourself -- it may be the wrong frequency at which the hammer bounces the wrong way. By changing the speed, amount of key drop, etc., you may be able to eliminate the problem. In normal staccato, gravity quickly returns the damper onto the strings. In hard staccato, the damper is actually bounced off the damper top rail, so that it returns even more quickly. At string contact, the hammer shank flex can be negative, which makes the effective mass of the hammer lighter; thus there is a considerable variety of tones that you can produce with staccato. Therefore, the motions of the hammer, backcheck, jack, and damper are all changed in staccato. ***Clearly, in order to play staccato well, it helps to understand how the piano works.***

Staccato is generally divided into three types depending on how it is played: (i) finger staccato, (ii) wrist staccato, and (iii) arm staccato, which includes both up-down motion and arm rotation. (i) is played mostly with the finger, holding the hand and arm still, (ii) is played mostly with wrist action, and (iii) is usually played as a thrust (III.4a), with the playing action originating at the upper arm. As you progress from (i) to (iii) you add more mass behind the fingers; therefore, (i) gives the lightest, fastest staccato and is useful for single, soft notes, and (iii) gives the heaviest feeling and is useful for loud passages and chords with many notes, but is also the slowest. (ii) is in between. In practice, most of us probably combine all three; since the wrist and arm are slower, their amplitudes must be correspondingly reduced in order to play fast staccato. Some teachers frown on the use of wrist staccato, preferring mostly arm staccato; however, it is probably better to have a choice (or combination) of all three. For example, you might be able to reduce fatigue by changing from one to the other, although the standard method of reducing fatigue is to change fingers. When practicing staccato, practice the three (finger, hand, arm) staccatos first before deciding on which one to use, or on how to combine them.

Because you cannot use the arm weight for staccato, the best reference is your steady body. Thus the body plays a major role in staccato play. Speed of staccato repetition is controlled by the amount of up-down motion: the smaller the motion, the faster the repetition rate, in exactly the same way as a basketball dribble.

2. Cycling (Chopin's Fantaisie Impromptu)

Cycling is the best technique-building procedure for things like new or fast passages you cannot handle. Cycling (also called "looping") is taking a segment and playing it repeatedly; usually continually, without breaks. If the conjunction needed for cycling continually is the same as the first note of the segment, this segment cycles naturally; it is called a self-cycling segment. An example is the CGEG quadruplet. If the conjunction is different, you need to invent one that leads to the first note so you can cycle without breaks.

Cycling is basically pure repetition, but it is important to use it almost as an anti-repetition procedure, a way to avoid mindless repetition. The idea behind cycling is that you acquire technique so rapidly that it eliminates unnecessary, mindless repetition. In order to avoid picking up bad habits, change the speed and experiment with different hand/arm/finger positions for optimum play and always work for relaxation; try not to cycle the exact same thing too many times. Play softly (even loud sections) until you attain the technique, get up to speeds at least 20% above final speed and, if possible, up to 2 times final speed. Over 90% of cycling time should be at speeds that you can handle comfortably and accurately. Then cycle down gradually to very slow speeds. You are done when you can play at any speed for any length of time, without looking at the hand, completely relaxed, and with full control. You might find that certain intermediate speeds give trouble. Practice these speeds because they may be needed when you start HT. Practice without the pedal (partly to avoid the bad habit of not pressing down completely through the key drop) until the technique is attained. *Change hands frequently to avoid injury.*

If a technique requires 10,000 repetitions (a typical requirement for really difficult material), cycling allows you to get them done in the shortest possible time. Representative cycle times are about 1 sec, so 10,000 cycles is less than 4 hours. If you cycle this segment for 10 min. per day, 5 days a week, 10,000 cycles will take almost a month. Clearly, very difficult material will take months to learn using the best methods, and *much* longer if you use less efficient methods.

Cycling is potentially the most injurious of any piano practice procedure, so please be careful. Don't over-do it the first day, and see what happens the next day. If nothing is sore the next day, you can continue or increase the cycling workout. Above all, whenever you cycle, always work on two at a time, one for the RH and another for the LH so that you can switch hands frequently. For young people, over-cycling can result in pain; in that case, stop cycling, and the hand should recover in a few days. In older people, over-cycling can cause osteo-arthritic flare-ups that can take months to subside.

Let's apply cycling to Chopin's FI: the left hand arpeggio, bar 5. The first six notes cycle by themselves, so you might try that. When I first tried it, the stretch was too much for my small hands, so I got tired too quickly. What I did was to cycle the first 12 notes. The second, easier six notes allowed my hands to rest a little and therefore enabled me to cycle the 12 note segment longer and at higher speed. Of course, if you really want to increase speed (not necessary for the LH but might be useful for the RH in this piece) cycle only the first parallel set (the first three or four notes for the LH).

Your ability to play the first segment does not automatically enable you to play all the other arpeggios. You will need to start practically from scratch even for the same notes one octave down. Of course, the second arpeggio will be easier after mastering the first one, but you may be surprised at how much work you need to repeat when a small change is made in the segment. This happens because there are so many muscles in the body that your brain can choose a different set of muscles to produce motions that are only slightly different (and it usually does). Unlike a robot, you have little choice about which muscles the brain is going to pick. Only when you have done a very large number of such arpeggios does the next one come easily. Therefore, you should expect to have to cycle quite few arpeggios.

In order to understand how to play this Chopin piece, it is helpful to analyze the mathematical basis of the 3 versus 4 timing part of this composition. The RH plays very fast, say 4 notes per half second (approximately). At the same time, the LH is playing at a slower rate, 3 notes per half second. If all the notes are played accurately, the audience hears a note frequency equivalent to 12 notes per half second, because this frequency corresponds to the smallest time interval between notes. *That is, if your RH is playing as fast as it can, then by adding a SLOWER play with the LH, Chopin succeeded in accelerating this piece to 3 times your maximum speed*!

But wait, not all of the 12 notes are present; there are actually only 7, so 5 notes are missing. These missing notes create what is called a Moiré pattern, which is a third pattern that emerges when two incommensurate patterns are superposed. This pattern creates a wavelike effect within each measure and Chopin reinforced this effect by using a LH arpeggio that rises and falls like a wave in synchrony with the Moiré pattern. The acceleration of a factor of 3 and the Moiré pattern are mysterious effects that sneak up on the audience because they have no idea what created them, or that they even exist. Mechanisms that affect the audience without their knowledge often produce more dramatic effects than ones that are obvious (such as loud, legato, or rubato). The great composers have invented an incredible number of these hidden mechanisms and a mathematical analysis is often the easiest way to flush them out. Chopin probably never thought in terms of incommensurate sets and Moiré patterns; he intuitively understood these concepts because of his genius.

It is instructive to speculate on the reason for the missing 1st note of the measure (bar 5) in the RH because if we can decipher the reason, we will know exactly how to play it. Note that this occurs at the very beginning of the RH melody. At the beginning of a melody or a musical phrase, composers always run into two contradictory requirements: one is that any phrase should (in general) begin softly, and the second is that the first note of a measure is a downbeat and should be accented. The composer can neatly satisfy both requirements by eliminating the first note, thus preserving the rhythm and yet start softly (no sound in this case)! You will have no trouble finding numerous examples of this device -- see Bach's Inventions. Another device is to start the phrase at the end of a partial measure so that the first downbeat of the first full measure comes after a few notes have been played (a classic example of this is the beginning of the first movement of Beethoven's Appassionata). This means that the first note of the RH in this measure of Chopin's FI must be soft and the second note louder than the first, in order to strictly preserve the rhythm (another example of the importance of rhythm!). We are not used to playing this way; the normal play is to start the first note as a downbeat. It is especially difficult in this case because of the speed; therefore this beginning may need extra practice.

This composition begins by gradually drawing the audience into its rhythm like an irresistible invitation, after calling attention to itself with the loud octave of bar 1 followed by the rhythmic arpeggio in the lower staff. The missing note in bar 5 is restored after several repetitions, thus doubling the Moiré repeat frequency and the effective rhythm. In the second theme (bar 13), the flowing melody of the RH is replaced by two broken chords, thus giving the impression of quadrupling the rhythm. This "rhythmic acceleration" culminates in the climactic forte of bars 19-20. The audience is then treated to a breather by a "softening" of the rhythm created by the delayed RH melodic (pinky) note and then its gradual fading, accomplished by the diminuendo down to PP. The whole cycle is then repeated, this time with added elements that heighten the climax until it ends in the descending crashing broken chords. For practicing this part, each broken chord might be individually cycled. These chords lack the 3,4 construct and bring you back out from the mysterious 3,4 nether-world, preparing you for the slow section.

As with most Chopin pieces, there is no "correct" tempo for this piece. However, if you play faster than about 2 seconds/bar, the 3x4 multiplication effect tends to disappear and you are usually left with mostly the Moiré and other effects. This is partly because of decreasing accuracy with speed but more importantly because the 12x speed becomes too fast for the ear to follow. Above about 20 Hz, repetitions begin to take on the properties of sound to the human ear. Therefore the multiplication device works only up to about 20 Hz; above that, you get a new effect, which is even more special than incredible speed – the "rapid notes" turn into a "low frequency sound". Thus 20 Hz is a kind of sound threshold. This is why the lowest note of the piano is an A at about 27 Hz. Here is the big surprise: there is evidence that Chopin heard this effect! Note that the fast part is initially labeled "Allegro agitato", which means that each note must be clearly audible. On the metronome, Allegro corresponds to a 12X speed of 10 to 20 Hz, the right frequency to hear the multiplication, just below the "sound threshold". "Agitato" ensures that this frequency is audible. When this fast section returns after the Moderato section, it is labeled Presto, corresponding to 20 to 40 Hz -- he wanted us to play it below and above the sound threshold! Therefore, there is mathematical evidence suggesting that Chopin knew about this sound threshold.

The slow middle section was described briefly in Section II.25. The fastest way to learn it, like many Chopin pieces, is to start by memorizing the LH. This is because the chord progression often remains the same even when Chopin replaces the RH with a new melody, because the LH mainly provides the accompaniment chords. Notice that the 4,3 timing is now replaced by a 2,3 timing played much more slowly. It is used for a different effect, to soften the music and allowing a freer, tempo rubato.

The third part is similar to the first except that it is played faster, resulting in a totally different effect, and the ending is different. This ending is difficult for small hands and may require extra RH cycling work. In this section, the RH pinky carries the melody, but the answering thumb octave note is what enriches the melodic line. The piece ends with a nostalgic restatement of the slow movement theme in the LH. Distinguish the top note of this LH melody (G# - bar 7 from the end) clearly from the same note played by the RH by holding it slightly longer and then sustain it with the pedal.

The G# is the most important note in this piece. Thus the beginning *sf* G# octave is not only a fanfare introducing the piece, but a clever way for Chopin to implant the G# into the listeners' minds. Therefore, don't rush this note; take your time and let it sink in. If you look throughout this piece, you will see that the G# occupies all the important positions. In the slow section, the G# is an Ab, which is the same note. This G# is another one of those devices in which a great composer is repeatedly "hitting the audience on the head with a two-by-four" (G#), but the audience has no idea what hit them. For the pianist, knowledge about the G# helps interpret and memorize the piece. Thus the conceptual climax of this piece comes at the end (as it should) when both hands must play the same G# (bars 8 and 7 from the end); therefore, this LH-RH G# must be executed with the utmost care, while maintaining the continuously fading RH G# octave.

Our analysis brings into sharp focus, the question of how fast to play this piece. High accuracy is required to bring out the 12-note effect and inhumanly accurate playing above the sound threshold. If you are learning this piece for the first time, the 12-note frequency may not be audible initially because of lack of accuracy. When you finally "get it" the music will all of a sudden sound very "busy". If you play too fast and lose the accuracy, you can lose that factor of three -- it washes out and the audience hears only the 4 notes. For beginners the piece can be made to sound faster by slowing down and increasing the accuracy. Although the RH carries the melody, the LH must be clearly heard; otherwise, both the 12-note effect and the Moiré pattern will disappear. This being a Chopin piece, there is no requirement that the 12-note effect be heard; this composition is amenable to an infinity of interpretations, and some may want to suppress the LH and concentrate on the RH, and still produce something magical.

An advantage of cycling is that the hand is playing continually which simulates continuous playing better than if you practiced isolated segments. It also allows you to experiment with small changes in finger position, etc., in order to find the optimum conditions for playing. The disadvantage is that the hand movements in cycling may be different from those needed to play the piece. The arms tend to be stationary while cycling whereas in the actual piece, the hands usually need to move. Therefore, in those cases in which the segment does not naturally cycle, you may need to use segmental practice, without cycling. One advantage of non-cycling is that you can now include the conjunction.

3. Trills & Tremolos

a.   Trills

There is no better demonstration of the effectiveness of the parallel set (PS) exercises (see III.7) than using them to learn the trill. There are two major problems to solve in order to trill: (1) speed (with control) and (2) to continue it as long as desired. The PS exercises were designed to solve exactly these types of problems and therefore work very well for practicing trills. Whiteside describes a method for practicing the trill which is a type of chord attack. Thus use of the chord attack for practicing the trill is nothing new. However, because we now understand the learning mechanism in more detail, we can design the most direct and effective approach by using PSs.

The first problem to solve is the initial two notes. *If the first two notes are not started properly, learning the trill becomes a difficult task. The importance of the first two notes applies to runs, arpeggios, etc., also.* But the solution is almost trivial -- apply the two note PS exercise. Therefore, for a 2323.... trill, use the first 3 as the conjunction and practice 23. Then practice the 32, then 232, etc. It's that simple! Try it! It works like magic! You may want to read section III.7 on PSs before applying them to the trill.

The trill consists of 2 motions: a finger motion and forearm rotation. Therefore, practice the 2 skills separately. First use only the fingers to trill, with the hand and arm completely still. Then keep the fingers fixed and trill only with arm rotation. This way, you will find out if it is the fingers or arm rotation that is slowing you down. Many students have never practiced rapid arm rotation (arm rocking), and this will often be the slower motion. For fast trills, this back-and-forth rotation is invisibly small, but necessary. Apply the PS exercises to both the finger and arm rotation motions. Exaggerate the motions for slow trills and increase the speed by reducing the magnitude of the motions. The final magnitude of both motions need not be the same because you will use a smaller motion for the slower one (arm rotation) in order to compensate for its slowness. As you practice these motions, experiment with different finger positions. See the Tremolo section where similar methods apply – the trill is just a shrunken tremolo.

Relaxation is even more critical for the trill than almost any other technique because of the need for rapid momentum balance; that is, the PSs, being only two notes, there are too many conjunctions for us to rely solely on parallelism to attain speed. Thus we must be able to change the momenta of the fingers rapidly. For trills, the momentum of the finger motion must be counteracted by the arm rotation. Stress will lock the fingers to the larger members such as palms and hands thus increasing the effective mass of the fingers. Larger mass means slower motion: witness the fact that the hummingbird can flap its wings faster than the condor and small insects even faster than the hummingbird. This is true even if the air resistance were ignored; in fact, the air is effectively more viscous to the hummingbird than to the condor and for a small insect, the air is almost as viscous as water is to a big fish; yet insects can flap their wings rapidly because the wing mass is so small. It is therefore important to incorporate complete relaxation into the trill from the very beginning, thus freeing the fingers from the hand. *Trilling is one skill that requires constant maintenance. If you want to be a good triller, you will need to practice trilling every day.* PS Exercise. #1 (2-note) is the best procedure for keeping the trill in top shape, especially if you had not used it for a while, or if you want to continue improving it.

Finally, the trill is not a series of staccatos. The fingertips must be at the bottom of the keydrop as long as possible; i.e., the backchecks must be engaged for every note. Take careful note of the minimum lift necessary for the repetition to work. Those who usually practice on grands should be aware that this lift distance can be almost twice as high for an upright. Faster trills require smaller lifts; therefore, on an upright, you may have to slow down the trill. Fast trills on electronic pianos are difficult because their actions are inferior.

    b.   **Tremolos** (Beethoven's Pathetique, 1st Movement)

    Tremolos are practiced in exactly the same way as trills. Let's apply this to the sometimes dreaded long octave tremolos of Beethoven's Pathetique Sonata (Opus 13). For some students, these tremolos seem impossible, and many have injured their hands, some permanently, by over-practicing them. Others have little difficulty. If you know how to practice them, they are actually quite simple. ***The last thing you want to do is to practice this tremolo for hours in the hopes of building endurance -- that is the surest way to acquire bad habits and suffer injury.***

    Since you need the octave tremolos in both hands, we will practice the LH and alternate with practicing the RH; if the RH catches on faster, you can use it to teach the LH. I will suggest a sequence of practice methods; if you have any imagination, you should be able to create your own sequence that may be better for you -- my suggestion is exactly that: a suggestion for illustration purposes. For completeness, I have made it too detailed and too long. Depending on your specific needs and weaknesses, you should be able to shorten the practice sequence.

    In order to practice the C2-C3 tremolo, first, practice the C2-C3 octave (LH). Bounce the hand up and down, comfortably, repeating the octave, with emphasis on relaxation -- can you keep playing the octave without fatigue or stress, especially as you speed it up? If you get tired, find ways of repeating the octave without developing fatigue by changing your hand position, motion, etc. For example, you might gradually raise the wrist and then lower it again – in this way, you can use 4 wrist positions for each quad. If you still get tired, stop and change hands; practice the RH Ab4-Ab5 octave that you will need later on. Once you can play the repetitive octave, 4 times per beat (include the correct rhythm) without fatigue, try speeding it up. At maximum speed, you will develop fatigue again, so either slow down or try to find different ways of playing that reduces fatigue. Change hands as soon as you feel tired. ***Do not play loud; one of the tricks for reducing fatigue is to practice softly. You can add dynamics later, once you have the technique.*** It is extremely important to practice softly so that you can concentrate on technique and relaxation. In the beginning, as you exert yourself to play faster, fatigue will develop. But when you find the right motions, hand positions, etc., you will actually feel the fatigue draining out of the hand and you should be able to rest and even rejuvenate the hand *while playing rapidly*. You have learned to relax!

    As with the trill, the tremolo consists of finger motion and arm rotation. First, practice finger tremolo using exaggerated finger motions, playing a very slow tremolo, lifting fingers as high as you can and lowering them with force into the keys. Same with arm rotation: fix the fingers and play tremolo using only arm rotation, in exaggerated way. All up and down motions must be rapid; to play slowly, simply wait between motions, and practice rapid and complete relaxation during this wait. Now gradually speed them up; this is accomplished by reducing the motions. After each is satisfactory, combine them; because both motions contribute to the tremolo, you need very little of each, which is why you will be able to play very fast.

    You can increase speed even more by adding the PS exercises to both the finger and arm rotation exercises, or their combination. First the 5,1 PS. Start with the repeated octaves, then gradually replace each octave with a PS. For example, if you are playing groups of 4 octaves (4/4 time), start by replacing the 4th octave with a PS, then 4th and 3rd, etc. Soon, you should be practicing all PSs. If the PSs become uneven or the hand starts to tire, go back to the octave to relax. Or change hands. Work the PSs until you can play the 2 notes in the PS almost "infinitely fast" and reproducibly, and eventually, with good control and complete relaxation. At the fastest PS speeds, you should have difficulty distinguishing between PSs and octaves. Then slow down the PSs so that you can play at all speeds with control. Note that in this case, the 5 note should be slightly louder than the 1. However, you should practice it both ways: with the beat on the 5 and with it on the 1, so that you develop a balanced, controllable technique. Now repeat the whole procedure with the 1,5 PS. Again, although this PS is not required to play this tremolo (only the previous one is necessary), it is useful for developing a balanced control. Once both the 5,1 and 1,5 are satisfactory, move on to the 5,1,5 or 5,1,5,1 (played like a short octave trill). If you can do the 5,1,5,1 right away, there is no need to do the 5,1,5. The objective here is both speed and endurance, so you should practice speeds that are *much* faster than the final tremolo speed, at least for these short tremolos. Then work on the 1,5,1,5.

Once the PSs are satisfactory, start playing groups of 2 tremolos, perhaps with a momentary pause between groups. Then increase to groups of 3 and then 4 tremolos. The best way to speed up the tremolos is to alternate between tremolos and octaves. Speed up the octave and try to switch to the tremolo at this faster speed. Now all you have to do is alternate hands and build up endurance. Again, building endurance is not so much building muscle, as knowing how to relax and how to use the correct motions. De-couple the hands from your body; do not tie the hand-arm-body system into one stiff knot, but let the hands and fingers operate independently from the body. You should breathe freely, unaffected by what the fingers are doing. ***Slow practice with exaggerated motions is surprisingly effective, so go back to it every time you run into trouble.***

For the RH (Bb octave of bar 149), the 1 should be louder than the 5, but for both hands, the softer notes should be clearly audible, and their obvious purpose is to double the speed compared to playing the octaves. Remember to practice softly; you can play louder whenever you want later, once you have acquired the technique and endurance. It is important to be able to play softly, and yet be able to hear every note, at the fastest speeds. Practice until, at the final speed, you can play the tremolos longer than you need in the piece. The final LH effect is a constant roar that you can modulate in loudness up and down. The lower note provides the rhythm and the upper note doubles the speed. Then practice the ascending tremolos as indicated on the music.

The Grave that starts this first movement is not easy, although the tempo is slow, because of its unusual rhythm and the fast runs in bars 4 and 10. The rhythm of the first bar is not easy because the first note of the second beat is missing. In order to learn the correct rhythm, use a metronome or supply single rhythm notes with the LH while practicing the RH. Although the rhythm is 4/4, it is easier if you double the notes of the LH and practice it like an 8/8. The run in bar 4 is very fast; there are 9 notes in the last group of 1/128 notes; therefore, they must be played as triplets, at twice the speed of the preceding 10 notes. This requires 32 notes per beat, impossible for most pianists, so you may have to use some rubato; ***the correct speed may be half the indicated, according to the original manuscript.*** The 10th bar contains so many notes that it spans 2 lines in the Dover edition! Again, the last group of 16 notes at 1/128 speed is played at twice the speed of the preceding 13 notes, impossibly fast for most pianists. The 4-note chromatic fingering (III.5h) may be useful at such speeds. Every student learning this Grave for the first time must carefully count the notes and beats so as to get a clear idea of what is involved. These crazy speeds may be an editor's error.

The first (and 3rd) movement is a variation on the theme in the Grave. That famous "Dracula" theme was taken from the LH of the first bar; clearly, the LH carries the emotional content, although the RH carries the melody. Pay attention to the hard staccato and sf in bars 3 and 4. In bars 7 and 8, the last notes of the three rising chromatic octaves must be played as 1/16, 1/8, and 1/4 notes, which, combined with the rising pitch and the cresc., create the dramatic effect. This is true Beethoven, with maximum contrast: soft-loud, slow-fast, single note-complex chords. In Beethoven's manuscript, there is no pedal indication.

4. Hand, Finger, Body Motions for Technique

a.   **Hand Motions** (Pronation, Supination, Thrust, Pull, Claw, Throw, Flick, Wrist)

Certain hand motions are required in order to acquire technique. For example we discussed parallel sets above, but did not specify what types of hand motions are needed to play them. ***It is important to emphasize from the start that the required hand motions can be extremely small, almost imperceptible***. After you have become expert, you can exaggerate them to any extent you desire. Thus during a concert by any famous performer, most of the hand motions will not be discernible (they also tend to happen too fast for the audience to catch) so that most of the visible motions are exaggerations or irrelevant. Thus two performers, one with apparently still hands, and one with flair and aplomb, may in fact be using the same hand motions of the type we discuss here. ***The major hand motions are pronation and supination, thrust (or push) and pull, claw and throw, flick, and wrist motions. They are almost always combined into more complex motions***. Note that they always come in pairs (there is a right and left flick, and similarly for wrist motions). They are also the major natural motions of the hands and fingers.

All finger motions must be supported by the major muscles of the arms, the shoulder blades in the back, and the chest muscles in front that are anchored to the center of the chest. The slightest twitch of the finger, therefore, involves all of these muscles. ***There is no such thing as moving only one finger -- any finger motion involves the entire body***. Stress reduction is important for relaxing these muscles so that they can respond to, and assist in, the movement of the fingertips. The major hand motions are discussed only briefly here; for more details, please consult the references (Fink or Sandor, and Mark for anatomy).

Pronation and Supination: The hand can be rotated around the axis of the forearm. The inward rotation (thumbs downward) is called ***pronation*** and the outward rotation (thumbs upward) is called ***supination***. These motions come into play, for example, when playing octave tremolos. There are two bones in your forearm, the inside bone (radius, connecting to the thumb) and the outside bone (ulna, connecting to the pinky). Hand rotation occurs by rotation of the inner bone against the outer one (hand position referenced to that of the piano player with palm facing down). The outer bone is held in position by the upper arm. Therefore, when the hand is rotated, the thumb moves much more than the pinky. A quick pronation is a good way to play the thumb. For playing the octave tremolo, moving the thumb is easy, but the pinky can only be moved quickly using a combination of motions. ***Thus the problem of playing fast octave tremolos boils down to solving the problem of how to move the pinky.*** The octave tremolo is played by moving the pinky with the upper arm and the thumb with the forearm (combined with the finger motions).

Thrust and Pull: Thrust is a pushing motion, towards the fallboard, usually accompanied by a slightly rising wrist. With curved fingers, the thrust motion causes the vector force of the hand moving forward to be directed along the bones of the fingers. This adds control and power. It is therefore useful for playing chords. The pull is a similar motion away from the fallboard. In these motions, the total motion can be larger than or smaller than the vector component downward (the key drop), allowing for greater control. Thrust is one of the main reasons why the standard finger position is curved. Try playing any large chord with many notes, first lowering the hand straight down as in a gravity drop, then using the thrust motion. Note the superior results with the thrust. Pull is useful for some legato and soft passages. Thus, when practicing chords, always experiment with adding some thrust or pull.

Claw and Throw: Claw is moving your fingertips into your palm and throw is opening the fingers out to their straight position. Many students do not realize that, in addition to moving the fingertips up and down, they can also be moved in and out to play. These are useful additional motions. They add greater control, especially for legato and soft passages, as well as for playing staccato. Like the thrust and pull, these motions allow a larger motion with a smaller keydrop. Thus, instead of always trying to lower the fingers straight down for the key drop, try experimenting with some claw or throw action to see if it will help. Note that the claw movement is much more natural and easier to conduct than a straight down. The straight down motion of the fingertip is actually a complex combination of a claw and a throw. The key drop action can sometimes be simplified by flaring the fingers out flat and playing with only a small claw movement. This is why you can sometimes play better with flat fingers than curved.

Flick: The flick is one of the most useful motions. It is a quick rotation and counter-rotation of the hand; a fast pronation-supination combination, or its reverse. We have seen that parallel sets can be played at almost any speed. ***When playing fast passages, the problem of speed arises when we need to connect parallel sets.*** There is no single solution to this connection problem. ***The one motion that comes closest to a universal solution is the flick, especially when the thumb is involved, as in scales and arpeggios.*** Single flicks can be conducted extremely quickly with zero stress, thus adding to the speed of play; however, quick flicks need to be "re-loaded"; i.e., continuous fast flicks is difficult. But this is quite suitable for connecting parallel sets because the flick can be used to play the conjunction and then be re-loaded during the parallel set. To re-emphasize what was pointed out at the beginning of this section, these flicks and other motions do not need to be large and are in general imperceptibly small; thus the flick can be considered more as a momentum flick than an actual motion.

Wrist Motion: We already saw that the wrist motion is useful whenever the thumb or pinky is played; the general rule is to raise the wrist for the pinky and lower it to play the thumb. Of course, this is not a hard rule; there are plenty of exceptions. The wrist motion is also useful in combination with other motions. By combining wrist motion with pronation-supination, you can create rotary motions for playing repetitive passages such as LH accompaniments, or the first movement of Beethoven's Moonlight Sonata. The wrist can be moved both up and down, and side-to-side. Every effort should be made such that the playing finger is parallel to the forearm; this is accomplished with the side-to-side wrist motion. ***This configuration puts the least amount of lateral stress on the tendons moving the fingers and reduces the chances of injuries such as Carpal Tunnel Syndrome.*** If you find yourself habitually playing (or typing) with the wrist cocked at a sideways angle, this may be a warning sign to expect trouble. A loose wrist is also a pre-requisite for total relaxation.

In summary, the above is a brief review of hand motions. An entire book can be written on this subject. And we did not even touch on the topics of adding other motions of the elbow, upper arm, shoulders, body, feet, etc. The student is encouraged to research this topic as much as possible because it can only help. The motions discussed above are seldom used alone. Parallel sets can be played with any combination of most of the above motions without even moving a finger (relative to the hand). This was what was meant, in the HS practice section, with the recommendation to experiment with and to economize the hand motions. Knowledge of each type of motion will allow the student to try each one separately to see which is needed. It is in fact the key to the ultimate in technique.

b.   Playing with Flat Fingers (FFP, Spider, Pyramid Positions)

We noted in section II.2 that the starting finger shape for learning the piano is the partially curled position. Many teachers teach the curled position as the "correct" position for playing the piano, and that the flat position is somehow wrong. However, V. Horowitz demonstrated that the flat, or straight, finger position is very useful. *Here we discuss why the flat finger position is not only useful but is also an essential part of technique and all accomplished pianists use it.*

We will initially define **"Flat Finger Position"** (FFP) as the one in which the fingers are stretched straight out from the hands, in order to simplify the discussions. We will later generalize this definition to mean specific types of "non-curled" positions; those positions are important because they are part of the finger position repertoire you need to become a complete pianist.

The most important advantages of the FFP are that it simplifies the finger motion and allows complete relaxation; that is, the number of muscles needed to control the finger motion is smaller than in the curled position because all you have to do is to pivot the entire finger around the knuckle. In the curled position, each finger must uncurl by just the right amount every time it hits a note, in order to maintain the correct finger angle to the key top surface. The motion of the FFP uses only the main muscles needed to depress the keys. *Practicing the FFP can improve technique because you are exercising only the most relevant muscles and nerves.* In order to demonstrate the complexity of the curled position, try the following experiment. First, stretch the forefinger of your RH out straight (FFP) and wiggle it up and down rapidly as you would when playing the piano. Now, keep this wiggling motion and gradually curl the finger in as far as you can. You will find that, as you curl the finger, it becomes more difficult to wiggle the fingertip until it becomes impossible when completely curled. I have named this phenomenon *"curl paralysis"*. If you do succeed in moving the fingertip, you can only do it very slowly compared to the straight position because you need to use a whole new set of muscles. In fact, the easiest way to move the fingertip rapidly in the completely curled position is to move the entire hand.

Therefore, with the curled position, you need more skill to play at the same speed compared to the FFP. *Contrary to the beliefs of many pianists, you can play faster with FFP than with the curled position because any amount of curl will invite a certain amount of curl paralysis.* This becomes particularly important when the speed and/or lack of technique produces stress while practicing something difficult. The amount of stress is greater in the curled position and this difference can be sufficient to create a speed wall.

There are discussions in the literature (Jaynes, Chapter 6), in which it is claimed that the lumbrical and interossei muscles are important in piano playing, but there is no research to support these claims, and it is not known whether these muscles play a part in FFP. It is generally believed that these muscles are used mainly to control the curvature of the fingers, so that FFP uses only the muscles in the arms to move the fingers and the lumbricals simply hold the fingers in position (curled or FFP), thus simplifying the movement and allowing for greater control and speed for FFP. Thus there is uncertainty today about whether the lumbricals enable higher speed or whether they cause curl paralysis.

Although the FFP is simpler, *all beginners should learn the curled position first and not learn the flat position until it is needed*. If beginners start with the easier FFP, they will never really learn the curled position well. Beginners who try to play fast with the flat position are likely to use fixed phase parallel set playing instead of finger independence. This leads to loss of control and uneven speeds. Once these bad habits are formed, it is difficult to learn finger independence. For this reason, many teachers forbid their students to play with flat fingers, which is a terrible mistake. Sandor calls the FFPs "wrong positions" but Fink recommends certain positions that are clearly FFPs (we will discuss several different FFPs below). *Trills often require the curled position because of their complex nature.*

Most pianists who learn on their own use mostly FFPs. Very young children (below 4 years of age) usually have difficulty curling their fingers. For this reason, jazz pianists use

FFPs more than classical pianists (because many were initially self-taught), and classical teachers correctly point out that early jazz pianists had inferior technique. In fact, early jazz had much less technical difficulty than classical music. However, this lack of technique resulted from a lack of instruction, not because they used FFPs. Thus FFPs are nothing new and are quite intuitive (not all intuitive things are bad) and are a natural way to play; after all, the thumb is *always* played FFP! Therefore, the road to good technique is a careful balance between practicing with curled fingers and knowing when to use the FFPs. ***What is new in this section is the concept that the curled position is not inherently superior and that FFPs are a necessary part of advanced technique.***

The 4th finger is particularly problematic for most people. Part of this difficulty arises from the fact that it is the most awkward finger to lift, which makes it difficult to play fast and avoid hitting extraneous notes inadvertently. These problems are compounded in the curled position because of the complexity of motion and curl paralysis. In the simplified flat finger configuration, these difficulties are reduced and the 4th finger becomes more independent and easier to lift. If you place your hand on a flat surface in the curled position and lift the 4th finger, it will go up a certain distance; now if you repeat the same procedure with the FFP, that fingertip will go up *twice* as far. Therefore, it is easier to lift the fingers, and particularly the 4th finger, in the FFP. The ease of lifting reduces the stress when playing fast. Also, when trying to play difficult passages fast using the curled position, some fingers (especially fingers 4 and 5) will sometimes curl too much creating even more stress and the need to fling these fingers out in order to play a note. These problems can be eliminated by using FFP.

Another advantage of the FFP is that it increases your reach because the fingers are stretched out straighter. For this reason, most pianists (especially those with small hands) already use the flat position for playing wide chords, etc., often without realizing it. However, such people can feel "guilty" about the lack of curl and try to incorporate as much curl as possible, creating stress.

Yet another advantage of the FFP is that the fingers are pressing the keys with the pads of the fingers instead of the fingertips. This fleshy pad is more sensitive to touch, and there is less interference from the fingernails. When people touch anything to feel it, they always use this part of the finger, not the fingertip. ***This extra cushion and sensitivity can provide better feel and control, and greater protection against injury.*** For the curled position, the fingers are coming down almost vertically to the key surfaces so that you are playing with the fingertips where there is the least amount of cushion between the bone and key top. If you injured the fingertips by practicing too hard using the curled position, you can give the fingertips a rest by using the FFP. Two types of injuries can occur at the fingertip when using the curled position and both injuries can be avoided using FFP. The first is simple bruising from too much pounding. The second is the detachment of the flesh from under the fingernail, which frequently results from cutting the fingernails too short. This second type of injury is dangerous because it can lead to painful infections. Even if you have fairly long fingernails, you can still play using the FFP.

More importantly, with FFP, ***you can play the black keys using most of the large underside areas of the fingers; this large surface area can be used to avoid missing the black keys*** that are easy to miss in the curled position because they are so narrow. ***For fast passages and large chords, play the black keys with FFP and the white keys with curled fingers***; this can greatly increase your speed and accuracy.

When the fingers are stretched out flat, you can reach further back towards the fallboard. In this position, it requires a little more force to depress the keys because of the lower leverage resulting from the shorter distance to the key bushing (at the balance rail pin).

The resulting (effectively) heavier key weight will allow you to play softer PP. Thus the ability to move closer to the key bushing results in the ability to increase the effective key weight. The heavier key weight allows more control and softer pianissimo. Although the change in key weight is small, this effect is greatly magnified at high speed. *Others argue that the tips of the keys give you more leverage so that you gain more control for PP.* Therefore, try both methods and see which one works best for you.

The FFP also allows louder fortissimo, especially for the black keys. There are two reasons. First, the area of the finger available for contact is larger and there is a thicker cushion, as explained above. Therefore, you can transmit a larger force with less chance of injury or pain. Second, the increased accuracy resulting from the larger contact area helps to produce a confident, authoritative, and reproducible fortissimo. In the curled position, the probability of missing or sliding off the narrow black keys is sometimes too scary for full fortissimo. Proponents of the curled position argue that the curled position is the only one strong enough to play the loudest fortissimo. This is false; athletes who do finger stands do so in FFP position, not the fingertips. In fact, pianists who over-practice using the curled position often suffer fingertip injury.

The ability to play fortissimo more easily suggests that the FFP can be more relaxing than the curled position. This turns out to be true, but there is an additional mechanism that increases the relaxation. With FFP, you can depend on the tendons under the finger bones to hold the fingers straight when you push down on the keys. That is, unlike the curled position, you need almost no effort to keep the fingers straight (when pressing down on the keys) because unless you are multiple jointed, the tendons on the palm side of the fingers prevent them from bending backwards. Therefore, when practicing FFP, learn to make use of these tendons to help you relax. Be careful when you first start using FFP for playing fortissimo. If you relax completely, you can risk injury to these tendons by hyper-extending them, especially for the pinky, because the pinky tendons are so small. If you start to feel pain, either stiffen the finger during key drop or stop the FFP and curl that finger. When playing fortissimo with curled fingers, you must control both the extensor and flexor muscles of every finger in order to keep them in the curled position. In the flat position, you can completely relax the extensor muscles and use only the flexor muscles, thus almost totally eliminating stress (which results from the two sets of muscles opposing each other), and simplifying the operation by over 50% when pressing the key down.

The best way to start practicing FFP is to practice the B major scale. In this scale, all fingers play the black keys except the thumb and pinky. Since these two fingers do not generally play the black keys in runs, this is exactly what you want to practice. The fingering for the RH is standard for this scale, but the LH must start with the 4th finger on B. You may want to read the following section (III.5) on playing fast scales before going on with this practice because you will need to know how to play thumb over and to use the glissando motions, etc. By feeling the keys, you will never miss a single note because you know where the keys are ahead of time. If one hand is weaker than the other, this difference will show up more dramatically with flat fingers. FFP reveals the technical skills/deficiencies more clearly because of the difference in leverage (the fingers are effectively longer) and the fingers are more sensitive. In that case, use the stronger hand to teach the weaker one how to play. Practicing with flat fingers may be one of the quickest ways to encourage the weaker hand to catch up to the other because you are working directly with the main muscles relevant to technique.

If you encounter any difficulties playing the FFP, try the black key parallel set exercises. Play all five black keys with the five fingers: the two-note group with thumb and forefinger and the three-note group with the remaining three fingers. Unlike the B major scale, this exercise will also develop the thumb and pinky. With this exercise (or with the B major scale), you can experiment with all kinds of hand positions. Unlike the curled position, *you can play with the palm of the hand touching the surface of the white keys. You can also raise the wrist so that the fingers actually bend backwards (opposite to the curl direction), as in the cartwheel motion (III.5.e). There is also an intermediate flat finger position in which the fingers remain straight, but are bent down only at the knuckles.* I call this the "pyramid" position because the hand and fingers form a pyramid with the knuckles at the apex. This pyramid position can be effective for very fast passages because it combines the advantages of the curled and straight positions.

The usefulness of these various positions makes it necessary to expand the definition of "flat finger" playing. The straight FFP is an extreme case, and there are any number of variations of positions between the totally flat position and the curled position. In addition to the pyramid position, you can bend the fingers at the first joint from the knuckle. This will be called the **"spider position"**. *The critical point here is that the last joint (closest to the fingernail) must be totally relaxed and allowed to straighten out when you press down on the key. Thus the generalized definition of FFP is that the third phalange is totally relaxed and straight.* Phalange (also called phalanx; plural is always phalanges) is the name for the small bones beyond the knuckle; they are numbered 1-3 (thumb has only 1 and 2), and the 3rd phalange is the "nail phalange" for fingers 2-5. We shall call both the pyramid and spider positions "flat finger" positions because all three FFPs share two important properties: the third phalange of the finger is never curled and is always relaxed, and you play with the sensitive palm side of the fingertip (see Prokop, P.13-15 for FFP photos). From here on, we shall use this broader definition of FFP. Although the fingers are bent in many of these positions, we shall call them FFP to distinguish them from the curled position. Most of curl paralysis comes from bending the third phalange. This can be demonstrated by bending only the third phalange (if you can) and then trying to move that finger rapidly. Note that total relaxation of the third phalange is now part of the definition of FFP. The FFP simplifies the computation in the brain because you almost totally ignore the flexor muscle of the third phalange. That is 10 fewer flexor muscles to control, and these are particularly awkward and slow muscles; therefore, ignoring them can increase finger speed. We have arrived at the realization that *the curled position is outright wrong for playing advanced material. The generalized flat finger position is what you need in order to play at the speeds needed by advanced players!* However, as discussed below, there are certain situations in which you need to quickly curl certain individual fingers for reaching some white keys and to avoid poking the fallboard with your fingernails. The importance of the generalized FFP cannot be over-emphasized because it is one of the key elements of relaxation that is often entirely ignored.

The flat finger position gives much more control because the front pad of the fingertip is the most sensitive part of the finger, and the relaxed third phalange acts like a shock absorber. This enables you to feel the keys; in the automobile, the shock absorber not only smoothes the ride, buy also keeps the wheels on the road for better control. If you have difficulty bringing out the color in a composition, using the FFPs will make it easier. *Playing with the fingertip using the curled position is like driving a car without shock absorbers, or playing a piano with worn hammers. The tone will tend to come out harsher. You are effectively restricted to one tone color.* By using FFP, you can feel the keys better and control tone and color more easily. Because you can completely relax the third phalanges and also ignore some of the extensor muscles, the flat finger motions are simpler and you can play faster, especially for difficult material such as fast trills. *We have therefore arrived at a most important general concept: we must liberate ourselves from the tyranny of the single fixed curled position.* We must learn to use all of the available finger positions because each has its advantages.

You may want to lower the bench in order to be able to play with the flat part of the fingers. When the bench is lowered, it usually becomes necessary to move it farther away from the piano so as to provide enough room for the arms and elbows to move between the keyboard and the body. In other words, many pianists sit too high and too close to the piano, which is not noticeable when playing with curled fingers. Thus the FFPs will give you a more precise way to optimize the bench height and location. At these lower heights, the wrists, and even the elbows might sometimes fall below the level of the keyboard while you are playing; this is perfectly permissible. Sitting farther away from the piano also gives you more space to lean forwards in order to play fortissimo.

All the flat finger positions can be practiced on a table. For the totally flat position, simply place all the fingers and the palm flat on a table and practice lifting each finger independently of the others, especially finger 4. Practice the pyramid and spider positions by pressing down with the fleshy front pad of the fingertips contacting the table and completely relaxing the third phalange so that it actually bends backwards. For the pyramid position, this becomes something like a stretching exercise for all the flexor tendons, and the last 2 phalanges are relaxed. You may also find that FFP works very well when typing on a keyboard.

The 4th finger in general gives everybody problems and you can perform an exercise to improve its independence using the spider position. At the piano, place fingers 3 and 4 on C# and D#, and the remaining fingers on white keys. Press down all five keys. The first exercise is to play finger 4, lifting it as high as you can. In all these exercises, you must keep all the non-playing fingers down. The second exercise is to play fingers 3 and 4 alternately (3,4,3,4,3,4, etc,), lifting 4 as high as you can, but lifting 3 only sufficiently to play the note, and keeping it always in contact with the key top (quite difficult, especially if you try to speed this up). Most people can lift the 4th finger highest in the spider position, indicating that this may be the best position for general playing. During key drop, play finger 3 louder than 4 (accent on 3). Repeat using fingers 4 and 5, with the accent on 5 and keeping it on the key as much as possible. In the 3rd and final exercise, play (3,4), (4,3), (5,4), and (4,5) parallel sets, with all the other fingers fully depressing their keys. These exercises may seem difficult at first, but you may be surprised at how quickly you will be able to play them after only a few days; however, do not stop as soon as you can do them, practice until you can do them very fast, with complete control and relaxation; otherwise they won't produce any benefits. These exercises simulate the difficult situation in which you are playing fingers 3 and 5 while lifting 4 above the keys.

The extra reach, the large contact area, and the added cushion under the fingers make FFP legato playing easier and different from legato using the curled position. The FFP also makes it easier to play two notes with one finger, especially because you can play with the fingers not parallel to the keys and use a very large area under the finger to hold more than one key down. Because Chopin was known for his legato, was good at playing several notes with one finger, and recommended practicing the B major scale, he probably used FFP. Mlle. Combe, who was the initial inspiration for this book, taught FFP and noted that it was particularly useful for playing Chopin. One legato trick she taught was to start with FFP and then roll the finger into the curled position so that the hand can move without lifting the finger off the key. The reverse can also be done when moving down from black keys to the white keys.

You can demonstrate the usefulness of the FFP by applying it to anything that is giving you difficulty. For example, I was running into stress problems with speeding up

Bach's inventions because they require finger independence, especially fingers 3, 4, & 5. While practicing with the curled position only, I felt that I was beginning to build speed walls at a few places where I didn't have enough finger independence. When I used FFP, they became much easier to play. This eventually allowed me to play at faster speeds and with greater control. The Bach Inventions are good pieces to use for practicing the FFPs, suggesting that Bach might have composed them with FFP in mind.

A discussion of FFP would be incomplete without discussing why you need the curled position, as well as some of its disadvantages. This position is not really an intentionally curled position but a relaxed position in which, for most people, there is a natural curl. For those whose relaxed position is too straight, they may need to add a slight curl in order to attain the ideal curled position. In this position, all the fingers contact the keys at an angle between 45 degrees and 90 degrees (the thumb might make a somewhat smaller angle). There are certain movements that are absolutely necessary for playing the piano that require the curled position. Some of these are: playing certain white keys (when the other fingers are playing black keys), playing between the black keys, and for avoiding poking your fingernails into the fallboard. Especially for pianists with large hands, it is necessary to curl fingers 2, 3, and 4 when 1 and 5 are playing the black keys in order to avoid jamming fingers 2, 3, and 4 into the fallboard. ***Thus, the freedom to play with any arbitrary amount of curl is a necessary freedom. One of the biggest disadvantages of the curled position is that the extensor muscles are not sufficiently exercised, causing the flexor muscles to overpower them and creating control problems. In FFP, the un-used flexor muscles are relaxed; in fact, the associated tendons are stretched, which makes the fingers more flexible. There are numerous accounts of the extraordinary flexibility of Liszt's fingers.***

The mistaken perception that FFP is bad for technique arises from the fact that it can lead to bad habits related to the incorrect use of parallel sets. This happens because with flat fingers, it is a simple matter to lay the fingers flat and jam them all down on the piano to play parallel sets masquerading as fast runs. This can result in uneven playing and beginning students might use it as a way of playing fast without developing technique. By learning the curled position first and learning how to use parallel sets correctly, we can avoid this problem. In my numerous communications with teachers, I have noticed that the best teachers are familiar with the usefulness of the FFP. This is especially true of the group of teachers whose teaching lineage traces to Liszt, because Liszt used this position. Liszt was Czerny's student, but did not always follow Czerny's teachings, and used FFP to improve tone (Boissier, Fay, Bertrand). In fact, it is hard to imagine that there are any advanced pianists who do not know how to use FFP. As proof, next time you attend a concert or watch a video, see if you can spot these FFPs -- you will find that every accomplished pianist uses them. However, because of the tradition of teaching mostly the curled position, you may notice that some pianists over-use the curled position. It is gratifying that the most celebrated pianist often chose to ignore his own teacher, Czerny.

If you had been taught only the curl position all your life, learning the FFPs may appear awkward at first because some important tendons have become shortened. Some teachers consider FFP a form of cheating, indicating a lack of curled finger skill, but it is not; it is a necessary skill. Start practicing FFP with care because some finger tendons may have to be stretched for the first time. All tendons must be stretched from time to time, but the curled position does not allow that.

What is the order of importance of all these positions -- which is the "default" FFP position that we should use most often? The spider position is the most important. The insect kingdom did not adopt this position without a good reason; they found out that it works best after hundreds of millions of years of research. Note that the distinction between the spider position and the curled position can be subtle, and many pianists who think they are using the curled position may in fact be using something closer to FFP. The second most important position is the flat out position because it is needed for playing wide chords and arpeggios. The third position is the curled position which is needed for playing the white keys and the pyramid position comes in fourth. The pyramid position uses only one flexor muscle per finger, the spider position uses two, and the curled position uses all three plus the extensor muscles during key drop. However, the final choice of finger position is personal, and this choice must be left to the pianist.

In general, you can use the following rule to decide which finger position to use: play the black keys using the completely flat FFP, and use the curled or pyramid position for the white keys. The spider position is versatile if you acquire it while young and can play both black and white keys. Note that if, within a group of notes, you must play both black and white keys, it is usually advantageous to use two types of finger positions. This might appear to be an added complication at first, but at high speed, this might be the only way. There are, of course, numerous exceptions; for example, in difficult passages involving the 4th finger, you may need more FFPs than curled positions even when most or all the keys are white, in order to make it easier to lift the 4th finger.

The above discussions on FFP are substantial, but they are by no means complete. In a more detailed treatment, we need to discuss how we apply FFP to specific skills such as legato, or playing two notes with one finger while controlling each note individually. Chopin's legato is documented to be particularly special, as was his staccato. Is his staccato related to the FFP? Note that in all the FFPs, you can take advantage of the spring effect of the relaxed third phalange, which might be useful in playing staccato. Clearly we need more research to learn how to use the FFPs. In particular, there is controversy as to whether we should play mostly with the curled position and add the FFP whenever necessary, as has been taught by most teachers, or vice versa, as Horowitz did, and as recommended here. FFP is also related to bench height. It is easier to play with flat fingers when the bench is lowered. There are numerous accounts of pianists discovering that they can play much better with a lower bench position (Horowitz and Glen Gould are examples). They claim to get better control, especially for pianissimo and speed, but no one has provided an explanation for why this is so. My explanation is that the lower bench height allowed them to use more FFPs. However, there appears to be no good reason to sit overly low, as Glen Gould did, because you can always lower the wrist to get the same effect.

In summary, Horowitz had good reasons to play with flat fingers and the above discussions suggest that part of his higher technical level may have been achieved by using more FFPs than others. ***The most important message of this section is that we must learn to relax the third phalange of the finger, play with the touch-sensitive part of the fingertip, and cultivate finger flexibility.*** The aversion to, or even prohibition of, FFP by some teachers turns out to be a mistake; in fact, any amount of curl will invite some degree of curl paralysis. However, beginners must learn the curled position first because it is frequently needed and is more difficult than the FFPs. If students learn the easier flat finger method first, they may never learn the curled position adequately. FFP is useful for speed, increasing your reach, playing multiple notes with one finger, avoiding injury, "feeling the keys", legato, relaxation, playing pianissimo or fortissimo, and adding color. Although the curled position is necessary, the statement "you need the curled position to play technically difficult material" is misleading – what you need is flexible fingers. Playing with flat fingers liberates us to use many useful and versatile finger positions. We now know how to play all those black keys and not miss a single note. Thank you, Johann, Frederic, Franz, Vladimir, Yvonne (Combe)!

c.   Body Motions

Many teachers encourage "use of the whole body for playing the piano" (see Whiteside). What does that mean? Are there special body motions that are required for technique? Not really; technique is in the hands and relaxation. However, because the hands are connected to and supported by the body, you can't just sit in one position and hope to play. When playing the upper registers, the body should follow the hands and you might even extend one leg in the opposite direction in order to balance the body, if it is not needed for the pedals. Also, even the smallest motion of any finger requires the activation of a series of muscles that lead all the way to at least the center of the body (near the sternum), if not all the way to the legs and other members that support the body. Relaxation is as important in the body as in the hands and fingers, because of the shear size of the muscles involved. Therefore, although most of the required body motions can be understood from simple common sense, and do not seem to be that important, the body motions are nonetheless absolutely essential to piano playing. So let's discuss these motions, some of which may not be totally obvious.

The most important aspect is relaxation. It is the same type of relaxation that you need in the hands and arms -- use of only those muscles required for playing, and only for the brief instants during which they are needed. Relaxation also means free breathing; if your throat is dry after a hard practice, you are not swallowing properly, a sure sign of tenseness. *Relaxation is intimately related to independence of every part of the body. The first thing you must do, before considering any useful body motions, is to make sure that the hands and fingers are totally decoupled from the body. If they are not decoupled, the rhythm will go awry, and you can make all sorts of unexpected mistakes. If, in addition, you don't realize that the body and hands are coupled, you will wonder why you are making so many strange mistakes for which you cannot find the cause.* This decoupling is especially important in HT play, because the coupling will interfere with the independence of the two hands. Coupling is one of the causes of mistakes: for example, a motion in one hand creates an involuntary motion in the other through the body. This does not mean that you can ignore body decoupling during HS practice; on the contrary, the decoupling should be consciously practiced during HS work. Note that decoupling is a simple concept and easy to execute once you learn it but, physically, it is a complex process. Any motion in one hand *necessarily* produces an equal and opposite reaction in the body, which is automatically transmitted to the other hand. Thus decoupling requires active effort; it is not a passive relaxation. Fortunately, our brains are sufficiently sophisticated so that we can easily grasp the concept of decoupling. This is why decoupling must be actively practiced. When you learn any new composition, there will always be some coupling until you practice it out. The worst type of coupling is the one acquired during practice, if you practice with stress or try to play something that is too difficult. During the intense efforts needed to try to play difficult material, a student can incorporate any number of unnecessary motions, especially during HT practice, which will eventually interfere with the playing as the speed increases. By getting up to speed HS, you can avoid most of these HT coupling mistakes.

The body is used to play fortissimo through the shoulders, as discussed above. It is also used for playing softly because in order to play softly, you need a steady, constant platform from which to generate those small, controlled forces. The hand and arm, by themselves, have too many possible motions to serve as a steady platform. When attached securely to a steady body, you have a much more stable reference platform. Thus the soft stillness of the pianissimo should emanate from the body, not the fingertips. And in order to reduce mechanical "noise" from extraneous finger motions, the fingers should be on the keys as much as possible. In fact, feeling the keys provides another stable reference from which to play. Once the finger leaves the key, you have lost that valuable reference, and the finger can now wander anywhere, making it difficult to accurately control the next note.

5. Playing Fast: Scales, Arpeggios, and Chromatic Scales
(Chopin's Fantaisie Impromptu and Beethoven's Moonlight, 3rd Movement)
a.   Scales: Thumb Under (TU), Thumb Over (TO)

Scales and arpeggios are the most basic piano passages; yet the most important method for playing them is often not taught at all! Arpeggios are simply expanded scales and can therefore be treated similarly to scales; thus we shall first discuss scales and then note how similar rules apply to arpeggios. There is one fundamental difference on how you must play the arpeggio (a flexible wrist) compared to the scale; once you learn that difference, arpeggios will become much easier, even for small hands.

There are two ways to play the scale. The first is the well-known "thumb under" method (TU) and the second is the "thumb over" method (TO). In the TU method, the thumb is brought under the hand in order to pass the 3rd or 4th finger for playing the scale. This TU operation is facilitated by two unique structures of the thumb; it is shorter than the other fingers and is located below the palm. *In the TO method, the thumb is treated like the other 4 fingers, thus greatly simplifying the motion. Both methods are required to play the scale but each is needed under different circumstances*; the TO method is needed for fast, technically difficult passages and the TU method is useful for slow, legato passages, or when some notes need to be held while others are being played.

For lack of a better terminology, I have named the TO method "Thumb Over" which is an obvious misnomer and might make it harder for a beginner to understand how to play it. I have tried other names, but none of them are any better than TO. The only possible advantage is that this outrageous nomenclature may call attention to the existence of TO.

Many piano teachers have been totally unaware of the TO method. This presented few difficulties as long as the students did not progress to advanced levels. In fact, with sufficient effort and work, it is possible to play fairly difficult passages using the TU method and *there are accomplished pianists who think that TU is the only method they need. In reality, for sufficiently fast passages, they have subconsciously learned (through very hard work) to modify the TU method in such a way that it approaches the TO method.* This modification is necessary because for such rapid scales, it is physically impossible to play them using the TU method. Therefore, it is important for the student to start learning the TO method as soon as they are past the novice stage, before the TU habit becomes ingrained into passages that should be played TO.

Many students use the method of playing slowly initially and then ramping up the speed. They do fine using TU at slow speed and consequently acquire the TU habit and find out, when they get up to speed, that they need to change to the TO method. This change can be a very difficult, frustrating, and time consuming task, not only for scales, but also for any fast run -- another reason why the ramping up method is not recommended in this book. *The TU motion is one of the most common causes of speed walls and flubs. Thus once the TO method is learned, it should always be used to play runs except when the TU method gives better results*.

The main piano playing muscles for the thumb are in the forearm, just as for the other 4 fingers. However, the thumb has other muscles in the hand that are used to move the thumb sideways in the TU method. The involvement of these extra muscles for the TU motion makes it a more complex operation, thus slowing down the maximum speed attainable. The extra complication also causes mistakes. *Teachers who teach TO claim that for those who use TU exclusively, 90% of their flubs originate with the TU motion.*

You can demonstrate the disadvantage of the TU method by observing the loss of thumb mobility in its tucked-in position. First, stretch your fingers out so that all the fingers are in the same plane. You will find that all the fingers, including the thumb, have mobility up and down (the motion needed to play the piano). Now, wiggle the thumb up and down rapidly -- you will see that the thumb can move 3 or 4 cm vertically with ease (without rotating the forearm), quite rapidly. Then, while still wiggling at the same rapid frequency, gradually pull the thumb under the hand -- you will see that as it goes under, it loses vertical mobility until it becomes immobile, almost paralyzed, when it is under the middle finger.

Now stop the wiggling and thrust the thumb down (without moving the wrist) -- it moves down! This is because you are now using a different set of muscles. Then, using these new muscles, try to move the thumb up and down as fast as you can -- you should find that these new muscles are much clumsier and the up and down motion is slower than the wiggle rate of the thumb when it was stretched out. Therefore, in order to be able to move the thumb in its tucked position, you not only need to use a new set of muscles but, in addition, these muscles are slower. It is the introduction of these clumsy muscles that creates mistakes and slows down the play in the TU method. The TO method eliminates these problems.

Scales and arpeggios are some of the most abused exercises in piano pedagogy -- novice students are taught only the TU method, leaving them unable to acquire proper techniques for fast runs and arpeggios. Not only that but, as the scale is speeded up, stress begins to mysteriously build up. Worse still, the student builds up a large repertoire with wrong habits that will need to be laboriously corrected. ***The TO method is easier to learn than the TU method because it does not require the sideways contortions of the thumb, hand, arm, and elbow.*** Beginners should be taught TU first because it is needed for slow passages and takes longer to learn. The TO method should be taught as soon as faster scales are needed, within the first two years of lessons. For talented students, the TO method must be taught within months of their first lessons, or as soon as they master TU.

Because there are two ways to play the scale, there are two schools of teaching on how to play it. The TU school (Czerny, Leschetizky) claims that TU is the only way that legato scales can be played and that, with sufficient practice, TU can play scales at any speed. The TO school (Whitesides, Sandor) has gradually taken over and the more insistent adherents *forbid* the use of TU, under any circumstances. See the Reference section for more discussions on TU vs. TO teaching. Both extreme schools are wrong because you need both skills.

The TO teachers are understandably angered by the fact that advanced students passed to them by private teachers often do not know the TO method and it takes six months or more to correct hours of repertoire that they had learned the wrong way. One disadvantage of learning both TU and TO is that when sight reading, the thumb might become confused and not know which way to go. This confusion is one reason why some teachers in the TO school actually forbid the use of TU. I recommend that you standardize to the TO method and use the TU as an exception to the rule. Note that Chopin taught both methods (Eigeldinger, P. 37).

Although the TO method was rediscovered by Whitesides, etc., the earliest account of its use dates back to at least Franz Liszt (Fay). Liszt is known to have stopped performing and returned to developing his technique for over a year when he was about 20 years old. He was dissatisfied with his technique (especially when playing scales) when compared to the magical performances of Paganini on the violin, and experimented with improving his technique. At the end of this period, he emerged satisfied with his new skills but could not teach others exactly what he had done to improve -- he could only demonstrate on the piano (this was true of most of Liszt's "teachings"). However, Amy Fay noticed that he now played the scale differently; instead of TU, Liszt was "rolling the hand over the passed finger" so that the thumb fell on the next key. It apparently took Fay many months to imitate this method but, according to her, "it completely changed my way of playing" and she claimed that it resulted in a marked improvement in her technique generally, not only for playing scales, because TO applies to any run and also to arpeggios.

b.   The TO Motion, Explanation and Video

Let us start by analyzing the basic fingering of scales. Consider the RH, C major scale. We begin with the easiest part, which is the RH descending scale, played 5432132,1432132,1 etc. Since the thumb is below the hand, the 3 or 4 finger rolls over the thumb easily, the thumb naturally folds under those fingers, and this descending scale fingering works well. This motion is basically the TU motion; the TO descending motion is similar, but we will need to make a slight but crucial modification to this in order to make it into a true TO method; however, this modification is subtle and will be discussed later.

Now consider the RH, C major ascending scale. This is played 1231234, etc. *In the TO method, the thumb is played like the 3 and 4 fingers; i.e., it is simply raised and lowered without the sideways TU motion under the palm.* Since the thumb is shorter than the other fingers, it can be brought down almost parallel to (and just behind) the passed finger without colliding with it. In order to hit the thumb on the right key, you will need to move the hand and use a slight twitch of the wrist. For scales such as the C major, both the thumb and passed finger are on white keys and will necessarily crowd each other somewhat. *In order to avoid any possibility of collision, the arm should be almost 45 degrees to the keyboard (pointing to the left), and the hand is rolled over the passed finger by using the passed finger as a pivot. The 3 or 4 finger must then be quickly moved away as the thumb comes down.* In the TO method, it is not possible to hold the 3 or 4 finger down until the thumb plays, unlike the TU method. When you first try the TO method, the scale will be uneven and there may be a "gap" when playing the thumb. Therefore, the transition must be very quick even in a scale played slowly. As you improve, you will notice that a quick flick/rotation of the wrist/arm is helpful. Beginners usually find TO to be easier than TU, but those who learned TU for many years will initially find TO clumsy and uneven. Also, rotate the forearm slightly clockwise (what Chopin called the "glissando position", see 5.c below) which automatically brings the thumb forwards. The RH ascending scale is more difficult than the descending scale because for the descending scale, you pivot and roll over the thumb, which is easy. But for the ascending scale, you roll over the 3 or 4 finger, but there are fingers above the rolled finger and these can interfere with the roll.

The logic behind the TO method is the following. *The thumb is used like any other finger.* The thumb only moves up and down. This simplifies the finger motions and, in addition, the hand, arms, and elbows do not need to contort to accommodate the TU movements. Thus the hand and arm maintain their optimum angle to the keyboard at all times and simply glide up and down with the scale. Without this simplification, technically difficult passages can become impossible, especially because you still need to add new hand motions to attain such speeds, and many of these motions are incompatible with TU. Most importantly, *the movement of the thumb to its correct location is controlled mostly by the hand* whereas in the TU method, it is the combined motion of the thumb and hand that determines the thumb location. Because the hand motion is smooth, the thumb is positioned more accurately than with the TU method, thus reducing missed notes and hitting of wrong notes and at the same time bestowing better tone control to the thumb. Also, the ascending scale becomes similar to the descending scale, because you always roll the fingers *over* for passing. This also makes it easier to play hands together since all fingers of both hands are always rolling over. Another bonus is that the thumb can now play a black key. It is this large number of simplifications, the elimination of the stress that results from the paralyzed thumb, and even more advantages discussed below, that reduce the potential for mistakes and enable faster play. There are exceptions: slow, legato passages, or some scales containing black keys, etc., are executed more comfortably with a TU-like motion. ***Most students who had used only TU will initially have a terrible time trying to understand how anyone can play TO.*** This is the clearest indication of the harm done by not learning TO as soon as possible; for these students, the thumb is not "free". We shall see that the free thumb is a versatile finger. But don't despair, because it turns out that most advanced TU students already know how to play TO -- they just don't know it.

The LH is the reverse of the RH; the TO method is used for the descending scale, and the ascending scale is somewhat similar to TU. If your RH is more advanced than the LH, perform the explorations to faster TO speeds using the RH until you decide exactly what to do, then pick up that motion with the LH.

Because students without teachers have difficulty visualizing TO, we examine a video clip comparing TO and TU. I have put this video in 2 formats because some computers can play only certain formats. Those with only printed pages will have to type in the URLs manually. First, open a video player such as QuickTime or Windows Media Player, then find the window where you can type in the URL of the video, usually under "File". Below are 2 URLs; one of them should work.

TO Video 1:   http://www.pianopractice.org/TOscale.mp4
TO Video 2:   http://www.pianopractice.org/TOscale.wmv

The video shows the RH playing two octaves TO, ascending and descending, played twice. This is then repeated using TU. To non-pianists, these may appear to be essentially the same, although the TU motion was slightly exaggerated. This illustrates why videos of piano motions are not as helpful as one might think. The TO motions ascending are basically correct. The TO motions descending has one error -- a slight bending of the nail phalange of the thumb. At these moderate speeds, this slight bending does not affect the play, but in strict TO, the thumb should remain straight for both ascending and descending play. This example illustrates the importance of learning TO as early as possible. My tendency to bend the nail phalange is the result of using only TU for many decades, before I learned TO. An important conclusion here is ***keep the thumb straight at all times for TO.***

c.   **Practicing TO: Speed, Glissando Motion**

We now discuss procedures for practicing fast TO scales. The RH C major ascending scale consists of the parallel sets (PSs) 123 and 1234. First, use the PS exercises (section III.7) to attain a fast 123, with 1 on C4. Then practice 1231 with the thumb going up and then coming down behind the 3, quickly moving the 3 out of the way as the thumb comes down. Most of the sideways motion of the thumb is accomplished by moving the hand. The last 1 in the 1231 is the conjunction required by the continuity rule (see section II.8). Repeat with 1234, with 1 on F4, and then 12341, with the last 1 rolling over, behind the 4, and landing on C5. Play fingers 234 close to the black keys in order to give the thumb more area to land on. Turn the forearm and wrist so that the fingertips of 2345 make a straight line parallel to the keyboard; thus, when playing middle C, the forearm should make an angle of about 45 degrees to the keyboard. Then connect the two PSs to complete the octave. After you can do one octave, do two, etc.

When playing fast scales, the hand/arm motions are similar to those of a glissando. The glissando type motion allows you to bring the thumb even closer to the passed fingers because all the fingers 2 to 5 are pointing slightly backwards. You should be able to play one fast octave (about 1 octave/sec.) this way after a few minutes of practice (let's not worry about evenness yet!). Practice relaxing to the point where you can feel the weight of your arm. When you become proficient with TO, you should find that long scales are no more difficult than short ones and that HT is not as difficult as TU. This happens because the contortions of the elbow, etc., for TU become difficult, especially at the high and low ends of the scales (there are many other reasons). It is important to stress here that *there is never any need to practice scales HT and, until you become quite proficient, HT practice will do more harm than good*. There is so much urgent material we must practice HS, that there is little to be gained by practicing HT, except for brief experimentation. Most advanced teachers (Gieseking) consider practicing fast HT scales to be a waste of time.

In order to control the phase angle (delay of successive fingers) in the PS accurately, raise your wrist (ever so slightly) as you play the PSs 123 or 1234. Then make the transition to the next PS by lowering the wrist to play TO. These wrist motions are extremely small motions, almost imperceptible to the untrained eye, and become even smaller as you speed up. You can accomplish the same thing by rotating the wrist clockwise (cw) to play the PSs and cycling back by rotating ccw to lower the thumb. However, the up and down wrist motion is preferred over the rotation because it is simpler, and the rotation can be reserved for other uses (Sandor). If you now try to play several octaves, it may initially come out like a washboard.

The fastest way to speed up scale playing is to practice only one octave. Once you are up to the faster speeds, cycle 2 octaves up and down. At high speeds, these shorter octaves are more useful because it is difficult to reverse direction at the top and bottom, and these short octaves give you more practice at the ends. With longer runs, you don't get to practice the ends as often, and the added stretch of the arm to reach the higher/lower octaves is an unnecessary distraction from concentrating on the thumb. *The way to play fast reverses at the top and bottom is to play them with a single downward pressure of the hand.* For example, to reverse at the top, play the last ascending PS, the conjunction, and the first PS coming down, all in one downward motion. In this scheme, the conjunction is effectively eliminated by incorporating it into one of the PSs. This is one of the most effective ways of playing a fast conjunction -- by making it disappear!

In the glissando motion, supinate or pronate the hands so that the fingers point away from the direction of motion of the hand. Now the keydrop motions of the fingers are not straight down, but have a horizontal backward component that enables the fingertips to linger a little longer on the keys as the hand moves along the keyboard. This is especially helpful for playing legato. Example: for RH ascending scale, turn forearm slightly clockwise so that the fingers point to the left. In other words, if the fingers were coming straight down (relative to the hand) and the hand is moving, the fingers would not come straight down onto the keys. By rotating the hand in the glissando direction, this error can be compensated. Thus the glissando motion allows the hand to glide smoothly. You can practice this motion by cycling one octave up and down; the hand should resemble the sideways motion of a skater, with alternate feet kicking sideways and the body tilting left and right while s/he skates forward. The hand should pronate or supinate with each change of direction of the octave. As in skating (where you must lean in the opposite direction before you can change the direction of motion) the rotation of the hand (reversal of glissando hand position) must precede the change in direction of the scale. This motion is best practiced by practicing one octave only.

For the RH descending TO scale, practice the PS 54321, and the other relevant PSs, with and without their conjunctions. *You need to make a small modification to avoid letting the thumb fold completely under the hand while the next PS is rolling over the thumb.* Lift the thumb as early as possible while keeping the scale smooth, by raising and/or rotating the wrist to pull the thumb up -- almost the reverse of what you did for the ascending scale. If you fold the thumb completely under the palm, it will become paralyzed and difficult to move to the next position. This is the "slight modification" referred to above and is somewhat similar to the thumb motion for the ascending scale. For TU play, the thumb can be allowed to fold completely under the palm. ***Because this motion is somewhat similar in TO and TU, and differ only in degree, it can be easily played incorrectly.*** Although the differences in motion are small visually, the difference in feeling to the pianist should be like night and day, especially for fast passages.

For ultra-fast scales (over one octave per second), think not in terms of individual notes, but in units of PSs. For the RH, naming 123=A, 1234=B, play AB instead of 1231234, i.e., two things instead of seven. For even faster play, think in units of pairs of PSs AB,AB, etc. As you progress in speed and start thinking in terms of larger units, the continuity rule should be changed from A1 to AB1 to ABA (where the final A is the conjunction). It is a bad idea to over-practice fast, at speeds you can not comfortably manage. ***The forays into very fast play are useful only for making it easier to practice accurately at a slower speed. Therefore practice most of the time at slower than maximum speed; you will gain speed faster that way.***

Try the following experiment in order to get the feel of truly fast scales. Cycle the 5 finger PS 54321 for the RH descending scale, according to the scheme described in the PS exercises (start with Ex. #1). Note that, as you increase the repetition speed, you will need to orient the hand and use a certain amount of thrust or rotation in order to attain the fastest, smooth, and even parallel play. You may need to study the arpeggio section below on "thrust" and "pull" (section f) before you can do this correctly. An intermediate level student should be able to get up to faster than 2 cycles per second. Once you can do this rapidly, comfortably, and relaxed, simply continue it down one octave at the same fast speed, making sure to play it TO. You have just discovered how to play a very fast run! How fast you can play depends on your technical level, and as you improve, this method will allow you to play even faster scales. Do not over practice these fast runs if they start to become uneven because you can end up with non-musical playing habits. ***These experiments are valuable mainly for discovering the motions needed at such speeds, and to train the brain to handle such speeds.*** Don't get into the habit of playing fast and listening to it; instead, the brain must first have a clear idea of what is expected before you play it.

It is best not to start playing scales HT until you are very comfortable HS. If you feel a need to practice scales HT (some use it for warm-ups) start HT practice with one octave, or part of one, such as one PS. For practicing by PSs, the C major scale is not ideal because the thumbs are not synchronized – use B major, where the thumbs of the 2 hands are synchronized, see below. Cultivate the habit of transitioning to HT at a fast speed (although it may seem much easier to start at slow speed and then gradually ramp up). To do this, play one octave LH at a comfortable fast speed several times, repeat the RH at the same speed several times, and then combine them at the same speed. Don't worry if at first the fingers don't match absolutely perfectly. First match the starting notes; then match both the start and final notes; then cycle the octave continually; then work on matching every note. *Then* practice at slow speed, maintaining the same motions, until the scales are very accurate and under complete control, relaxed.

Before going too far with the C major scale, consider practicing the B major scale. See table below for scale fingerings. In this scale, only the thumb and pinky play the white keys, except for the bottom finger (4) of the LH. All other fingers play the black keys. This scale has the following advantages:

(1) It is easier to play initially, especially for those with large hands or long fingers. Each key falls naturally under each finger and there is plenty of room for every finger. For this reason, Chopin taught this scale to beginners before teaching the C major scale.

(2) It allows you to practice playing the black keys. The black keys are more difficult to play (easier to miss) because they are narrower, and require greater accuracy.

(3) It allows play with flatter fingers (less curled), which is better for practicing legato and for tonal control.

(4) TO play is much easier with this scale. This is the reason why I used the C major scale to illustrate the TO method. With the B major, it is more difficult to see the difference between the TU and TO motions. However, for purposes of practicing the proper motions, B major may be superior, if you already understand the difference between TU and TO because it is easier to get to the faster speeds without acquiring bad habits.

(5) The thumbs are synchronized in the B major scale, making it possible to practice HT, PS by PS. Thus HT play is easier than for the C major scale. Once you become proficient with this scale HT, learning C major HT becomes simpler, thus saving you time. You will also understand exactly why the C major is more difficult.

This paragraph is for those who grew up learning TU only and must now learn TO. At first, you might feel as if the fingers get all tangled up and it is difficult to get a clear idea of what TO is. The main cause of this difficulty is the habit you have acquired playing TU which must be unlearned. TO is a new skill you need to learn and is no harder to learn than a Bach Invention. *But the best news of all is that you probably already know how to play TO! Try playing a very fast chromatic scale.* Starting with C, play 13131231313 . . . . . The flat finger position may be useful here. If you can play a very fast chromatic scale, the thumb motion is exactly the same as for TO because it is impossible to play a fast chromatic scale TU. Now slow down this fast chromatic thumb motion and transfer it to the B major scale; think of B major scale as a chromatic scale in which only a few white keys are played. Once you can play the B major TO, transfer this motion to C major.

Of course, learning scales and arpeggios (below) TO is only the beginning. The same principles apply to any situation involving the thumb, in any piece of music, anywhere that is reasonably fast. Once the scale and arpeggios are mastered, these other TO situations should come almost as second nature. For this to develop naturally, you must use a consistent and optimized scale fingering; these are listed in the tables below.

Those who are new to the TO method and have learned many pieces using the TU method will need to go back and fix all the old pieces that contain fast runs and broken chords. Ideally, all the old pieces that were learned using TU should be redone so as to completely get away from the TU habit where TO is more appropriate. It is a bad idea to play some pieces TU and others TO for similar fingerings. One way to accomplish the switch to TO is to practice scales and arpeggios first so that you become comfortable with TO. Then learn a few *new* compositions using TO. After about 6 months or so, when you have become comfortable with TO, you can start converting all your old pieces.

TO and TU should be considered as the extremes of two different ways to use the thumb. That is, there are many other motions in between. *One unexpected benefit of learning TO is that you become much better at playing TU. This happens because your thumb becomes technically more capable: it becomes free.* And you gain the ability to use all those motions between TO and TU that may be required depending on what other notes are being played or what type of expression you want to create. *The thumb is now free to use all of its available motions and for controlling tone. This freedom, plus the ability to now play much more technically difficult material correctly, is what transforms the thumb into a very versatile finger.*

d.   Scales: Origin, Nomenclature and Fingerings

Repeating scales and exercises mindlessly is discouraged in this book. However, it is critically important to develop the skill to play exquisite scales and arpeggios, in order to acquire some basic techniques and standard fingerings for routine playing and sight reading. Scales and arpeggios in all the major and minor keys should be practiced until you are familiar with their fingerings. They should sound crisp and authoritative, not loud but confident; just listening to them should lift up one's spirits. The most important objective to achieve is to practice until the fingering of each scale becomes automatic.

Before describing the fingerings, let's discuss some basic properties of scales: the key nomenclature and the question: what is a scale? *There is nothing magical or musical about the C major scale; it arises simply from the desire to include as many chords as possible into an octave that can be played with one hand.* This is a design feature (just as the most modern features are incorporated into every new car design) that makes it easier to learn/play the keyboard. From the size of the human fingers/hand, we can assume that the largest interval should span 8 keys. How many chords can these keys accommodate? We need the octave, thirds, fourths, fifths, and sixths. Starting from C4, we have now placed E4, F4, G4, A4, and C5, a total of 6 notes, leaving space for only 2 more notes, a full tone and a semitone. Note that even the minor third is already present as A4-C5. If you place the semitone above C4, you end up with one accidental (black key) near C4 and 4 accidentals near C5 in order to complete the chromatic scale, so it is better to place the semitone near C5 so that the octave is better balanced with 2 accidentals near C4 and 3 near C5. This completes the construction of the C major scale, with its accidentals (Sabbatella, Mathiew).

In the nomenclature process, it is unfortunate that C major was not named A major. Thus the octave numbers change at C, not A; therefore, at C4, the notes are numbered . . . . . A3,B3,C4,D4,E4, . . . For any scale, the first note is called the **tonic**, so C is the tonic of the C major scale. The lowest note of an 88 key keyboard is A(-1) and the highest note is C8.

The standard **major scale ascending fingerings** are 12312345 (RH, one octave), 54321321(LH) for C,G,D,A,E major scales (with 0,1,2,3,4 sharps, respectively); these fingerings will be abbreviated as S1 and S2, where **S stands for "standard"**. The sharps increase in the order F,C,G,D,A, (G-major has F#, D-major has F# and C#, A-major has F#, C#, and G#, etc.) and for the F,Bb,Eb,Ab,Db,Gb, major scales, the flats increase in the order B,E,A,D,G,C; **every interval between adjacent letters is a fifth**. They are therefore easy to remember, especially if you are a violinist (the violin's open strings are G,D,A,E). The letters always appear in the sequence GDAEBFC which represents the complete circle of fifths, and this sequence is worth memorizing. Look at B or Gb major scales in a music book and you will see how the 5 sharps or 6 flats line up in the same sequence. Thus 2 sharps will have sharps at F, C, three sharps will be F, C, G, and so on. The flats increase in reverse order compared to the sharps. Each scale is identified by its **key signature**; thus the key signature of the G major scale has one sharp (F#). *Once you learn to recognize the interval of a fifth, you can generate all the scales in order of increasing sharps (by going up in fifths from C) or in order of increasing flats (by going down in fifths)*; this is useful when you want to practice all the scales in sequence without having to refer to the printed scales. See **Table 1.III.5.a below for the ascending major scales** (reverse the fingerings for descending scales).

The minor scales are complex because there are 3 families of them, and can be confusing because they are often just called "minor" without specifying which of the three, or worse, each has been given several different names. They were created because they produce moods different from the others. The simplest minor scale is the **relative minor** (also called **natural minor**); it is simple because it shares the same key signature as its major relative,

Table 1.III.5.a   Ascending Major Scales

RH	LH	Scale	Sharps/Flats
S1=12312341	S2=54321321	C,G,D,A,E	0,1,2,3,4 Sharps
S1	43214321321	B	5 Sharps
12341231	S2	F	1 Flat
41231234	32143213	Bb	2 Flats
31234123	32143213	Eb	3 Flats
34123123	32143213	Ab	4 Flats
23123412	32143213	Db	5 Flats
23412312	43213214	Gb	6 Flats

Table 1.III.5.b   Ascending Harmonic Minor Scales

S1(RH)	S2(LH)			
S1(RH)	S2(LH)	A	0 Sharp	G sharp
S1	S2	E	1 Sharp	D Sharp
S1	43214321	B	2 Sharps	A Sharp
34123123	43213214	F#	3 Sharps	E Sharp
34123123	32143213	C#	4 Sharps	B Sharp
34123123	32143213	G#	5 Sharps	F Sharp
S1	S2	D	1 Flat	C Sharp
S1	S2	G	2 Flats	F Sharp
S1	S2	C	3 Flats	B Nat.
12341231	S2	F	4 Flats	E Nat.
21231234	21321432	Bb	5 Flats	A Nat.
31234123	21432132	Eb	6 Flats	D Nat.

but its tonic moves up to the sixth note of its major relative. I find it easier to remember this as a minor 3rd down instead of a 6th up. Thus the relative minor of G major has its tonic at E and the key signature is F#, and is called E (relative) minor. Another minor is the **melodic minor**; it is created by raising the 6th and 7th notes of the relative minor by a semitone **only when ascending**; the descending part is unchanged. The third, and the most frequently used, minor is the **harmonic minor** which is created from the relative minor by raising the 7th note a semitone.

      Fingerings for the harmonic minor scales are shown in Table 1.III.5.b (the last column lists the raised note for the minor scale: thus A [harmonic] minor is ABCDEFG#A, and its relative major is C major). As stated earlier, there is nothing magical about scales; they are simply human creations constructed for convenience -- just a framework on which to hang your music. Therefore, you can create any number of them, and the ones covered here, though most widely used, are not the only ones.

      We can never play scales too well. When practicing scales, always try to accomplish something -- smoother, softer, clearer, faster. Make the hands glide, the scale sing; add color, authority or an air of excitement. Quit as soon as you start to lose concentration. There is no such thing as a maximum speed in parallel playing. Therefore, in principle, you can keep increasing the speed and accuracy all your life -- which can be quite a bit of fun, and is certainly addicting. If you want to demonstrate your speed to an audience, you can probably do that using scales and arpeggios at least as well as with any piece of music.

      e.   **Arpeggios** (Chopin's FI, Cartwheel Motion, Finger Splits)

      Playing arpeggios (arps) correctly is technically complex. This makes arps particularly suitable for learning some important hand motions, such as thrust, pull, and the "cartwheel motion". "Arpeggio", as used here, includes broken chords and combinations of short arpeggic passages. We shall illustrate these concepts here using Beethoven's Moonlight Sonata (3rd Movement) for the thrust and pull, and Chopin's Fantaisie Impromptu (FI) for the cartwheel motion. Recall that suppleness of the hands, especially at the wrist, is critical for playing arps. The technical complexity of arps arises from the fact that in most cases, this suppleness must be combined with everything else: thrust, pull, cartwheel motion, glissando (or finger splits) motion, and TU or TO. One note of caution: the Moonlight is difficult because of the required speed. Many Beethoven compositions cannot be slowed down because they are so intimately tied to rhythm. In addition, this movement requires a minimum reach of a 9th, comfortably. Those with smaller hands will have more difficulty learning this piece than those with adequate reach.

      Let's first discuss how to play TO arps. Arps extending over several octaves are played TO just like scales. Therefore, if you know how to play TO scales, you know, in principle, how to play TO arps. However, the method of playing TO arps is a more extreme example of the TO motion than for scales and therefore serves as the clearest example of this motion. We noted above that the easiest TO motion is that used in playing chromatic scales (1313123131312 ... for the RH). The chromatic TO motion is easy because the horizontal motion of the thumb is small. The next slightly more difficult motion is that for playing the B major scale. This TO motion is easy because you can play the entire scale with flat fingers so that there is no collision problem with the passing thumb. The next in difficulty is the C major scale; it is more difficult because all the fingers are crowded into the narrow white key area. Finally, the most difficult motion is the TO arp in which the hand must move rapidly and accurately. This motion requires a slight flex and flick of the wrist, sometimes described as a "throwing" motion. The nice thing about acquiring the TO arp motion is that, once you learn it, you simply have to make a smaller version of the same motion in order to play the easier TO motions.

The standard fingering for the CEGCEG . . . .C arp is 123123....5, RH, and 5421421....1, LH ascending, and reverse for descending. See Michael Aaron, Adult Piano Course, Book Two for fingerings of all arps and scales.

Because arps jump over several notes, most people spread the fingers to reach those notes. For fast arps, this is a mistake because spreading the fingers slows down their motion. The key method for fast arps is to move the hand instead of spreading the fingers. If you move the hand and wrist appropriately, you will find that it is not necessary to spread the fingers. This method also makes it easier to relax.

The Cartwheel Method (Chopin's FI). In order to understand the cartwheel motion, place your left palm flat on the piano keys, with the fingers spread out like the spokes of a wheel. Note that the fingertips from pinky to thumb fall on an approximate semi-circle. Now place the pinky above C3 and parallel to it; you will have to rotate the hand so that the thumb is closer to you. Then move the hand towards the fallboard so that the pinky touches the fallboard; make sure that the hand is rigidly spread out at all times. If the 4th finger is too long and touches the fallboard first, rotate the hand sufficiently so that the pinky touches the fallboard, but keep the pinky as parallel to C3 as possible. Now *rotate the hand like a wheel counter clockwise (as viewed from above) so that each successive finger touches the fallboard (without slipping) until you reach the thumb. This is the cartwheeling motion in the horizontal plane. If your normal reach is one octave with your fingers spread out, you will find that the cartwheeling motion will cover almost two octaves!* You gain extra reach because this motion makes use of the fact that the center three fingers are longer than the pinky or thumb, and the circumference of a semi-circle is much larger than the diameter. Now repeat the same motion with the hand vertical (palm parallel to fallboard), so the fingers point downwards. Start with the pinky vertical and lower the hand to play C3. Now if you roll the hand up towards C4, (don't worry if it feels very awkward), each finger will "play" the note that it touches. When you reach the thumb, you will again find that you have covered a distance almost twice your normal reach. *In this paragraph, we learned three things: (1) how to "cartwheel" the hand, (2) this motion expands your effective reach without making any jumps, and (3) the motion can be used to "play" the keys without moving the fingers relative to the hand.* In actual practice, cartwheeling is used with the hand somewhere between vertical and horizontal, and the fingers will be in the pyramid position or slightly curved. Although cartwheeling will add some keydrop motion, you will also move the fingers in order to play.

Believe it or not, *the reach can be stretched even more by use of "finger splits" (Fraser), which is a form of glissando motion.* Picture applying an exaggerated glissando motion to the arp, RH, ascending, CEGCEG..... ; you can now spread the distance between fingers more than the cartwheel. To demonstrate this, make a "V" with fingers 2 & 3 and place the "V" on a flat surface, at the edge, so that only the "V" is on the surface. Spread the "V" as far as you can with comfort and ease. Then rotate your arm and hand 90 degrees clockwise so the fingers are now touching the surface with their sides. This is an exaggerated glissando position. Now you can spread the fingers even more. This works with any pair of fingers.

Therefore, by using a combination of TO, FFP, cartwheel motion and finger splits, you can easily reach and play fast arps with little stress on the stretching muscles. Notice that this complex combination of motions is enabled by a supple wrist. Once you become comfortable with this combination of motions, you will have enough control so that you gain the confidence that you will never miss a note. Practice the CEG arp using these motions.

We apply this method to the LH broken chords of Chopin's FI. In Section III.2, we discussed the use of cycling to practice the LH. We will now add the cartwheel motion, etc., to the cycling. Cycle the first 6 (or 12) LH notes of bar 5 (where the RH first joins in). Let's start with just the cartwheel motion. If you position the hand almost horizontally, then practically all the keydrop must be accomplished by finger motion. However, if you raise the hand more and more towards the vertical, the cartwheeling motion will contribute more keydrop and you will need less finger motion to play. *Cartwheeling is especially useful for those with small hands because it automatically expands the reach. Cartwheeling also makes it easier to relax because there is less need to keep the fingers spread widely apart. You will also find that your control increases because the motions are now partly governed by the large motions of the hand which makes the playing less dependent on the motion of each finger and gives more uniform, even results.* Use as much FFP as you need, and add a small amount of glissando motion.

The RH is an even bigger challenge. Most of the fast runs should be practiced using the basic keystroke (practicing slowly) and parallel sets (for speed). The part starting at bar 13 should be practiced like the tremolo (section 3.b), and then applying the parallel sets. That is, practice first (slowly) using only the fingers with no hand motion. Then use mostly arm/hand rotation to play the 15. Exaggerate these motions while practicing slowly; then gradually speed up by reducing each motion, then combine them to play even faster. Then apply parallel sets, playing all 4 notes in one down motion of the hand. Play white keys with curled fingers and black keys with FFP. Use the palm widening muscles (section 7.e) instead of the finger spreading muscles and practice rapid relaxation after playing each 15 octave.

f.   Thrust and Pull, Beethoven's Moonlight, 3rd Movement

For those who are learning Beethoven's Moonlight Sonata for the first time, the most difficult section is the two-hand arpeggic ending of the 3rd movement (bars 196-198; this movement has 200 bars). By illustrating how to practice this difficult passage, we can demonstrate how arpeggios should be practiced. Let's try the RH first. In order to simplify the practice, we skip the first note of bar 196 and practice only the following 4 ascending notes (E, G#, C#, E), which we will cycle. *As you cycle, make an elliptical, clockwise motion (as seen from above) of the hand.* We divide this ellipse into two parts: the upper part is the half towards the piano and the lower part is the half towards your body. When playing the upper half, you are "thrusting" your hand towards the piano, and when playing the lower half, you are "pulling" the hand away from it. First, play the 4 notes during the upper half and return the hand to its original position using the lower half. This is the thrust motion for playing these 4 notes. Your fingers tend to slide towards the piano as you play each note. Now make a counter clockwise motion of the hand and play the same 4 ascending notes during the lower half of the ellipse. Each finger tends to slide away from the piano as it plays each note. Those who have not practiced both motions may find one much more awkward than the other. Advanced players should find both motions equally comfortable.

The above was for the RH ascending arp. For the RH descending arp, let's use the first 4 notes of the next bar (same notes as in preceding paragraph, an octave higher, and in reverse order). Again, the pull motion is needed for the lower half of the clockwise motion, and the thrust is used for the upper half of the counter clockwise rotation. For both ascending and descending arps, practice both thrust and pull until you are comfortable with them. Now see if you can figure out the corresponding exercises for the LH. *Notice that these cycles are all parallel sets and therefore can eventually be played extremely fast.*

Having learned what the thrust and pull motions are, you might reasonably ask, "why do you need them?" First, it should be pointed out that *the thrust and pull motions use different sets of muscles. Therefore, given a specific application, one motion has to be*

100

better than the other. We will learn below that one motion is stronger than the other. Students who are not familiar with these motions may randomly pick one or switch from one to the other without even knowing what they did. This can result in unexpected flubs, unnecessary stress, or speed walls. The existence of the thrust and pull is analogous to the situation with TU and TO. Recall that by learning both TU and TO, you get to fully utilize all the capabilities of the thumb. In particular, at high speed, the thumb is used in a way which is about midway between TU and TO; however, the important thing to keep in mind is that the thumb motion must be on the TO side of dead center. If you are even slightly on the TU side, you hit a speed wall.

The analogy of thrust and pull to TU and TO go even further, because thrust and pull also have a neutral motion, just as TU and TO have a range of motions in between. ***You get the neutral motion by reducing the minor axis of the ellipse to zero***; i.e., you simply translate the hand right and left without any *apparent* elliptical motion. But here again, it makes a big difference whether you approach the neutral position from the thrust side or the pull side, because the seemingly similar neutral motions (approached from thrust or pull side) are actually being played using a different set of muscles. Let me illustrate this with a mathematical example. Mathematicians will be horrified if you tell them that $0 = 0$, which at first glance seems to be trivially correct. Reality, however, dictates that we must be very careful. This is because we must know the true meaning of zero; i.e., we need a mathematical definition of zero. It is defined as the number $1/N$, when N is allowed to go to infinity. You get to the "same" number zero, whether N is positive or negative! Unfortunately, if you try to divide by zero: $1/0$, you get a different answer depending on whether N is positive or negative. $1/0 = $ +infinity when N is positive, and $1/0 = $ -infinity when N is negative! If you had assumed the two zeros to be the same, your error after the division could have been as large as two infinities depending on which zero you used! In a similar way, the "same" neutral positions achieved by starting with TU or TO are fundamentally different, and similarly with thrust and pull. That is, under certain circumstances, a neutral position approached from either thrust or pull is better. The difference in feel is unmistakable when you play them. This is why you need to learn both.

This point is so universally important, especially for speed, that I will illustrate it with another example. The Samurai's life depends on the speed of his sword. In order to maximize this speed, the sword must always be in motion. If he simply raises the sword, stops, and lowers it, the motion is too slow and his life is endangered. The sword must continually move in some circular, elliptical, or curved motion, even when it looks like he is simply raising and lowering it. This is one of the first lessons in swordsmanship. Thus the use of generically circular motions to increase speed has universal validity (tennis serve, badminton slam, etc.), and applies to the piano also.

OK, so we have established that thrust and pull are both needed, but how do we know when to use which? In the case for TU and TO, the rules were clear; for slow passages you can use either one, and for certain legato situations, you need TU; for all others you should use TO. For arps, the rule is to use the strong motions as a first choice and the weak motions as a secondary choice. Each person has a different strong motion, so you should first experiment to see which is strongest for you. The pull motions should be stronger because our pulling muscles in the arms are stronger than the pushing muscles. Also, the pull motions use the fleshy parts of the fingers whereas the thrust motions tend to use the fingertips which tends to injure the fingertips and to strain the attachment of the fingernails.

Finally, one can ask the question, "why not always play neutral - neither thrust nor pull?" Or learn one (pull only), and become very good at it? Here again, we are reminded of the fact that there are two ways to play neutral depending on whether you approach it from the thrust side or pull side, and for a particular application, one is always better than the other. As for the second question, a second motion may be useful for endurance because it uses a different set of muscles. Not only that, but in order to play the strong motions well, you must know how to play the weak motions. That is, you play best when the hand is balanced in the sense that it can play both motions. Therefore, whether you decide to use thrust or pull for a particular passage, you should always practice the other one also. That is the only way that you will know which motion is best for you. For example, ***as you practice this ending of Beethoven's sonata, you should find that you make faster technical progress by practicing every cycle using both thrust and pull.*** In the end, most students should end up playing very close to neutral, although a few may decide to use exaggerated thrust or pull motions.

There is much more new material to practice in this 3rd movement before we should be playing HT, so at this stage, you probably do not need to practice anything HT, except as experimentation to see what you can or cannot do. In particular, trying HT at the highest speeds will be counter-productive and is not recommended. However, cycling a short segment HT can be quite beneficial; but this should not be over-practiced if you still cannot play it satisfactorily HS. The main difficulties in this movement are concentrated in the arps and Alberti accompaniments ("do-so-mi-so" type); once these are mastered, you have conquered 90% of this movement. For those without sufficient technical skill, you should be satisfied with getting up to about quarter-note = MM120. Once you can play the entire movement comfortably at that speed, you might try to mount an effort towards presto (above 160). It is probably not a coincidence that with the 4/4 signature, presto corresponds to the rapid heart beat rate of a very excited person. Note how the LH accompaniment of bar 1 actually sounds like a beating heart.

We shall now outline our plan of attack for learning this movement. We started with the most difficult part, the two-hand arp at the end. Most students will have more difficulty with the LH than the RH; therefore, once the RH is fairly comfortable, start practicing the RH arp of the first two bars of this movement, while still practicing the LH part of the ending. One important rule for playing arps rapidly is to keep the fingers near the keys as much as possible, almost touching them. Do not lift the fingers far off the keys. Remember to use flat finger positions for black keys and the curled position for white keys. Thus in the first 2 bars of this 3rd movement, only the D is played with curled fingers. This habit of curling only specific fingers for each ascending arp is best cultivated by cycling parallel sets. Clearly, a major technical skill you must learn is the ability to quickly change any finger from flat to curl, independently of the others.

The pedal is used in only two situations in this piece: (1) at the end of bar 2, at the double staccato chord and all following similar situations, and (2) bars 165-166, where the pedal plays a critical role. The next segment to practice is the tremolo type RH section starting at bar 9. Work out the fingering of the LH carefully -- those with smaller hands may not be able to hold the 5th finger down for the duration of the 2 bars. If you have difficulty interpreting the rhythm of this section, listen to several recordings to get some ideas. Then comes the LH Alberti accompaniment starting at bar 21, and similar RH parts that appear later. The Alberti accompaniment can be practiced using parallel sets, as explained starting at section II.8. The next difficult segment is the RH trill of bar 30. This first trill is best performed using 3,5 fingering and the second one requires 4,5. For those with small hands, these trills are as difficult as the ending arps, so they should be practiced from the very beginning, when you first start learning this movement. These are the basic technical requirements of this piece. The cadenza of bar 186 is an interesting combination of a "scale" and an arp; if you have difficulty interpreting it, listen to several recordings to get some ideas. Don't overlook the fact that bars 187 and 188 are adagio.

Start HT practice after all these technical problems are solved HS. ***There is no need to practice using the pedal until you start HT.*** Note that bars 163, 164, are played without pedal. Then application of the pedal to bars 165, 166, gives meaning to these last 2 bars. Because of the fast pace, there is a tendency to practice too loud. This is not only musically incorrect, but technically damaging. ***Practicing too loud can lead to fatigue and speed walls; the key to speed is relaxation.*** It is the P sections that create most of the excitement. For example, the FF of bar 33 is only a preparation for the following P, and in fact, there are very few FF's in the entire movement. The whole section from bar 43 to 48 is played P, leading to just one bar, #50, played F.

Finally, if you have practiced correctly, you should find certain speeds at which it is easier to play faster than slower. This is completely natural in the beginning, and is one of the best signs that you have learned the lessons of this book well. Of course, once you have become technically proficient, you should be able to play at any speed with equal ease.

g.   **Thumb: the Most Versatile Finger**

The thumb is the most versatile finger; it lets us play scales, arpeggios, and wide chords (if you don't believe it, try playing a scale without the thumb!). Most students do not learn how to use the thumb correctly until they practice scales. Therefore it is important to practice scales as soon as possible. Repeating the C major scale over and over, or even including the B major, is not the way to practice scales. It is important to practice all the major and minor scales and arpeggios; the objective is to ingrain the correct fingering of each scale into the fingers.

Play with the tip of the thumb, not the first joint. This makes the thumb effectively as long as possible, which is needed because it is the shortest finger. In order to produce a smooth scale, all the fingers need to be as similar as possible. In order to play with the tip of the thumb, you may have to raise the wrist slightly. Using the tip is helpful at high speeds, for better control, and for playing arpeggios and chords. Playing with the tip facilitates TO and the "glissando motion" in which the fingers point away from the direction of motion of the hand. Do not exaggerate the glissando motion, you only need a small amount.

It is most important to liberate the thumb by practicing TO and a very flexible wrist. Except for TU, the thumb is always straight and is played by pivoting at the wrist joint and is moved into position by wrist and hand motion. One of Liszt's most significant technical improvements occurred when he learned to use the thumb correctly.

h.   **Fast Chromatic Scales**

The chromatic scale consists of semitone steps. The most important consideration for chromatic scales is the fingering, because there are so many ways to finger them. The standard fingering, starting from C, is 1313123131345 for ascending RH, and 1313132131321 for ascending LH for one octave (the top is fingered for a return) and the reverse for descending. This fingering is difficult to play fast because it is composed of the shortest possible parallel sets and therefore contains the largest number of conjunctions; it is usually the conjunctions that limit the speed. Its main advantage is simplicity which makes it applicable to practically any chromatic segment, starting from any note, and is the easiest to remember. One variation of this is 1212123121234, which enables a little more speed and legato, and is more comfortable for those with large hands.

In attempts to speed up the chromatic scale, several sequences using longer parallel sets have been devised; all of the "accepted" sequences avoid the use of the thumb on a black key. The most commonly used is, starting from E, 123123412312 (Hauer, Czerny, Hanon). One complication with this fingering is that the starting sequence should be changed depending on the starting key in order to maximize velocity. Also, the RH and LH are different; this sequence uses 4 parallel sets. You can shrink it to 3 parallel sets by playing, starting at C, 123412312345. With good TO technique, this scale might be playable, but even with TO, we rarely use a 51 or 15 transition, which is difficult. Clearly, the restriction of avoiding the thumb on a black key limits the choice of fingering and complicates matters because the fingering will depend on the starting note.

If we allow one thumb on a black key, a good scale is, starting from C:
1234,1234,1234; 1234,1234,12345,   2 octaves RH ascending,
5432,1432,1432; 1432,1432,14321,   2 octaves LH ascending,
with the thumb on G# for both hands and 3 identical parallel sets per octave - the simplest and fastest possible configuration. Reverse to descend. I call this the **"4-finger chromatic scale"**; as far as I know, this fingering has not been discussed in the literature because of the thumb on a black key followed by passing over the 4th finger. In addition to speed, the biggest advantage is simplicity; you use the same fingering no matter where you start (for example, use finger 3 for starting the RH with D), ascending or descending, the fingering is the same for both hands (in reverse), the thumbs and fingers 3 are synchronized, and the beginning and end is always 1,5. With good TO technique, this scale is unbeatable; you only need to pay attention to the 14 or 41 where 1 is on G#. Try this on the last chromatic run in the Grave of Beethoven's Pathetique and you should notice a marked decline in the number of flubs and eventually a significant increase in speed. Once you learn it for this run, it will work for any other chromatic run. In order to develop a smooth run, practice with the beat on every note, every other note, every third note, etc.

In summary, although most exercises are not helpful, exercising scales, arpeggios and the 4-finger chromatic scale have a special place in piano technique acquisition. Because you can use them to learn so many fundamental technical skills, they must be part of a pianist's daily practice program.

6. Memorizing
a.   Why Memorize?
The reasons for memorizing are so compelling that it is surprising that many people have been unaware of them. *Advanced pianists must play from memory because of the high level of technical skill that is expected*. For practically all students (including those who consider themselves to be non-memorizers) the most difficult passages are played from memory. *Non-memorizers may need the sheet music in front of them for psychological support* and for small cues here and there, but in fact, they are playing difficult passages from "hand memory" (explained below).

The rewards of this book accrue because it is a total package; i.e., the whole is larger than the sum of its parts. Memorizing is a good example. In order to understand this, let's look at those students who do not memorize. Once a new piece is "learned", but not yet perfected, non-memorizers typically abandon the piece and go on to the next one, partly because it takes so long to learn new pieces and partly because reading the score is not conducive to performing difficult pieces. Statistically, students who do not memorize never learn any piece well, and this handicap limits technical development. *Now if they were able to learn quickly and memorize at the same time, they will be performing and making music with all their finished pieces <u>the rest of their lives</u>!* We are not just talking about memorizing or not memorizing a piece -- we are talking about a *lifetime* of difference in your development as an artist, and whether you really have a chance to make music. It is the difference between a performing artist and a student who never has a performable piece. There are many more advantages to memorizing; instead of listing them here, we will discuss them as we encounter them while learning how to memorize below.

Finally, memorizing benefits brain development in youth and decelerates its deterioration with age. Memorizing piano music will not only improve your memory in daily life but will also slow down memory loss with age and even improve the brain's capacity to memorize. You will become a "memory expert", giving you confidence in your ability to remember; lack of confidence is a major cause of poor memory as well as many other problems, such as low self esteem. Memory affects intelligence and good memory raises the effective IQ.

In my youth, life seemed so complicated that, in order to simplify it, I intuitively subscribed to the "principle of least knowledge" which posits that the less unnecessary information you stuff into your brain, the better. This theory is analogous to that for disk memory in a computer: the more clutter you delete, the more memory you have left for use. I now know that this approach breeds laziness and an inferiority complex that you are not a good memorizer, and is harmful to the brain because it is like saying that the less muscle you use, the stronger you will become because there is more energy left over. The brain has more memory capacity than anyone can jam into it in a lifetime but if you don't learn how to use it, you will never benefit from its full potential. I suffered a lot from my early mistake. I was afraid to go bowling because I could not keep score in my head like everyone else. Since I changed my philosophy so that I now try to memorize everything, life has improved dramatically. I even try to memorize the slope and break on every golf green I play. That can have a huge effect on the golf score. Needless to say, the corresponding benefits to my piano career have been beyond description.

Memory is an associative function of the brain. An associative function is one in which one object is associated with another by a relationship. Practically everything we experience is stored in our brains whether we like it or not, and once the brain transfers this information from temporary to permanent storage (an automatic process that usually takes 2 to 5 minutes), it is there practically for life. Therefore, when we memorize, storing the information is not the problem -- retrieving it is the problem because unlike the computer, in which all data have addresses, our memory is retrieved by a process that is not yet understood. The best understood retrieval process is the associative process: to recall John's telephone number, we first think of John, then recall that he has several phones and then remember that his cell phone number is 123-4567. That is, the number is associated with the cell phone, which is associated with John. Each digit in the phone number has a huge array of associations related to our life's experience with numbers, starting with the first time we learned numbers as a young child. Without these associations, we wouldn't have any idea what numbers are and would therefore not be able to recall them at all. "John" also has many associations (such as his house, family, etc.) and the brain must filter them all out and follow the "telephone" association in order to find the number. Because of the huge information processing power of the brain, the retrieval process is more efficient if there are more associations and these associations quickly increase in size as more items are memorized because they can be cross-associated. Therefore the human memory is almost diametrically opposite to the computer memory: the more you memorize, the easier it becomes to memorize because you can create more associations. Our memory capacity is so large that it is effectively infinite. Even good memorizers never "saturate" their memory until the ravages of age take their toll. As more material is put into memory, the number of associations increases geometrically. This geometrical increase partly explains the enormous difference in the memorizing capacity between good and poor memorizers. Thus everything we know about memory tells us that memorizing can only benefit us.

b. Who can, What to, and When to, Memorize.

Anyone can learn to memorize if taught the proper methods. A proper integration of the memorizing and learning procedures can reduce the time required to learn, in effect assigning a negative time to memorizing. Almost all of the procedures for memorizing are the same as the learning procedures that we have already covered. If you separate these processes, you will end up having to go through the same procedure twice. Few people would be able to go through such an ordeal; this explains why those who do not memorize during the initial learning process never memorize well. If you can play a piece well but had not memorized it, it can be very frustrating to try to memorize it. Too many students have convinced themselves that they are poor memorizers because of this difficulty.

Because memorizing is the fastest way to learn, you should memorize every worthwhile piece you play. Memorizing is a free byproduct of the process of learning a new piece of music. *Thus in principle, the instructions for memorizing are trivial: simply follow the learning rules given in this book, with the additional requirement that everything you do during those learning procedures be performed from memory.* For example, while learning a LH accompaniment bar-by-bar, memorize those LH bars. Since a bar is typically 6 to 12 notes, memorizing that is trivial. Then you will need to repeat these segments 10, 100, or over 1,000 times, depending on difficulty, before you can play the piece -- that is many more repetitions than needed to memorize. You can't help but memorize it! Why waste such a priceless, one-time opportunity?

We saw, in sections I and II, that the key to learning technique quickly was to reduce the music to trivially simple segments; those same procedures also make these segments trivial to memorize. Memorizing can save tremendous amounts of time. You don't need to look for the music each time and you can jump from segment to segment as you desire. You can concentrate on learning the technique without distractions from having to refer to the music every time. *Best of all, the numerous repetitions you need, to practice the piece, will commit it to memory in a way that no other memorizing procedure will ever achieve, at no extra cost of time.* These are some of the reasons why memorizing before you learn is the only way.

c. Memorizing and Maintenance

A memorized repertoire requires two investments of time: the first is for memorizing the piece initially and a second "maintenance" component for implanting the memory more permanently and for repairing any forgotten sections. During the lifetime of a pianist, the second component is by far the larger one because the initial investment is zero or even negative. Maintenance is one reason why some give up memorizing: why memorize if I am going to forget it anyway? Maintenance can limit the size of a repertoire because after memorizing, say, five to ten hours of music, the maintenance requirements may preclude memorizing any more pieces depending on the person. There are several ways to extend your repertoire beyond any maintenance limit. An obvious one is to abandon the memorized pieces and to re-memorize later as needed. *Pieces that are well memorized can be re-polished quickly, even if they haven't been played for years.* It is almost like riding a bicycle; once you learn how to ride a bicycle, you never need to re-learn it all over again. We now discuss maintenance procedures that can greatly increase your memorized repertoire.

Memorize as many pieces as possible before the age of 20. Pieces learned in those early years are practically never forgotten and, even if forgotten, are most easily recalled. This is why youngsters should be encouraged to memorize all their repertoire pieces. Pieces learned after age 40 require more memorizing effort and maintenance, although many people have no trouble memorizing new pieces past age 60 (albeit more slowly than before). Note the word "learn" in the preceding sentences; they do not have to have been memorized and you can still memorize them later with better retention properties compared to pieces learned or memorized at an older age.

There are times when you do not need to memorize, such as when you want to learn large numbers of easy pieces, especially accompaniments, that would take too long to memorize and maintain. Another class of music that should not be memorized is the group of pieces that you use to practice sight reading. Sight reading is a separate skill that is treated in III.11. *Everyone should have a memorized repertoire and a sight reading repertoire*.

d.   Hand Memory

A large component of your initial memory will be hand memory, which comes from repeated practice. The hand goes on playing without your really remembering each note. Although we will discuss all the known types of memory below, we will start with analyzing hand memory first because historically, it was frequently thought of as the only and best method of memory although, in reality, it is the least important. "Hand memory" has at least two components: a reflex hand motion that comes from touching the keys and a reflex in the brain from the sound of the piano. Both serve as cues for your hand to move in a pre-programmed way. For simplicity, we will lump them together and call them hand memory. Hand memory is useful because it helps you to memorize at the same time that you practice the piece. In fact, everybody must practice common constructs, such as scales, arpeggios, Alberti accompaniments, etc., from hand memory so that your hands can play them automatically, without having to think about every note. Therefore, when you start to memorize a new piece, there is no need to consciously avoid hand memory. Once acquired, you will never lose hand memory, and we show below how to use it to recover from blackouts.

When we talk about hand memory, we usually mean HT memory. *Because hand memory is acquired only after many repetitions, it is one of the most difficult memories to erase or change.* This is one of the main reasons for HS practice -- to avoid acquiring incorrect HT habits that will be so difficult to change. HS memory is fundamentally different from HT memory. HS play is simpler and can be controlled directly from the brain. In HT memory, you need some kind of feedback in order to coordinate the hands (and probably the two halves of the brain) to the accuracy needed for music. Therefore, HS practice is the most effective method for avoiding the dependence on hand memory, and to start using the better methods of memory discussed below.

e.   Starting the Memorizing Process

Start the memorizing process by simply following the instructions of sections I and II, and memorizing each practice segment before you start practicing it. *The best test of your memory is to play that segment in your mind, without the piano -- this is called Mental Play (MP)*, which will be discussed at length below. How well you understand and remember a piece depends on speed. As you play faster, you tend to remember the music at higher levels of abstraction. At very slow play, you must remember it note by note; at higher speeds, you will be thinking in terms of musical phrases and at even higher speeds you may be thinking in terms of relationships between phrases or entire musical concepts. These higher level concepts are always easier to memorize. This is why HS practice, and getting quickly up to speed, will help the memorizing step. However, to test your memory, you must do the opposite – play slowly, as explained below.

Even if you can play HT, you should memorize it HS. This is one of the few instances in which memorizing and learning procedures differ. If you can play a section HT easily, there is no need to practice it HS for technique. However, for performing the piece, memorizing it HS will be useful for recovering from blackouts, for maintenance, etc. If you test the memory (e.g., by trying to play from somewhere in the middle of a piece), you will find that it is easier if you had memorized it HS.

Memory is an associative process; therefore there is nothing as helpful as your own ingenuity in creating associations. So far, we saw that HS, HT, music, and playing at different speeds are elements you can combine in this associative process. Any music you memorize will help you memorize future pieces of music. The memory function is extremely complex; its complex nature is the reason why intelligent people are often also good memorizers, because they can quickly think of useful associations. Conversely, if you learn to memorize, your effective IQ will go up. *By memorizing HS, you add two more associative processes (RH and LH) with much simpler structure than HT.* Once you have memorized a page or more, break it up into logical smaller musical phrases of about 10 bars and start playing these phrases randomly; i.e., practice the art of starting play from anywhere in the piece. If you had used the methods of this book to learn this piece, starting randomly should be easy because you learned it in small segments. *It is really exhilarating to be able to play a piece from anywhere you want and this skill never ceases to amaze the audience.* Another useful memorizing trick is to play one hand and "play" the other hand in your mind at the same time. If you can do this, you have memorized it very well!

Memory is first stored in temporary or short-term memory. It takes 2 to 5 minutes for this memory to be transferred to long term memory. This has been verified innumerable times from tests on head trauma victims: they can remember only up to 2 to 5 minutes before the trauma incident; we saw a most vivid example of this from the survivor of Princess Diana's fatal accident – he could not remember the accident or the few minutes prior to the accident. After transferal to long term memory, your ability to recall this memory decreases unless there is reinforcement. If you repeat one passage many times, you are acquiring hand memory and technique, but the total memory is not reinforced proportionately to the number of repeats. It is better to wait 2 to 5 minutes and to re-memorize again.

In summary, memorize in phrases or groups of notes; never try to memorize each note. The faster you play, the easier it is to memorize because you can see the phrases and structure more easily. This is why memorizing HS is so effective. Many poor memorizers instinctively slow down and end up trying to memorize individual notes when they encounter difficulties. This is precisely the wrong thing to do. Poor memorizers can not memorize, not because their memory is not good, but because they do not know how to memorize. *One cause of poor memory is confusion.* This is why memorizing HT is not a good idea; you cannot play as fast as HS and there is more material that can cause confusion. Good memorizers have methods for organizing their material so that there is less confusion. Memorize in terms of musical themes, how these evolve, or the skeletal structure which is embellished to produce the final music. Slow practice is good for memory, not because it is easier to memorize playing slowly, but because it is a tough test of how well you have memorized.

f.   Reinforcing the Memory

One of the most useful memory devices is reinforcement. *A forgotten memory, when regained, is always better remembered.* Many people fret that they forget. Most people need to forget and re-memorize three or four times before anything is permanently memorized. In order to eliminate the frustrations from forgetting and to reinforce memory, try to purposely forget, for example, by not playing a piece for a week or more and then re-learning it. Or quit before you completely memorize so you must start all over again the next time. Or instead of repeating short sections (the method you used initially to memorize the piece), play the entire piece, only once a day, or several times a day but several hours apart. Find out ways of making you forget (like memorizing many things at once); try to create artificial blackouts -- stop in the middle of a phrase and try to restart.

Memorizing new material tends to make you forget whatever you had memorized previously. Therefore, spending a lot of time memorizing a small section is not efficient. If you choose the right number of things to memorize, you can use one to control the "forgetting" of the other so that you can re-memorize it for better retention. This is an example of how experienced memorizers can fine-tune their memorizing routines.

g.   Practicing Cold

Practice playing memorized pieces "cold" (without warming up your hands); this is obviously more difficult than with warmed up hands but practicing under adverse conditions is one way of strengthening your ability to perform in public and improve the memory. This ability to sit down and play cold, with an unfamiliar piano or environment, or several times a day when you have a few minutes, is one of the most useful advantages of memorizing. And you can do this anywhere, away from home, when your music score may not be available. Practicing cold prepares you to play at a gathering, etc., without having to play Hanon for 15 minutes before you can perform. Playing cold is an ability that is surprisingly easily cultivated, although it may seem almost impossible at first. If you have never practiced cold before, you will be surprised at how quickly you can improve this skill. This is a good time to find those passages that are too difficult to play with cold hands and to practice how to slow down or simplify difficult sections. If you make a mistake or have a blackout, don't stop and backtrack, but practice keeping at least the rhythm or melody going and playing through the mistake.

The first few bars of even the simplest pieces are often difficult to start cold, and will require extra practice, even if it is well memorized. Often, the more technically difficult beginnings are easier to remember, so don't get caught unprepared by seemingly easy music. Clearly, it is important to practice the starts of all pieces cold. Of course, don't always start from the beginning; another advantage of memorizing is that you can play little snippets from anywhere in the piece, such as the most interesting parts, and you should always practice playing snippets (see section III.14, on "Performances and Recitals"). Gather as many associations as you can: What are the key/time signatures? What is the first note and its absolute pitch?

h.   Slow Play

An important way to reinforce memory is slow play, VERY slow play, less than half speed. Slow speed is also used to reduce the dependence on hand memory and supplant it with "real memory" (we shall discuss true memory below) because when you play slowly, the stimulus for hand memory recall is changed and reduced. The stimulation from the piano sound is also materially altered. The biggest disadvantage of slow play is that it takes a lot of time; if you can play twice as fast, you practice the piece twice as often in the same time, so why play slowly? Besides, it can get awfully boring. Why practice something you don't need when playing full speed? You really have to have good reasons to justify practicing very slowly. In order to make slow play pay off, try to combine as many things as possible into your slow play so that it does not waste time. Playing slowly, without well defined objectives, *is* a waste of time; you must simultaneously seek numerous benefits by knowing what they are. So let's list some of them.

(1) Slow play is surprisingly beneficial to good technique, especially for practicing relaxation and correct keystroke.
(2) Slow play reinforces your memory because there is time for the playing signals to travel from your fingers to the brain and back several times before succeeding notes are played. If you only practiced at speed, you could be reinforcing hand memory and losing true memory.
(3) Slow play allows you to practice getting mentally ahead of the music you are playing

(next section), which gives you more control over the piece and can even allow you to anticipate impending flubs. This is the time to work on your jumps and chords (sections III.7e, f). Always be at least a split second ahead of the music and practice feeling the keys before playing to guarantee 100% accuracy. As a general rule, think about one bar ahead -- more on this below.

(4) Slow play is one of the best ways to purge your hands of bad habits, especially those that you might have unconsciously picked up during fast practice (FPD, II.5). FPD is mostly hand memory which bypasses the brain; this is why you are usually unaware of them.

(5) You now have time to analyze the details of the structure of the music as you play, and pay attention to all the expression markings. Above all, concentrate on making music.

(6) One of the primary causes of blackouts and flubs during a performance is that the brain is racing much faster than usual, and you can "think" many more thoughts in the same amount of time between notes than during practice. This extra thinking introduces new variables that confuse the brain, leading you into unfamiliar territory, and can disrupt your rhythm. Therefore you can practice inserting extra thoughts between notes during slow practice. What are the preceding and following notes? Are they just right, or can I improve them? What do I do here if I make a mistake? etc., etc. Think of typical thoughts you might encounter during a performance. You can cultivate the ability to detach yourself from those particular notes you are playing, and be able to mentally wander around elsewhere in the music, as you play a given section.

If you combine all the above objectives, the time spent playing slowly will be truly rewarding, and keeping all these objectives going at once will be a challenge that will leave no room for boredom.

i.   Mental Timing
When playing from memory, you need to be mentally ahead of what you are playing at all times so that you can plan ahead, be in complete control, anticipate difficulties, and adjust to changing conditions. For example, you can often see a flub coming, and use one of the tricks discussed in this book (see section III.9 on polishing a piece) to get around it. You won't see this flub coming unless you are thinking ahead. One way to practice thinking ahead is to play fast, and then to slow down. By playing fast, you force the brain to think more quickly, so that when you slow down, you are now automatically ahead of the music. You cannot think ahead unless the music is well memorized, so thinking ahead really tests and improves the memory.

You can think ahead on many different levels of complexity. You can think ahead one note when playing very slowly. At faster speeds, you may have to think in terms of bars or phrases. You can also think about themes or musical ideas or different voices or chord transitions. These are all different associations that will help your memory process.

The best way to play very fast, of course, is HS. This is another valuable byproduct of HS practice; you will be surprised at first, what really fast playing will do to your brain. It is a totally new experience, if you have never played this fast before. Every brain has its maximum speed, which varies widely among individuals. You should make sure that this maximum is sufficient to cover piano music. The best way to practice such speeds is by use of parallel sets. Since you have to go really fast in order to beat the brain, such speeds are not easily attainable HT. Fast play is a good way to speed up the brain so that it can think ahead.

j.   Establishing Permanent Memory, Mental Play
There are at least five basic methods of memorizing; they are: (1) hand memory (audio/tactile), (2) music memory (aural), (3) photographic memory (visual), (4) keyboard memory/mental play (visual/tactile, brain), and (5) theoretical memory (brain). Practically everybody uses a combination of them. Most people rely mainly on one and use the others as

supplementary help.

We already discussed **hand memory** above (III.6.d). It is acquired by simple repetition until the "music is in the hands". In the intuitive school of teaching, this was thought to be the best way to memorize, because of a lack of better methods. What we want to do now is to replace it with true memory in order to establish a more permanent and reliable memory.

Music memory is based on the music: the melody, rhythm, expression, emotion, etc. This approach works best for artistic and musical types of persons who have strong feelings associated with their music. Those with absolute pitch will also do well because they can find the notes on the piano from the memory of the music. People who like to compose also tend to use this type of memory. Musicians do not automatically have good musical memory. It depends on the type of brain they have, although it is trainable, as discussed in section III.6.m below. For example, people with good music memory can also remember other things, such as the name of the composer and the name of the composition. They have good melody recall, so that they can hum the music if you tell them the title, for most compositions that they have heard a few times.

The most important function of music memory is to serve as the memory algorithm. We shall see in section "m" below that all super memorizers use some type of algorithm for memorizing. The keys to successful memorizing are having an algorithm and knowing how to use it. Musicians are lucky because they don't have to invent an algorithm – music is one the best algorithms around! This is the main reason why concert pianists can play for hours without missing a note. Until we understood this aspect of memory, we had attributed such memory feats to "talent" or "genius", but in reality, it is a memory skill that is easily learned, as described below.

Photographic memory: You memorize the entire sheet music and actually picture it and read it in the mind. Even those who think that they do not have photographic memory, can achieve it if they practice photographic memory routinely as they practice the piece from the *very beginning*. Many people will find that, if they are diligent about this procedure from day one (of when they start the piece), there will be only an average of a few bars per page that are not photographically memorized by the time they can play the piece satisfactorily. One way to photographically memorize is to follow exactly the methods outlined here for technique and memory, but to also photographically memorize the sheet music at the same time, hand by hand, bar-by-bar, and segment by segment.

Another way to approach photographic memory is to start memorizing the general outline first, like how many lines there are in the page and how many bars per line; then the notes in each bar, then the expression markings, etc. That is, start with the gross features, and then gradually fill in the details. Start photographic memory by memorizing one hand at a time. You really need to take an accurate photograph of the page, complete with its defects and extraneous marks. If you have difficulty memorizing certain bars, draw something unusual there, such as a smiley face or your own markings that will jolt your memory. Then next time you want to recall this section, think of the smiley face first.

One advantage of photographic memorization is that you can work on it without the piano, anytime, anywhere. In fact, once acquired, you must read it in your mind, away from the piano, as often as you can until it is permanently memorized. Another advantage is that if you get stuck in the middle of playing a piece, you can easily restart by reading that section of the music in your mind. Photographic memory also allows you to read ahead as you play which helps you to think ahead. Another advantage is that it will help your sight reading.

The main disadvantage is that most people cannot retain photographic memory for long periods of time since maintenance requires more work than other methods because of the high bandwidth of visual images. Another disadvantage is that picturing the printed music in the mind and reading it is a comparatively slow mental process that can interfere with the playing. However, if you follow the methods discussed here, you may find it much easier than you thought. In principle, once you have memorized a piece, you know every note and therefore should be able to map it back to the sheet music, thus helping the photographic memory. ***Once you have acquired most of the types of memories discussed here, adding photographic memory requires very little additional work,*** and you reap considerable rewards. Thus every pianist should use a certain minimum of photographic memory. The first line, containing the key and time signatures, is a good place to start.

For those who think that they do not have photographic memory, try the following trick. First memorize a short piece of music. Once each section is memorized, map it back onto the score from which you learned the piece; that is, for each note you play (from memory), try to picture the corresponding note on the sheet music. Since you know every note, HS, mapping it back from the keyboard to the sheet music should be simple. When mapping back, look at the score to make sure that every note is in the correct position on the right page. Even the expression markings should be memorized. Go back and forth, playing from photographic memory and mapping back from the keyboard to the sheet music until the photograph is complete. Then you can amaze your friends by writing down the score for the entire piece, starting from anywhere! Note that you will be able to write the whole music, forwards or backwards, or from anywhere in the middle, or even each hand separately. And they thought only Wolfgang could do it!

Keyboard memory and mental play: In keyboard memory, you remember the sequence of keys and hand motions, with the music, as you play. It is as if you have a piano in your mind, and can play it. Start the keyboard memory by memorizing HS, then HT. Then when you are away from the piano, play the piece in your mind, again HS first. ***Playing in your mind (mental play – MP), without the piano, is our ultimate memory goal.*** Keyboard memory is a good way to start practicing MP. Playing HT in your mind is not necessary at first, especially if you find it to be too difficult, although you will eventually be playing HT with ease. During MP, take note of which sections you forgot, then go to the music/piano and refresh your memory. You might try photographic memory on parts that you tend to forget using keyboard memory because you need to look at the score anyway in order to re-memorize. MP is difficult not only because you have to have it memorized, but also because you don't have hand memory or the piano sound to help; however, this is precisely why it is so powerful.

Keyboard memory has most of the advantages of photographic memory but has the added advantage that the memorized notes are piano keys instead of tadpoles on a sheet of paper; therefore, you do not have to translate from tadpoles to the keys. This allows you to play with less effort compared to photographic memory, since there is no need to go through the extra process of interpreting the music score. The expression markings are not markings on paper, but mental concepts of the music (music memory). Every time you practice, keyboard memory (as well as hand memory and music memory) automatically maintains itself, whereas photographic memory does not. You can practice MP without a piano, thus more than doubling the time available for practice, and you can play ahead, just as with photographic memory.

When using keyboard memory, you tend to make the same mistakes, and get stuck at the same places, as when playing at the piano. This makes sense because all mistakes originate in the brain. This suggests that we may be able to practice and improve certain aspects of piano playing by using only MP -- that would be a truly unique advantage! Most of the suggestions for memorizing given in this book apply best to keyboard memory, which is another one of its advantages. MP is the best test of true memory – when you conduct MP, you will realize how much you still depend on hand memory even after you thought that you had acquired keyboard memory. Only after acquiring sufficient MP can you be free of hand memory. However, hand memory is always a good backup – even when you have lost mental memory, you can usually restore it without looking at the score by playing it out on the piano using hand memory.

For those who wish to learn sight singing and acquire absolute (or perfect) pitch, MP automatically develops those skills. The keyboard memory visualizes the keyboard, which helps in finding the right key for absolute pitch, a skill you will need when composing, or improvising at the piano. Therefore, those practicing MP should also practice sight singing and absolute pitch, since they have already partly learned those skills. See sections 11 and 12 below for more details. In fact, MP does not work well without absolute pitch. Doubtless, MP is one of the ways by which the musical geniuses got to be what they were. Thus many of these "genius feats" are achievable by practically all of us if we know how to practice them. Conclusion: memory leads to keyboard/mental play, which leads to relative/absolute pitch! In other words, these are essential components of technique -- when you achieve them all, your ability to memorize and to perform will make a quantum jump. Moreover, *MP is the key that opens the doors to the world of concert pianists and composers.*

As with any memory procedure, MP must be practiced from the very first year of piano lessons. If you are over 20 years old, and never practiced MP, it may take a year of diligent practice for you to become comfortable with it, and to use it properly; learning MP is only slightly easier than absolute pitch. Therefore, as soon as you memorize a segment, play it in your mind, and maintain it like as any other type of memory. You should eventually be able to play the entire composition in your mind. You will think back in amazement and say to yourself "Wow! That was easier than I thought!" because this book provides the basics needed for learning MP.

MP will give you the ability to start anywhere within a segment -- something that is difficult to learn in any other way. You can also gain a much clearer concept of the structure of the composition and the sequence of melodies, because you can now analyze all those constructs in your head. You can even "practice" at speeds that your fingers cannot manage. The fingers can never achieve speeds that the brain cannot; you can certainly try it with partial success, but it will be uncontrollable. *Thus MP at fast speeds will help the fingers play faster.* When you become good at it, playing in your mind does not have to take much time because you can play it very fast, or in abbreviated fashion, skipping easy sections and concentrating only on places where you normally encounter difficulties. Perhaps the single greatest benefit of MP is that your memory will improve so much, that you will gain the confidence to perform flawlessly. Such confidence is the best known way for eliminating nervousness. If you experienced any enlightenment as you learned the other methods of this book, wait till you master MP -- you will wonder how you ever had the courage to perform anything in public without being able to play it in your mind -- you have entered a new world, having acquired abilities that are highly admired by any audience.

There is another advantage of MP -- the more pieces you memorize in your mind, the easier it becomes to memorize more! This happens because you are increasing the number of associations. Hand memory is the opposite -- it becomes harder to memorize as your repertoire increases because the possibility for confusion increases. Also, your MP skill will increase rapidly as you practice it and discover its numerous powers. Because MP is useful in so many ways, you will automatically practice it more and more, and become even better at it. All concert pianists conduct MP out of necessity, whether they were formally taught MP or not. A few lucky students were taught MP; for the rest, there is a mad scramble to learn this "new" skill that they are expected to have when they reach a certain skill level. Fortunately, it is not a difficult skill to master for the serious student because the rewards are so immediate and far-reaching that there is no problem with motivation.

Theoretical memory: At the advanced level, learning MP is easy because such students have studied some theory. A good solfege course should teach this skill, but solfege teachers do not always teach memorizing skills or MP. Theory lessons will give you the best way to memorize. By associating the music with the underlying theory, you can establish firm associations with basic concepts. Unlike all the other memories, theoretical memory has deeper associations because theory leads to a better understanding of the music and the associations are more detailed – small details that you hardly noticed before can take on major significance. At the very least, you should note the main characteristics of the composition such as key signature, time signature, rhythm, chord structure, chord transitions, harmony, melodic structure, etc.

In summary, keyboard memory should be your primary method of memory. You must hear the music at the same time, so musical memory is a part of this process. Enlist the help of photographic memory whenever it comes easily, and add as much theoretical memory as you can. *You have not really memorized until you can play the piece in your mind* -- this is the only way in which you can gain confidence to perform musically and with confidence. You can use it to reduce nervousness and it is the fastest and easiest way to learn relative/absolute pitch. In fact, MP is a powerful method that affects practically every musical activity you conduct at and away from the piano. This is not surprising because everything you do originates in the brain, and MP is how the music was composed. It not only solidifies keyboard memory but also helps musicality, music memory, photographic memory, performances, pitch accuracy, playing cold, etc. Don't be passive and wait for the music to come out of the piano, but actively anticipate the music you want to produce – which is the only way to execute a convincing performance. MP is how the great geniuses accomplished much of what they did, yet too many teachers have not taught this method: it is little wonder that so many students view the achievements of the great pianists as unattainable. *We have shown here that Mental Play is not only attainable, but must be an integral part of learning piano.*

k.   Maintenance

There is no more effective maintenance procedure than using keyboard memory and MP. Make a habit of playing in your mind at every opportunity you have. The difference between a good memorizer and a poor memorizer is not so much "memory power" as mental attitude -- what do you do with your brain during your waking and sleeping hours? Good memorizers have developed a habit of continually cycling their memory at all times. Therefore, when you practice memorizing, you must also train your mind to constantly work with the memorization. Poor memorizers will require a lot of effort at first because their brains are not accustomed to automatically perform memory functions continually, but is not that difficult if practiced over an extended period of time (years). Once you learn MP, this task will become much easier. Savants generally have problems of repetitive motions: their brains are cycling the same activity over and over again at all times. This can explain why they cannot perform many normal functions but can have incredible memories and amazing musical abilities, especially when we view these savants in the light of our above discussions about memory and playing music in your mind.

Maintenance time is a good time to revisit the score and check your accuracy, both for the individual notes and the expression marks. Since you used the same score to learn the piece, there is a good chance that if you made a mistake reading the score the first time, you will make the same mistake again later on, and never catch your mistake. One way around this problem is to listen to recordings. Any major difference between your playing and the recording will stand out as a jarring experience and is usually easy to catch.

A good maintenance procedure is to go through the process first used to learn/memorize the piece, such as starting from arbitrary places, playing very slowly, playing cold, etc. *Make sure that you still remember it HS.* This can become a real chore for major pieces, but is worth it, because you don't want to find out that you need it during a performance. These HS maintenance sessions are not just for memory. This is the time to try new things, playing much faster than final speed, and generally cleaning up your technique. Extended HT playing often introduces timing and other unexpected errors and this is the time to fix them by using the metronome. *Therefore, playing HS for both memory and technique enhancement is a very worthwhile endeavor.* The best preparation for recovery from flubs during a performance is HS practice and MP. Then, if you flub or have a blackout, you have many options for recovery, such as: keep on playing with one hand, first recovering one hand, and then adding the other, or simply keep the melody or rhythm going.

l.   **Sight Readers versus Memorizers:** Learning Bach's Inventions

Many good sight readers are poor memorizers and vice versa. This problem arises because good readers initially find little need to memorize and enjoy reading, so they end up practicing reading at the expense of memorizing. The more they read, the less memory they need, and the less they memorize, the worse memorizers they become, with the result that one day they realize that they are unable to memorize. Of course, there are naturally "talented" readers who have genuine memory problems, but these comprise a negligibly small minority. *Therefore, the memorizing difficulties arise mainly from a psychological mental block built up over long periods of time.* Good memorizers can experience the reverse problem; they can't sight read because they automatically memorize everything and rarely have a chance to practice reading. However, this is not a symmetric problem because practically all advanced pianists know how to memorize; therefore, *poor memorizers also had the misfortune of never having acquired advanced technique; that is, the technical level of poor memorizers is generally lower than that of good memorizers.*

"Sight reading" is used loosely in this section to mean true sight reading as well as practicing music with the help of the score. The distinction between sight reading a piece one had never seen and a piece that had been played before is not important here. In the interest of brevity, that distinction will be left to the context of the sentence.

It is more important to be able to memorize than to sight read because you can survive as a pianist without good reading ability, but you can't become an advanced pianist without the ability to memorize. Memorizing is not easy for the average pianist who was not trained in memory. Good readers who cannot memorize face an even more formidable problem. Therefore, *poor memorizers who wish to acquire a memorized repertoire must do so by starting with a mental attitude that this is going to be a long term project with numerous obstacles to overcome*. As shown above, the solution, in principle, is simple -- make it a practice to memorize everything *before* you learn the piece. In practice, the temptation to learn quickly by reading the score is often too irresistible. You need to fundamentally change the way you practice new pieces.

The most difficult problem encountered by poor memorizers is the psychological problem of motivation. For these good readers (poor memorizers), memorizing seems like a waste of time because they can quickly learn to play many pieces reasonably well by reading. They might even be able to play difficult pieces by using hand memory, and if they have a blackout, they can always refer back to the music in front of them. Therefore, they can manage without memorizing. After years of practicing piano this way, it becomes very difficult to learn how to memorize because the mind has become dependent on the score.

Difficult pieces are impossible under this system, so they are avoided in favor of a large number of easier compositions. With this awareness of potential difficulties, let's try to work through a typical program for learning how to memorize.

__The best way to learn how to memorize is to memorize a few, new, short pieces, instead of memorizing something you can already play.__ Once you successfully memorize a few pieces without too much effort, you can start building confidence and improving the memorizing skills. When these skills are sufficiently developed, you might even think of memorizing old pieces you had learned by reading but had not memorized well.

Piano sessions should be either memorizing sessions or technical practice sessions. This is because playing other things during memory sessions will confuse the material being memorized. During technical practice sessions, you almost never need the score. Even during memorizing sessions, use the score only in the beginning and then put it away.

As an example of short pieces to memorize, let's learn three of **Bach's 2-part Inventions: #1, #8, and #13**. I will go through #8 with you. After learning #8, try #1 yourself and then start on #13. The idea is to learn all three simultaneously, but if that proves too taxing, try two (#8 and #1), or even just #8. It is important that you try only what you think you can comfortably handle, because the objective here is to demonstrate how easy it is. The schedule given below is for learning all three at once. We are assuming that you have learned the material of sections I to III, and that your technical level is sufficient to tackle the Bach Inventions. The pedal is not used in any of the Bach Inventions.

Bach's Invention #8, day one. The time signature is 3/4 so there is one beat per quarter note and each bar (measure) has 3 beats. The key signature shows one flat, which places the key one step counter-clockwise from C major on the circle of fifths -- or F major (not D minor because the music does not use C# and starts and ends with notes of the F major chord).

Begin by memorizing bars 2 to 4 of the LH, including the first two notes (conjunction) of bar 5. It should take less than a minute to memorize; then start playing it at speed. Take your hands off the piano, close your eyes, and play this section in your head (MP), visualizing every note and key that you play (photographic and keyboard memory). Then do the same for the RH, bars 1 to 4, including the first 4 notes of bar 5. Now return to the LH and see if you can play it without the score, and similarly with the RH. If you can, you should never have to refer to this part of the score again, unless you have a blackout, which will happen once in a while. Go back and forth between the LH and RH until you are comfortable. This should take only a few minutes more. Let's say that this whole procedure takes 5 minutes; less for a fast learner. You will find fingering suggestions on most sheet music; for example, W. A. Palmer's "J. S. Bach, Inventions and Sinfonias" by Alfred.

Now learn bars 5 to 7, including the first 2 notes of the LH and the first 4 notes of the RH in bar 8. This should be completed in about 4 minutes. These are all HS practices; we will not start HT until we finish memorizing the whole piece HS. However, you are free to try HT at any time, but do not waste time practicing HT if you do not make immediate, fast progress because we have a schedule to follow! When starting bars 5 to 7, don't worry about forgetting the previously memorized bars -- you should put them out of your mind. This will not only reduce mental tension and confusion (by not mixing different memorized sections), but also make you partially forget the previously memorized section, forcing you to rememorize for better retention. Once you are comfortable with bars 5-7, connect bars 1-7, including the conjunctions in bar 8. It may take 3 minutes to do both hands, separately. If you forgot bars 2-4 while learning 5-7, repeat the learning process -- it will come very quickly and the memory will be more permanent. Don't forget to play each section in your mind.

Next memorize bars 8-11, and add them to the previous sections. Let's assign 8 minutes to this part, for a total of 20 minutes to memorize bars 1-11 and to bring them up to speed, HS. If you have technical difficulties with some parts, don't worry about it, we will work on that later. You are not expected to play anything to perfection at this time.

Next, we will abandon bars 1-11 (don't even worry about trying to remember them -- it is important to remove all sense of anxiety and to let the brain concentrate on the memory task), and work on bars 12-23 only. Break this section up into the following segments (the conjunctions should be obvious): 12-15, 16-19, and 19-23. Bar 19 is practiced twice because this provides extra time to practice the difficult 4th finger in the LH. Work only on bars 12-23 until you can play them all in succession, HS. This should take another 20 minutes.

Then finish off bars 24 to end (34). These might be learned using the following segments: 24-25, 26-29, and 30-34. This may require another 20 minutes, for a total of 1hr to memorize the whole thing. You can now either quit and continue tomorrow, or review each of the three sections. The important thing here is not to worry about whether you will remember all this tomorrow (you probably won't), but to have fun, maybe even trying to connect the three sections or to put the beginning parts HT to see how far you can go. Work on parts that give you technical problems when you try to speed them up. Practice these technical workouts in as small segments as you can; this frequently means two-note parallel sets. That is, practice only the notes you can't play satisfactorily. Jump from segment to segment. The total time spent for memorizing on the first day is 1 hour. You can also start on the second piece, Invention #1. Between days 1 and 2, practice playing in your mind whenever you have extra time.

Day two: review each of the three sections, then connect them. Start by playing each section in your mind before playing anything on the piano. You might need the sheet music in some places. Then put the music score away -- you will seldom need them again except for emergencies and to double check the accuracy during maintenance. The only requirement on the 2nd day is to be able to play the whole piece HS from beginning to end, both on the piano and in your mind. Concentrate on bringing up the speed, and go as fast as you can without making mistakes. Practice relaxation. If you start to make mistakes, slow down and cycle the speed up and down. Note that it may be easier to memorize playing fast, and you might get memory lapses playing very slowly, so practice at different speeds. Don't be afraid to play fast, but make sure that you balance this with sufficient intermediate speed and slow play so as to erase any FPD. Beginners have most difficulties at chord changes, which often take place at the beginning of a bar. Chord changes create difficulties because after the change, you need to play a new set of unfamiliar notes.

If you are completely comfortable HS on the 2nd day, you might start HT, using the same small segments used to learn HS. The first note of bar 3 is a collision of the two hands, so use only the LH for this note, and similarly in bar 18. Play softly, even where "f" is indicated, so that you can accentuate the beat notes to synchronize the two hands and practice relaxation. You will probably be slightly tense in the beginning, but concentrate on relaxing as soon as possible.

Moderate speed is often the easiest speed to play from memory because you can use the rhythm to keep you going and you can remember the music in phrases instead of individual notes. Therefore, pay attention to the rhythm from the very beginning. Now slow down and work on accuracy. To prevent the slow play from speeding up, concentrate on each individual note. Repeat this fast-slow speed cycle and you should improve noticeably with each cycle. The main objectives are to completely memorize it HS and to speed up the HS play as much as possible. Wherever you have technical difficulties, use the parallel set exercises to develop technique quickly. You should not need more than 1 hour.

Day three: learn HT in the three major sections as you did with HS. As soon as you notice confusion setting in HT, go back to HS to clear things up. This is a good time to further increase the speed HS, up to speeds faster than final speed (more on how to do this later). Of course, those with insufficient technical skill will have to play slower. Remember: relaxation is more important than speed. You will be playing faster HS than HT, and all attempts at increasing speed should be conducted HS. Since the hands are not yet well coordinated, you should have some memory lapses and it may be difficult to play HT without mistakes unless you play slowly. From here on, you will have to depend on the slower post practice improvement to gain any major improvement. However, in 3 hours over 3 days, you have basically memorized the piece and can play, perhaps haltingly, HT. You can also play the entire piece in your mind.

Now start on Invention #1, while you polish up the first piece. Practice the two pieces alternately. Work on #1 until you start to forget #8, then go back and refresh #8 and work on it until you start to forget #1. Remember that you *want* to forget a little so that you can relearn, which is what is needed to establish long term memory. There are psychological advantages to using these "win-win" programs: if you forget, that is exactly what you were looking for; if you can't forget, that's even better! This program will also give you an idea of how much you can/cannot memorize in a given amount of time. Youngsters should find that the amount you can memorize at one time increases rapidly as you gain experience and add more memorizing tricks. This is because you have a run-away situation in which the faster you memorize, the faster you can play, and the faster you play, the easier it becomes to memorize. Increased confidence also plays a major role. Ultimately, the main limiting factor will be your technical skill level, not the memorizing ability. If you have sufficient technique, you will be playing at speed in a few days. If you can't, that may mean that you need more technique -- it does not mean that you are a poor memorizer.

Day four: There is not much you can do to rush the first piece technically after two or three days. For several days, start practicing #8 by playing HS, then HT, at different speeds according to your whim of the moment. As soon as you feel ready, practice HT, but return to HS if you start making mistakes, have memory lapses HT, or if you have technical problems getting up to speed. Practice playing the piece HT in segments, jumping from segment to segment at random throughout the piece. Try starting with the last small segment and work backwards to the beginning.

Isolate the trouble spots and practice them separately. Most people have a weaker LH, so bringing the LH up to faster than final speed may present problems. For example, the last four notes of the LH in bar 3 (Inv. #8), 4234(5), where (5) is the conjunction, may be difficult to play fast. In that case, break it up into three parallel sets: 42, 23, and 345 and practice them using the parallel set exercises. Then connect them: 423 and 2345. 423 is not a parallel set (4 and 3 play the same note), so you cannot play this as fast as parallel sets. First bring them up to nearly infinite speed (almost a chord) and then learn to relax at those speeds, playing in rapid quads (see section III.7b). Then gradually slow down to develop finger independence. Join the parallel sets in pairs and, finally, string them all together. This is actual technique enhancement and therefore will not happen over-night. You may see little improvement during practice, but you should feel a distinct improvement the next day, and a lot of improvement after a few weeks.

When you can play it HT, start playing HT in your mind (MP). This HT practice should take a day or two. *If you don't complete the task of playing MP at this step, for most people, you never will.* But if you succeed, it will become the most powerful memory tool you have ever used.

By day 5 or 6, you should be able to **start piece #13** and begin practicing all three pieces every day. An alternate approach is to learn only piece #8 well first, then after you have gone through the entire procedure so that you are familiar with it, start #1 and #13. The main reason for learning several pieces at once is that these pieces are so short that you will be playing too many repetitions in one day if you only practiced one. Remember, from day one, you will be playing at speed (HS), and from day two, you should be playing at least some sections faster than final speed. Also, it takes longer to learn these three pieces, one at a time, than three together.

Beyond day two or three, how fast you progress will depend more on your skill level than memory ability. Once you can play the entire piece HS at will, you should consider the piece memorized. This is because, if you are above the intermediate level, you will be able to play it HT very quickly, whereas if you are not that advanced, the technical difficulties in each hand will slow the progress. Memory will not be the limiting factor. For HT work, you will obviously have to work with coordinating the two hands. Bach designed these Inventions for learning to coordinate the two hands and, at the same time, to play them independently. This is the reason why there are two voices and they are superimposed; also, in #8, one hand plays staccato while the other plays legato.

All three pieces discussed above should be completely memorized in one to two weeks and you should begin to feel comfortable with at least the first piece. Let's say that for over a week, all you did was to concentrate on memorizing new pieces. Now if you go back to old pieces that were memorized previously, you will find that you don't remember them as well any more. This is a good time to re-polish those old pieces and to alternate this maintenance chore with further polishing of your new Bach pieces. You are basically done. Congratulations!

How well you can play from memory depends on your technique as well as how well you have memorized. ***It is important not to confuse lack of technique with the inability to memorize,*** because most people who have difficulty memorizing have adequate memory but inadequate technique. Therefore, you will need methods for testing your technique and your memory. If your technique is adequate, you should be able to play comfortably at about 1.5 times final speed, HS. For #8, the speed is about MM = 100 on the metronome, so you should be able to play both hands at about 150 HS. At 150, you got Glenn Gould beat (albeit HS - he plays at around 140)! If you cannot do well above 100 HS, then you must improve your technique before you can expect to play HT at anything close to 100. The best test for memory is whether you can play it in your mind. By applying these tests, you can determine whether you need to work on technique or memory.

Most people have a weaker LH; bring the LH technique up as close to the RH level as possible. As illustrated above for bar 3 of the LH, use the parallel set exercises to work on technique. Bach is particularly useful for balancing the LH and RH techniques because both hands play similar passages. Therefore, you know immediately that the LH is weaker if it cannot get up to the same speed as the RH. For other composers, such as Chopin, the LH is usually much easier and does not provide a good LH test. Students with inadequate technique may need to work HS for weeks before they can hope to play these inventions HT at speed. In that case, play HT at comfortably slow tempi and wait for your HS technique to develop before speeding up HT.

Bach's music has a notorious reputation of being difficult to play fast, and is highly susceptible to FPD (fast play degradation, see section II.25). The intuitive solution to this problem has been to patiently practice slowly. You don't have to play very fast to suffer FPD with many of Bach's compositions. If your maximum speed is MM = 20, whereas the suggested speed is 100, then for you, 20 is fast and at that speed, FPD can rear its ugly head. This is why playing slowly HT and trying to speed it up will only generate more confusion and FPD. Now we know the reason for that notorious reputation -- the difficulty arises from too many repetitions of slow HT play, which only increases the confusion without helping your memory or technique. The better solution is HS, segmental practice. For those who had never done this before, you will soon be playing at speeds you never dreamed possible.

Quiet hands: Many teachers justifiably stress "quiet hands" as a desirable objective. *In this mode, the fingers do most of the playing, with the hands moving very little. Quiet hands is the litmus test for technique acquisition.* The elimination of unnecessary motions not only allows faster play, but also increases control. Many of Bach's music were designed for practicing quiet hands. Some of the unexpected fingerings indicated on the music score were chosen so as to be compatible with, or facilitate, quiet hands play. *Some teachers impose quiet hand playing on all students at all times, even for beginners, but such an approach is counter-productive because you can't play quiet hands slowly so there is no way to teach it at slow speed.* The student feels nothing and wonders why it is any good. When playing slowly, or if the student does not have sufficient technique, some extra motion is unavoidable, and is appropriate. To force the hands to be motionless under those conditions would only make it more difficult to play and creates stress. Those who already have quiet hands technique can add a lot of motion without detriment when playing slowly or fast. Some teachers try to teach quiet hands by placing a coin on the hand to see if it is quiet enough so that the coin will not fall off. This method only demonstrates the teacher's recognition of the importance of quiet hands, but it harms the student by creating stress. If you are playing Bach at full speed using quiet hands, a coin placed on your hand will immediately fly off. Only when playing beyond a certain speed does quiet hands become obvious to the pianist, and necessary. When you acquire quiet hands for the first time, it is absolutely unmistakable, so don't worry about missing it. The best time to teach the student what quiet hands means, is when playing sufficiently fast so that you can feel the quiet hands. Once you have it, you can then apply it to slow play; you should now feel that you have much more control and a lot more free time between notes. Thus quiet hands is not any specific motion of the hand but a feeling of control and the near total absence of speed walls.

In the case of the Bach pieces discussed here, the quiet hands become necessary at speeds close to final speed; without it, you will start to hit speed walls at the recommended speeds; obviously, the speeds were chosen with quiet hands in mind. HS practice is important for quiet hands because it is much easier to acquire and feel it in your hands when played HS, and because HS play allows you to get to quiet hands speed more quickly than HT. In fact, *it is best not to start HT until you can play in the quiet hands mode with both hands because this will reduce the chances of locking in bad habits.* That is, HT with or without quiet hands is different, so that you don't want to get into the habit of playing HT without quiet hands – you will never get up to speed! Those with insufficient technique may take too long a time to attain quiet hands, so that such students may have to start HT without quiet hands; they can then gradually acquire quiet hands at a later time, by using more HS practice. This explains why those with sufficient technique can learn these inventions so much faster than those without. Such difficulties are some of the reasons for not trying to learn pieces that are too difficult for you, and provide useful tests for whether the composition is too difficult or appropriate for your skill level. Those with insufficient technique will certainly risk building up speed walls. Although some people claim that the Bach Inventions can be played "at any speed", that is true only for their musical content; these compositions need to be played at their recommended speeds in order to take full advantage of the technical lessons that Bach had in mind. There is an over-emphasis on speed in this section because of the need to demonstrate/achieve quiet hands; however, do not practice speed for speed's sake since that will not work because of stress and bad habits; musical play is still the best way to increase speed -- see section III.7.i.

For those with stronger RHs, quiet hands will come first with the RH; once you know the feel, you can transfer it to the LH more quickly. Once it kicks in, you will suddenly find that playing fast becomes easier. This is why HT practice doesn't work for learning new Bach pieces -- there is no way to get to quiet hands quickly HT.

Bach wrote these Inventions for technical development. Thus he gave both hands equally difficult material; this provides more challenges for the LH because the bass hammers and strings are heavier. Bach would have been mortified to see exercises such as the Hanon series because he knew that exercises without music would be a waste of time, as demonstrated by the effort he put into these compositions to incorporate music. The amount of technical material he crammed into these compositions is incredible: finger independence (quiet hands, control, speed), coordination as well as independence of the two hands (multiple voices, staccato vs. legato, colliding hands, ornaments), harmony, making music, strengthening the LH as well as the weaker fingers (fingers 4 and 5), all major parallel sets, uses of the thumb, standard fingerings, etc. Note that the ornamentals are parallel set exercises; they are not only musical ornaments but are also an integral part of technical development. Using the ornaments, Bach asks you to practice parallel sets with one hand while simultaneously playing another part with the other hand, and producing music with this combination!

Be careful not to play Bach too loud, even where F is indicated. Instruments of his time produced much less sound than modern pianos so that Bach had to write music that is filled with sound, and with few breaks. One of the purposes of the numerous ornaments and trills used in Bach's time was to fill in the sound. Thus his music tends to have too much sound if played loudly on modern pianos. Especially with Inventions and Sinfonias, in which the student is trying to bring out all the competing melodies, there is a tendency to play each succeeding melody louder, ending up in loud music. The different melodies must compete on the basis of musical concept, not loudness. Playing more softly will also help to achieve total relaxation and true finger independence.

If you want to learn one of the **3-part Inventions, you might try Sinfonia #15** which is easier than most of the others. It is very interesting, and has a section in the middle where the two hands collide and play many of the same notes. As with all Bach compositions, this one contains a lot more than first meets the eye, so approach it with care. First of all, it is allegro vivace! The time signature is a strange 9/16, which means that the groups of six 1/32 notes in bar 3 must be played as 3 beats, not 2 (three pairs of notes instead of two triplets). This time signature results in the three repeat notes (there are two in bar 3) that have thematic value and they march across the keyboard in characteristic Bach fashion. When the two hands collide in bar 28, raise the RH and slide the LH under it, both hands playing all the notes. If the thumb collision is problematic, you might eliminate the RH thumb and play only the LH thumb. In bar 36, be sure to use the correct RH fingering: (5),(2,3),(1,4),(3,5),(1,4),(2,3).

Finally, let's discuss the last necessary step in memorizing -- analyzing the structure, or the "story", behind the music. The memorizing process will be incomplete until you understand the story behind the music. We shall use Invention #8. The first 11 bars comprise the "exposition". Here, the RH and LH play basically the same thing, with the LH delayed by one bar, and the main theme is introduced. The "body" consists of bars 12 to 28, where the roles of the two hands are initially reversed, with the LH leading the RH, followed by some intriguing developments. The ending starts at bar 29 and brings the piece to an orderly finish, with the RH re-asserting its original role. Note that the ending is the same as the end of the exposition -- the piece effectively ends twice, which makes the ending more convincing. Beethoven developed this device of ending a piece multiple times and raised it to incredible heights.

We now present some explanations for why developing such a "story" is the best way to memorize a composition permanently. That is how all great musicians organized their music.

m.   Human Memory Function; Music = Memory Algorithm

The memory function of the brain is only incompletely understood. ***There is no proof for the existence of "photographic memory" in the strict sense of the phrase***, though I have used this terminology in this book. ***All memory is associative.*** Thus when we visually "memorize" a Monet painting, we are actually associating the subjects of the painting with something deeper in our memory, not just a two dimensional picture composed of so many pixels. This is why great paintings or unusual photographs are easier to remember than similar images of lesser significance, though both may have the same bandwidth (number of pixels). As another example, if you take a photograph of a circle on a sheet of paper, the photo will be accurate; the diameter and location of the circle will be exactly correct. But if you make a "photographic memory" of the same circle in your mind and then try to redraw it on another sheet of paper, the diameter and location will be different. This means that you memorized it conceptually (associating with some previous knowledge about circles and approximate sizes and locations). How about photographic memory of the music score? I can actually see it in my mind! Isn't that photographic? It is easy to prove that this, too, is associative -- in this case, associated with music. If you ask a musician with "photographic" memory to memorize a full page of random music notes, he will have great difficulty memorizing even a single page, although he may have no trouble photographically memorizing a 20 page sonata quickly. This is why there is no better way to memorize music (photographic or otherwise) than from the standpoint of music theory. All you have to do is to associate the music with the theory and you have it memorized. In other words, when humans memorize something, they don't store the data bits in the brain like a computer, but they associate the data with a basic framework or "algorithm" consisting of familiar things in the brain. In this example, music theory is the framework. Of course, a super memorizer (who may not be a musician) can develop methods for memorizing even a random sequence of notes by devising an appropriate algorithm, as we now explain.

The best evidence for the associative nature of human memory comes from tests on good memorizers who can perform incredible feats such as memorizing hundreds of telephone numbers from a phone book, etc. There are numerous memory contests in which good memorizers compete. These good memorizers have been extensively interviewed and it turns out that none of them memorize photographically, although the end result is almost indistinguishable from photographic memory. When asked how they memorize, it turns out that they all use associative algorithms. The algorithm is different for every person (even for the same task), but they are all devices for associating the objects to be memorized with something that has a pattern that they can remember. For example, for remembering hundreds of numbers, one algorithm is to associate a sound with each number. The sounds are chosen such that they form "words" when strung together, not in English, but in a new "language" that is created for that purpose. Japanese is a language with such a property. For example, the square root of 2 is 1.41421356 which can be read as a phrase that translates roughly to, "good people, good people are worth looking at", and the Japanese routinely use such algorithms to remember strings of numbers such as telephone numbers. To 7 decimals, the square root of 3 reads "Treat the entire world!" and the root of 5 reads "On the 6th station of Mt. Fuji, an owl is crying." The amazing thing is the speed with which good memorizers can map the object to be memorized onto their algorithm. It also turns out that these good memorizers are not born that way, although they may be born with mental capabilities that can lead to good memory. ***Memorizers develop after much hard work in perfecting their algorithms and practicing every day, just like pianists.*** This "hard work" comes effortlessly because they enjoy it.

A simple, but less efficient, algorithm is to map the numbers into a story. Suppose that you want to memorize the sequence of 14 numbers 53031791389634. The way to do it is to use something like the following story: "I woke up at 5:30 AM with my 3 brothers and 1 grandmother; the ages of my brothers are 7, 9, and 13, and my grandmother is 89 years old, and we went to bed at 6:34 PM." This is an algorithm based on life's experience, which makes the random numbers "meaningful". What is so intriguing is that the algorithm contains 38 words, yet it is much easier to remember than the 14 numbers. In fact, you have memorized 132 letters and numbers with greater ease than the 14 numbers! You can easily test this for yourself. First memorize both the 14 numbers (if you can -- it is not easy for me) and the above algorithm. Then 24 hours later, try to write down the numbers from memory and from the algorithm; you will find the algorithm to be much easier and more accurate. All good memorizers have devised incredibly efficient algorithms and have cultivated the art of rapidly transferring any memory job onto their algorithms.

Can pianists take advantage of this use of efficient algorithms? Of course we can! How do you think Liszt memorized and could perform more than 80 compositions within a short period of time? There is no reason to indicate that he had any special memory abilities, so he must have used an algorithm. But that algorithm is all around us – it is called music! Music is one of the most efficient algorithms for memorizing huge amounts of data. Practically all pianists can memorize several Beethoven sonatas easily. From the point of view of data bits, each sonata represents over 1,000 telephone numbers. Thus we can memorize the equivalent of over 10 pages of phone numbers – something that would be considered miraculous if they were actually phone numbers. And we can probably memorize more if we did not have to spend so much time practicing for technique and musicality. Therefore, what pianists achieve routinely is not that different from what those "genius memorizers" are famous for. Music is an especially efficient algorithm because it follows some strict rules. Composers such as Liszt were familiar with these rules and formulas and could memorize faster (see IV.4 for Mozart's formula). Moreover, musical logic is inborn in all of us, which is a part of the music algorithm that we do not have to learn. Therefore, musicians have an advantage over practically any other profession when it comes to memorizing, and most of us should be able to achieve a level of memory close to that of good memorizers in memory contests. This is because we now know a lot about how it is done.

It is now possible to understand how memorizers can memorize many pages of phone numbers. They simply end up with a "story", instead of a string of numbers. Note that a 90 year old man may not be able to remember your name, yet he can sit down and tell you stories for hours or even days from memory. And he doesn't have to be any kind of memory specialist to do this. Thus if you know how to use your brain, you can do things that seemed at first to be utterly impossible.

So then, what is it about associations that actually enable us to do something we otherwise cannot do? Perhaps the simplest way to describe this is to say that associations enable us to <u>understand</u> the subject to be memorized. This is a very useful definition because it can help anyone to do better in school, or in any learning endeavor. If you really understand physics or math or chemistry, you don't need to memorize it, because you can't forget it. This might seem pointless because we shifted our question from "what is memory?" to "what is association?" and then to "what is understanding?". It is not pointless if we can define *understanding*: it is a mental process of associating a new object with other objects (the more the better!) that are already familiar to you. That is, the new object now becomes "meaningful".

What do "understand" and "meaningful" mean? The human memory function has numerous components, such as visual, auditory, tactile, emotional, conscious, automatic, short term, long term, etc. Therefore, any input into the brain can result in an almost infinite number of associations. However, most people make only a few. Good memorizers have brains that continually make numerous associations with every input, in an almost automatic or habitual way. The large number of associations ensures that even if some of them are forgotten there are enough left to maintain the memory. However, that is not enough. We saw that in order to memorize, we must understand, which means that these associations are connected and ordered in some logical way. Understanding is like filing everything in a well organized way into a file cabinet. If the same information is strewn randomly all over the desktop and on the floor, you won't easily find the information you need. The brains of good memorizers are constantly seeking "interesting" or "amazing" or "mysterious" or "outrageous", etc., associations (file cabinet locations) that make recall easier. The "meaningful" and "understanding" associations of memory make good memorizers effectively more intelligent; thus good memory can raise the effective IQ. This is somewhat analogous to computers: adding memory can speed up a slow computer.

The associative nature of memory explains why keyboard memory works: you associate the music with the particular motions and keys that must be played to create the music. This also tells us how to optimize keyboard memory. Clearly, it is a mistake to try to remember each keystroke; we should think in terms of things like "RH arpeggio starting from C, which is repeated in the LH an octave down, staccato, with happy feeling", etc., and to associate these motions with the resulting music and its structure; i.e., memorize groups and families of notes and abstract concepts. You should make as many associations as possible: Bach's music may have certain characteristics, such as special ornaments and colliding hands and parallel sets. What you are doing is making the action of playing "meaningful" in terms of how the music is produced and how well you "understand" the music. This is why practicing scales and arpeggios is so important. When you encounter a run of 30 notes, you can remember it simply as a section of a scale, instead of 30 notes to memorize. Learning absolute pitch or at least relative pitch is also helpful for memory because they can provide additional associations with specific notes. The most common associations musicians make are with emotions evoked by the music. Some use color or scenery. In conclusion, "Born memorizer" is a phrase without a definition, because every good memorizer has a system, and all the systems appear to follow some very similar basic principles that anyone can learn.

n.   How to Become a Good Memorizer

Nobody becomes a good memorizer without practice, just as nobody becomes a good pianist without practicing. This means that anyone can become a good memorizer with proper training, just as anyone can learn any language under the right conditions. Most students have enough desire to memorize and therefore are willing to practice; yet many fail. Why do they fail, and are there simple solutions? The answer is yes!

Poor memorizers fail to memorize because they quit before they start. They were never introduced to effective memory methods and had experienced enough failures to conclude that it is useless to try to memorize. One helpful device in becoming a good memorizer is to realize that our brains record everything whether we like it or not. The only problem is that we can't recall that data easily.

We saw that the ultimate goal of all the memory procedures we discussed is good, solid MP. ***My initial understanding of MP was that it could be performed only by gifted musicians. This turned out to be false.*** We all conduct MP in our daily lives! MP is just a process of recalling items from memory and arranging them or using them, for planning our actions, solving problems, etc. We do this practically every moment of our waking hours, and probably even during sleep. When a mother with 3 kids wakes up in the morning and plans the day's activities for her family and what to eat and how to cook each dish for breakfast, lunch, and dinner, she is conducting a mental procedure just as complex as what Mozart did when he played a Bach Invention in his head. We don't think of this mother as a genius on the level of Mozart only because we are so familiar with these mental processes which we conduct effortlessly every day. Therefore, although Mozart's ability to compose music was indeed extraordinary, MP is nothing unusual – we can all do it with a little practice. *In today's teaching/training practices, MP has become standard in most disciplines that require utmost mental control, such as golf, figure skating, dance, downhill ski, etc. It should also be taught to piano students from the very beginning.*

Another way to improve memorization is to apply the "forget 3 times" rule; namely, that *if you can forget and re-memorize the same thing 3 times, you will usually remember it indefinitely*. This rule works because it eliminates the frustration from forgetting and it provides 3 chances to practice various memorization/recall methods. Frustration with, and fear of, forgetting is the worst enemy of poor memorizers, and this method alleviates that frustration.

Finally, you must "understand" and organize anything you memorize. Maintain an orderly filing cabinet of information, not memories scattered randomly all over the brain, that can't be easily retrieved. Everything you memorize must be classified and associated with other things in memory that are related to it. For example, instead of memorizing the sequence of sharps and flats in the key signature (CGDAEBF), you can "understand" it as a result of the circle of fifths, which is easy to visualize on a keyboard. Because of the large number of associations, this "understanding" is retained permanently in memory. These techniques will make you a good memorizer in just about everything, not only piano. In other words, *the brain becomes constantly active in memorizing and it becomes an effortless, automatic routine. The brain automatically seeks interesting associations and constantly maintains the memory with no conscious effort.* For older folks, establishing this "automation" habit is harder, and will take longer. As you succeed in memorizing these initial items (such as a piano repertoire), you will begin to apply the same principles to everything else and your general memory will improve. Therefore, in order to become a good memorizer, you must change the way you use the brain, in addition to knowing all the memory tricks/methods discussed here. This is the hardest part -- changing how your brain operates.

o.   **Summary**

Memorizing is necessary for learning a piece quickly and well, playing musically, acquiring difficult technique, performing flawlessly, eliminating nervousness, etc. To memorize piano music, simply use the rules for learning, with the added proviso that you memorize everything before you start to practice that section. It is the repetition during practice, from memory, that automatically implants the memory with little or no additional effort compared to the effort needed to learn the piece. The first important step is HS memorization. When you memorize something beyond a certain point, you will almost never forget it. For memorizing, you can use music (melodic) memory, hand memory, photographic memory, keyboard memory, and music theory. You should have two repertoires: memorized and sight reading. The human memory function is associative and a good memorizer is good at finding associations and organizing them into an "understanding" of the subject matter. A super memorizer is an expert in the development and use of efficient algorithms for memory. Music is an efficient algorithm; absolute pitch will also help. All these memory methods should culminate in Mental Play -- you can play the music, and hear it, as if you have a piano in your head. MP is essential for practically anything you do at the piano and it enables you to practice memorizing at any time. Good memorizers are good because their brains are always memorizing something automatically; you can train the brain to do this only if you can do MP. MP brings with it a whole new world of musical capabilities such as playing a piece from anywhere in the middle, absolute pitch, composing, performing without flubs, etc., which we had mistakenly attributed to "talent". Good memory can raise your effective IQ. Many of those miraculous feats that the musical geniuses are fabled to have performed are within reach of all of us!

7. Exercises
a.   Introduction: Intrinsic, Limbering, and Conditioning Exercises
Most finger exercises are not useful because of a number of disadvantages [see section (h)]. They can waste a lot of time. If the exercises are for developing the technique to play difficult pieces, the time will be better spent practicing the difficult pieces directly. Most exercises are repetitious, requiring no musical input which will turn off the musical brain. *Mindless practice is harmful.* Exercises are supposed to increase stamina; however, most of us have plenty of physical stamina to play but insufficient brain stamina; therefore mindless repetitive exercises can decrease our total musical stamina. Without proper guidance, students will practice these repetitions mechanically and, after a short time, gain no new skills. It is one way to create closet pianists who can practice only when no one is listening because they never practiced making music. Some accomplished pianists routinely use exercises for warming up, but this habit arose as a result of (incorrect) early training and concert pianists do not need them for their practice sessions.

Historically, the Hanon type exercises became widely accepted because of several misconceptions: (i) that technique can be acquired by learning a limited number of exercises, (ii) that music and technique can be learned separately, (iii) that technique requires mostly muscular development without brain development, and (iv) technique requires finger strength. Such exercises became popular with many teachers because, if they worked, the students could be taught technique with little effort from the teachers! This is not the fault of the teachers because these misconceptions were passed down through the generations, involving such famous teachers as Czerny, Hanon, and many others. The reality is that piano pedagogy is a challenging, time-consuming, knowledge-based profession.

If we define technique as the ability to play, then it has at least three components. It has an **intrinsic technique** component, which is simply your skill level. Having the skill, however, doesn't mean you can play. For example, if you haven't played for several days and the fingers are frozen cold, you probably won't be able to play anything satisfactorily. So there is a second component, the degree to which the fingers are limbered up (**warming up** component). There is also a third component, which will be called **conditioning**. For example, for a person who had been chopping down huge trees for weeks, or someone who had done nothing but knit sweaters for days, the hands may not be in condition to play the piano. The hands have adapted to a different job. On the other hand, practicing at least three hours every day for months will enable the hands to perform incredible feats. Defining the components of technique is important because these definitions enable the identification of the exercises that are needed.

The intrinsic skill level and warming up of the hands are easy to understand, but conditioning is complex. Important factors controlling conditioning are the length and frequency of practice and the state of the brain/nerve/muscle system. *In order to keep the hands in their best playing condition, most people will need to play every day.* Skip a few days of practice, and the conditioning will deteriorate. Thus, *although it was remarked elsewhere that practicing a minimum of three days a week can yield significant progress, this will clearly not result in the best conditioning.* Conditioning is a much larger effect than some people realize. Advanced pianists are always acutely aware of conditioning because it affects their ability to play. It is probably associated with physiological changes such as dilation of blood vessels and the accumulation of certain chemicals at specific locations of the nerve/muscle system. As the skill level rises, this conditioning factor becomes more important for dealing with difficult technical material and the higher musical concepts such as color or the characteristics of different composers.

A more elusive factor that affects conditioning is the state of the brain/nerve system. *Thus for no obvious reason, you can have "good" days and "bad" days.* This is probably analogous to the "slumps" that afflict athletes. In fact "bad days" can last for extended periods of time. With the awareness of this phenomenon and experimentation, this factor can be controlled to some extent. Musicians, like golfers, etc., must learn how to diagnose their own problems. This awareness can help to better cope psychologically with those "bad" days. Professional athletes, such as golfers and those who practice meditation, etc., have long known the importance of mental conditioning. Discovering the causes of such bad days would be even more helpful. One common cause is FPD, which was discussed near the end of section II.25. Another common cause is deviation from fundamentals: accuracy, timing, rhythm, correct execution of expressions, etc. Playing too fast, or with too much expression, can be detrimental to conditioning. This is why it is so difficult to perform twice in a row, and it is necessary to know how to "reset" the conditioning between performances. Possible cures are to listen to a good recording, enlist the help of a metronome or to revisit the music score. *Playing a composition slowly once before quitting is one of the most effective preventive measures against inexplicable "bad playing" of that composition later on.* Thus conditioning depends not only on how frequently you practice, but also on what and how you practice. Solid mental play can prevent slumps; at least, you can use it to know that you are in a slump *before* you play. Better yet, you can use mental play to get out of the slump, by adjusting the time when your performance peaks. We all use a certain amount of mental play whether we know it or not. If you do not consciously use mental play, then slumps can come and go, seemingly for no reason, depending on the condition of your mental play. That is why mental play is so important for performers.

Fast vs. Slow Muscles

Understanding the difference between (1) control and speed, and (2) finger strength for technique, is important. *All muscle bundles consist mainly of fast and slow muscles.* The slow muscles provide strength and endurance. The fast muscles are necessary for control and speed. Depending on how you practice, one set grows at the expense of the other. Obviously, when practicing for technique, we want to grow the fast muscles and reduce the slow ones. Therefore, *avoid isometric or strength type exercises. Practice quick movements, and as soon as the work is done, rapidly relax those muscles*. This is why any pianist can outrun a sumo wrestler on the keyboard, even though the wrestler has more muscle. The fast muscles control the basic rapid finger stroke and these muscles are driven by a brain which has also been speeded up; see "speed stroke" in (i) below.

Most of the muscles that move the fingers are in the forearm (Prokop). There are some reports claiming that the most important piano playing muscles are the lumbricals (Jaynes) and the interossei (in the hands), but these are minority views that must await further research to carry any weight. It is clear, however, that "finger strengthening exercises" such as squeezing spring devices sold for this purpose, are bad for technique, especially speed.

The research on "piano muscles" and brain speed are woefully inadequate. Because those who designed exercises in the past had little idea or research results on what the exercises need to achieve, most of those exercises are only marginally helpful, and how useful they were depended more on how you used them than their original design. For example, the main objective behind most exercises was to develop finger strength, which is wrong. Another concept was that the more difficult the exercise, the more advanced technique you learned. This is obviously not true; the only truth is that if you are advanced, you can play difficult material. Some of the simplest exercises (as we shall see) can teach the most advanced techniques, and that is the kind of exercise that is most useful.

b.   Parallel Set Exercises for Intrinsic Technical Development

For exercises to be useful, they must be able to identify weaknesses and then strengthen those skills. *We need a complete set of exercises, and they must be arranged in some logical order so that an exercise that addresses a particular need can be quickly located.* I propose that the concept of parallel play provides the framework for devising a universal set of exercises. *Parallel sets (PSs) are groups of notes that can be played simultaneously, like a chord.* Any arbitrary musical passage can be constructed from combinations of PSs. Of course, PSs alone do not comprise a complete set of exercises; conjunctions, repetitions, jumps, stretching, etc., are also needed, and are addressed below. Apparently, Louis Plaidy taught exercises resembling PS exercises in the late 1800s.

All the PS exercises are HS exercises. However, you can practice them HT also, and in any combination, even 2 notes against 3, etc. At first, try a few of each exercise, then read section (c) on how to use them. There is no need to practice PSs by themselves because, if expanded, there will be an infinite number (as they should be, if they are complete), so you will never practice them all. You will never need all of them either, and probably over half are redundant. Use these exercises only when needed (*all the time!*), so that the only requirement at this point is that you become familiar with them so that you can instantly call upon a specific, required exercise when the need arises – no more wasting of time doing unnecessary exercises! Once the problem is solved using a particular exercise, there is no need to keep repeating it, because you have acquired the desired skill. *PS exercises should not be practiced every day like Hanon exercises; they are to be used for diagnosing difficulties and correcting them.*

PS exercises are designed to test your technique. A beginner with no technique should fail all of them. Most students will initially have no idea how to play them correctly. It would be very helpful if someone could demonstrate a few for you if you had never done them before. I will make videos available as soon as I find the time. Intermediate students with 2 to 5 years of lessons should be able to play over half of them satisfactorily. Thus these exercises provide a means for measuring your progress. This is total technique development and therefore involves tone control and musical playing. Advanced students will still need them but, unlike developing students, they will need them only briefly, often for just a few seconds of practice and experimentation.

Exercise #1. This exercise teaches the basic motion that is needed for all following exercises. *Play one note,* for example, finger 1, e.g. thumb of RH, as four repetitions: 1111. In this exercise, we are learning how to repeat one "thing" rapidly; later, we will replace the "thing" with a PS so that we can save time by playing as many PSs as possible in a short time. Remember, one reason for practicing exercises is to save time. This repetition motion is needed in most PS exercises.

Play the 1111 as quadruplets ("quads") of equal strength, or as one measure of a 4/4 or a 2/4 time signature. ***The idea is to play them as fast as possible, up to speeds of over one quad per second, with complete relaxation.*** When you can play a quad to your satisfaction, try two: 1111,1111. The comma represents a pause of any arbitrary length, which should be shortened as you progress. Then string three, then four quads in rapid succession: 1111,1111,1111,1111. You "pass" this exercise at about one quad per second, 4 quads in succession, with only a brief pause between quads. Play them softly, relaxed, and not staccato, as explained in more detail below. If you pass the 4-quad test, you should be able to play the quads as long and as fast you want, with control and without fatigue. This seemingly trivial motion is much more important than appears at first sight because it is the basis for all velocity motions, as will become apparent when we come to PSs involving many fingers such as those in fast Alberti accompaniments or tremolos. That is why we devote so many paragraphs below to this exercise.

The thumb has four major ways to move down; the other fingers have three. **The first motion is finger motion**: with the hand motionless, you can press the keys with only finger motion, mainly by pivoting each finger at the knuckle (the "thumb knuckle" is at the wrist). **The second motion is wrist motion**: with the forearm motionless and rigid fingers, you can press a key with wrist motion only. **The third motion is arm motion.** With the fingers and wrist rigid, you can lower the finger by moving the entire forearm down. This motion originates at the shoulder. **The fourth motion, which applies mostly to the thumb, is forearm rotation.** Practice each of these motions separately, eliminating all stress. First, practice each slowly, with large, exaggerated motion. Then increase speed by decreasing the motion. You can further increase speed by combining the motions, because when you combine them, you need even smaller individual motions to accomplish the same key drop.

Let's try this whole routine with the thumb as an example. In all of the following, stretch the thumb out comfortably; do not tuck it under the hand. (1) Thumb finger motion: Use only thumb motion to play the quad, moving it as far up and down as you can. Hand, arm, etc., do not move. Because of the large motion, you can play at only about one note per second (don't worry if your speed is different, because each person can have very different numbers – same comment applies to other numbers discussed below). Let's also assume that your maximum thumb motion is about 10 cm. Now move the thumb only 5 cm – you can play faster! Then try 3 cm, and so on, until the smallest motion that will still play the note. As you speed it up, stress will start to build – this is your maximum speed. There is no need to practice faster at this time. (2) Wrist motion: play the thumb by keeping the thumb rigid and pivoting the hand up and down at the wrist. The maximum motion will be about 10 cm, and as you decrease this motion, you will be able to increase the speed. The maximum speed with which you can play with wrist motion without stress should be about the same as for thumb motion alone. Now combing motions (1) and (2); you should be able to play faster than the maximum of either motion. (3) Arm motion: keep thumb and wrist fixed and play the thumb by only moving the arm up and down. Start by lifting the thumb about 10 cm, and increase speed by decreasing this distance. You can reduce stress with a thrust motion of the arm with each quad, because this makes use of different muscles for each downstroke. You can also raise the wrist with each quad and further reduce stress. (4) Forearm rotation: now keep everything rigid and play the thumb by only rotating the forearm. Again, rotate the thumb up about 10 cm and play the note. Increase speed by reducing this distance. In principle, you should be able to combine all four motions, and even the arm thrust and raised wrist, to play the fastest motion humanly possible. Combining so many motions is very difficult; practice it by combining them in pairs. Some may decide to depend mostly on one motion, and add just a little of the others.

Every part of the body must be involved: fingers, hand, arm, shoulder, etc., not only the fingers. This does not mean that every part must move by a visible amount - they may appear stationary, but must participate. A large part of the "involvement" will be conscious relaxation because the brain tends to use too many muscles for even the simplest tasks. Try to isolate only the necessary muscles for each motion and relax all others. The final motion may give the appearance that only the finger is moving. From more than several feet away, few people will notice a 1 mm movement; if each part of the body moved less than one mm, the sum of those motions can easily add up to the several mm needed for the key drop, even without finger movement.

As the repetition speed increases, the fingers/hands/arms will automatically go into positions that are ideal; PSs will make sure of that. These positions will resemble those of famous pianists playing at a concert -- after all, that is why they can play it. Therefore it is important, when attending concerts, to bring your opera glass and watch the details of the motions of professional pianists. To the untrained observer, a concert pianist may seem to be doing nothing unusual, but if you know the hand motions as explained here, you will see them executed beautifully.

Beginners, in their first year, may not be able to play at one quad per second. Do not force yourself to practice at speeds you cannot handle without stress. However, periodic, brief, excursions into your fastest playing are necessary for exploration purposes. Even students with over five years of lessons will find some of the following exercises difficult. Those practicing PSs for the first time should practice exercise #1 for a while, then practice #2 (below); if #2 becomes problematic at certain speeds (fatigue, stress), those problems can be solved by practicing #1 again (try it; you will find out what I mean). Then briefly examine the other exercises, but there is no need to do them all now, because there will be plenty of chances to practice them as the need arises when practicing with real music later on.

Practice Exercise #1 until all stress disappears and you can feel gravity pulling the arm down. As soon as stress builds up, you will not be able to feel the gravitational pull. Don't try too many quads at once if you begin to lose control. Don't keep practicing with stress because playing with stress can quickly become a habit. As stress builds up, the quads will start to slow down; therefore, the slowing down is a sign of stress – it is time to switch hands. Get one quad down well before adding another. The reason for stopping at four quads is that, once you can do four, you can usually do a large number in succession. However, *exactly* how many are needed, before you can play an indefinite number in succession, depends on the individual. If, after stringing two quads together, you can then play the quads indefinitely at any speed, then you have passed the test for Exercise #1, and don't have to practice it again.

For the first few days of practice, there should be some improvements *during* practice because you are rapidly learning new motions and eliminating wrong ones. In order to make further progress, use the post practice improvement (PPI), because muscle/nerve growth throughout your body and brain will eventually be required. For PPI, instead of pushing for speed *during* practice, wait for the hand to automatically develop quickness so that you play faster the *next time* you practice; this can happen when you switch hands, or when you practice the next day.

This is technique acquisition, not muscle building. ***Technique means making music and these exercises are valuable for developing musical playing.*** Do not bang away, like a jack hammer. If you can't control the tone of one note, how can you control it with more? One key trick in controlling tone is to practice softly. By playing softly you get yourself out of the mode of practice in which you totally ignore the nature of the sound and bang away, just trying to achieve the repetitions. Press down on the key completely and hold it down momentarily (very short -- a fraction of a second). ***Read section III.1 (basic keystroke)*** *which is mandatory reading before you do any serious PS exercises.*

In order to increase speed and accuracy, and to control the tone, *keep the playing finger near the key as much as possible.* If the finger does not touch the key once in a while, you lose control. Do not rest the finger on the key all the time, but touch the key as lightly as you can so that you know where it is. This will give an added feel for where all the other keys are, and when it comes time to play them, the fingers will find the right keys more accurately. *Determine the minimum key lift needed for repetition and practice playing with as little key lift as possible.* The key lift is larger for uprights than grands. Faster speeds are achieved with smaller key lifts.

Experiment with controlling the tone using finger sliding: try the pull motion or thrust motion. Sliding increases control because you are creating a small key drop using a larger motion. The result is that any errors in the motion will be decreased by the ratio of key drop to total motion, which is always less than one. Therefore, you can play more uniform and softer quads by sliding than by coming straight down. Sliding also simplifies the finger motion because the finger does not have to come straight down -- any motion with a downward component will do, which increases your options. The thumb may be the easiest finger to slide. *Play with the tip of the thumb, not the joint;* this will enable the thumb to slide and the wrist to be raised, thus reducing the chances of the other fingers accidentally hitting some keys. Playing with the tip also increases the effective range and speed of the thumb movement; that is, for the same thumb movement, the tip moves farther and faster than the joint. Knowing how to slide the fingers will let you play with confidence even when the keys are slippery or if they get wet from perspiration. *Do not develop a dependence on the friction of the key surface to play the notes because it will not always be there for you.* Playing with a raised wrist will cause the fingers to slide towards you during the key drop. With a low wrist, the fingers will tend to slide away from you, especially for fingers 2-5. Practice each of these sliding motions: practice all five fingers with the wrist up for a while; then with the wrist down. At an intermediate wrist height, the fingers will not slide, even if the keys are slippery!

Repeat Exercise #1 with all the fingers, one at a time. Some fingers (typically, 4 and 5) may be slower than the others. This is an example of how to use these exercises as a diagnostic tool to find the weak fingers.

Proper regulation of the piano action and voicing of the hammers is critical to successful execution of these exercises, both for acquiring new skills and for avoiding non-musical playing. This is because it is impossible to produce soft (or powerful, or deep) musical tones with worn hammers and defective actions. You will need expert guidance to avoid acquiring bad habits if you practice on such pianos.

Exercise #2. The *2-finger Parallel Set exercises:* play 23 of the RH on CD as fast as you can, like a grace note. The idea is to play them rapidly, but under complete control. Obviously, the methods of Sections I and II will needed here. For example, if the RH can do one exercise easily, but a related exercise is difficult for the LH, use the RH to teach the LH. Practice with the beat on the 2 as well as with the beat on the 3. When that is satisfactory, play one quad as in exercise #1: 23,23,23,23. If you have difficulty with accelerating a 23 PS quad, play the two notes together as a "chord" and practice the chord quad exactly as you did the single note quad in exercise #1. Again, bring the quad up to speed, about a quad per second. Then increase the number of quads until you can string 4 quads in succession. Repeat the entire exercise with each of 12, 34 and 45. Then come down: 54, 43, etc. *All the comments about how to practice for exercise #1 apply.*

In this and subsequent exercises, the comments in preceding exercises almost always apply to succeeding exercises and will not generally be repeated. Also, I will list only representative members of a family of exercises and leave it to the reader to figure out all the other members of the family. The total number of exercises is much larger than you would initially think. Furthermore, if the different PS exercises are combined HT, the number of possibilities quickly becomes mind boggling. For beginners who have difficulty playing HT, these exercises may provide the best ways to practice HT play.

One objective of PSs is to teach the brain the concept of extreme velocity, up to almost infinity. Once the brain gets used to a certain maximum velocity, all slower velocities become easier to execute. Perform all the exercises initially using only the white keys. Once all the white key exercises are done, work on similar exercises including the black keys.

In the beginning, you may be able to play the 2 notes in succession very fast, but without much independent control. *You can initially "cheat" and increase speed by "phase-locking" the two fingers, e.g., holding the two fingers in a fixed position (locked phase, 3 slightly higher than 2) and simply lowering the hand to play the two notes.* One easy way to do this is to curl 2 a little more than 3. *The phase angle is the delay between successive fingers in parallel play. Eventually, you must play with finger independence.* The initial phase locking is used only to get up to speed quickly. This is one reason why some teachers do not teach parallel play, because they think that parallel play means phase locking, which is bad technique. One reason for this problem is that after phase locked play, both fingers stay on their keys and the two notes overlap. It is as important to lift the finger at some precise time as it is to lower it. For independent finger playing, the first finger must rise just as the second finger plays so that successive notes are clearly separated. Therefore, the ability to play 23 quads rapidly is not enough. What takes time to develop is the independent control of each finger.

Once you can play fast PSs relaxed, slow down and work on playing each note more correctly. Beginners will have difficulty lifting the fingers at the right time to control the note duration. In that case, either wait for technique to develop further, or practice the lifting exercises of section (d) below.

Exercise #3. *Larger PSs*: e.g., 123 and its family, 234, etc. Repeat all of the procedures as in exercise #2. Then work with the 1234 group, and finally, the 12345 sets. With these large sets, you may have to slow down the quad repetition speed slightly. *The number of possible exercises for these larger sets is very large.* The beat can be on any note and you can start on any note. For example, 123 can be practiced as 231 and 312. When coming down, the 321 can be played 213 or 132; - all six are distinct because you will find that some are easy but some are difficult. If you include the beat variations, there are 18 exercises for just three fingers on white keys.

Exercise #4. *Expanded PSs:* start with the 2-note sets 13, 24, etc. (the 3rds group). These sets also include the 14 (fourths), and 15(fifth and octave), type groups. Then there are the 3-note expanded PSs: 125, 135, 145 (fifth and octave) groups. Here, there are several choices for the middle note. Then there are the expanded sets played with 12: thirds, fourths, fifths, etc.; these can also be played using 13, etc.

Exercise #5. *The compound PSs:* 1.3,2.4, where 1.3 represents an interval, i.e., CE played simultaneously. Then do the 1.4,2.5 group. I have often found sets that are easy going up but difficult coming down, or vice versa. For example, 1.3,2.4 is easier for me than 2.4,1.3. *These compound sets will require quite a bit of skill.* Unless you have had at least several years of lessons, do not expect to be able to play these with any proficiency.

This is the end of the repetitive quad exercises based on exercise #1. In principle, Exercises #1 to #5 are the only exercises you need because they can be used to construct the PSs we discuss below. Exercises #6 and #7 are too complex to be repeated in rapid quads.

Exercise #6. *Complex PSs:* these are best practiced individually instead of as rapid quads. In most cases, they should be broken up into simpler PSs that can be practiced as quads; at least, initially. "Alternating sets" are of the type 1324, and "mixed sets" are of the type 1342, 13452, etc., mixtures of alternating and normal sets. Clearly, there is a large number of these. ***Most of the complex PSs that are technically important can be found in Bach's lesson pieces, especially his 2-part Inventions,*** see section III.20. This is why Bach's lesson pieces (by contrast to Hanon) are some of the best practice pieces for acquiring technique.

    Exercise #7. Now practice ***connected PSs***; e.g., 1212, that contain one or more conjunctions. This can be either a trill (CDCD) or a run (CDEF, use thumb over). ***Now these sets cannot be played infinitely fast because the speed is limited by your ability to connect the PSs.*** The objective here is still speed -- how fast you can play them accurately and relaxed, and how many of them you can string together. This is an exercise for learning how to play conjunctions. These can be practiced by "adding overlapping PSs": practice 12, then 21, then 121, then 1212. Play as many notes as possible during one motion of the hand. For example, practice playing 1212 in one down motion of the hand.

    Connected PSs are the main practice elements in Bach's 2-part Inventions. Therefore, look into these Inventions for some of the most inventive and technically important connected PSs. ***As explained in section III.19.c, it is often difficult for students to memorize certain Bach compositions and to play them beyond a certain speed***. This has limited the popularity of playing Bach, and limited the use of this most valuable resource for acquiring technique. ***However, when analyzed in terms of PSs and practiced according to the methods of this book, Bach's compositions can become quite simple to learn.*** Therefore, this book should greatly increase the popularity of playing Bach.

    The nearly infinite number of PS exercises needed demonstrates how woefully inadequate the older exercises are (e.g., Hanon - I will use Hanon as a generic representative of what is considered the "wrong" type of exercise here; I don't mean to keep picking on Hanon because it *can* help your technique). There is one advantage of the Hanon type exercises, however, which is that they start with the most commonly encountered fingerings and the easiest exercises; i.e., they are nicely prioritized. However, chances are nearly 100% that they will be of little help when you hit a difficult passage in an arbitrary piece of music. The PS concept allows us to identify the simplest possible series of exercises that form a more complete set that will apply to practically anything that you might encounter. As soon as these exercises become slightly complex, their number becomes enormous. By the time you get to the complexity of even the simplest Hanon exercise, the number of possible PS exercises becomes intractably large. Even Hanon recognized this inadequacy and suggested variations such as practicing the exercises in all possible transpositions. This certainly helps, but still lacks whole categories such as Exercises #1 and #2 (the most fundamental and useful ones), or the incredible speeds anyone can readily achieve with PS exercises.

    It is easy to bring Hanon up to ridiculous speeds by using the methods of this book. Try that just for the fun of it -- you will quickly find yourself asking, "What am I doing this for?" Even those ridiculous speeds cannot approach what you can readily achieve with PSs because every Hanon exercise contains at least one conjunction and therefore cannot be played infinitely fast. ***This is clearly the biggest advantage of PS exercises: there is no speed limit in theory as well as in practice, and therefore allows you to explore speed in its entire range*** .

    As one illustration of the usefulness of these exercises, suppose that you want to practice a four-finger compound trill based on exercise #5 (e.g., C.E,D.F,C.E,D.F, . . .). By following the exercises in order from #1 to #7, you now have a step-by-step recipe for diagnosing your difficulties and acquiring this skill. First, make sure that your 2-note intervals are even by applying exercises #1 and #2 (12 & 34). Then try 1.3,2 and then 1.3,4. When these are satisfactory, try 1.3,2.4. Then work on the reverse: 2.4,1 and 2.4,3, and finally 2.4,1.3. The rest should be obvious if you have read this far. These can be rough workouts, so remember to change hands frequently, before fatigue sets in.

It is re-emphasized here that there is no place in the methods of this book for mindless repetitive exercises. Such exercises have another insidious disadvantage. Many pianists use them to "limber up" and get into great playing condition. This can give the wrong impression that the wonderful playing condition was a consequence of the mindless exercises. It is not; the limbered up playing condition is the same regardless of method. Therefore, the pitfalls of mindless exercises can be avoided by using more beneficial ways of limbering up. Scales are useful for loosening the fingers and arpeggios are useful for loosening the wrists. And they are useful for learning some very basic skills, as we saw in section (5) above.

    c.   **How To Use The Parallel Set Exercises** (Beethoven's Appassionata, 3rd Movement)

    PS exercises are not intended to replace the Hanon, Czerny, etc., or any type of exercise. The philosophy of this book is that time can be better spent practicing "real" music than "exercise" music. The PS exercises were introduced because there is no known faster way to acquire technique. Thus, technical pieces like Liszt's and Chopin's etudes or Bach's Inventions are not "exercise music" in this sense. *The PS exercises are to be used in the following ways:*

    (i) *For diagnostic purposes:* going through these exercises systematically will reveal your strengths and weaknesses. More importantly, for practicing a passage you cannot play, PSs provide a method for identifying the problem. In hindsight, it seems obvious that any effort to improve some technical aspect will require a diagnostic tool. Otherwise it is like going to a hospital for an operation without knowing the cause of the malady. According to this medical analogy, practicing Hanon is like going to the hospital to get the same "universal" checkups/treatments every day regardless of whether the patient is seriously ill or healthy – the correct approach is a good diagnosis and targeted treatment only when the person is sick; moreover, once cured, there is no need to keep taking the same medication.

    (ii) *For acquiring technique:* the weaknesses found in (i) can now be corrected using the same exercises that diagnosed them. In principle, these exercises never end, because the upper limit of speed/technique is open ended. However, in all practicality, they end at speeds of around one quad per second because few, if any, music requires higher speeds. This demonstrates the beauty of these exercises in enabling practice speeds that are faster than needed, thus providing that extra margin of safety and control.

    Procedures (i) and (ii) will solve many problems in playing difficult material. Several successful applications to previously "impossible" situations will generate the confidence that nothing is unconquerable, within reason. As an example, consider one of the most difficult passages of the third movement of Beethoven's Appassionata, bar 63, the LH accompaniment to the climactic RH run, and similar, ensuing passages. Listen to recordings carefully, and you will find that even the most famous pianists have difficulty with this LH and tend to start it slowly and then accelerate it, or even simplify the score. This accompaniment consists of the compound PSs 2.3,1.5 and 1.5,2.3, where 1.5 is an octave. Acquiring the required technique simply boils down to perfecting these PSs and then joining them. For most people, one of the above two PSs will be difficult, and that is the one you need to conquer. Trying to learn this by playing it slowly and accelerating it HT would take much longer to learn and brings no guarantee of success, because it becomes a race between success and building a speed wall. Instead, practice HS and change hands frequently to avoid stress and fatigue. Also, practice it softly in the beginning in order to learn to relax.

In summary, the parallel set exercises comprise one of the main pillars of the methods of this book. They are one of the reasons for the claim that nothing is too difficult to play if you know how to practice. They serve both as diagnostic tools and as technique development tools. Practically all technique should be acquired using PSs during HS practice to bring up the speed, to learn to relax, and to gain control. They form a complete set of necessary tools. Unlike Hanon, etc., they can be immediately summoned to help when you hit *any* difficult passage and they allow practice at any speed, including speeds higher than anything you will ever need. They are ideal for practicing to play without stress and with tone control. In particular it is important to get into the habits of sliding the fingers over the keys and feeling the keys before playing them. Sliding the fingers (caressing the keys) provides tone control and feeling the keys improves accuracy. Without breaking up a difficult passage into simple PSs, it is impossible to incorporate these extra refinements into your playing. We now move on to other useful exercises.

d.   Scales, Arpeggios, Finger Independence and Finger Lifting Exercises

Scales and arpeggios must be practiced diligently. They are not in the class of mindless repetitive exercises because of the numerous necessary techniques that are most quickly acquired using them (such as thumb over, flat finger positions, feeling the keys, velocity, PSs, glissando motion, tone/color, how to reverse directions, supple wrist, etc.). Scales and arpeggios must be practiced HS; practicing them HT all the time will place them in the same category as Hanon. Two exceptions to this "no HT rule" are: (A) when you are using them for warm-ups (before recitals, etc.), and (B) when practicing to make sure that the two hands can be synchronized accurately. Learning to play them well is very difficult and you will certainly need PSs, see sections III.4.b and III.5 for more details.

The finger independence and lifting (see below) exercises are performed by first pressing all five fingers down, e.g., from C to G using the RH. Then play each finger three to five times: CCCCDDDDEEEEFFFFGGGG. While one finger is playing, the others must be kept down. Do not press down firmly as this is a form of stress, and will cause fatigue very quickly. Also, you don't want to grow any more slow muscles than is necessary. All the depressed keys must be completely down, but the fingers are resting on them with only enough downward force to keep the keys down. The gravitational weight of the hand should be enough. Beginners may find this exercise difficult in the beginning because the non-playing fingers tend to collapse from their optimum positions or lift involuntarily, especially if they begin to tire. If they tend to collapse, try a few times and then switch hands or quit; do not keep practicing in the collapsed position. Then try again after a rest. One variation of this exercise is to spread out the notes over an octave. This type of exercise was already in use during F. Liszt's time (Moscheles). They should be done using the curled as well as all the flat finger positions.

For the finger independence exercise, try to increase the speed. Note the similarity to PS exercise #1, section (b). For general technique development, exercise #1 is superior to this one. The main objective of exercise #1 was speed; the emphasis here is different -- it is for finger independence. Some piano teachers recommend doing this exercise once during every practice session, once you can play it satisfactorily. Until you can play it satisfactorily, you may want to practice it several times at every practice session. Practicing it many times at once and then neglecting it in subsequent sessions will not work.

All the practice methods and exercises discussed in this book deal mostly with the muscles used to press the key down (flexors). It is possible for those muscles to become far more developed than the ones used to lift the fingers (extensors), especially for those who practice loud all the time and never develop the art of playing fast, thus causing control problems. Eventually, the flexors can end up overpowering the extensors. Therefore, it is a good idea to exercise the relevant extensors by performing lifting exercises. The flat finger positions are valuable for exercising the extensors for lifting the fingers and, at the same time, relaxing the extensors near the fingertips. These two extensors use different muscles.

For finger lifting exercises, repeat the above exercise, but lift each finger as high as you can, quickly and immediately down. The motion should be as fast as you can, but slow enough that you have complete control; this is not a speed contest, you just have to avoid growing the slow muscles. Again, keep all the other fingers down with minimal pressure. As usual, it is important to reduce stress in the fingers that are not being lifted. Practice rapid relaxation immediately after a hard lift.

Everyone has problems with lifting the 4th finger. There is a mistaken belief by many that we must be able to lift the 4th finger as high as all the others and therefore they expend an inordinate amount of effort trying to achieve this. Such efforts have been proven to be futile and even harmful. This is because the anatomy of the 4th finger does not allow it to be lifted beyond a certain point. The only requirement on the 4th finger is not to depress a key inadvertently, which can be met with only a small amount of lift. Therefore you can play at all times with the 4th finger barely off the keys or even touching them. Practicing difficult passages with inordinate effort at lifting this finger higher can cause stress in fingers 3 and 5. It is more productive to learn to play with less stress as long as the 4th finger is not interfering in any way. The exercise for lifting the 4th finger independently is performed as follows. Press all fingers down, CDEFG, as before. Then play 1,4,1,4,1,4, . ., with the accent on 1 and lifting 4 as quickly and as high as you can. Then repeat with 2,4,2,4,2,4, . . . Then 3,4, then 5,4. You can also do this exercise with 4 on a black key.

Both the finger independence and lifting exercises can be performed without a piano, on any flat surface. This is the best time to practice relaxing the extensor muscles of the last two phalanges (the nail phalange and middle phalange) of fingers 2 to 5; see section III.4.b for more details. During the entire exercise, those two phalanges for all the fingers should be completely relaxed, even for the finger being lifted.

e.   **Playing (Wide) Chords, Finger/Palm Spreading Exercises**

In section II.10 the gravity drop was used to improve chord accuracy. However, if there is still unevenness after using the gravity drop, then there is a fundamental problem that must be diagnosed and treated using the PS exercises. Chords become uneven when the control over individual fingers is uneven. Let's take an example. Suppose that you are playing a LH C.E interval against a G in octave 3. The C3.E3 and G3 are played with the fingers 5.3 and 1, a series of 5.3,1,5.3,1,5.3,1, etc. Let's further assume that there is an interval problem with the 5.3. These two fingers do not land simultaneously. The way to diagnose this problem is to try the 5,3 PS, and then test 3,5. If you have a problem, chances are that you have more of a problem with one than the other, or both. Typically, 3,5 is more difficult than 5,3 because of the bone structure in the forearm. Work on the problematic PS(s). Once you can play both PSs well, the interval should come out better. There is a smaller possibility that the problem lies in the 5,1 or 3,1 PSs, so if the 5,3 did not work, try these.

The hand has two sets of muscles that spread the fingers/palm to reach wide chords. One set mainly opens the palm and the other mainly spreads the fingers apart. When stretching the hand to play wide chords, use mainly the set of muscles that open the palm. The feeling is that of spreading the palm but with free fingers; i.e., spread the knuckles apart instead of the fingertips. The second set of muscles simply spread the fingers apart. This spreading helps to widen the palm but it interferes with the finger movement because it tends to lock the fingers to the palm. *Cultivate the habit of using the palm muscles separately from the finger muscles.* This will reduce both stress and fatigue when playing chords, and improve control. Of course, it is easiest to use both sets of muscles simultaneously, but it is useful to know that there are 2 sets of muscles when planning exercises and for deciding how to play chords.

Finger spreading: In order to test whether the fingers are fully stretched, open the palm to its maximum and spread the fingers for maximum reach; do this on a flat surface with the wrist touching the surface. If the pinky and thumb form a almost straight line, the fingers will not stretch any more. If they form a "V", then the reach can be expanded by performing spreading exercises. Another way to test this alignment is to place the palm on a table top at the edge of the table with the thumb and pinky down the edge, so that only fingers 2, 3, and 4 are resting on the table top. *If the thumb and pinky form a triangle with the edge of the table, the stretch can be expanded.* It is possible to "cheat" by raising the wrist, but this results in an awkward position and a smaller reach. Perform a spreading exercise by pushing the hand towards the table edge so as to spread the thumb and pinky apart. You can save some time by stretching one hand using the top edge of the piano while practicing HS with the other.

Palm spreading: *It is more important, but more difficult, to stretch the palm instead of the fingers.* One way is to place the right palm over the left palm, right arm pointing left and left arm pointing right, with the hands in front of the chest. In this position, thumb meets pinky; interlock the thumbs and pinkies so that fingers 2,3,4 are on the palm side and 1,5 protrude on the back side of palm. Then push the hands towards each other so that thumbs and pinkies push each other back, thus spreading the palm. This is illustrated in the photo III.7a. Also, exercise the palm and finger spreading muscles while simultaneously applying the pushing force. This is not an isometric exercise, so the stretching motions should be quick and short. This ability to quickly stretch and immediately relax is important for relaxation. Regular stretching when young can make a considerable difference in the reach when you get older, and periodic maintenance will prevent the reach from decreasing with age. The webbings between fingers can be stretched by jamming them against each other using the two hands. For example, to stretch the webbings between fingers 2 and 3, spread those 2 fingers on both hands to form Vs. Then jam the vertices of the 2 Vs against each other. For maximum effectiveness, use the palm and finger spreading muscles to stretch the palm with every jamming motion. Again, don't perform these like isometric exercises but use quick motions. Most people have a slightly larger left hand, and some can reach more by using fingers 1,4 than 1,5.

When playing wide chords, the thumb should be curved slightly inwards, not fully stretched out. For those who have thumbs that can bend backwards, pay attention to this thumb position for maximum stretch; if you form the habit of bending the thumb all the way backwards, this habit will be almost impossible to reverse and make TO difficult. It is counter-intuitive that, by bending the thumb in, you can reach further; this happens because of the particular curvature of the thumb's fingertip. When playing chords, the hand must move to those chord positions, and these motions must be very accurate if the chords are to come out right. This is the "jump" motion discussed below; you will need to develop proper jump motions as well as a habit of feeling the keys in order to execute chord play. You can't just raise the hand high above the keys, position all the fingers in the right position, smash them down, and expect to hit all the correct notes exactly at the same instant. Great pianists often appear to do that, but as we shall see below, they are not. Therefore, until you have perfected the jump movement and are able to feel the keys, any problems with playing chords may not be caused by lack of reach or finger control. It is now time to study how to execute jumps.

f.   Practicing Jumps

Many students watch famous pianists make quick, wide jumps and wonder why they can't do jumps themselves, no matter how hard they practice. These great pianists appear to jump effortlessly, playing notes or chords accurately from position to position no matter where they are. In reality, they are making several motions that are too fast for the eye to see unless you know what to look for. Students with no jump training tend to move the hand along an inverted V motion. With this type of motion, it is difficult to hit a note or chord accurately because the hand is coming down at some arbitrary angle. This angle is never the same because it depends on the distance of jump, the tempo, how high the hand was lifted, etc. Coming down at an angle increases the possibility of missing the correct location, and the keys are played by a sideways motion instead of straight down. Fast jumps are impossible because you can never get there in time.

Jumps consist of two principal motions: (1) a horizontal translation of the hand to the correct position and (2) the actual downward motion to play. In addition, there are two optional motions: feeling the keys and the take-off motion. The combined motion should look more like an inverted "U" than an inverted "V". This inverted U has short legs and a flat top. *The first skill to practice is to make the horizontal motion as fast as possible so as to reserve enough time to locate the keys after the hand reaches its destination.* Locate the keys by feeling them before the actual playing. Feeling the keys is optional because it is not always necessary and sometimes, there is not enough time for it. When this combination of motions is perfected, it looks as if it is done in one motion.

Feeling the keys can be done surprisingly quickly. There is usually plenty of time to do this. *Therefore, it is a good policy to always feel the keys when practicing jumps slowly.* When all the skills listed here are perfected, there will be enough time to feel the keys even at the final speed. There are a few instances in which there is no time to feel the keys, and those few can be played accurately if you had located most of the other jumps accurately by feeling them.

Another component of the jump is the take-off. Get into the habit of making quick takeoffs regardless of the speed of the jump. There is nothing wrong with getting there way ahead of time. Even when practicing slowly, you should practice quick takeoffs so that the skill will be there when you speed up. Start the take-off with a small downward and sideways kick of the wrist; unlike the downward motion at the end, the take-off does not have to be straight up and it can be combined with the rapid horizontal travel. Obviously, the entire jump procedure is designed for the hand to arrive at the destination quickly, accurately, and reproducibly so that there is plenty of time to play straight down and feel the keys.

The most important motion to practice once you know the components of a jump is to accelerate the horizontal travel. You will be surprised at how fast the hand can move horizontally. You may be amazed at how much faster you can move with only a few days of practice -- something some students never achieve in a lifetime because they were never taught to practice it. *This horizontal speed is what provides that extra time needed to ensure 100% accuracy and to effortlessly incorporate all the other components of the jump.* Practice feeling the keys whenever possible so that it becomes second nature and you can find the keys without looking at your hands. Once it is smoothly incorporated into your play, the audience will not notice that you are feeling the keys because it is done in a fraction of a second. Like an accomplished magician, the hands will move faster than the eye can see.

Now that you know the components of a jump, look for them when you watch concert pianists performing. You should now be able to identify each component, and you may be amazed at how often they feel the keys before striking them and how they can execute these components in the blink of an eye. These skills will also enable you to play, and even make long jumps, without looking at the hands.

The best way to practice fast horizontal motions is to do it away from the piano. Sit down with the elbow straight down, forearm pointing forward, fingers spread out in horizontal plane or in piano playing position. ***Quickly move the hand sideways, parallel to the floor, as in a jump motion.*** Move the hand rapidly away from you and stop, then immediately relax; the shoulder does not move. Then move rapidly back to its original position. Practice these out and in motions, as fast as you can, but completely relaxing after each motion. *Do not* try to learn these motions in one day, although from day one, you should see immediate improvements in your jumps if you had never done this before. The most significant improvements will have to await post practice improvement, so it is futile to try to accomplish it in one day.

As you learn to accelerate the horizontal motion, jumps will immediately become easier. ***In order to reduce stress, relax all muscles as soon as the horizontal motion is over, and as soon as the notes are played.***. A good piece to practice the jump for the LH is the 4th variation in Mozart's famous Sonata in A, #16 (K300). This variation has large jumps in which the LH crosses over the RH. One popular piece you can use to practice RH jumps is the 1st movement of Beethoven's Pathetique Sonata (Opus 13), right after the LH octave tremolos, where the RH makes jumps crossing over the LH. A more challenging passage to practice is in Chopin's Ballade Op. 23, at the end, the LH jumps in the first half of the "Presto con fuoco".

Practice accelerating the horizontal motion by playing at a slow tempo, but moving horizontally as quickly as you can, stopping over the correct position, feeling the keys and waiting before playing. Feeling the notes will guarantee 100% accuracy. The idea here is to establish a habit of always getting to the destination ahead of time. Once the quick horizontal motion is satisfactory, speed up the tempo by reducing the waiting time before playing the notes. Then gradually combine all four jump components into one smooth motion. Now your jump looks like that of those great pianists you envied! Better yet, jumps aren't that difficult or scary, after all.

g.   Stretching and Other Exercises

Most stretching exercises for the large muscles of the body are helpful (see Bruser). To stretch the flexor muscles (for the fingers): with the palm of one hand, push the fingers of the other hand back towards the top of the forearm (for photos, see Prokop, P. 75). People have very different flexibility and some will be able to push the fingers back so that the fingernails will touch the arm (180 degrees from the straight forward position!), while others may be able to push back only about 90 degrees (fingers pointing up with the forearm horizontal). The ability of the flexor muscles to stretch decreases with age; therefore, it is a good idea to stretch them frequently throughout life in order to preserve their flexibility. For stretching the extensor muscles, press the back of the fingers towards the bottom of the forearm. You might perform these stretching exercises just before "playing cold".

There are numerous exercises in Sandor and Fink. These are interesting because each exercise is chosen to demonstrate a particular hand motion. In addition, the motions are often illustrated using passages taken from classic compositions by famous composers.

h.   Problems with Hanon Exercises

Since about 1900, Charles Louis Hanon's (1820-1900) exercises have been used by numerous pianists in the hopes of improving technique. There are now two schools of thought: those who think that the Hanon exercises are helpful and those who think they are a waste of time. There is one "reason" some people give for using Hanon: that is to warm up the hands before starting practice. I suspect that this habit grew out of having learned Hanon early in the person's piano career, and that this same person would not be using Hanon if s/he were not so habituated.

I used Hanon exercises extensively in my youth but I am now firmly in the anti-Hanon school. Below, I list some reasons why. Czerny, Cramer-Bulow, and related lesson pieces share many of these disadvantages. ***Hanon is possibly the prime example of how intuitive methods can suck entire populations of pianists into using methods that are essentially useless, or even harmful.***

(i) ***Hanon makes some surprising claims in his introduction with no rationale, explanation or experimental evidence. This is exemplified in his title, "The Virtuoso Pianist, in 60 Exercises".*** His introduction shows that he simply felt that these are useful exercises and so wrote them down, a prime example of the "intuitive approach". ***Most advanced teachers reading this introduction would conclude that this approach to acquiring technique is amateurish and would not work.*** Hanon implies that the ability to play these exercises will ensure that you can play anything -- this is not only totally false, but also reveals a surprising lack of understanding of what technique is. ***Technique can only be acquired by learning many compositions from many composers.*** There is no question that there are many accomplished pianists who use Hanon exercises. However, ***all advanced pianists agree that Hanon is not for acquiring technique,*** but might be useful for warming up or keeping the hands in good playing condition. There are many better pieces for warming up than Hanon, such as etudes, numerous Bach compositions, scales, and arps. The skills needed to play any significant piece of music are incredibly diverse - almost infinite in number. ***To think that technique can be reduced to 60 exercises reveals the naiveté of Hanon and any student who believes that is being misled.***

(ii) ***All 60 are almost entirely two-hand exercises***, in which the two hands play the same notes an octave apart, plus a few contrary motion exercises in which the hands move in opposite directions. ***This locked HT motion is one of the greatest limitations of Hanon's exercises because the better hand cannot practice skills more advanced than the weaker hand.*** At slow speed, neither hand gets much workout. At maximum speed, the slow hand is stressed while the better hand is playing relaxed. ***Because technique is acquired mostly when playing relaxed, the weaker hand develops bad habits and the stronger hand gets stronger.*** The best way to strengthen the weaker hand is to practice that hand only, *not* by playing HT. In fact, the best way to learn Hanon is to separate the hands as recommended in this book, but Hanon seems to have been unaware of that. To think that by playing HT, the weaker hand will catch up to the stronger hand, reveals a surprising ignorance for someone with so much teaching experience. This is what I meant by "amateurish" above; more examples below. Locking the two hands does help to learn how to coordinate the hands, but does nothing to teach independent control of each hand. In practically all music, the two hands play different parts. Hanon doesn't give us any chance to practice that. Bach's Inventions are much better and (if you practice HS) will really strengthen the weaker hand. ***Hanon is very limited; it teaches only a fraction of the total technique.***

(iii) ***There is no provision for resting a fatigued hand. This leads to stress and injury.*** A diligent student who fights the pain and fatigue in an effort to carry out Hanon's instructions will almost surely build up stress, acquire bad habits, and risk injury. ***The concept of relaxation is never even mentioned.*** Piano is an art for producing beauty; it is not a macho demonstration of how much punishment your hands, ears, and brain can take. ***Dedicated students often end up using Hanon as a way of performing intense exercises in the mistaken belief that piano is like weight lifting and that "no pain, no gain" applies to piano.*** Such exercises might be performed up to the limit of human endurance, even until some pain is felt. This reveals a lack of proper education about what is needed to acquire technique. The wasted resources due to such misconceptions can mean the difference between success and failure for a large number of students, even if they don't suffer injury. Of course, many students who routinely practice Hanon do succeed; in that case, they work so hard that they succeed *in spite* of Hanon.

(iv) ***The Hanon exercises are devoid of music so that students can end up practicing like robots.*** It does not require a musical genius to compile a Hanon type of exercises. The joy of piano comes from the one-on-one conversations with the greatest geniuses that ever lived, when you play their compositions. For too many years, Hanon has taught the wrong message that technique and music can be learned separately. Bach excels in this respect; his music exercises both the hands and the mind. ***Hanon probably excerpted most his material from Bach's famous Toccata and Fugue, modified so that each unit is almost self cycling. The remainder was probably also taken from Bach's works, especially the Inventions and Sinfonias.***

(v) ***Many pianists use Hanon as warm-up exercises. This conditions the hands so that it becomes impossible to play "cold", something any accomplished pianist should be able to do, within reasonable limits.*** Since the hands are cold for at most 10 to 20 minutes, "warming up" robs the student of this precious, tiny, window of opportunity to practice playing cold. Those who use Hanon for warm-ups can be misled into thinking that it is Hanon that is making their fingers fly, while in reality, after any good practice session, the fingers will be flying, with or without Hanon. It is unfortunate that the Hanon type of thinking has bred a large population of students who think that only Mozart can just sit down and play, and that the rest of us are not supposed to perform such "magical feats". In order to be able to "play on demand", start by quitting Hanon exercises.

(vi) ***Some technique can be acquired using Hanon. But Hanon gives no instructions on how to acquire technique.*** If students used their "Hanon time" to practice real music, they would acquire a lot more technique. Who wouldn't rather play Mozart, Bach, Chopin, etc., than Hanon with better results and build a repertoire they can perform? Hanon cannot help if you get stuck at a difficult passage in another composition; it does not provide any diagnostics for telling you why you can't play a given passage. The PS exercises provide both diagnostics and solutions for most situations.

(vii) ***What little advice he does dispense, have <u>all</u> been shown to be wrong!*** So let's look into them:

(A) He recommends "lifting the fingers high", an obvious no-no for fast playing, since that will be the biggest source of stress. I have never seen a famous pianist in concert lift the fingers high to play a fast run; in fact, I have never seen *anyone* do that! Hanon's advice has misled students into thinking that piano should be played by lifting the finger and plonking it down. It is true that the extensor muscles are often neglected, but there are exercises for treating this problem directly.

(B) He recommends continuous practicing of both hands, as if piano technique is some kind of weight lifting exercise. Students must never practice with fatigued hands. This is why the HS method of this book works so well.

(C) He recommends playing his exercises every day, but once any skill is acquired, it doesn't need to be reacquired over and over. Once all 60 pieces are learned, every hour that Hanon is repeated is a wasted hour -- what will we gain?

(D) He is apparently aware of only the thumb under method, whereas the thumb over method is more important at faster speeds.

(E) In most of the exercises, he recommends fixed wrists which is only partially correct. His recommendation reveals a lack of understanding of what "quiet hands" means.

(F) There is no way to practice a majority of the important hand motions, although there are a few wrist exercises for repetitions. His format of locked 2-hand practice limits the options for practicing different hand motions.

(viii) *The Hanon exercises do not allow for practicing at the kinds of speeds possible with the PS exercises.* Without the use of such speeds, certain fast speeds cannot be practiced and there is no possibility of practicing "over-technique" (more technique than necessary to play that passage - a necessary safety margin for performances).

(ix) *Hanon wastes time.* The student ends up with insufficient time to develop their repertoire or acquire real technique. A person who has 2 hrs to practice every day, playing Hanon for 1 hr as recommended, would waste half of his piano lifetime! A person who has 8 hours to practice, on the other hand, doesn't *need* Hanon. All the editions I have seen print out the entire runs, whereas all you need are at most 2 bars ascending and 2 bars descending and the final ending bar. Although the number of trees cut down to print Hanon is negligible in the broader picture, this reveals the mentality behind these exercises of simply repeating the intuitively "obvious" without really understanding what you are doing, or even pointing out the important elements in each exercise. "*Repetition is more important than the underlying technical concepts" -- this is probably the worst mentality that has hindered students most in the history of piano*; we now know that this mentality evolved because of a lack of knowledge concerning practice methods.

(x) *Teachers can be classified into two types according to whether they teach Hanon or not.* Those who do not teach Hanon tend to be more knowledgeable because they know the real methods for acquiring technique and are busy teaching them -- there is no time left for Hanon. Thus if you are looking for a piano teacher, choose from among those that do not teach Hanon, and you will increase the chances of finding a superior one.

i.   Practicing for Speed

Piano playing is all about exquisite finger control. As we increase speed, such control becomes progressively difficult because human hands were not created for such speeds. However, the hands are complex and adaptable, and we know from history that such fast playing is possible.

Speed Stroke, Relaxation

It seems obvious that fast keystroke motion is the key to fast play, yet it is often not taught. The single most important concept for speed is finger motion at the knuckle joint. Every finger has 3 bones. The knuckle joint is the joint between finger and palm. For the thumb, the knuckle joint is very close to the wrist. In speed play, consider each finger as a unit and simply move it at the knuckle joint. This motion has innumerable advantages. It uses only one finger-moving muscle which is also the fastest muscle. Moving the finger at the knuckle is especially important for the thumb. You can't play anything fast if the thumb can't keep up with the other fingers. Involving any other finger-bending muscle would complicate the motion, creating nerve-impulse delays that start all the way from the brain. This is the explanation of why TU doesn't work for fast play – in TU, the other 2 thumb joints must bend, which is a slower motion. This also explains why flat finger positions are faster than curled positions. Thus when playing fast, don't concentrate on the fingertips, but use the feeling that the fingers are moving at the knuckles. Motion at the knuckle is also most conducive to relaxation -- in speed play, rapid relaxation becomes more important.

The 3 components of the basic keystroke (1.a above) must now be accelerated. The downstroke must be as fast as possible. The hold is important because you must instantly relax during the hold, yet not lift the finger so that the backcheck is not prematurely released. Then the lift stroke must come at exactly the correct time, and likewise accelerated. In section (7.a), we saw that all muscle bundles consist of fast and slow muscles; therefore, we need to develop fast muscles and fast nerve responses when practicing for speed, and reduce the amount of slow muscles. Practicing with all your strength for hours will be counterproductive. Playing faster doesn't usually work either, because it only makes it harder to practice any of these stroke components. It also means that speed is going to take some time to develop because of the need to grow the necessary cells in the brain, muscles, and nerves. It is important to learn the speed motions. Don't lean into the piano in order to keep all the notes down, because that will grow slow muscles -- carefully control the finger pressure when "playing deeply for good tone". Practice each stroke component separately, then assemble them after they are all accelerated. This means practicing each note slowly, but executing each component rapidly. If you play lots of notes rapidly, you may *never* get it right.

The simplest way to practice the speed stroke is to play the 5 notes, C-G, in succession, carefully practicing each stroke component. For the downstroke, practice the motion as rapidly as you can, yet retain the ability to control the loudness, and to keep a steady residual pressure for the hold component, and immediately relaxing. This is similar to the basic keystroke except that everything must now be accelerated. During the transition to the hold, practice immediate relaxation while maintaining enough pressure to hold the backcheck in place. Then rapidly raise the finger for the lift component at the same time that the next finger executes the downstroke. All the non-playing fingers should be touching the key tops, not waving high above the keys. It may be easier to first practice the notes in pairs, 121212 . . ., then 232323. . . ., etc. Play at one or two notes per second initially, and speed up gradually. Exaggerate the lift stroke because the extensor muscles are too weak for most people and need extra workout. Involve the whole body while staying relaxed; the feeling is that each note originates from the bottom of the stomach. For these exercises, the objective is quick strokes, not how fast you can play successive notes.

Fast play cannot be accomplished by learning one skill; it is a combination of many skills, and that is another reason why it takes time to learn. Speed is like a chain, and the maximum speed is limited by the weakest link in the chain. As the speed is increased, it becomes obvious that the basic keystroke must be abbreviated in order to play beyond a certain speed. The first change is to discard the hold which only wastes time. There must be an instant of relaxation between the downstroke and lift. Bad habits often creep in when practicing for speed. Some students might "simplify" the motion by keeping all extensor muscles tense (lifting all fingers) and playing fast by overpowering them with the flexors. That is clearly one way to create stress and build a speed wall because opposing muscles are fighting each other.

Other Speed Methods

Now, add all the other motions that lead to speed. We consider several *general* speed motions here; there are additional *particular* tricks for practically every difficult fast passage. This is why exercises such as Hanon are so harmful – they deprive students from learning these particular tricks, by misleading them into thinking that learning Hanon will solve all general and particular problems. An example of a particular speed trick is the unusual fingering of the RH starting at bar 20 of the 3rd movement of Beethoven's Appassionata (actually, there are several possible fingerings). Here are a few general methods that apply to broad classes of applications.

The parallel sets teach all the fingers to move simultaneously so that successive notes can be played much more rapidly than the speed of each finger. But without first establishing a solid basic keystroke, the parallel sets can end up teaching numerous bad habits resulting in sloppiness. **Flat finger positions** can be faster than curled positions because they avoid curl paralysis and the fingertips of extended fingers can move faster than the tips of curled fingers. Also, by relaxing the last two phalanges at the fingertips, the motion is simplified.

Speed is the second most difficult skill to acquire, after musicality. The most common intuitive misunderstanding is that you need to practice playing fast in order to acquire speed. Experienced teachers know the futility of such a simplistic approach and have tried to devise methods for acquiring speed. One common approach has been to discourage students from playing fast -- this approach will at least prevent all kinds of potentially irreversible problems: psychological, physical, musical, technical, etc., but does not address the speed problem directly and can slow down the learning process unnecessarily.

The mistaken notion that you must build piano muscles in order to play fast has led many to practice louder than they need to. Speed is skill, not strength. Difficult passages tend to cause stress and fatigue during practice. Playing softly reduces both, thereby accelerating technique acquisition. Students who play loud are masking their lack of technique with loudness, and growing slow muscles at the expense of fast muscles. Good tone is produced by "pressing deeply" into the piano. However, you must also relax. Do not keep pushing down after the notes are played. This **constant down pressure not only wastes energy (causing fatigue) but also prevents the fingers from moving rapidly**. *Rhythm* is important for speed. Rhythm involves not only the music as played by the fingertips, but also the entire body, so that one part does not move against another. *Balance* is another important factor. Not only the balance of your body on the bench, but also the center of gravity of each playing hand and of the two hands. **Speed alone does not mean success.** Speed, without proper technique, will ruin the music. Therefore, music is the criterion for acquiring speed -- in order to acquire speed, we must play musically. We can play fast, but only up to speeds at which we can maintain musicality. This is why it is so important to play your finished pieces – *don't always practice new difficult material and ignore the finished pieces*. These are the pieces that can be played at full speed, with relaxation, and allow you to practice speed.

Speed Walls

What are speed walls (SW), how are they created, how many are there, and how are they overcome? There is always a maximum speed that you can play. When first learning a piece, this speed is often below the final speed. If practiced incorrectly, the speed does not increase beyond a certain value no matter how hard you practice – this is called a speed wall. SWs are caused mainly by stress and bad habits, and are therefore erected by the pianists. There are as many SWs as bad habits, so there can be an unlimited number of them. Clearly, the best way to avoid them is not to create them in the first place. *HS practice is one of the best weapons against SWs because most SWs are HT SWs.* Outlining is another effective weapon because it allows the large motions to be correctly played at final speed, thus avoiding the SWs in these motions. Quiet hands is also helpful for similar reasons. Parallel sets are useful because you immediately start at speeds above the speed wall, and come down in speed. Relaxation is essential at all times, but especially necessary for avoiding SWs because stress is a major cause. Any method for increasing the efficiency of motion helps; thus mixing flat finger and curled positions, keeping the fingers on the keys, and the various hand motions, such as glissando, cartwheel, arm rotation, flick, wrist motion, etc., are all needed to prevent SWs. Musical play is not possible at SWs because any SW will be audible; thus in principle, if you always practice musically, you will never meet a SW. Clearly, practically every recommended practice method in this book is aimed at preventing speed walls.

What if you already have a SW – can you get rid of it? The best solutions are not to play it, or only playing it slowly, for weeks or months and learning something new during that time. Learning new things is a good way to erase old memories. Properly designed HS, PS practice with relaxation might work. Early detection of SWs is the key to removing them successfully – this is why we need to know all about SWs. Students who used intuitive methods for a long time will have many speed walls that are so well established that they are nearly impossible to tear down. The best solution is to abandon those pieces for a year or more, learn new pieces, and come back to them when your technique has improved by a significant amount.

In conclusion, speed can't be acquired by forcing the fingers to play faster than they can at their technical level because you will lose relaxation, develop bad habits and erect speed walls. Speed is a combination of many skills. The basic keystroke must be maintained even at high speed. The best way to stay within your technical limitation is to play musically. Use PSs, cycling, etc., briefly to increase speed with less attention to musicality, but make that an exception, not the rule. Therefore, even repetitive cycling for long periods must be practiced musically. Making music frees you from the speed demon and leads you into that magical realm of the wonderful sound of the piano.

8. Outlining (Beethoven's Sonata #1)

Outlining is a method for accelerating the learning process by simplifying the music. It allows you to maintain the musical flow or rhythm, and to do this at the final speed almost immediately. This enables you to practice musically long before that segment can be played satisfactorily or at speed. *It helps you to acquire difficult technique quickly by teaching the larger playing members (arms, shoulders) how to move correctly; when this is accomplished, the smaller members often fall into place more easily.* It also eliminates many pitfalls for timing and musical interpretation errors. The simplifications are accomplished by using various devices, such as deleting "less important notes" or combining a series of notes into a chord. You then get back to the original music by progressively restoring the simplified notes. Whiteside has a good description of outlining on P.141 of the first book, and P.54-61, 105-107, and 191-196 of the second book, where several examples are analyzed.

For a given passage, there are many ways to simply the score, and a person using outlining for the first time will need some practice before s/he can take full advantage of the method. It is obviously easiest to learn outlining under the guidance of a teacher. The idea behind outlining is that, by getting to the music first, the technique will follow more quickly because music and technique are inseparable. In practice, it requires a lot of work before outlining can become useful. Unlike HS practice, etc., it cannot be learned so easily. Use it only when absolutely necessary (where other methods have failed). It can be helpful when you find it difficult to play HT after completing the HS work. Outlining can also be used to increase the precision and improve the memorizing.

I will demonstrate two very simple outlining examples. Common methods of simplification are (1) deleting notes, (2) converting runs, etc., into chords, and (3) converting complex passages into simpler ones. An important rule is: although the music is simplified, retain the same fingering that was required before the simplification.

Chopin's music often employs tempo rubato and other devices that require exquisite control and coordination of the two hands. In his Fantaisie Impromptu (Op. 66), the six notes of each LH arpeggio (e.g., C#3G#3C#4E4C#4G#3) can be simplified to two notes (C#3E4, played with 51). There should be no need to simplify the RH. This is a good way to make sure that all notes from the two hands that fall on the same beat are played accurately together. Also, for students having difficulty with the 3-4 timing, this simplification will allow play at any speed with the difficulty removed. By first increasing the speed in this way, it may be easier to pick up the 3-4 timing later, especially if you cycle just half a bar.

The second application is to Beethoven's Sonata #1 (Op. 2, No. 1). I noted in the Reference that Gieseking was remiss in dismissing the 4th movement as "presenting no new problems" in spite of the difficult LH arpeggio which is very fast. Let's try to complete the wonderful job Gieseking did in getting us started on this Sonata by making sure that we can play this exciting final movement.

The initial 4 triplets of the LH can be learned by using parallel set exercises applied to each triplet and then cycling. Parallel set exercise #1 is useful here (play the triplets as chords) and practice relaxing. The first triplet in the 3rd bar can be practiced in the same way, with the 524524 . . . fingering. Here, I have inserted a false conjunction to permit continuous 524 cycling, in order to work on the weak 4th finger. When the 4th finger becomes strong and under control, add the real conjunction, 5241. Here, TO is required. Then practice the descending arpeggio, 5241235. Practice the ensuing ascending arpeggio using the same methods, but be careful not to use TU in the ascending arpeggio as this is easy to do. Remember the need for supple wrists for all arpeggios. For the RH, you can use the rules for practicing chords and jumps (sections 7.e and 7.f above). So far, everything is HS work.

In order to play HT, use outlining. Simplify the LH and play only the beat notes (starting with the 2nd bar): F3F3F3F3F2E2F2F3, with fingering 55515551, which can be continually cycled.

These are the first notes of each triplet. When this is mastered HS, you can start HT. Once this HT becomes comfortable, adding the triplets will be easier, and you can do it with much less chance of incorporating mistakes. Since these arpeggios are the most challenging parts of this movement, by outlining them, you can now practice the entire movement at any speed.

In the RH, the first 3 chords are soft, and the second 3 are forte. In the beginning, practice mainly accuracy and speed, so practice all 6 chords softly until this section is mastered. Then add the forte. To avoid hitting wrong notes, get into the habit of feeling the notes of the chords before depressing them. For the RH octave melody of bars 33-35, be sure not to play with any crescendo, especially the last G. And the entire Sonata, of course, is played without pedal. In order to eliminate any chance of a disastrous ending, be sure to play the last 4 notes of this movement with the LH, bringing it into position well before it is needed.

For technique acquisition, the other methods of this book are usually more effective than outlining which, even when it works, can be time consuming. However, as in the Sonata example above, a simple outlining can enable you to practice an entire movement at speed, including most of the musical considerations. In the meantime, you can use the other methods of this book to acquire the technique needed to "fill in" the outlining.

9. Polishing a Piece - Eliminating Flubs

There are 5 things we want to accomplish when polishing a "finished" piece: ensure good memory, eliminate flubs, make music, further develop technique, and prepare for performances. *The first step is to ensure memory and we saw in III.6 that the best way is to play the entire piece in your mind, away from the piano.* Mental play (MP) guarantees that the memory is practically infallible. If some parts are slightly shaky, you can work on them at any time, even away from the piano. MP is the most secure memory because it is pure mental memory: it is not dependent on aural, tactile, or visual stimuli. It also eliminates most flubs because flubs originate in the brain. Let's look at a few common causes of flubs. Blackouts occur because of too much dependence on hand memory. Stuttering is a habit formed by stopping at every mistake while practicing HT without sufficient HS practice. You hit wrong notes because the hands are not always feeling the keys and you lose track of where the keys are. Missing notes result from lack of relaxation and inadvertent lifting of the hands -- a habit that is usually acquired from too much slow HT practice. We have discussed solutions that eliminate all these sources of mistakes. Finally, playing musically and bringing out the "color" of the composition is the ultimate task in polishing. You can't just play the notes accurately and expect music and color to magically appear -- you must actively create them in your mind before playing the notes – MP allows you to do all this. If the fingers can't reproduce these mental images, perhaps the piece is too difficult. You will develop technique faster by practicing pieces that you can polish to perfection. However, don't give up too easily because the cause of the difficulty may not lie with you but with some other factor, such as the quality or condition of the piano.

A large part of polishing is attention to detail. The best way to ensure correct expression is to go back to the music and review every expression mark, staccato, rest, notes that are held down, lifting of the finger or pedal, etc. These will give you the most accurate picture of the logical construct of the music that is needed to bring out the proper expressions. The weaknesses of each individual are different, and are often not evident to that individual. A person whose timing is off usually cannot hear the incorrect timing. *This is where teachers play key roles in detecting these weaknesses.*

Making music is the most important part of polishing a piece. Some teachers emphasize this point by saying that you use 10% of your time learning technique and 90% of the time learning to make music. Most students use over 90% of their time struggling with technique in the mistaken belief that practicing what you can't play will develop technique. This mistake arises from the intuitive logic that if you practice anything you can't play, you should eventually be able to play it. But this is true only for material that is within your skill level. For material that is too difficult, you never know what is going to happen, and frequently such an attempt will lead to irreversible problems such as stress and speed walls. For example, if you want to increase speed, the fastest way is to play easy pieces that you have polished and to speed up that play. Once the finger speed increases, then you are ready to play more difficult material at faster speed. ***Thus the polishing time is also the best time for technical development, and it can be a lot of fun.***

Perfecting your performance skills is part of polishing; this will be discussed in section 14 below. Many pianists experience the following strange phenomenon. There are times when they can do no wrong and can play their hearts out with no mistakes or difficulties. At other times, any piece becomes difficult and they make mistakes where they normally have no problems. What causes these ups and downs? Not knowing which one you will experience can be a terrifying thought that can cause nervousness. Obviously, there are many factors, such as FPD and judicious use of slow play, etc. However, the most important factor is mental play (MP). All pianists use some MP whether they consciously do it or not. The performance often hinges on the quality of that MP. Unless you conduct MP consciously, you never know what condition it is in. For example, practicing a new piece will confuse the MP of another piece. This is why it is so important to know what MP is, establish good MP, and know when to review/maintain it. If your MP had deteriorated for some reason, reviewing it before a performance will alert you to the impending danger and give you a chance to repair the damage.

A common problem is that students are always learning new pieces with no time to polish pieces. This happens mostly to students using the intuitive learning methods. It takes such a long time to learn each piece that there is no time to polish them before you have to start another piece. The solution, of course, is better learning methods.

In summary, ***solid mental play is the first requisite for polishing a piece and preparing it for performances.*** Advanced technique is acquired not only by practicing new skills, but also by playing finished pieces. In fact practicing new skills all the time is counter productive and will lead to speed walls, stress, and non-musical play.

10. Cold Hands, Slippery (Dry/Sweaty) Fingers, Illness, Hand Injury (Carpal Tunnel), Ear Damage (Tinnitus)

Cold Hands: Cold, stiff, hands, on a cold day, is a common affliction caused mainly by the body's natural reaction to cold. A few people suffer from pathological problems that may need medical attention. But the majority of cases are natural body reactions to hypothermia. In that case, the body withdraws blood, mostly from the extremities, towards the center of the body in order to conserve heat. The fingers are most susceptible to this cooling, followed by the hands and feet.

For such cases, the solution is, in principle, simple. You need to raise the body temperature. In practice, it is often not that easy. In a cold room, even raising the body temperature so high (with extra clothing) that you feel too warm does not always eliminate the problem. Clearly, any method of conserving heat should help. ***Of course, it is best if you can raise the room temperature. If not, common aids are: (1) soaking the hands/arms in warm water, (2) use of a room heater, such as a portable radiant heater (about 1KW) that you can aim directly at the body, (3) thick socks, sweaters, or thermal underwear, and (4) gloves without fingers (so you can play the piano with the gloves on).*** If you just want to keep the hands warm before playing, mittens are better than gloves. Hair dryers do not have sufficient power, are not designed to be used for more than about 10 minutes without overheating dangerously, and are too noisy for creating warm air around a pianist.

It is not clear whether it is better to stay warm all the time or only when practicing piano. If you keep warm all the time (such as by wearing thermal clothing), the body may not detect hypothermia and therefore will maintain the desired blood flow. On the other hand, the body may become more sensitive to cold and eventually develop cold hands even when the body is warm, if the room is cold. For example, if you wear the gloves without fingers all the time, the hands may become accustomed to this warmth and feel very cold when you take them off. And the warming effect of these gloves may wear off once the hands get accustomed to them. Therefore, it is best to wear them only when practicing or just before practicing. The counter argument is that wearing them all the time will allow you to play piano at any time, without warm-ups or having to soak the hands in warm water. Clearly, this is a complex problem and wearing gloves does not always solve the problem and can make it worse.

The playing muscles are in the arms, so if you want to warm up the piano muscles, it is more important to warm the forearms/elbows than the fingers. In fact, every muscle from the forearms all the way to the center of the body is involved in piano play. Therefore, if you are using warm water to heat the hands before a performance, try to soak the forearms, especially the upper half (near the elbows) where the flexor and extensor muscles are concentrated. If this is not possible, then you have to soak the hands long enough so that the warm blood can flow from the hands into the arms. The interossei and lumbricals are in the hand, so these need to be warmed also.

Cold fingers of this type are clearly the body's reaction to cool temperature. *The best solution might be to soak the hands several times a day in very cold water to acclimate them to cold temperatures. Then they may not react to cold at all. This might provide a permanent solution.* For example, you might cool them this way right after practice so that it does not interfere with the practice. The objective of the cooling is to get the skin acclimated to cold temperatures. Dip in cold water for no more than 5 to 10 seconds; do not cool the entire hand down to the bone. In fact what you might do is to first warm the hands in warm water, and then cool only the skin in ice cold water. Such a treatment should feel good, without any cold shock or pain. This is exactly the principle behind the Nordic practice of jumping into an opening in a frozen lake after a hot sauna. This seemingly masochistic practice is actually completely painless and has beneficial consequences, such as acclimating the skin to cold temperatures and stopping perspiration that would otherwise cause the clothes to become soggy and freeze up in the extreme cold. In fact, without jumping into cold water, a person with clothes wet from perspiration after a sauna could freeze to death! The pores in the skin can be closed by dipping the hands into cold water after warming, thus preventing perspiration and retaining heat in the hands.

Slippery (Dry/Sweaty) Fingers: When the fingers are overly dry or wet, they may become slippery. Too much washing using strong detergents can cause the hands to become dry. Application of most quality moisturizing lotions such as Eucerin will solve this problem. In order to avoid smearing the piano keys with excess lotion, apply in small amounts and wait until the lotion is completely absorbed into the skin before applying more. Several small applications will last longer than a single large amount. Wipe off any excess before playing the piano. People who tend to perspire while playing must also be careful about slippery fingers. If you initially apply a lotion because the hands were dry, but you begin to perspire while playing, you can get into terrible problems with slipperiness if the fingers have excess lotion. Therefore, if you tend to perspire, be careful about using any kind of lotion. Even without any lotion, wet or dry fingers can be slippery. In that case, practice using thrust and pull motions so that you can control the finger positions more accurately. These motions require some slippage of the fingers over the keys and are therefore more compatible with slippery fingers.

Illness: *Some people might think that a harmless illness, such as a cold, might still allow them to practice piano. After all, there is nothing to do while resting with a cold and piano is not considered strenuous work. That is a bad idea.* It is particularly important for parents to understand that playing the piano involves significant exertion, especially of the brain, and not treat piano as a relaxing pastime when illness strikes. Thus youngsters with even mild colds should not be made to practice piano, unless the child is willing to do so on her/is own. There is much more brain activity

148

during piano play than most people realize. Infections do not affect the whole body equally; they usually settle opportunistically in stressed organs. If the person is running a fever and then plays the piano, there will be some risk of brain damage. Fortunately, most people lose the urge to practice the piano even when only mildly sick, and this is a clear signal that you should not practice.

Whether one can play piano when sick is an individual matter. To play or not is quite clear to the pianist; most people will feel the stress of piano playing even before the symptoms of the illness become clear. Thus it is probably safe to leave the decision to practice or not, to the pianist. *It is useful to know that, if you feel sudden fatigue or other symptoms that make it difficult to play, it might be an indication that you are coming down with some illness.* The problem with not playing during an illness is that if the illness lasts for more than a week, then the hands will lose a considerable amount of conditioning. Exercises that do not strain the brain, such as scales, arpeggios, and Hanon, might be appropriate in such a situation.

Healthy/Unhealthy Practice: Learning the health consequences of piano practice is important because any activity can be conducted in a healthy or unhealthy way. *Stress-free, psychologically sound approach to piano practice can enhance a person's health whereas practicing without concern for well-being can be unhealthy.* It is important to learn proper breathing so as to avoid hypoxia. Frustrations resulting from an inability to memorize or acquire certain skills must be prevented by learning efficient practice methods. This book discusses methods for avoiding fatigue. Hand injuries are avoidable. Excessive nervousness is bad for health, not only the performance. We must think through, or learn from experience, the correct relationships among students, teachers, parents and the audience. Therefore, by paying attention to health concerns, piano practice can be made into a beneficial activity as effective as proper diet and exercise.

Hand Injuries (Carpal Tunnel, etc.): Hand injury is generally not a major issue for students up to about the intermediate level. For advanced pianists, it is a major issue because the human hand was not made to withstand such extreme use. Injury problems with professional pianists are similar to those of professionals in sports, such as tennis, golf, or football. *Therefore, the limitations from possible injury may be the second most important limitation after availability of time to practice.* It might appear that, because relaxation is an essential component of piano technique, injury should not occur. Unfortunately, the physical requirements of playing at advanced levels are such that (as in sports) injury is likely to occur in spite of well known precautions and other measures that professionals take. Injury tends to occur while practicing to acquire difficult technique. Students who use the methods of this book must be particularly aware of the possibility of injury because they will quickly start practicing material that require high technical skills. Thus is it important to know the common types of injuries and how to avoid them.

Every injury has a cause. Although there are numerous documented accounts of injury and success/failure of cures, definitive information on causes and cures has been elusive. The only general cures mentioned are rest and a gradual return to playing using stress-free methods. I injured the flexor tendons in my left palm by using golf clubs with worn, hard grips although I always wore golf gloves. My hand doctor immediately diagnosed the cause of my pain (a notch in my tendon), but could not tell me how I injured my hand, so he could not really tell me how to cure it. I figured out later that the pressure of the golf grip had created notches in my tendons, and these notches moved up and down in my hand during piano playing; the resulting friction caused inflammation and pain after long piano practice sessions. The doctor showed me how to feel these notches by pressing on the tendon and moving my finger. Now I replace the grips on my clubs frequently and have added pads in my golf glove (cut out from Dr. Scholl's self-stick foot-pads), and my pain problem has been eliminated. However, years of gripping the club too hard (I knew nothing about relaxation in those days) has done permanent damage to my hands so that my fingers are not as independent as I would like them to be.

You can accidentally sprain certain muscles or tendons, especially in the shoulders and back.

These are generally caused by poor alignment of the hands or body, and non-balanced playing. The best approach here is caution -- pianists must be extra cautious and avoid such injuries because they can take years to heal. Stop practicing if you feel any pain. A few days of rest will not harm your technique and may prevent serious injury. Of course, it is best to see a doctor; however, most hand doctors are not familiar with piano injuries.

Fingertips can be injured by playing too hard (loud). This condition can be temporarily alleviated by proper bandaging. *The curled finger position can cause bruising of the fingertips because there is minimum padding between the bone and skin at the tip.* In the curled position, you can also peel the flesh off from under the fingernail if the fingernail is cut too short. Avoid both of these types of injury by using the flat finger position (section III.4b).

Most hand injury is of the repetitive stress injury (RSI) type. *Carpal Tunnel Syndrome (CTS) and tendonitis are common ailments. Anecdotal accounts suggest that surgery usually does not solve the CTS problem and can do more harm than good.* In addition, surgery is irreversible. Fortunately, massage therapists have recently solved the problem of curing CTS. Why massage therapists? Because both pianists and massage therapists use the fingers as their main tools of their professions. Therefore, they both suffer from the same injuries. However, massage therapists are in a better position to experiment and find cures while pianists are not medically trained and have no idea how to even diagnose their ailments. It turns out, fortunately, that pain is felt long before irreversible damage occurs so that the syndrome can be cured if treated as soon as you feel pain. Although pain is usually felt near the wrists, the cause of the pain is not at the wrists but mainly in the arms and neck where large muscles and tendons can exert harmful forces on the tendons running through the transverse ring of tendons at the wrist that bundle all the tendons running to the fingers. This is why treating the wrist may not cure the pain and wrist surgery can aggravate the problem. The group with the most advanced methods for CTS is the SET (Structural Energetic Therapy) massage specialists; they start with cranial and then progress to deep tissue treatments of the relevant areas of the head, arms, and body. Cranial is necessary because it gives the quickest relief and the tissue work alone does not cure the problem. Until you receive treatment, it is hard to believe that the bones of the skull are related to CTS. See the SET site for more details. Although this site is for massage therapists, you can learn what is involved in treating CTS, to what extent it is curable, and how to find the appropriate therapist. There are still few therapists trained in this art, but at the very least, you can contact the experts and discuss your problem. There is a simple test for advanced cases of CTS. Stand in front of a mirror and dangle the arms straight down, completely relaxed, and in their "normal" positions. If the thumbs are closest to the mirror, you are OK. If more knuckles are visible (arms turned inwards), you have more advanced cases of CTS. Also, the body stance should be straight. Practically no one has a perfectly straight stance, and it may also be necessary to straighten any inappropriate stance in order to treat the CTS completely. The asymmetric playing motions of athletes such as golfers and tennis players create asymmetric changes in bone density, bone structure and musculature. *Right handed golfers will have higher bone densities in their right hips; it may be beneficial for RH golfers to practice hitting lefty to reduce asymmetry injuries/problems.*

Stress reduction methods of piano practice, such as Taubman, Alexander, and Feldenkrais, can be effective both for preventing injury, and for recovering from injury. In general, it is best to keep the playing finger (except the thumb) in line with the forearm as much as possible in order to avoid RSI. Of course, the best preventive measure is not to over-practice with stress. The HS method is especially beneficial because stress is minimized and each hand gets to rest before damage can occur. The "no pain, no gain" approach is extremely harmful. Piano playing can require tremendous exertion and energy, but it must never be painful. See the Reference section for some informative web sites on hand injury for pianists.

Ear Damage (Tinnitus, etc.): *Ear damage generally occurs as a function of age; hearing loss can start as early as age 40 and by age 70, most people have lost some hearing.* Hearing loss can occur from over-exposure to loud sounds and can also be caused by infections and other pathological causes. The person may lose hearing in the low frequency or high frequency range. This is often accompanied by tinnitus (ringing sound in the ear). Those who lose hearing in the low frequency range tend to hear a low, roaring or throbbing tinnitus, and those who lose hearing in the high frequency range tend to hear a high pitched whine. Tinnitus may be caused by uncontrollable firing of the hearing nerves in the damaged section of the ear; however, there are many other causes. See the Reference section for information on the internet on hearing damage.

Although severe hearing loss is easily diagnosed by an audiologist, its cause and damage prevention are not well understood. A damaged ear is more easily damaged than a healthy ear. For example, those with mild hearing loss have difficulty hearing conversations, but are extremely sensitive to loud sounds -- even moderately loud sounds that do not bother normal people can be painfully loud because even moderately loud sounds can cause further damage and damage generally causes pain. Ironically, those with hearing loss can be more sensitive to loud sounds; that is why hearing aid technology is so difficult – you can't simply amplify all sounds. Soft sounds must be amplified but loud sounds must be attenuated. There is no method for diagnosing tinnitus except from the comments of the patient. For tests and treatments you need to see an ENT specialist (Ear Nose Throat). For non-pathological cases, damage is generally caused by exposure to loud sounds. Yet a few people exposed to very loud sounds, such as pianists who play every day for hours on concert grands, piano tuners who routinely use "pounding" during tuning, or members of rock bands, may not suffer hearing loss. On the other hand, some, who are exposed to less sound, can lose their hearing, especially with age. Therefore, there is a wide difference in susceptibility to hearing loss. However, *there certainly is a tendency for those exposed to louder sounds to suffer more hearing loss. It is likely that hearing loss by pianists and piano tuners (as well as rock band members, etc., and people who routinely listen to very loud music) is much more widespread than is generally known because most of them go unreported.*

Tinnitus is present in essentially 100% of people 100% of the time, but is so soft in normal people that it cannot be heard unless the person is in a soundproofed room. It may be caused by spontaneous firing of the hearing nerves in the absence of sufficient stimulus. That is, the human hearing mechanism effectively "turns up the amplification" when there is no sound. Totally damaged regions produce no sound because the damage is so severe that they cannot function. Partially damaged regions apparently produce tinnitus because they are sufficiently damaged to detect almost no ambient sound; this silence causes the brain to fire the detectors, or the system develops a leak in the sound signal circuit. These detectors are either piezo-electric material at the base of hairs inside the cochlea, or ion channels opened and closed by molecules associated with the hairs -- there is conflicting literature on this topic. Of course, there are many other causes of tinnitus, and some may even originate in the brain. *Tinnitus is almost always an indication of the onset of hearing loss.*

For those who do not have audible tinnitus, there is probably no need to avoid loud music, within reasonable limits. Thus practicing the piano at any loudness should be harmless up to about age 25. Those who already have tinnitus should avoid exposure to loud piano. However, *tinnitus usually "sneaks up" on you, so that the onset of tinnitus often goes unnoticed until it is too late. Therefore, everybody should receive tinnitus education and wear ear protection after age 40 during piano practice. Ear protection is an abhorrent idea to most pianists but when you consider the consequences (see below), it is definitely worthwhile.* Before wearing protection, do everything possible to reduce sound intensity, such as soundproofing the room (adding carpets to hard floors, etc.), voicing the hammers, and generally practicing softly (even loud passages -- which is a good idea even without possibility of ear damage).

Ear protectors are readily available from hardware stores because many workers using construction or yard equipment need such protection. For pianists, an inexpensive unit will suffice because you need to hear some music. You can also use most of the larger headphones associated with audio systems. Commercial protectors completely surround the ear and provide a better sound barrier. Since protectors available today are not designed for pianists, they don't have a flat frequency response; that is, the sound of the piano is altered. However, the human ear is very good at adapting to different types of sound and you can get used to the new sound very quickly. The piano sound will also be quite different when you take the protection off (as you will need to do once in a while to see what the REAL sound is like). These different sounds can be quite educational for teaching us how much the brain influences what sounds you hear or don't hear and how different persons will interpret the same sounds. *It is worthwhile to try ear protection just to experience these different sounds. For example, you will realize that the piano makes many strange sounds you never noticed before!* The differences in sound are so startling and complex that they cannot be expressed in words. For lower quality pianos, ear protection will result in sound simulating a higher quality instrument because the undesirable high harmonics and extraneous sounds are filtered out.

The brain automatically processes any incoming data, whether you want it to or not. This is, of course, part of what music is -- it is the brain's interpretation of incoming sounds, and most of our reaction to music is automatic. Thus when you wear ear protection, much of this stimulus disappears, and a large amount of the brain's processing power is freed to do other jobs. In particular, you now have more resources to apply to your HS practice. After all, that is why you practice HS, and not HT -- so that you can concentrate more on the difficult task of acquiring technique. Thus you may find that progress is faster HS when wearing ear protection! This is the same principle behind why many pianists close their eyes when they want to play something with high emotional content -- they need all the resources available to produce the high level of emotion. With eyes closed, you eliminate a tremendous amount of information coming into the brain because vision is a two-dimensional, multi-color, moving source of high bandwidth information that must be immediately and automatically interpreted in many complex ways. Therefore, although most audiences admire that a pianist can play with the eyes closed, it is actually easier. *Thus, in the near future, most piano students will probably wear ear protection, just as many athletes and construction workers use helmets today.* It doesn't make any sense for us to spend the last 10, 30, or more years of our lives without hearing – a most important lesson Beethoven taught us.

How does piano sound damage the ear? Clearly, loud sound containing many notes should be most damaging. Thus it is probably not an accident that Beethoven became prematurely deaf. This also cautions us to practice his music with ear damage in mind. The specific type of piano is also important. *Most uprights that do not produce sufficient sound are probably least damaging. Large grands that transfer energy efficiently into the strings with long sustain probably do not cause as much damage as medium quality pianos in which a large amount of energy is imparted into the initial, instantaneous bang associated with the hammer striking the strings.* Although much of this damaging sound energy may not be in the audible range of the ear, we can detect it as an unpleasant or harsh sound. Thus the medium size grands (about 6 ft) may be most damaging. In this regard, the condition of the hammer is important, since a worn hammer can produce a much louder initial bang than a properly voiced hammer. This is why worn hammers cause more string breakage than new or well voiced hammers. With old, hardened hammers, probably most pianos can cause ear damage. *Thus proper voicing of the hammer may be much more important than many people realize, for pianissimo, playing musically, technical development, and protecting the ear.* If you have to close the lid of a grand in order to play softly, or to reduce the sound to a pleasant level, the hammers probably need voicing.

Some of the loudest sounds are produced by those ear phones used to listen to music. Parents should warn their youngsters not to keep turning up the volume, especially if they subscribe to the culture that plays loud music. Some youngsters will fall asleep with their ear phones blasting; this can be very damaging because the damage is cumulative. *It is a bad idea to give gadgets with ear phones to youngsters -- postpone it as long as possible.* However, sooner or later, they will end up with one; in that case, warn them *before* they suffer ear damage.

Except for some special cases of tinnitus (especially those cases in which you can alter the sound by moving your jaws, etc.), there is no cure yet. Large doses of aspirin can cause tinnitus; in that case, stopping its use can sometimes reverse the process. Small amounts of aspirin taken for cardiac purposes (81mg) apparently do not cause tinnitus, and there are some claims in the literature that these small amounts may delay the onset of tinnitus. Loud tinnitus can be extremely debilitating because it cannot be changed and is present all the time, and it only increases with time. Many sufferers have been driven to thoughts of suicide. Although there is no cure, there are remedies, and all indications are that eventually, we should be able to find a cure. There are hearing aids that reduce our perception of tinnitus, for example, by supplying sufficient sound so that the tinnitus is masked or the person is distracted from the tinnitus. Thus for tinnitus suffers, absolute quietness can cause the tinnitus to become annoying.

One of the most annoying traits of hearing loss is not that the ear has lost its sensitivity (frequently, sensitivity tests reveal very little deterioration), but the inability of the person to properly process the sound so as to understand speech. People with normal hearing can understand speech mixed with a large amount of extraneous sound. *Understanding speech is usually the first ability that is lost with onset of hearing loss.* Modern hearing aids can be quite helpful, both by amplifying only those frequencies needed to understand speech and for suppressing sounds that are loud enough to cause damage. *In other words, if your hearing aid just amplifies all sounds, it may cause even more damage.* Another approach to tinnitus is to train the brain to ignore the tinnitus. The brain is amazingly trainable, and part of the reason why tinnitus causes suffering is the inappropriate brain response of the person. *The brain has the ability to either concentrate on the sound, thereby driving you crazy, or to ignore it, in which case you won't hear it unless you are reminded of it.* The best example of this effect is the metronome. Most pianists do not know that if they practice with the metronome too long, the brain will play tricks so that you either do not hear the click at all, or hear it at the wrong time, especially if the metronome click is sharp and loud. This is one reason why modern metronomes have flashing lights. In addition to enabling you to time yourself without the sound, it allows you to check to see if what you hear matches the light flashes. Thus modern treatments of tinnitus start with teaching the patient that others have succeeded in living with it with minimal discomfort. Then the patient receives ear training in such a way as to be able to ignore the tinnitus. Fortunately, the brain is quite adept at learning to ignore a constant sound that is always there.

If you read enough stories about tinnitus suffers, you will probably follow the advice to wear ear protection after age 40, at least when practicing loud passages for long periods of time. At the first hint of tinnitus, it is imperative that you start ear protection procedures because once the tinnitus starts, ear deterioration can proceed rapidly with exposure to loud sounds, with significant deterioration every year. Use of a digital piano and turning the volume down is one solution. Look for an ENT specialist immediately, especially one experienced in tinnitus treatments. Ear protection applies to other members of the household; therefore, if at all possible, isolate the piano room acoustically from the rest of the house. Most quality (glass) doors will be sufficient. There are a few herbs and "natural" medications that claim effectiveness against tinnitus. Most of these do not work, and the ones that seem to benefit some people have dangerous side effects. Although it is true that there are precious few specialists treating tinnitus, the situation is improving and there are many sites on the internet with information on tinnitus, such as The American Tinnitus Association.

11. Sight Reading
"Sight Reading" has been used loosely by many beginner students to mean playing compositions that have not been memorized, by looking at the score. These compositions may have been played before and the melodies may already be familiar. *The correct definition is reading*

unfamiliar music that had not been practiced before, and it is the topic of this section. It means playing unfamiliar music at the correct speed and is a skill that is distinct from the mere ability to figure out the notes in order to learn a new composition. Beginning students should be taught reading first, then memorizing, and then sight reading. At advanced levels, sight reading involves the application of basic music theory, such as chord progressions and harmonies, and interpretation of the music. Here are the basic rules for sight reading (also, see Richman):

(a) ***Keep the eyes on the music; do not look at the keyboard/fingers.*** Glance at the hands occasionally when it is necessary for large jumps. Try to develop a peripheral vision towards the keyboard so that you have some idea of where the hands are while still looking at the score. With peripheral vision, you can keep track of both hands simultaneously. ***Develop a habit of feeling the keys before playing them.*** Although this rule applies whether you are sight reading or not, it becomes critical in sight reading. It also helps to "get there ahead of time" for jumps, see section 7.e and 7.f above; therefore, you should practice the jump maneuvers in conjunction with the sight reading practice.

(b) ***Play through mistakes and make them as inaudible as possible.*** The best way to do this is to make it sound as if you had modified the music -- then the audience does not know whether you made a mistake or changed it. This is why students with basic music theory training have such an advantage in sight reading. Three ways to make mistakes less audible are (i) keep the rhythm intact, (ii) maintain a continuous melody (if you can't read everything, carry the melody and omit the accompaniment), and (iii) practice simplifying those parts that are too complicated to sight read. The first thing that must be done is to eliminate the habits of stopping and backtracking (stuttering), at every mistake. ***The best time to develop the skill of not stopping at every mistake is when you begin your first piano lessons.*** Once the stuttering habit is ingrained, it will take a lot of work to eliminate it. For those with a stuttering habit, the best thing to do is to decide that you will never backtrack again (whether you succeed or not) -- it will slowly go away. Learning to anticipate flubs is a great help, and this will be discussed below. The most powerful tool is the ability to simplify the music. Eliminate ornamentals, fish out the melody from fast runs, etc.

(c) ***Learn all the common musical constructs: Alberti accompaniments, major and minor scales and their fingerings as well as their corresponding arpeggios, common chords and chord transitions, common trills, ornaments, etc.*** When sight reading, you should recognize the constructs and not read the individual notes. Memorize the locations of those very high and very low notes as they appear on the score so that you can find them instantly. Start by memorizing all the octave C's, then fill in the others, beginning with notes closest to the C's.

(d) ***Look ahead of where you are playing; at least one bar ahead, but even more, as you develop the skill at reading the music structure.*** Get to the point where you can read one structure ahead. By looking ahead, you can not only prepare ahead of time but also anticipate flubs before they occur. You can also anticipate fingering problems and can avoid painting yourself into impossible situations. Although fingering suggestions on the music are generally helpful, they are often useless because, although they may be the best fingerings, you may not be able to use them without some practice. Therefore, you should develop your own set of fingerings for sight reading.

(e) "Practice, practice, practice". ***Although sight reading is relatively easy to learn, it must be practiced every day in order to improve. It will take most students from one to two years*** of diligent practice to become good. Because sight reading depends so heavily on recognition of structures, it is closely related to memory. This means that you can lose the sight reading ability if you stop practicing. However, just as with memory, if you become a good sight reader when young, this ability will stay with you all your life. After practicing sight reading, try to play in your mind (section III.6j), some of the common structures that you encountered.

Keep adding to the "tricks of the trade" as you improve. Practice the art of scanning through a composition before sight reading it, in order to get some feel for how difficult it is. Then you can figure out ahead of time how to get around the "impossible" sections. You can even practice it quickly, using a condensed version of the learning tricks (HS, shorten difficult segments, use parallel sets, etc.), just enough to make it sound passable. I have met sight readers who would talk to me about some sections of a new piece for a while, then play through an entire piece with no trouble. I later realized that they were practicing those sections in the few seconds they had while they were distracting me with their "discussions".

Gather several books with easy pieces. Because it is initially easier to practice "sight reading" with familiar pieces, you can use the same compositions to practice sight reading several times, a week or more apart. "Sonatina" books, Mozart's easier sonatas, and books of easy popular songs, are good books for practicing. For the easiest pieces, you might use Beyer, the beginner books listed in III.18c, or the easiest Bach pieces for beginners. Although you can develop a lot of sight reading skills with familiar pieces, you should also practice with pieces that you had never seen before in order to develop true sight reading skills. The most useful skill for help with true sight reading is sight singing, which we now discuss.

12. Learning Relative Pitch and Absolute Pitch (Sight Singing, Composing)

Relative pitch (RP) is the ability to identify a note, given a reference. Absolute pitch (AP), is the ability to identify a note without using a reference note. AP is used here instead of Perfect Pitch, PP, because PP can be confused with pianissimo. The quality of your AP is determined by how accurately you can reproduce a pitch, how quickly you can identify a note, and how many notes you can identify when they are played simultaneously. People with good AP will instantly (within 3-5 seconds) identify 10 notes played simultaneously. The standard test for AP uses 2 pianos; the tester sits at one and the student at the other, and the student tries to repeat the note played by the tester. If there is only one piano, the student names the note played by the tester (do, re, mi . . . . or C, D, E, ...). In the following exercises use CDE first because most theory books use this notation. However, there is nothing wrong with using doremi if that works better for you. *Nobody is born with absolute pitch; it is a learned skill, because the chromatic scale is a human invention - there is no physical relationship between the pitches of the chromatic scale and nature.* The only physical relationship between the chromatic scale and the ear is that both operate on a logarithmic scale in order to accommodate a large frequency range. We know that the ear operates on a logarithmic scale because harmonies have a special meaning and harmonies are ratios and ratios are easiest to manipulate on a logarithmic scale. Thus, although we are not born with AP, we are born to recognize harmonies. The effect of the logarithmic human hearing is that the ear hears a large difference in pitch between 40 and 42.4 Hz (a semitone or 100 cents), but hears almost no difference between 2000Hz and 2002.4 Hz (about 2 cents), for the same difference of 2.4 Hz. The human ear responds to all frequencies within its range and is not calibrated on an absolute scale at birth. This is in contrast to the eye, which responds to color on an absolute scale (everyone sees red as red from birth without any training, and this perception never changes with age) because color detection is achieved using chemical reactions that respond to specific quanta (wavelengths) of light. Some people who can identify certain pitches with specific colors can acquire AP by the color that the sound evokes. They are effectively calibrating the ear to an absolute reference.

Absolute and relative pitch are best learned in very early youth. Babies who cannot understand a single word will respond appropriately to a soothing voice or a lullaby or a scary sound, which demonstrates their readiness for musical training. *The best way for toddlers to acquire AP is to be exposed almost daily to well tuned pianos from birth.* Therefore, every parent who has a piano should keep it tuned and play it with the baby nearby. Then they should test the child from time to time for AP. This test can be performed by playing a note (when the child is not looking) and then asking her/im to find that note on the piano. Of course, you have to first teach the child the piano scale: starting with the C major scale near the middle, and then the fact that all the other notes are related to this scale by octaves. If the child can find it after several tries, s/he has RP; if s/he can find it the first time every time, s/he has AP. The particular temperament to which the piano is tuned (Equal, Well temperament, etc.) is not important; in fact many people with AP know nothing about temperaments and when notes on pianos tuned to different temperaments are played, they have no trouble in identifying the notes because different temperaments change most frequencies by less than 5%, and no one has AP with that kind of accuracy. RP and AP can be acquired later in life but becomes more difficult after age 20 to 30. In fact, *even those with AP will slowly lose it starting around age 20, if it is not maintained.* Many piano schools routinely teach AP to all their students with over 90% success. The problem with teaching a group of older students is that there is always a certain percentage of "pitch deprived" students who had never been trained in pitch and who will have difficulty learning even RP. Instructions on how to teach AP to very young children are given in 16.b below because they are trivially simple and are an integral part of teaching the very young; instructions for adults are given in this section, below.

Having AP is clearly an advantage. It is a great help for memorizing, sight reading, recovering from blackouts, and composing music. You can be the pitch pipe for your choir, and easily tune string or wind instruments. It is a lot of fun because you can tell how fast a car is going by listening to the tires whine, you can tell the differences between different car horns and locomotive whistles, especially by noting whether they use thirds or fifths. You can remember telephone numbers easily by their tones. However, there are disadvantages. Music played off tune can be annoying. Since so much music is played off tune, this can present quite a problem. The person can sometimes react strongly to such music; physical reactions such as teary eyes or clammy skin can occur and out-of-tune pianos can become especially difficult to play. Transposed music is OK because every note is still correct. *AP is a mixed blessing.*

There is a method that makes learning RP and AP quick and easy! This method is not generally taught at music schools or in the literature, although it has been used by those with AP (usually without their explicit knowledge of how they acquired it), since the beginning of music. With the method described here, the pitch skills become simple by-products of the memory process. You expend little extra effort to acquire pitch recognition because memorizing is necessary anyway, as explained in III.6. In that section we saw that the final objective of memorizing is to be able to play the music in your mind (mental play, MP). It turns out that, by paying attention to RP and AP during the process of practicing MP, you naturally acquire the pitch skills! *Thus, you do not only play music in your mind, but you must always play it at the correct pitch.* This makes perfect sense because, without playing at the correct pitch, you lose so many of the benefits of MP. Conversely, MP will not work well unless it is done in AP, because MP is a memory function, and memory is associative and AP is one of the most important associations – AP is what gives music its true melodic lines, color, expression, etc. For most, memorizing two significant compositions is sufficient to acquire AP to within a semitone, which is faster than any known method being taught today; for most, this should take a few weeks to a few months. Young children will accomplish this with zero effort, almost automatically (see 16.b below); as you grow older, you will need more effort because of all the confusing sounds that are already in memory.

Two useful compositions for practicing RP and AP are Bach's Invention #1 and Beethoven's Moonlight Sonata, 1st Movement. The Bach gives you middle C (its first note) and the C Major scale; these are the most useful note and scale to learn in AP. The Moonlight has compelling melodies that make the memorizing process easy and enjoyable. Yet the complex chord transitions provide a variety of notes and intervals and the complexity prevents you from guessing the notes -- you need a considerable amount of practice and repetition before you can play it in your mind perfectly. It is also technically simple enough for everybody. Both compositions should be practiced HS for pitch practice initially, and HT later on.

When creating notes in your mind, do not try to hum or sing them because the dynamic range of the piano is larger than your singing range and you need to train the mind to deal with these higher and lower notes. Also, the memory of each note for AP must include everything -- the harmonics, timbre, etc., of your piano -- you need as many memory associations as possible. Therefore, use the same piano until you feel that you have AP. Unless you have an electronic piano, make sure that the piano is in tune. Once you acquire a strong AP, it will work with any source of sound. Unless you are a singer who can sing on pitch (in which case you should have AP), you will not be able to accurately sing the pitch. The resultant incorrect sound will confuse the brain and destroy any AP that you might have acquired. Just as MP frees the pianist from the limitations of the piano, MP (instead of singing them) frees you from the limitations of the vocal chords.

Procedure for learning relative pitch and absolute pitch: After you have memorized Bach's Inv. #1, and can play the entire piece in your head, start practicing RP. Play the first note (C4) on the piano, and use it as a reference to MP the first bar or two, and check the last note with the piano. Most beginners will MP all intervals narrow because the brain automatically tries to "increase the singing range". Thus ascending notes will be sung flat and descending notes sharp. Start with one or two bars, correct any errors, and repeat until the errors disappear. Then add more bars, etc. By the time you work through the whole Bach in this way, your RP should be pretty good. Then start on AP. MP the first few bars without a reference note from the piano and see if you got the starting C4 right. Everyone has a maximum and minimum note s/he can hum. Therefore, check your C4 without a piano by humming up to the maximum and down to the minimum; for example, your low and high may be F3 and C5; then C4 should be a fourth above F3. After this check, double-check the C4 with the piano. Repeat until your C4 is correct to within a semitone. After that, further success depends on practice; every time you walk by the piano, try to guess C4 (by using the first few bars of the Bach) and test it. You can find the C4 directly by concentrating on exactly how it sounds at the piano, but it is easier with real music because music has more associations. Success depends on how many associations you can make with the note – harmonics, tone, melody, etc. When the C4 is fairly correct, start testing notes randomly all over the piano and trying to guess what they are (white keys only). At first, you may fail miserably. There are too many notes on the piano. In order to improve the success rate, guess the notes by referencing to the C4-C5 octave; for example, C2 is C4, two octaves down. In this way, the task of memorizing 88 notes on the keyboard is reduced to just 8 notes and one interval (octave). This simplification is possible because of the logarithmic nature of the chromatic scale; further simplification of the notes within the octave is accomplished using RP (semitone, 3rd, 4th, 5th). Acquaint yourself with all the notes on the piano by playing them in octaves and training the mind to recognize all octave notes; all octave C's, D's, etc. Until you learn some rudimentary absolute pitch, practice AP mostly at the piano so that you can correct yourself as soon as you wander off key. Do not practice mentally with the wrong pitch for extended periods (this will only confuse the brain); always have the piano nearby to correct yourself. Start practicing away from the piano after your AP is at least within two semitones.

Then memorize the whole Moonlight (first movement) and start work on the black keys. Successful AP depends on how you test yourself. Invent ways to test; I'll show you a few examples. Let's use the first 3 RH notes of the Moonlight. Memorize the sound of these notes in AP, and check this several times a day. See if you can get the first note (G#3) right every time you sit down at the piano. Practice relative pitch by checking the second note, C#4 (a fourth from G#3), then MP a half tone down to C4, and check. Go to the 3rd note, E4, check, then MP down to C4 and check. From G#3, MP a half step down, then up to C4. Now jump to some arbitrary place in this movement and repeat similar procedures (these tests are easier with the Bach).

Progress may seem slow at first, but your guesses should get closer with practice. At first, identifying notes takes time because you need to check your guess by humming to your highest and lowest notes, or by recalling the beginnings of the Bach or Moonlight. Then suddenly, one day, you should experience that magical moment when you are able to identify any note directly, without any intermediate steps. You have acquired true AP! This initial AP is fragile and you may lose it and regain it several times. The next step is to strengthen your AP by practicing to identify the notes as rapidly as you can. The strength of your AP is measured by the speed with which you can identify notes. After that, start practicing with 2-note intervals, then 3, etc. Once you have a strong AP, practice humming the notes and singing on pitch, and sight reading on pitch. Congratulations, you have done it!

The biological mechanism underlying AP is not well understood. It appears to be entirely a memory function. Therefore, in order to truly acquire AP, the daily mental habits must change, just as for becoming a good memorizer. In memorizing, we saw that the change needed was to develop a mental habit of constantly inventing associations (the more outrageous or shocking, the better!) and repeating them automatically in the brain. For good memorizers, this process occurs naturally, or effortlessly, and that is why they are good. The brains of poor memorizers either become quiescent when not needed, or wander into logical or other interests instead of performing memory work. *People with AP tend to continually make music mentally; music keeps running around in their heads, whether it is their own compositions or music they had heard. This is why most musicians with AP will automatically start to compose music.* The brain always returns to music when it has nothing else to do. This is probably a prerequisite to acquiring permanent AP. Note that AP does not make you into a composer; MP does. Therefore, MP is more important than AP; those with strong MP can easily learn AP and maintain it, and enjoy all the advantages discussed here. As with memorization, the hardest part of acquiring permanent AP is not the practice, but the changing of your mental habits. In principle, it's easy -- MP as much as you can, and keep checking it for AP at the piano.

AP and memorizing using MP must be periodically maintained as part of the memory maintenance program. This program automatically performs maintenance on pitch recognition -- check, from time to time, that your MP is on pitch. This too, should happen automatically because you should always MP at least the beginning of every piece before playing it at the piano. By first playing it in your mind, you ensure that the speed, rhythm, and expression are correct. *Your music will sound more exciting when you mentally lead it, and less exciting if you play it and wait for the piano to make the music.* Combining AP, MP and keyboard memory results in a powerful set of tools that will make composing music easy, both for composing in your mind and for playing it out on the piano.

Conventional methods of learning AP take a long time, typically more than 6 months, and usually, much longer, and the resultant AP is weak. One way to start is by memorizing one note. You might pick A440 because you hear it every time at a concert and can perhaps recall it most easily. However, A is not a useful note for getting to the various chords of the C major scale, which is the most useful scale to memorize. Therefore, pick C, E, or G, whichever you tend to remember best; C is probably the best. The standard way to learn AP in music classes is via the solfege (singing exercises) route. *Solfege books are readily available in stores or over the internet. It consists of increasingly complex series of exercises involving different scales, intervals, time signatures, rhythms, accidentals, etc, for voice training. It also covers pitch recognition and dictation.* Solfege books are best used in a class environment with a teacher. AP is taught as an adjunct to these exercises by learning to sing them at the correct pitch. Therefore, there are no special methods for acquiring AP -- you simply repeat until the correct pitch is implanted in memory. Because AP is learned together with many other things, progress is slow.

In summary, every pianist must learn AP because it is so easy, useful, and even necessary in many situations. We demonstrated above that AP is easier to learn using music instead of rote memory. AP is inseparably associated with MP, which frees you from the mechanical limitations of musical instruments. These MP and AP abilities automatically qualify you as "talented" or even "genius" by past standards, but such labels are important mainly to the audience; for yourself, it is comforting to know that you have acquired skills needed to become an accomplished musician.

Sight singing and composing: RP and AP do not automatically enable you to immediately write down a music you had just heard, or play it out on the piano. Those skills must be practiced just as you need to practice for technique, sight reading, or memorizing, and will take time to learn. Developing RP and AP are the first steps towards those goals. In order to be able to write down a music or your composition, it is obviously necessary to study and practice dictation. A quick way to practice dictation is to practice sight singing. Take any music and read a few bars and sing it or play it using MP (one voice only). Then check it out on the piano. If you do this with enough music that you had never heard before, you will learn sight singing and develop most of the dictation skills you need. For practicing to play any melody on the piano, practice sight reading. Once you become fairly good at sight reading (this may take over 6 months), start playing out your own melodies on the piano. The idea behind learning sight reading is to familiarize yourself with common runs, chords, accompaniments, etc., so that you can find them quickly on the piano. Another way is to start playing from fake books and learning improvisation (section V). When composing, don't worry if at first you find it difficult to start a piece or end it – those are some of the most difficult elements of composition. Start by building a collection of ideas that you can later assemble into a composition. Don't worry that you have never had any lessons in composition; it is best to develop your own style first, then study composition to help you to nurture that style. Music never comes "on demand", which can be frustrating; therefore, when ideas come, you must work on them immediately. Listening to music you like, or composing at a good concert grand can be inspirational. Although digital pianos are adequate for composing popular music and practicing jazz improvisations, a quality grand can be very helpful when composing high level classical music.

13. Video Recording and Audio Recording Your Own Playing

One of the best ways to improve musical playing and to practice for recitals is to videotape or record it and watch/listen to it. You will be surprised at how good and how bad the different parts of your playing are. They are often very different from what you imagine yourself to be doing: good touch? rhythm? tempo accurate and constant? What motions are breaking up the rhythm? Do you clearly bring out the melodic lines? Is one hand too loud/soft? Are the arm/hands/fingers in their optimum positions? Are you using the whole body -- i.e., is the body in synch with the hands or are they fighting each other? All these and much more become immediately obvious. The same music sounds quite different when you are playing it or listening to its recording. You hear much more when listening to a recording than when playing it. Video recording is the best way to prepare for recitals and can sometimes eliminate nervousness because you have a clearer picture of your performance.

Initially, most pianists made only audio recordings, thinking that the musical output was the most important; in addition, the older camcorders could not adequately record music. Audio recording has the disadvantage that proper recording of the piano sound is more difficult than most people realize and such attempts often result in failure and abandonment of the effort. Camcorders have become so affordable and versatile that videotaping is now unquestionably the better method. Although the resulting sound may not be CD quality (don't believe the claims of digital video camera manufacturers), you do not need such quality to achieve all the useful pedagogical objectives. Make sure to select a camcorder with the option of turning the automatic gain control off in audio; otherwise, the pianissimo passages will be amplified and distorted. Many sales persons in camcorder dealers are unfamiliar with this feature because it is usually an option in the software settings. You will also need a fairly sturdy tripod; a light one might shake if you really pound away at the piano. Only concert pianists need more advanced audio recording systems; for the best and cost effective results, seek out a recording studio. You may need high quality audio recording for various uses; the audio recording technology is changing so rapidly that it is best to surf the internet for the latest equipment and methods and will not be further discussed here.

Start by making a one-to-one map between what you *think* you are playing and the actual output (video or audio). That way, you can modify your general playing tendencies so that the output will come out right. For example, if you are playing faster than you think in easy sections and slower in difficult sections, you can make the proper adjustments. Are the pauses long enough? Are the endings convincing?

The recording session will reveal how you react in an actual performance, for example, if you make a mistake or have a blackout. Do you react negatively to mistakes and become discouraged, or can you recover and concentrate on the music? During a performance, you tend to get blackouts, etc., at unexpected places where you generally had no trouble during practice. Recording sessions can flush out most of those problem spots. Pieces are not "finished" unless you can record them satisfactorily. Videotaping is a good simulation of playing in recitals. Thus, if you can play satisfactorily during videotaping, you should have little trouble playing that piece in a recital. Once you start taping, you may want to send the tapes to other people!

What are the disadvantages? The main disadvantage is that it will take a lot of time, because you must watch and listen to the recordings. You might be able to save some time by listening while you are doing some other chore. The recording session itself takes little extra time because that counts as part of practice time. However, every time you correct a section, you must re-record and listen again. Thus there is no escaping the fact that watching/listening to yourself is going to be a time consuming operation. However, it is something that every piano student must do. One problem with camcorders is that they all have motors that make noise which is picked up by the built-in mike. If you find this to be a problem, find a model with either an attachable mike of good quality, or a mike input and buy a separate quality mike, such as a boundary or PZM mike.

14. Preparing for Performances and Recitals

a. Benefits and Pitfalls of Performances/Recitals: The benefits and pitfalls of performing determine our daily piano learning programs. For the amateur pianist, the benefits of performances, even casual ones, are immeasurable. The most important benefit is that technique is never really acquired until it is demonstrated in a performance. For young students, the benefits are even more fundamental. They learn what it means to complete a real task, and they learn what "making music" means. Most youngsters (who don't take music lessons) don't learn these skills until they go to college; piano students must learn them at their *first recital*, regardless of age. Students are never as self-motivated as when preparing for a recital. Teachers who have held recitals know those enormous benefits. Their students become focused, self-motivated, and results oriented; they listen intently to the teacher and really try to understand the meaning of the teachers' instructions. The students become deadly serious about eliminating all errors and learning everything correctly -- it is capitalism at its best, because it is *their* performance. Teachers without recitals often end up with students who practice maybe a few times just before lesson day.

Because the psychology and sociology of piano playing is not well developed, there are pitfalls that we must seriously consider. The most important one is nervousness and its impact on the mind, especially for the young. Nervousness can make recitals a frightful experience that requires careful attention in order to avoid not only unhappy experiences but also lasting psychological damage. At the very least, reducing nervousness will alleviate stress and fright. There is not enough attention paid to making recitals a pleasant experience and reducing the tension and stress, including the piano competitions. This whole subject will be treated more completely in the section on nervousness. The point here is that any discussions on performing must include a treatment of stage fright. Even great artists have stopped performing for long periods of time for one reason or another, and some of the reasons were undoubtedly related to stress. *Therefore, although good piano teachers always hold recitals of their students and enter them into competitions, they have tended to be poor sociologists or psychologists, concentrating only on piano playing and ignoring nervousness.* It is important for any person guiding youngsters through recitals and competitions to learn the fundamentals of what causes nervousness, how to deal with it, and its psychological consequences. When teachers fail, it is the job of the parents to look out for the social and psychological welfare of their children; therefore, the following section (section 15) on nervousness is a necessary companion to this section.

There are numerous other psychological and sociological implications of recitals and competitions. The judging systems in music competitions are notoriously unfair, and judging is a difficult and thankless job. Thus students entered into competition must be informed of these shortcomings of the "system" so that they do not suffer mental damage from perceived unfairness and disappointment. It is difficult, but possible, for students to understand that the most important element of competitions is that they participate, not that they win. There is too much emphasis on technical difficulty and not enough on musicality. The system does not encourage communication among teachers to improve teaching methods. It is no wonder that there is a school of thought that favors eliminating competitions. There is no question that recitals and competitions are necessary; but the present system can certainly be improved. We discuss some ideas in section 15.

b. Basics of Flawless Performances: The basic requirements for a flawless performance are: technical preparation, musical interpretation, MP, and a good performance preparation routine. When all these elements come together, you can virtually guarantee a perfect performance.

Of course, there are plenty of excuses for not being able to perform. Knowing these excuses is one of the prerequisites for learning how to perform. Perhaps the most common excuse is that you are always learning new pieces so that there is insufficient time to really finish a piece or maintain the finished pieces in playable condition. We saw that learning a new piece is the best way to mess up old pieces. For those who have never performed, the second most important reason is that they probably never really finished anything. There is always that one difficult section you can't quite manage in every "interesting" piece worth performing. Another excuse is that pieces that are easy for you are somehow always uninteresting. Note that the learning methods of this book are designed to counter every one of these excuses, mainly by accelerating the learning process and by mandating memorization, so that by the time you can play a piece well in your mind, none of these excuses will be valid. Thus all the necessary elements for flawless performances can be found in this book. We now discuss a few more ideas for learning how to perform.

c. Practicing for Performances: Most pianists use a special practice speed for preparing for performances, a speed slightly slower than the performance speed. This speed allows for accurate practice without picking up unexpected bad habits and creates a clear picture of the music in the mind. It also conditions the hand for playing with control at the faster performance speed and improves technique. This slower speed is not necessarily easier than the performance speed. The rationale for the two speeds is that, during a performance, it is easier to bring out the expression if you play slightly faster than the last time you played. If you play the same composition twice in a row (or on the same day) the music comes out flat the second time unless it is played faster than the first time because the slower play sounds less exciting and this feeling starts a negative feedback cycle, in addition to FPD. *After such repeat performances (in fact, after every performance), play it slowly as soon as you can, in order to erase the FPD and "reset" the music in your mind.* A similar process takes place in a computer: after continuous use, data fragmentation occurs and the main memory disk must be "defragged" to restore the data to their proper locations.

Inexperienced performers often play too fast for their skill level because of nervousness during the recital. Such inappropriate speeds can be easily detected by video recording. Therefore, during routine practice (not immediately before a performance), it is important to practice speeds faster than performance speed, just in case you make that mistake during a performance. Obviously, the performance speed must be slower than your fastest speed. Remember that the audience has not

161

heard this piece innumerable times like you have during practice, and your "final speed" can be too fast for them. A piece played with careful attention to every note can sound faster than one played at a faster speed, but with indistinct notes. You need to "spoon feed" every note to the audience or they will not here it.

Practice recovering from mistakes. Attend student recitals and watch how they react to their mistakes; you will easily spot the right reactions and the inappropriate ones. A student showing frustration or shaking the head after a mistake is creating three mistakes out of one: the original mistake, an inappropriate reaction, and broadcasting to the audience that a mistake was made. More on this in section "g" below.

d. Practicing Musically: What does it mean to play musically? This question can only be answered by application of the myriad micro-rules that apply to specific passages of specific compositions; this is where a teacher can show you what to do. Incorporating all of the musical notations and markings into the music will build a sound foundation. There are some general rules for playing musically:

(i) carefully connect each bar to the next bar (or measure, or phrase). These bars/measures do not stand alone; one logically flows into the other and they all support each other. They are connected rhythmically as well as conceptually. This point may appear to be trivially obvious; however, if performed consciously, you might be surprised by the improvement in your music.

(ii) there must always be a conversation between the RH and LH. They don't play independently. And they won't talk to each other automatically even if they were timed perfectly. You must consciously create a conversation between the two hands, or voices.

(iii) "cresc." means that most of the passage should be played softly; only the last few notes are loud, which means that it is important to start softly. Similarly, for other indications of this nature (rit., accel., dim., etc); make sure that you have reserved space for the action to take place and don't start the action immediately, wait until the last moment. These "expression tools" should create mental illusions; for example, if you ramp up a cresc. gradually, it is like climbing up a slope, whereas if you wait till the last moment and increase it exponentially, it is like being thrown up in the air, which is more effective.

(iv) strive more for accuracy than expressive rubato; rubato is often too easy, incorrect, and not in tune with the audience. This is the time to use the metronome to check the timing and rhythm.

(v) when in doubt, start and end each musical phrase softly, with the louder notes near the middle. It is usually incorrect to have loud notes at the beginning; of course, you can also make music by breaking this rule.

Musicality has no limit -- it can be improved no matter where you are on the musicality scale. The terrifying part of this is the flip side. If you do not pay attention, you can develop non-musical playing habits that can keep on destroying your musicality. This is why it is so important to focus on musicality and not only on technique; it can make the difference between becoming a performer and a non-performer.

Always listen to your own music (when practicing) and mentally lead the music using MP -- that is the only way it is going to attract the audience's attention. If a mistake occurs, don't get depressed because the depression will make it harder to play well. On the other hand, if you get a good start, the audience will be drawn in, and the music will feed on itself and the performance becomes easier. Thus playing becomes a feedback cycle of leading the music using MP and listening to the actual music emanating from the piano, and they must reinforce each other.

Many students hate to practice when others are around to listen; some even think that intense piano practice is necessarily unpleasant and punishing to the ear. These are symptoms of common misconceptions resulting from inefficient practice methods, and a sign of weak mental stamina. With correct practice methods and musical play, there should be nothing unpleasant about piano practice sessions. ***The best criterion that you are practicing correctly is the reaction of others -- if your*** *practice sounds good to them, or at least it doesn't bother them, then you are doing it right*. Musical practice improves mental stamina because it requires so much concentration.

   e. Casual Performances: Common types of casual performances are playing pieces for testing pianos in stores or playing for friends at parties, etc. These are different from formal recitals because of their greater freedom and reduced mental pressure. There is usually no set program, you can pick anything that is appropriate for the moment. It may be full of changes and interruptions. Nervousness is not even an issue, and is in fact one of the best ways to practice methods for avoiding nervousness. Even with these alleviating factors, this is not easy in the beginning. For an easy start, play little snippets (short segments from a composition). Start with simple ones; pick out the best sounding sections. If it doesn't work out too well, start on another one. Same, if you get stuck. You can start and quit at any time. This is a great way to experiment and find out how you perform and which snippets work. Do you tend to play too fast? It is better to start too slow and speed up than the other way round. Can you play a beautiful legato, or is your tone harsh? Can you adjust to a different piano -- especially one that is out of tune or difficult to play? Can you keep track of the audience reaction? Can you make the audience react to your playing? Can you pick the right types of snippets for the occasion? Can you put yourself in the right frame of mind to play? What is your level of nervousness, can you control it? Can you play and talk at the same time? Can you gloss over mistakes without being bothered by them? Another way to practice performing is to introduce youngsters, who have never had piano lessons, to the piano. Teach them how to play the C major scale, or "Chopsticks" or Happy Birthday.

   Playing snippets has one interesting advantage which is that most audiences are very impressed by your ability to stop and start anywhere in the middle of a piece. Most people assume that all amateur pianists learn pieces by finger memory from beginning to end, and that the ability to play snippets requires special talent. Start with short snippets, then gradually try longer ones. Once you have done this type of casual snippet performance on 4 or 5 different occasions, you will have a good idea of your performance capabilities. Obviously, one of the routines you should practice "cold" are snippet playing routines.

   There are a few rules for preparing for snippet performances. Don't perform a piece you had newly learned. Let it stew for at least 6 months; preferably one year (practicing snipets during that time). If you had spent 2 weeks learning a difficult new piece, don't expect to be able to play snippets that had not been played at all in those 2 weeks -- be prepared for all kinds of surprises, such as blackouts. ***Don't practice the snippets fast on the day on which you might be performing them. Practicing them very slowly will help.*** Can you still play them HS? You can break a lot of these rules for very short snippets. Above all, make sure that you can mentally play them (away from the piano) -- that is the ultimate test of your readiness.

   In general, don't expect to perform anything well, casual or otherwise, unless you have performed that piece at least three times, and some claim, at least 5 times. Sections that you thought were simple may turn out to be difficult to perform, and vice versa. Thus the first order of business is to lower your expectations and start planning on how you are going to play this piece, especially when unexpected things happen. It is certainly not going to be like the best run you made during practice. Without this mental preparation, you can end up very disappointed after every attempt at performing and develop psychological problems.

   A few mistakes or missed notes goes unnoticed in practice, and your assessment of how they sound during practice is probably much more optimistic than your own assessment if you had played exactly the same way for an audience. After a practice, you tend to remember only the good parts, but after a performance, you tend to remember only the mistakes. Usually, you are your worst critic; every slip sounds far worse to you than to the audience. Most audiences will miss half of the mistakes and forget most of what they do catch after a short period of time. Casual performances are more relaxed, and they provide an avenue for easing gradually into formal performing, in preparation for recitals.

Classical music is not always the best venue for casual performances. Thus every pianist should learn popular music, jazz, cocktail music, music from fake books, and improvisation. They provide some of the best ways to practice for formal recitals. See section V.

f. Performance Preparation Routines: Even if a student can play perfectly during practice, s/he can make all kinds of mistakes and struggle with musicality during a recital if the preparation is incorrect. ***Most students intuitively practice hard and at full speed during the week preceding the recital, and especially on the day of the recital. In order to simulate the recital, they imagine an audience listening nearby and play their hearts out, playing the entire piece from beginning to end, many times. This practice method is the single biggest cause of mistakes and poor performance.*** The most telling remark I hear so often is, "Strange, I played so well all morning but during the recital, I made mistakes that I don't make during practice!" To an experienced teacher, this is a student practicing out of control without any guidance about right and wrong methods of recital preparation.

Teachers who hold those recitals in which the students perform wonderfully keep a tight leash on their students and control their practice routines closely. Why all this fuss? Because during a recital, the most stressed element is the brain, not the playing mechanism. And this stress cannot be replicated in any kind of simulated performance. Thus the brain must be rested and fully charged for a one-time performance; it cannot be drained by playing your heart out. All mistakes originate in the brain. All the necessary information must be stored in an orderly manner in the brain, with no confusion. This is why improperly prepared students always play worse in a recital than during practice. When you practice at full speed, a large amount of confusion is introduced into the memory. The environment of the recital is different from that of the practice piano, and can be very distracting. Therefore, you must have a simple, mistake-free memory of the piece that can be retrieved in spite of all the added distractions. This is why it is difficult to perform the same piece twice on the same day, or even on successive days. The second performance is invariably worse than the first, although intuitively, you would expect the second performance to be better because you had one extra experience performing it. As elsewhere in this section, these types of remarks apply only to students. Professional musicians should be able to perform anything any number of times at any time; this skill comes from continuous exposure to performing, and honing the proper rules of preparation.

Through trial and error, experienced teachers have found practice routines that work. The most important rule is to limit the amount of practice on recital day, so as to keep the mind fresh. The brain is totally unreceptive on recital day. It can only become confused. Only a small minority of experienced pianists have sufficiently "strong" musical brains to assimilate something new on recital day. By the way, this also applies to tests and exams at school. Most of the time, you will score better in an exam by going to a movie the night before the exam than by cramming. ***A typical recommended piano practice routine for the recital day is to play nearly full speed once, then medium speed once and finally once slowly.*** That's it! No more practice! Never play faster than recital speed. Notice how counter intuitive this is. Since parents and friends will always use intuitive methods, it is important for the teacher to make sure that any person associated with the student also knows these rules, especially for the younger students. Otherwise, in spite of anything the teacher says, the students will come to the recital having practiced all day at full speed, because their parents made them do it.

Of course, this is only the starting point. It can be altered to fit the circumstances. This routine is for the typical student and is not for professional performers who will have much more detailed routines that depend not only on the type of music being played, but also on the particular composer or particular piece to be played. Clearly, for this routine to work, the piece will have had to be ready for performance way ahead of time. However, even if the piece has not been perfected and can be improved with more practice, this is still the best routine for the recital day. If you make a mistake that is stubborn and which will almost certainly recur during the recital, fish out the few bars containing the mistake and practice those at the appropriate speeds (always ending with slow play), staying away from fast playing as much as possible. If you are not sure that the piece is completely memorized, play it very slowly several times. Again, the importance of secure MP must be emphasized -- it is the ultimate test of memory and readiness to perform. Practice MP at any speed and as often as you want; it can also calm any nervous jitters.

Also, avoid extreme exertion, such as playing a football game or lifting or pushing something heavy (such as a concert grand!). This can suddenly change the response of your muscles to a signal from the brain and you can end up making totally unexpected mistakes when you play. Of course, mild warm-up exercises, stretching, calisthenics, Tai Chi, Yoga, etc., can be beneficial.

For the week preceding the recital, always play at medium speed, then slow speed, before quitting practice. You can substitute medium speed for slow speed if you are short of time, or the piece is particularly easy, or if you are a more experienced performer. Actually, this rule applies to any practice session, but is particularly critical before a recital. The slow play erases any bad habits that you might have picked up, and re-establishes relaxed playing. Therefore, during these medium/slow plays, concentrate on relaxation. There is no fixed number such as half speed, etc., to define medium and slow, although medium is generally about 3/4 speed, and slow is about half speed. More generally, medium speed is the speed at which you can play comfortably, relaxed, and with plenty of time to spare. Slow is the speed at which you need to pay attention to each note separately.

Up to the last day before the recital, you can work on improving the piece, especially musically. But within the last week, adding new material or making changes in the piece (such as fingering) is not recommended, although you might try it as a training experiment to see how far you can push yourself. Being able to add something new during the last week is a sign that you are a strong performer; in fact, purposely changing something at the last minute is good performance training. *For working on long pieces such as Beethoven Sonatas, avoid playing the entire composition many times. It is best to chop it into short segments of a few pages at most and practice the segments.* Practicing HS is also an excellent idea because no matter who you are, you can always improve technically. Although playing too fast is not recommended in the last week, you can practice at any speed HS. Avoid learning new pieces during this last week. That does not mean that you are limited to the recital pieces; you can still practice any piece that was previously learned. New pieces will often cause you to learn new skills that affect or alter how you play the recital piece. In general, you will not be aware that this happened until you play the recital piece and wonder how some new mistakes crept in.

Make a habit of playing your recital pieces "cold" (without any warming up) when you start any practice session. The hands will warm up after one or two pieces, so you may have to rotate the recital pieces with each practice session, if you are playing many pieces. Of course, "playing cold" has to be done within reason. If the fingers are totally sluggish from inaction, you cannot, and should not try to, play difficult material at full speed; it will lead to stress and even injury. Some pieces can only be played after the hands are completely limbered up, especially if you want to play it musically. However, the difficulty of playing musically must not be an excuse for not playing cold because the effort is more important than the result in this case. You need to find out which ones you can play cold at full speed, and which ones you should not. Slow down so that you can play with cold hands; you can always play at final speed after the hands have warmed up.

Practice the starting few bars, from several days prior to the recital. Whenever you have time, pretend that it is recital time and play those few starting bars. Choose the first 2 to 5 bars and practice a different number of bars each time. Don't stop at the end of a bar, always end by playing the first note of the next bar.

g. During the Recital: *Nervousness is usually worst just before you start to play. Once you start, you will be so busy with the playing that the nervousness will tend to be forgotten and will decrease.* This knowledge can be quite reassuring, so there is nothing wrong with starting play as soon as you sit down at the piano for the recital. Some people will delay starting by adjusting the bench or some clothing item in order to have time to double check that the starting tempo, etc., are correct, using MP.

Do not assume that there won't be any mistakes; that assumption can only invite more trouble because you will feel terrible when a mistake does occur. Be ready to react correctly with each mistake, or more importantly, anticipate an impending mistake that you may be able to avoid. It is amazing how often you can feel an impending mistake before it hits, especially if you are good at MP. *The worst thing that most students do when they make a mistake or when they expect one is to get scared and start playing more slowly and softly.* This can *lead* to disaster. Although hand memory is not something you want to depend on, this is one time you can take advantage of it. Hand memory depends on habit and stimuli -- the habit of having practiced many times, and the stimuli of previous notes leading to succeeding notes. Therefore, in order to enhance hand memory, you must play slightly faster and louder, exactly the opposite of what an anxious person would do during a recital (another counter-intuitive situation!). The faster play makes better use of the playing habit, and leaves less time for moving some wrong muscle that might derail you from the habit. The firmer play increases the stimuli for the hand memory. Now playing faster and louder are scary things to do during a recital, so you should practice this at home just as you practice anything else. Learn to anticipate mistakes and to avoid them by using these avoidance methods. Another method of playing through mistakes is to make sure that the melodic line is not broken, even at the cost of missing some "accompaniment" notes. With practice, you will find that this is easier than it sounds; the best time to practice this is when you are sight reading. Another way to play through mistakes is to at least keep the rhythm. Of course, none of this would be needed if you have a really secure MP.

If you have a blackout, don't try to restart from where you blacked out unless you know exactly how to restart. Restart from a preceding section or a following section that you know well (preferably a following section because mistakes usually cannot be corrected during the recital and you will probably repeat the same blackout). *Secure MP will eliminate practically all blackouts.* If you decide to replay the blackout part, play slightly faster and louder; not slower and softer because that will almost guarantee a repeat of the blackout.

In a concert hall with good acoustics, the sound of the piano will be absorbed by the hall and you will hear very little of the piano sound. It is obviously important to practice with the recital piano in the recital hall before the event. *For a grand piano, if the music stand it up, you will hear even less sound from the piano; always make sure that the music stand is down.* If you need to read music, place it flat over the tuning pin area.

h. That Unfamiliar Piano: Some students fret that the recital piano is a huge grand whereas they practice on a small upright. Fortunately, the larger pianos are easier to play than the smaller ones. Therefore the issue of a different piano is usually not something to worry about for the typical student recital. Larger pianos generally have better action, and both louder and softer sounds are easier to produce on them. In particular, grands are easier to play than uprights, especially for fast, difficult passages. Thus the only time you may have to be concerned about the piano is when the recital piano is decidedly inferior to your practice piano. The worst situation is the one in which your practice piano is a quality grand, but you must perform using a low quality upright. In that case, technically difficult pieces will be difficult to play on the inferior piano and you may need to make adjustments, for example, by playing at a slower tempo, or shortening or slowing down the trill, etc.

Another important factor is the tuning of the piano. A piano in tune is easier to play than one out of tune. Therefore, it is a good idea to tune the recital piano before the recital. Conversely, it is not a good idea to tune the practice piano just before the recital unless it is badly out of tune. If the recital piano is out of tune, it may be best to play slightly faster and louder than you intended.

i. After the Recital: Review the recital and evaluate your strengths and weaknesses so that the practice/preparation routines can be improved. A few students will be able to play consistently without audible mistakes. Most of the others will make several mistakes every time they play. Some will tend to bang on the piano while others are timid and play too softly. There is a cure for every problem. Those who make mistakes probably have not yet learned to play sufficiently musically and almost always cannot play in their minds. Those who tend to play flawlessly invariably have learned MP, whether they do it consciously or not.

As noted elsewhere, *playing several recitals in succession is the hardest thing to do. But if you must, then you will need to recondition the recital pieces immediately following the recital. Play them with little or no expression, medium speed, then slow speed.* If certain sections or pieces did not come out satisfactorily during the recital, work on them, but only in small segments. If you want to work on the expression at full speed, do this also in small segments.

15. Origin and Control of Nervousness

Nervousness is a natural human emotion like happiness, fear, sadness, etc. Nervousness arises from a mental perception of a situation in which performance is critical. *Therefore, nervousness, like all emotions, is a performance enhancing reaction to a situation.* Happiness feels good, so we try to create happy situations, which helps us; fear helps us to escape danger, and sadness makes us avoid sad situations which tends to improve our chances of survival. Nervousness makes us concentrate all our energies towards the critical task at hand and is therefore another survival tool. Most people dislike nervousness because it is too often accompanied, or is caused, by fear of failure. Therefore, although nervousness is necessary for a great performance, it needs to be kept under control; it should not be allowed to interfere with the performance. The history of the great artists is full of legends of very nervous as well as totally non-nervous performers, indicating that this phenomenon has not been studied in any scientific, medical, or psychological way, with practical results, even at music conservatories where this ought to be a major component of their curricula.

Emotions are basic, primitive, animal reactions, somewhat like instinct, and are not totally rational. Under normal circumstances, emotions guide our daily, moment-by-moment actions nicely. However, *under extreme conditions, emotions can get out of control, and become a liability.* Clearly, emotions were designed to work only under normal circumstances. For example, fear makes the frog escape long before a predator can catch it. However, when cornered, the frog freezes in fear and this makes it an easier meal for the snake than if the overwhelming fear hadn't paralyzed it. Likewise, *nervousness normally is mild and helps us to perform a critical task better than if we were lackadaisical.* However, under extreme conditions, it can spin out of control and hinder our performance. The requirement to perform a difficult piano solo flawlessly in front of a large audience eminently qualifies as an extreme situation. It is no surprise that nervousness can grow out of control, unless our name is Wolfie or Franz (Freddy apparently didn't qualify, as he was a nervous wreck and disliked public performances; however, he seemed more comfortable in a salon environment). Thus, although violinists do get nervous, it does not spin out of control when they are playing in an orchestra because the conditions are not as extreme as for solo performances. Youngsters, who are too frightened to perform solo, almost always enjoy performing in a group. This shows the importance of the mental perception of the situation.

Clearly, the way to control nervousness is to first study its cause and nature and to develop methods for controlling it based on this knowledge. Since it is an emotion, any method for controlling emotions will work. Some have claimed that, under a doctor's supervision, medications such as Inderal and Atenolol, or even Zantac will work to calm nerves. Conversely, you can make it worse by drinking coffee or tea, not getting enough sleep, or taking certain cold medications. Emotions can also be controlled by use of psychology, training, or conditioning. Knowledge is the most effective means of control. For example, experienced snake handlers do not suffer any of the emotions most of us would experience when we come close to a poisonous snake because of their knowledge of snakes.

By the time nervousness becomes a problem, it is usually a compound emotion spinning out of control. In addition to nervousness, other emotions such as fear and worry, join in. A lack of understanding of nervousness also creates fear because of the fear of the unknown. Thus the simple knowledge of what stage fright is, can be a calming factor by reducing the fear of the unknown.

How does nervousness grow out of control, and are there ways to prevent it? One way to approach this question is to visit some principles of fundamental science. *Practically anything in our universe grows by a process known as the Nucleation-Growth (NG) mechanism. The NG theory states that an object forms in two stages, nucleation and growth.* This theory became popular and useful because it is in fact the way in which the majority of objects in our universe form, from raindrops to cities, stars, humans, etc. *Two key elements of NG theory are: (1) nucleation and (2) growth.* Nuclei are always forming and disappearing, but there is a thing called a critical nucleus which, when formed, becomes stable -- it does not disappear. In general, the critical nucleus does not form unless there is a supersaturation of the material that aggregate to form it. For the object to grow to its final size, the critical nucleus needs a growth mechanism by which to increase its size. In general, the growth mechanism is totally different from the nucleation mechanism. One interesting aspect of nucleation is that there is always a barrier to nucleation -- otherwise, everything would have nucleated a long time ago. Growth is a two-way street: it can be positive or negative.

Let's examine one example: rain. Rain occurs when water droplets form critical nuclei in air that is supersaturated with water vapor (relative humidity greater than 100%). The oft misquoted "scientific truth" that relative humidity never exceeds 100% is routinely violated by Nature because that "truth" is valid only under equilibrium conditions, when all forces have been allowed to equilibrate. Nature is almost always dynamic, and it can be far from equilibrium. This happens, for example, when the air cools rapidly and becomes supersaturated with water vapor; that is, relative humidity higher than 100%. Even without supersaturation, water vapor is constantly forming water droplets, but these evaporate before they can form critical nuclei. With supersaturation, critical nuclei can suddenly form, especially if there are hydrophilic dust particles (the seeds) in the air or compressive disturbances such as thunderclaps that bring the molecules closer together, thus increasing the supersaturation. The air filled with critical nuclei is what we call a cloud or fog. If the formation of the cloud reduces the supersaturation to zero, a stable cloud is created; if not, the nuclei will keep growing to reduce the supersaturation. Nuclei can grow by other mechanisms. This is the growth stage of the NG process. The nuclei can bump into each other and aggregate, or start to fall and hit other water molecules and nuclei, until rain drops form.

Let's apply NG theory to nervousness. In everyday life, your sense of nervousness comes and goes, without becoming anything serious. However, in an unusual situation such as a performance, there is a supersaturation of factors that cause nervousness: you must perform flawlessly, you didn't have enough time to practice the piece, there is a big audience out there, etc. However, this still may not cause any problem because there are natural barriers to nucleating nervousness, such as a flow of adrenalin, a sense of accomplishment, or even being unaware of nervousness, or you might be too busy finalizing the preparations for the recital. But then, a fellow performer says, "Hey, I got butterflies in my stomach," and you suddenly feel a lump in your throat and realize that you are nervous -- the critical nucleus has formed! This may still not be that bad, until you start to worry that perhaps your piece is not yet ready to perform or the nervousness might interfere with the playing -- these worries cause the nervousness to grow. These are exactly the processes described by NG theory. The nice thing about any scientific theory is that it not only describes the process in detail, but also provides solutions. So how does NG theory help us?

We can attack nervousness at the nucleation stage; if we can prevent nucleation, it will never form a critical nucleus. Merely delaying the nucleation will be helpful because that will reduce the time available for it to grow. Playing easier pieces will reduce the supersaturation of worry. Mock recitals will give you more experience and confidence; both will reduce the fear of the unknown. Generally, you need to perform a piece 3 or more times before you know whether you can perform it successfully or not; thus performing pieces that had been performed several times will also help. *Nervousness is generally worst before a performance; once you start playing, you are so busy with the task at hand that there is no time to dwell on nervousness, thus reducing the growth factor.* This knowledge helps because it alleviates the fear that things might get worse during the performance. Not dwelling on nervousness is another way of delaying the nucleation as well as slowing the growth stage. Thus it is a good idea to keep yourself occupied while waiting for the recital to begin. *MP is useful because you can check your memory and keep yourself occupied at the same time; thus it is the most important tool for preventing or delaying nucleation and for reducing growth.* See sections 16.c & d for suggestions on how teachers can provide performance training.

For an important recital, avoiding nucleation is probably not possible. Therefore we should examine ways to discourage growth. Since nervousness generally decreases after the performance starts, this knowledge can be used to reduce the worry and therefore the nervousness. This can feed on itself, and as nervousness begins to decrease, you feel more assured, and it can often dissipate entirely, if you can reduce it below the critical nucleus. Another important factor is mental attitude and preparation. A performance is always an interactive process between you and the audience. Playing musically, of course, is always the answer -- when you can involve your entire brain in the business of creating music, there is little brain resources left to worry about nervousness. These are all measures for reducing the growth.

It is not a good idea to pretend that nervousness does not exist, especially with youngsters who can more easily suffer long term psychological damage. Kids are smart and they can easily see through the pretense, and the need to play along with the pretense can only increase the stress. This is why performance training, in which nervousness is discussed openly, is so important. For young students, the parents and friends attending the recital need to be educated also. Statements like "I hope you aren't nervous!" or "How can you perform without getting nervous?" are almost certain to cause nucleation and growth. On the other hand, to completely ignore nervousness and send kids out to perform with no performance training is irresponsible and can even cause serious, lifelong psychological damage.

Developing the proper mental attitude is the best way for controlling stage fright. If you can get into the frame of mind that performing is a wonderful experience of making music for others and develop proper reactions when you do make mistakes, nervousness will not be problematic. There is this huge difference between, for example, (1) creating humor out of a mistake or recovering nicely from it and (2) letting that mistake look like a disaster that mars the entire performance. Performance training must include lessons on how to react to various circumstances. *It is important, early in a student's career, to play easy pieces that can be performed without nervousness, Eeven one such experience can provide the existence proof that performing without nervousness is possible. That single experience can influence your performance attitude for the rest of your life.* The best way to guarantee such a flawless performance is to develop a secure MP, which will allow you to start playing from any note in the piece, stay mentally ahead of the music, create musicality in your mind, recover from flubs, avoid them or cover them up, keep your mind occupied (thus preventing nervousness from developing), practice any part of the music at any time or place, write out the entire score from memory (one hand at a time!), etc.; these achievements will give you the confidence of an accomplished musician. The audience will conclude that they are being treated to great, rare talent.

In summary, stage fright is nervousness that has spiraled out of control. A certain amount of nervousness is normal and helpful. You can minimize nervousness by delaying its nucleation by keeping busy and reducing its growth by playing musically; MP is the most effective tool for this purpose. Thus it doesn't make sense, and is a mistake, to ask "do you get nervous when you perform?" Everyone does, and should. We only need to contain nervousness so that it does not grow out of control. *Realizing that a certain amount of nervousness is normal is the best starting point for learning to control it.* Of course, there is a wide range of individuals from those who don't get nervous at all, to those who suffer terribly from stage fright. The best policy for nervousness is honesty -- we must acknowledge its effect on each individual and treat it accordingly. Gaining confidence in your ability to perform can usually eliminate nervousness and perfecting the art of MP is the best way to achieve such confidence.

16. Teaching

a. Types of Teachers. Teaching piano is a difficult profession because practically everything you try to do contradicts something else that should be done. If you teach reading, the student may end up unable to memorize. If you teach slow, accurate play, the student may not acquire sufficient technique in any reasonable amount of time. If you push them too fast, they may forget all about relaxation. If you concentrate on technique, the student might lose track of musical playing. You need to devise a system that successfully navigates through all these types of contradictory requirements and still satisfies the individual wishes and needs of each student. There was no standard text book until this book was written, and starting teachers had to invent their own teaching systems with very little guidance. *Teaching piano is a Herculean task that is not for the faint of heart.*

Historically, teachers generally fell into at least three categories: teachers for beginners, intermediate students, and advanced students. The most successful approach involved a group of teachers composed of all three categories; the teachers were coordinated in such a way that their teachings were mutually compatible, and the appropriate students were passed on to the appropriate teachers. Without such coordination, many teachers of advanced students often refused to take students from certain teachers because the latter "do not teach the proper fundamentals". This should not happen if the fundamentals are standardized. The last thing an advanced teacher wanted was a student who was initially taught all the "wrong" methods. Thus, standardization using a textbook, such as this one, will solve such problems.

b. Teaching Youngsters, Parental Involvement, Mental Play, Absolute Pitch. *Children should be tested for their readiness to take piano lessons at ages between 2 and 8. The first lessons for beginners, especially children under 7 years old, should be brief, 10 to 15 minutes.* Increase the lesson time only as their attention time span and stamina increase. If more time is necessary, divide the lesson into sessions with breaks in between ("cookie time", etc.). The same rules apply to practice times at home. You can teach a lot in 10 min.; it is better to give 15 min. lessons every other day (3 days/wk) than to give hour long lessons every week. This principle applies at any age, although the lesson times and time between lessons will increase with age and skill level.

It is important for youngsters to listen to recordings. They can listen to, and play, Chopin at any age. They should also listen to recordings of their own playing; otherwise, they may not understand why you are criticizing their mistakes. Do not feed them music just because it is classical or it was written by Bach. Play what you and the youngsters enjoy.

Youngsters develop in spurts, both physically and mentally, and they can only learn what they are mature enough to learn. *Therefore, part of the teaching must consist of a constant testing of their level of readiness: pitch, rhythm, absolute pitch, reading, finger control on the keyboard, attention span, interest in music, which instrument is best?, understanding musical concepts, communications ability, intelligence, etc.* On the other hand, most youngsters are ready for many more things than most adults realize and once they are ready, the sky is the limit. Therefore, it is also a mistake to assume that all kids must be treated as kids all the time. They can be surprisingly advanced in many respects and treating them as kids only holds them back (for example, by letting them listen only to "kiddie music") and deprives them of the opportunity to fulfill their potential. **Kiddie music exists only in the minds of adults, and generally does more harm than good.**

Brain development and physical development can proceed at very different rates. *The brain is generally way ahead of the physical. Because of this physical lag, too many parents assume that the brain development is also slow.* It is important to test the brain and support its development and not let the physical development slow brain development. This is especially important because the brain can accelerate physical development. Language, logic, and music, as well as visual stimuli, are most important for brain development.

For at least the first 2 years of lessons (longer for youngsters) teachers must insist that the parents participate in the teaching/learning process. The parents' first job is to understand the methods that the teacher is teaching. *Since so many practice methods and recital preparation procedures are counter-intuitive, the parents must be familiar with them so that they can not only help to guide the students, but also avoid negating the teacher's instructions.* Unless the parents participate in the lessons, they will fall behind after a few lessons and can actually become a hindrance to the child's development. The parents must participate in deciding how long the students practice each day, since they are most familiar with all the time demands on the students. The parents also know the students' ultimate objectives best -- are the lessons for casual playing, or for advancing to much higher levels? What types of music do the students eventually want to play? Beginning students always need help at home in working out the optimum routine for daily practice as well as keeping track of weekly assignments. Once the lessons start, it is surprising how often the teachers need the parents' help -- where and how to buy sheet music, how often to tune the piano, or when to upgrade to a better piano, etc. The teachers and parents need to agree on how fast the students are expected to learn and to work towards attaining that learning rate. The parents need to be informed of the students' strengths and weaknesses so as to be able to match their expectations and plans with what is or is not achievable. *Most importantly, it is the parents' job to evaluate the teacher and to make proper decisions on switching teachers at the appropriate time.*

This book should serve as a textbook for both the student and the parents. This will save the teacher a lot of time and the teacher can then concentrate on demonstrating technique and teaching music. Parents need to read this book so that they do not interfere with the teacher's teaching methods.

Students need a lot of help from their parents, and the kinds of help change with age. When young, the students need constant help with daily practice routines: are they practicing correctly and following the teacher's instructions? It is most important at this stage to establish correct practice habits. *The parents must make sure that during practice, the students make it a habit to play through mistakes instead of backtracking, which will create a stuttering habit and makes the student mistake-prone during performances.* Most youngsters will not understand the teacher's instructions given hurriedly during their lessons; the parents can more readily understand them. As the students advance, they need feedback on whether they are playing musically, whether their tempo and rhythm are accurate or if they need to use the metronome, and whether they should stop practicing and start listening to recordings.

Mental development is the main reason for letting youngsters listen to classics -- the "Mozart Effect". The reasoning goes something like this. Assume that the average parent has average intelligence; then there is a 50% chance that the child is smarter than the parents. That is, the parents cannot compete on the same intellectual level as their baby! So, how do parents teach music to babies whose musical brain can quickly develop to much higher levels than their parents'? By letting them listen to the great classics! Let them talk to, and learn directly, from Mozart, Chopin, etc. Music is a universal language; unlike the crazy adult languages that we speak, music is inborn, so babies can communicate in music long before they can say "dada". Therefore, classical music can stimulate a baby's brain long before the parents can communicate with the baby even on the most basic levels. And these communications are conducted at the levels of the genius composers, something few parents can hope to match!

How to teach your child: Here, we consider musical and brain development. Brain development is important long before birth. Thus the mother must strive for a stress-free environment and balanced diet, with no smoking, excessive alcohol consumption, etc. After birth, there is general agreement that breast feeding is best. A side benefit is that breast feeding is a form of birth control – while breast feeding, women usually do not get pregnant (up to 4 years!). Some women with small breasts fear that they will not produce enough milk, but this fear is unfounded. All women have the same number of mammary glands; the difference in breast size is caused only by the variation in the amount of fat stored in the breasts. The important factor in breast feeding is regular feeding, equally with both breasts – any interruption can stop milk production in that breast. Babies do best in a "normal" environment; the baby room does not need to be extra quiet while the baby is sleeping (this will create fussy sleepers that can't get enough sleep if there is any noise); in fact there is some argument for maintaining some noise in the baby room in order to nurture stronger sleeping habits. Babies should be acclimated to normal temperature swings – no need to cover them with extra blankets or clothe them in more clothes than adults. Babies can use any amount of stimulation you can give them; the main ones are auditory, visual, taste, smell, touch-pressure, and touch-temperature. Thus carrying a baby around is very good for sensory stimulation to develop the brain; touch the baby everywhere and supply lots of visual and auditory stimuli. Feed foods with as many different smells and tastes as soon as possible. There are reports that the baby has more brain cells at birth than adults, though the brain volume is only one quarter of adult size. Stimulation causes some cells to grow and lack of stimuli causes others to atrophy and disappear.

For teaching babies, the most important step is constant testing to see what they are ready to learn. Not all babies will become pianists, although at this stage, they can be guided towards practically any talent, and parents are best equipped to mold their children into careers in which the parents have expertise. ***Babies can hear right after birth.*** Many hospitals routinely screen babies immediately after birth in order to identify hearing impaired babies who will need special treatments immediately. Because hearing impaired babies do not receive sound stimuli, their brain development will be retarded; this is another evidence that music helps brain development. For babies, the memory of external sounds in the brain is initially empty. Thus any sound heard at that stage is special, and all subsequent sounds are referenced to those initial sounds. In addition, babies (of most species, not only humans) use sound to identify and bond to the parents (usually the mother). Of all the sound characteristics that the baby uses for this identification, absolute pitch is probably a major characteristic. These considerations explain why almost every youngster can readily pick up absolute pitch (AP). Some parents expose babies to music before birth to accelerate the babies' development, but I wonder if this will help AP, because the sound velocity in amniotic fluid is different from that in air with a resultant change in apparent frequency. Therefore, this practice might confuse the AP, if it works at all. For implanting AP, the electronic piano is better than an acoustic because it is always in tune.

Practically every world class musician, athlete, etc., had parents who taught them at an early age; thus "prodigies" are created, not born, and parents exert greater control over "prodigy" production than teachers or brain power. Test the child for hearing, rhythm (clapping hands), pitch (singing), motor control, attention span, what interests them, etc. As soon as they are ready (walking, speech, music, art, math, etc.), they must be taught. Teaching babies and adults is different. Adults must be taught; in young children, you only have to awaken the concept in their brains, and provide a supportive environment as their brains take off in that direction. They can quickly advance so far that you can't teach them any more.

Good examples are Mental Play (MP) and AP. Awaken MP by letting them listen to music and asking if they can sing it back to you. Let them get the idea that there is music in their head, not only the music coming in through the ears. Make sure that they listen to music in perfect tune, then teach them the scale (use C, D, E . . ., not do re mi, which should come later), then test them in the C4 octave. At this age, learning AP is automatic and almost instantaneous; when you teach them C4, they will recognize that no other note is C4, because they have no other memory to confuse them. This is why it is so critical to teach them as soon as they are ready. Then teach them the higher and lower notes – the concept of relative pitch, such as octaves; then 2-note intervals (child has to identify both notes), then 3 note chords or any 3 random notes played simultaneously -- all the way up to 10 notes, if possible. These musical lessons can be taught between the ages of 2 and 8.

MP should be taught from the very beginning in order to train the students to play music in their minds all the time. If this is done at the correct pitch, youngsters will acquire AP after only a few lessons with little effort. Support their MP by providing lots of good music to listen to, and train them to recognize compositions by name and composer. Singing or a simple musical toy (in tune) is a good way to teach pitch, rhythm, and motor control. As soon as they start piano lessons, MP is further developed by memorizing and creating a memorized repertoire. Be prepared to support them if they immediately start composing – provide ways to record their music or teach them dictation.

Long before their first piano lesson, you can show them pictures of enlarged music notes (tadpoles!) and familiarize them with the music staff, where the notes go, and where to find them on the piano. This will simplify the teacher's task of teaching them how to read music. If you are not a pianist, you can take piano lessons at the same time as your child; this is one of the best ways to get them started. This is a good time to identify those students who have little idea of pitch and to devise programs to help them. Advanced students automatically develop MP skills because MP is so necessary; however, if they are taught from the beginning, it will speed their learning rates for everything else. If MP is not taught, the students may not even realize that they are doing it, and not develop it properly. Moreover, because they are not aware of what they are doing, they will tend to neglect MP as they get older and their brains get bombarded with other pressing matters. As they neglect the MP, they will lose their AP and their ability to perform with ease. For older students and adults who want to learn MP and AP, see III.12 above.

Most importantly, remember that each child has strengths and weaknesses. It is the parents' job to find the strengths and support them, and the strengths will not always point towards a pianist career. They must be tested in sports, literature, science, art, etc., because each child is an individual. Don't be disappointed if the tests indicate that the child is not yet ready most of the time – that is normal. However, a basic piano education, following a knowledge based, project management type of method used in this book, will benefit children no matter what career they choose.

Parents must balance the physical and mental developments of their children. Because learning piano can be so fast, those olden days -- when dedicated pianists had insufficient time for sports and other activities -- are over. Techies and artists don't have to turn into wimps. There is this disturbing tendency to classify each youngster as brainy or brawny, creating a wall or even antagonism between art and physical activity, science, etc. Actually, they all follow eerily similar principles. As an example, the rules for learning golf and piano are so similar that this book can be turned into a golf manual with just a few changes. The Greeks had it right a long time ago -- mental and physical development must proceed in parallel – today, we can do even more because our knowledge base is much larger and our information infrastructure has exploded. If the parents do not provide proper guidance, some youngsters will devote all their time in one direction, neglecting everything else, developing psychological problems, and wasting precious time. Health and injury is another issue. Those music players with earphones can damage the ears so that you begin to lose hearing and suffer maddening tinnitus before age 40. Parents must educate their children to turn the volume down on those earphones, especially if they are listening to genres of music that are often played extremely loud.

c. Memorizing, Reading, Theory. The teacher must choose, at an early stage, whether the student should be taught to play from memory or learn to read music. This choice is necessitated by the fact that the details of the teaching program and how the teacher interacts with the students depend on it. ***The Suzuki violin method emphasizes playing from memory at the expense of reading, especially for youngsters, and this is the best approach for piano also.*** It is easier to practice reading *after* you can play reasonably well, just as babies learn to speak before they learn to read. The abilities to speak and to make music are natural evolutionary traits that we all have; reading is something that was added later as a consequence of our civilization. Learning to speak is simply a process of memorizing all the sounds and logical constructs of each language. Therefore, reading is more "advanced" and less "natural", and therefore cannot logically precede memory. For example, there are many musical concepts in memory (from listening to recordings) that can never be written down, such as color, playing with authority and confidence, etc. This is why memory must be taught from the very beginning.

However, reading should not be totally neglected in the beginning. It is only a matter of priority. Since music notation is simpler than any alphabet, young children can learn to read music long before they can learn to read books. Thus reading should be taught from the very beginning, but only enough to read music for learning a piece and memorizing it. ***Reading should be encouraged as long as it does not interfere with playing from memory and there should be no pressure to develop advanced reading skills.*** This means that, once a piece is memorized, the music score should not be used for daily practice. However, the teacher must make sure that this lack of emphasis on reading does not result in a poor reader who automatically memorizes everything and can't read. There is a tendency in most beginners to become either good readers (and poor memorizers) or vice versa, because when you become good at one, you need less of the other. By monitoring the student carefully, a parent or teacher can prevent the student from becoming a poor reader or a poor memorizer. Parental help is often necessary for this monitoring to succeed because the teacher is not always there when the student is practicing. In fact, many parents unwittingly create poor memorizers or poor readers by helping their children out instead of letting them practice their weaker skills. Because becoming a poor reader or memorizer happens over a long period of time, usually many years, there is ample time to detect the trend and correct it. ***Just like talent, prodigy, or genius, readers and memorizers are not born, they are created.***

Reading music is an indispensable teaching tool for teachers; the teacher's job can be made easier if the student can be taught to read. Teachers who emphasize reading are certainly justified because of the enormous amount of information that is contained in even the simplest printed music, and practically every beginning student will miss a large fraction of that information. Even advanced pianists often return to the music score to make sure that they haven't missed anything. Clearly, the best program is one based on memory, but with enough reading training so that the student does not become a poor reader. Especially for beginners, it does not pay to embark upon an intensive reading program just to be able to read (because the fingers can't play them anyway), although the initial slow reading speed can be awfully frustrating to both teacher and student. It is actually beneficial to allow the student to struggle through this slow reading stage. A major learning trick in piano pedagogy is to learn several skills simultaneously, especially because many of them take a long time to learn. Thus memorizing, reading, theory, etc., can all be learned simultaneously, saving you a lot of time in the long run. Trying to learn one of these skills quickly at the expense of the others often leads to learning difficulties.

You can never teach too much music theory (solfege): notation, dictation, absolute pitch, rhythm, etc. Learning music theory helps the students to acquire technique, memorize, understand the structure of the composition, and perform it correctly. It will also help with improvisation and composition. Statistically, the majority of successful piano students will end up composing music. The only problem with solfege lessons is that many teachers teach it inefficiently, wasting a lot of the students' time. Modern music (pop, jazz, etc.) nowadays uses very advanced musical concepts and music theory is helpful for understanding chord progressions, music structure and improvisation. Therefore, *there are advantages to learning both classical and modern music. Modern music provides contemporary theory and helps develop rhythm and performance skills, and also appeals to a wider audience.*

   d. Some Elements of Piano Lessons and performance skills. The piano lesson should not be a routine in which the student plays the lesson piece and the teacher assigns a new piece. *It is the teacher's job, when starting a new piece, to go through it in segments, examining the fingerings, analyzing the music, and basically bringing the student up to speed during the lesson, at least HS or in segments.* After the technical problems are solved, the job shifts into playing it musically -- examining the musical content, bringing out the expression, the attributes of the composer (Mozart is different from Chopin, etc.), the color, etc. A good teacher can save the students a tremendous amount of time by demonstrating all the necessary elements of technique. It should not be left to the student to try to find these out by trial and error. Because of these requirements, lessons beyond beginner level can become quite intense and time consuming. *Scales should be taught thumb-under for beginners but, within a year, they should be taught thumb-over also.* Although most exercises such as Hanon are now considered unhelpful, it is very important to be able to play scales and arpeggios (in all transpositions) well; this will require many years of hard work.

   Practicing 30 minutes every 2 or 3 days is the absolute minimum necessary to make any progress. Half an hour every day is adequate for significant progress for youngsters. As they get older, they will need progressively more time. These are minimum practice times; more time will be needed for faster progress. If the practice methods are efficient and the students are making good progress, the question of how much practice time is enough becomes meaningless – there is so much music and enjoyment that there is never enough time.

   The best way to motivate students to practice, and the best way to teach the art of making music, is to hold recitals. When the students must perform, all the teacher's instructions, the necessary practice time, etc., take on an entirely new meaning and urgency. *The students will become self-motivated.* It is a mistake to teach piano without any program of performance. There are numerous possibilities for such programs and experienced teachers will be able to design an appropriate one for each student at every level. Formal recitals and music competitions are full of pitfalls and must be approached with care and a lot of planning. However, teachers can organize informal recitals using much less stressful formats, with tremendous benefits to the students.

   Although recitals and competitions are important, it is even more important to avoid their pitfalls. The main pitfall is that recitals can be self-defeating because the stress, nervousness, extra effort and time, and sense of failure after even small mistakes, can do more harm than good in molding the performance capability/psychology of the student at any age. Therefore *teachers must have a clearly defined program or approach to teaching the art of performing in addition to the art of playing.* The preparatory methods for recitals discussed in section 14 above should be part of this program. Popular, or "fun" music is especially useful for performance training. Above all, the program must be designed to produce a rewarding atmosphere of accomplishment and not a competitive one where anything short of miraculous perfection, playing the most difficult pieces the student can manage, is a failure. In competitions, students must be taught early on that judging is frequently imperfect or unfair; that it is not the winning, but the participatory process, that is most important for its pedagogical value. Given the same piece of music to play, a relaxed and less

175

nervous student will perform better, and develop a better attitude towards performing. Students must understand that it is the process, not the winning, that is the final objective of having competitions. One of the most important components of this objective is to cultivate the ability to enjoy the experience instead of becoming nervous. One of the worst pitfalls of most competitions is the emphasis on the most difficult material that the student can play. The correct emphasis should be on the music, not the acrobatics.

Of course we must aim to win competitions and play flawless recitals. But there are stressful and less stressful approaches to these objectives. ***It is the teacher's job to teach stress control.*** Unfortunately, the majority of teachers today totally ignore performance stress control or worse, parents and teachers frequently pretend that there is no such thing as nervousness even when they themselves are nervous. This can have the effect of creating a permanent problem with nervousness. See section 15 above for discussions on controlling nervousness.

It is important to first teach a student all about nervousness and stress and not to shove them out on a stage to perform with no preparation in the vain hope that they will somehow learn to perform on their own. Such action is quite analogous to throwing a person into the middle of a deep lake to teach them how to swim; that person can end up with a lifelong fear of water. Playing for the teacher at every lesson is a good start, but is woefully insufficient preparation. Thus the teacher should design a "performance training" routine in which the student is gradually introduced to performances. This training must start with the first piano lessons. Various skills, such as recovering from blackouts, preventing blackouts, covering mistakes, sensing mistakes before they occur, snippet playing, starting from arbitrary places in a piece, choice of pieces to perform, audience communication, etc., should be taught. Above all, they must learn mental play. We saw that HS practice, slow play, and "playing cold" are the important components of preparation. Most students will not know which "finished" pieces they can perform satisfactorily until they actually play them in recitals several times; therefore, even among finished pieces, every student will have a "performable" and a "questionable" repertoire. ***One of the best ways to train for performances is to record the student's finished pieces and produce an album of finished repertoire that is periodically updated as the student advances.*** This should be done from the very beginning of lessons so as to cultivate the skill as early as possible. The first mistake most pianists make is to think that "I am still a beginner, so my playing is not worth recording". Once you buy that argument in the beginning, you will end up following it the rest of your life because it becomes a self-fulfilling prophesy. That argument is false because music is supreme -- easy compositions, played musically, is as good as it gets; Horowitz cannot play "chopsticks" any better than a well-taught beginner.

Without performance training, even good performers will not perform to their best ability, and the majority of students will end up thinking that piano performance as a kind of hell that is associated with music or piano. Once that attitude is ingrained in youth, they will carry it into adulthood. The truth should be the exact opposite. Performance should be the final goal, the final reward for all the hard work. It is the demonstration of the ability to sway an audience, the ability to convey the grandest designs of the greatest musical geniuses that every lived. ***Secure mental play is the single most effective method for reducing stage fright.***

One way to introduce students to performing at recitals is to hold mock recitals among the students themselves and to have them discuss their fears, difficulties, weaknesses, and strengths to get them all acquainted with the main issues. How do you play mentally? Do you do it all the time? Do you use photographic memory or keyboard memory, or mostly music memory? Does it happen automatically or do you do it at certain times? Students will understand the issues better when they can actually feel them and then discuss them openly with their peers. Any nervousness they might feel becomes less scary when they realize that everyone experiences the same things, that nervousness is perfectly natural, and that there are various ways to combat them or even take advantage of them. In particular, once they go through the entire process from start to finish of a mock recital, the whole procedure becomes much less mysterious and frightening. *Students must be taught that learning to enjoy performing is part of the art of piano. That "art of performing" also requires study and practice, just like finger technique.* In a group of students, there is always one that is good at performing. The others can learn by watching and discussing how these good ones cope with each issue. Then there are students who just freeze on a stage – these need special help, such as learning very simple pieces to perform, or given several chances to perform in one recital, or perform with a group or in duets.

Another way to introduce students to performances and at the same time have some fun is to schedule an informal recital in which the students play a game of "who can play fastest". In this game, every student plays the same piece, but the amount of practice time is limited, say, to three weeks. Note that in this ruse, the hidden agenda is to teach the students how to enjoy giving recitals, not to teach them how to play fast. The students themselves vote for the winner. At first, the teacher gives no instructions; students must choose their own practice methods. After the first recital, the teacher holds a group lesson in which the students discuss their practice methods and the teacher adds any useful information. Of course, clarity, accuracy, and music must be considered in choosing a winner. Music can be made to sound faster by playing more slowly but more accurately. There will be wide differences in the practice methods and achievements of the various students and, in this way, they will learn from each other and will understand the basic teachings better. While the students are participating in a "contest", it is the teacher's job to ensure that it is a fun experience, a way to experience the joy of performing, a way to completely forget about nervousness. Mistakes evoke laughter, they are not to be frowned upon. And refreshments might be served afterwards. The teacher must not forget to intersperse instructions for learning to perform, together with the "contest" skills.

Once the students are taught the basics of performance, how should recitals be organized? They should be designed to strengthen performance capability. *One of the hardest things to do is to perform the same composition several times on the same day or on successive days.* Therefore, such repeat performances provide the best training for strengthening the performance capability. For teachers or schools with a sufficient number of students, the following is a good scheme to use. Group the students into beginner, intermediate, and advanced. On Friday, hold a recital of the beginners, with their parents and friends as audience. Beginners should participate in recitals from their first year of lessons, as early as 4 or 5 years of age. At the end of this recital, the advanced students also play, which makes it really worthwhile for the audience to attend. On Saturday, the intermediate students play, with their parents and friends as audience; again, the advanced students play at the end. On Sunday, the advanced students hold their recital, with their parents/friends as the audience; some special guests might be invited. In this way, the advanced students get to perform the same piece three days in a row. The Sunday recital of the advanced students should be recorded and copied onto CD's, as they make excellent souvenirs. If this type of recital is held twice a year, each advanced student will have six recitals under their belt every year. If these students are also entered into competitions (typically involving an audition, a final, and, if they win, a winner's concert), they will have adequate performance training (at least 9 performances a year). Since most pieces are not "secure" until they are performed 3 times, this recital scheme will also serve to make the recital piece "secure" so that it can now be included in the "performable" repertoire, after just one weekend of recitals.

Teachers should be willing to communicate with other teachers, exchange ideas, and learn from each other. There is nothing as potentially damaging to a student as a teacher whose teaching methods are inflexible and frozen in time. In this information age, there is no such thing as secret methods of teaching piano, and the success of the teacher depends on open communications. An important topic of communication is the exchange of students. Most students can benefit greatly by having been taught by more than one teacher. Teachers of beginners should pass their students to higher level teachers as soon as they are ready. Of course, most teachers will try to keep their best students and to teach as many students as they can. One way to solve this problem is for teachers to form groups consisting of teachers with different specialties so that the group forms a complete school. This also helps the teachers because it will make it much easier for them to find students. For students looking for good teachers, it is clear from these considerations that it is best to look for groups of teachers rather than teachers who operate individually. Teachers can also benefit by banding together and sharing students and costs of facilities.

Starting teachers often have difficulty finding their first students. Joining a group of teachers is a good way to get started. Also many established teachers often have to turn away students because of a lack of time, especially if the teacher has a good reputation in that local area. Those teachers are good sources of students. One way to increase the pool of potential students is to offer to go to the students' homes to teach. For at least the first few years when a new teacher starts to teach, this might be a good approach for increasing the potential student pool.

e. Why the Greatest Pianists Could Not Teach. Very few of the greatest pianists were good teachers. This is eminently natural because artists train all their lives to be artists, not teachers. I experienced an analogous situation as a graduate physics student at Cornell University where I took courses taught by professors who specialized in teaching, and where I also attended weekly lectures by famous physicists including Nobel Prize winners. Some of those renowned physicists could certainly present exciting lectures that attracted great interest, but I learned most of the skills needed to find a job as a physicist from the teaching professors, not the Nobel laureates. This difference in teaching ability between teaching and practicing scientists pales in comparison with the chasm that exists in the arts world because of the nature of the scientific discipline (see IV.2). *Learning and teaching are an integral part of being a scientist. By contrast, the greatest pianists were either reluctantly, or by economic necessity, pushed into teaching for which they received no meaningful training.* Thus there are plenty of reasons why the great performers were not good teachers.

Unfortunately, we have historically looked to the famous artists for guidance, under the rationale that if they can do it, they should be able to show us how. Typical historical accounts reveal that, if you were to ask a famous pianist how to play a certain passage, s/he will sit at the piano and play it out because the language of the pianist is spoken by the hands and the piano, not the mouth. That same great artist may have little idea about how the fingers are moving or how they are manipulating the piano keys. In order to move the hands in the proper way, you must learn to control thousands of muscles and nerves, and then train the hands to execute those motions. There are two extremes among the ways to acquire technique. One extreme is the analytical one, in which every motion, every muscle and every physiological information is analyzed. The other extreme is the artist's approach, in which the person simply imagines a certain musical output and the body responds in different ways until the desired result is obtained. This artist's approach can not only be a quick shortcut, but can also yield unexpected results that may exceed the original idea. It also has the advantage that a "genius" without analytical training can be successful. The disadvantage is that there is no assurance of success. Technique acquired in this way cannot be taught analytically, except by saying that "you must feel the music this way" in order to play it. Unfortunately, for those who do not know how to do it yet, this kind of instruction is of little help, except as a demonstration that it can be done. Also, even knowing the practice methods isn't enough. You need the correct explanation of why they work. This requirement is often outside the expertise of the artist or piano teacher. Thus there is a fundamental impediment to proper development of piano teaching tools: artists and piano teachers do not have the training to develop such tools; on the other hand, scientists and engineers who may have such training have insufficient piano experience to research piano methods.

The old masters were geniuses, of course, and had some remarkable insights and inventiveness as well as intuitive feel of mathematics and physics which they applied to their piano playing. Therefore, it is incorrect to conclude that they had no analytical approaches to technique; practically every analytical solution to piano practice that we know of today was re-invented many times by these geniuses or at least used by them. It is therefore unbelievable that no one ever thought of documenting these ideas in a systematic way. It is even more amazing that there does not seem to have been even a general realization by both teachers and students that practice methods were the key to acquiring technique. A few good teachers have always known that talent is more created than born (Olson). The main difficulty seems to have been the inability of the artist approach to identify the correct theoretical basis (explanation) for why these practice methods work. Without a sound theoretical explanation or basis, even a correct method can be misused, misunderstood, changed, or degraded by different teachers so that it may not always work and be viewed as unreliable or useless. These historical facts prevented any orderly development of piano teaching methods. Thus the understanding, or the explanation of why a method works, is at least as important as the method itself. This situation was aggravated by emphasis on "talent" as the road to success. This was a convenient ruse for successful pianists who got more credit than they deserved and at the same time were freed from the responsibility for their inability to teach the "less talented". And, of course, the "talent" label contributed to their economic success.

In addition, piano teachers tended to be poor communicators in the sense that they tended not to share teaching ideas. Only at large conservatories was there any significant mixing of ideas so that the quality of teaching at conservatories was better than elsewhere. However, the problems of the preceding paragraph prevented any truly systematic developments of teaching methods even at these organizations. An additional factor was the stratification of piano learning into beginners and advanced students. Conservatories generally accepted only advanced students; yet, without conservatory type teaching, few students attained the advanced levels necessary to be accepted. This gave piano learning a reputation as something far more difficult than it really was. The bottleneck created by a lack of good teaching methods was historically attributed to lack of "talent". When all these historical facts are assembled, it is easy to understand why the great masters could not teach, and why even dedicated piano teachers did not have all the tools they needed.

Although I started writing this book as just a compilation of some remarkably effective teaching tools, it has evolved into a project that solves many of the historical deficiencies responsible for the difficulties of acquiring technique. Fate has suddenly turned the future of piano into a wide, open future with limitless possibilities. We are entering a brave, new, exciting era that can finally be enjoyed by everyone because *we are unlocking the secrets of how to be a "genius"*. Example: Mozart was fabled to have the ability to speak sentences backwards. If you have any MP skills, that is easy. Simply write "kiss me" in your mind and read it backwards! Practice with two-word sentences, then longer ones. You will quickly discover that you don't need to be a genius to do what he did, and you can demonstrate to your friends that you are as good as Mozart.

17. Upright, Grand & Electronic Pianos; Purchasing and Care

a. Grand, Upright, or Electronic? Grands have certain advantages over uprights. However, these advantages are minor compared to the importance of the skill level of the pianist. *There are great pianists who became technically advanced practicing mostly on uprights. There is no evidence that you need a grand for initial technical development*, although a few piano teachers will insist that any serious student must practice on a grand. An argument can be made in favor of uprights, at least for beginners, because uprights require firmer playing and may be better for early finger development (you need to press harder in order to make louder sounds). They may be superior even for intermediate students because uprights are less forgiving and require greater technical skill to play. These arguments are controversial, but do illustrate the point that, for students up to intermediate level, any differences among uprights and grands are small compared to other factors such as student motivation, quality of teachers, practice methods, and proper piano maintenance.

Another factor is piano quality: good uprights are superior to low quality grands (which includes most grands under 5.2 feet). The rule concerning uprights is simple: if you already have one, there is no reason to get rid of it until you buy an electronic or a grand; if you don't have a piano, there is no compelling reason to buy an upright. Students above intermediate level will need a grand piano because the most technically difficult music is harder (if not impossible) to play on most uprights and electronics.

Electronics are fundamentally different from acoustics (grands and uprights). The construction of their actions is not as good (not as expensive) and most electronics do not have good enough speaker systems to compete with the acoustics. Acoustics, therefore, produce sound in a fundamentally different way which causes many critics to favor acoustics because of better control over "tone". Thus the question of which instrument is best is a complex one depending on the person's circumstances, and specific requirements. We will now discuss each type below so that we can make an intelligent decision on which type of instrument is best for which student.

b. Electronic Pianos. Today's electronic (or digital) pianos are still inferior to good grands for technical development but are improving rapidly. Even the best electronics are inadequate for advanced pianists; their mechanical response is poorer, the musical output and dynamic range are inferior, and fast, technically advanced material becomes difficult to execute. Most inexpensive speakers can not compete with the soundboard of a grand. The electronic pianos do not allow the control of tone, color, pianissimo, staccato, and the special manipulations of the damper and soft pedals, that good grands provide. Thus there is no question that an advanced pianist will prefer a grand piano over an electronic; however, this conclusion assumes that the grand is tuned at least twice a year, and is regulated and voiced whenever necessary. Most uprights do not provide sufficient advantage for technical development to warrant their use over quality electronics that are readily available, comparatively inexpensive, and costs little to maintain.

The electronic pianos have some unique advantages, so we discuss them here. Because of these advantages, most serious pianists will own both an acoustic and an electronic.

(i) For less than half the price of an average acoustic upright, you can buy a new electronic piano with all the features you need: headphone and volume control, touch control, organ, string, harpsichord, metronome, recording and midi/analog out, transposition, different tunings and canned accompaniments. Most electronics provide much more, but these are the minimum features you can expect. The argument that an acoustic piano is a better investment than an electronic is false because an acoustic piano is not a good investment, especially when the initial cost is so much higher and initial depreciation is large. The electronic piano requires no maintenance, whereas the maintenance costs of acoustics are substantial, since they require tuning, voicing, and regulation about twice a year, plus occasional repairs.

(ii) The electronics are always in perfect tune. Very young children exposed sufficiently to perfectly tuned pianos acquire absolute pitch automatically, although most parents never discover this because, if it is not discovered and maintained, it is lost during the teen years. The acoustic piano begins to go out of tune the minute the tuner leaves your house, and some notes will be out of tune most of the time (in fact, most of the notes will be out of tune most of the time). However, these small deviations from tuning will not affect the learning of absolute pitch unless the piano is allowed to go way out of tune. Because too many acoustic pianos are inadequately maintained, the fact that the electronics are always in tune can be a big advantage. ***The importance of a well tuned piano for musical and technical development cannot be over-emphasized, because without the musical development, you will never learn how to perform.*** The sound of an electronic can be greatly improved by hooking it up to a set of good speakers or sound system.

(iii) You can use headphones or adjust the volume so that you can practice without disturbing others. The ability to turn down the volume is also useful for reducing ear damage when practicing loud passages: an important factor for anyone over 60 years old, when many will start to suffer from

hearing loss or tinnitus. If you are an advanced player, even an electronic will create considerable "playing noise" (with the volume turned off) that can be quite loud to anyone nearby and these vibrations can transmit through the floor to rooms under the piano. Therefore it is a mistake to think that the sound from an electronic (or an acoustic with "silent" feature) can be completely turned off.

(iv) They are more portable than acoustics. Although there are light keyboards with similar features, it is best for piano practice to use the heavier electronics so that they do not shift while playing loud, fast music. Even these heavier electronics can be easily carried by two persons, and will fit in many cars.

(v) Variable touch weight is more important than many people realize. However, you have to know what "touch weight" means before you can use it to advantage; see the following paragraphs for details. In general, the touch weight of electronics is a little lighter than that of acoustics. This lighter weight was chosen for two reasons: to make it easier for keyboard players to play these electronics (keyboards are even lighter), and to make them easier to play compared to the acoustics. The disadvantage of the lighter weight is that you may find it slightly more difficult to play an acoustic after practicing on an electronic. The touch weight of acoustics needs to be heavier in order to produce a richer tone. One advantage of heavier weight is that you can feel the keys of an acoustic while playing, without inadvertently playing some wrong notes. However, this can also lead to careless playing with some inadvertent finger motions because you can lightly hit a key of an acoustic without making any sound. You can practice getting rid of these uncontrolled motions by practicing on an electronic and choosing a light touch weight so that any inadvertent strike will produce a sound. Many people who practice only on acoustics don't even know that they have such uncontrolled motions until they try to play on an electronic, and find out that they are hitting a lot of extra keys. The light touch is also useful for acquiring difficult technique quickly. Then, if you need to play on an acoustic later on, you can practice with increased weight after you acquire the technique. This two-step process is usually faster than trying to acquire technique at heavy key weight.

(vi) Recording piano music is one of the most difficult things to do using conventional recording equipment. With an electronic piano, you can do it with the push of a button! You can easily build up an album of all the pieces you learned. Recording is one of the best ways not only to really finish and polish your pieces but also to learn how to perform for an audience. Everyone should cultivate a habit of recording every finished piece from the very beginning of her/is lessons. Of course, the initial performances will not be perfect, so you may want to go back and re-record them as you improve. Too many students never record their performances, which is the main reason for excessive nervousness and difficulties during performances.

(vii) Most pianists who follow good practice methods and become proficient when young will end up composing their own music. *Electronic pianos are helpful for recording your compositions so that you don't need to write them down, and for playing them in different instruments*, as appropriate for each composition. With some additional software or hardware, you can even compose entire symphonies and play every instrument yourself. There is even software that will transcribe (though imperfectly) your music onto sheet music. However, there is nothing like a quality grand to help you compose – the sound from a great piano somehow inspires the composing process; therefore, if you are a serious composer, most electronics will be inadequate.

(viii) If you can acquire technique rapidly, there is nothing stopping you from broadening your horizon beyond classical music and playing popular music, jazz, blues, etc. You will appeal to a wider audience if you can mix music genres and you will have more fun. The electronic piano can help by providing the accompaniments, drums, etc., for those types of music. Thus these extra capabilities of the electronic pianos can be very useful and should not be ignored. They are more easily transportable for gigs.

(ix) Buying electronic pianos is very simple, especially when compared to buying acoustics (see

section e). All you need to know is your price range, the features you want, and the manufacturer. You don't need an experienced piano technician to help you evaluate the piano. There are no questions about whether the piano dealer made all the proper "prepping", whether the dealer will honor the agreements to ensure that the piano functions after delivery, whether the piano was properly "stabilized" during the first year of ownership, or whether you got one with good or inferior tone and touch. Many established manufacturers, such as Yamaha, Roland, Korg, Technic, Kawai, and Kurzweil, produce electronics of excellent quality.

(x) And this is only the beginning; electronics will improve in leaps and bounds with time. One recent development is piano modeling (see <u>Pianoteq</u>), instead of the sampling used before. Good sampling requires a tremendous amount of memory and processing power, which can slow down the piano response. Modeling is more versatile and enables things you can not do even on a grand, such as partial soft pedal, control the hammer shank flex or let you play Chopin's Pleyel.

(xi) We should all move towards WT (Well Temperaments – see Chapt. Two, 2.c) and away from ET (Equal Temperament that is universally accepted today). Once you decide to use WT, you will need several of them. Learning to discern and bring out key color is a most valuable skill. ET is the worst tuning for this. With electronic pianos, you can get most of the common WTs.

The *touch weight* of a piano is not a simple matter of adding or subtracting lead weights to the keys to change the force required to depress them. The touch weight is a combination of the *down weight*, the inertia of the keys and hammers, and the force required to produce a certain volume of sound. ***The down weight is the maximum weight that the key will support before it will start to move down.*** This is the weight that is adjusted using lead weights, etc. The down weight of all pianos, including the "weighted key" electronics, is standardized at about 50 grams and varies little from piano to piano regardless of touch weight. When playing a piano, this 50 gram weight is a small fraction of the force required to play -- most of the force is used to produce the sound. In acoustic pianos, this is the force needed to impart velocity to the hammer. In electronics, it is the electronic reaction to the key motion and a fixed mechanical resistance. In both cases, you also have to overcome the inertia of the mechanism in addition to supplying the force for producing the sound. For example, when playing staccato, most of the force required is for overcoming the inertia whereas when playing legato, the inertial component is small. Electronics have a smaller inertial component because they have only the inertia of the keys whereas the acoustics have the additional inertia of the hammers; this makes the acoustics less sensitive to inadvertent hitting of the keys. Therefore, you will feel the most difference between acoustics and electronics when playing fast or staccato and little difference when playing slow legato. ***For the pianist, touch weight is the effort required to produce a certain volume of sound and has little to do with down weight.*** For acoustics, touch weight is determined mostly by hammer mass and voicing (hardness of the hammer). There is only a narrow range of hammer masses that is ideal because you want heavier hammers for larger sound but lighter ones for faster action. Thus a lot of the touch weight can be adjusted by the piano technician by hammer voicing, rather than by changing the down weight. For electronic pianos, touch weight is controlled in the software by switching to the sound of a softer hammer for heavier touch weight and vice versa, which simulates an acoustic grand; there is no mechanical change to the down weight of the keys or the inertial component. Thus if you switch to the heaviest key weight, you might feel that the sound is somewhat muffled and if you switch to the lightest weight, the sound might be more brilliant. In electronic pianos, it is easier to decrease the touch weight without adversely affecting the sound because there is no hammer to adjust. On the other hand, the maximum dynamic range of most electronic pianos is limited by the speakers, so that it is generally easier to play a larger dynamic range with acoustic grands. In summary, ***touch weight is mainly a subjective judgment by the pianist about how much effort is required to produce a certain volume of sound; it is not the down weight (resistance of the keys to the keydrop).*** Some pianists have asked their tuners to increase the down weight (with the hope of increasing finger strength), but this throws the piano out of regulation and is bad for technical development (velocity, musicality).

You can demonstrate this subjective judgment by turning the volume up or down using the electronic piano and trying to achieve the same loudness. Thus if you practice on an electronic for a long time with the volume turned down, and then play an acoustic, the acoustic can feel downright light. Unfortunately, things are a little more complicated because when you switch to a heavier touch weight with the electronic piano, it gives you the sound of a softer hammer. In order to reproduce the sound of a properly voiced hammer, you need to strike harder. This adds to the perception of a heavier key weight, and this effect cannot be simulated by changing the volume control. From these discussions, we can conclude that: there are small differences in the touch weight between grands and electronics, with the grands tending to be heavier, but those differences are not sufficient to cause major problems when switching from one to the other. Thus the fear that practicing on an electronic will make it difficult to play on a grand is unfounded; in fact, it is more likely to be easier, although it may take a few minutes of playing on the grand to get used to it.

If you are a beginner purchasing your first piano, an electronic is the obvious choice, unless you can afford a quality grand and have space for it. Even in that case, you will probably want an electronic piano also because the cost of the electronic will be negligible compared to the grand, and it gives you so many features that the grand does not have. *Most acoustic uprights are now obsolete.*

c. Uprights. Acoustic uprights do have some advantages. They are less expensive than grands. They take up less space, and for small rooms, large grands may produce too much sound so that they cannot be played full blast with the lid fully open without hurting or even damaging the ears. However, the electronics have these same advantages plus many more. Owners of uprights too often neglect hammer voicing entirely because this neglect results in more sound. Since uprights are essentially closed instruments, the neglect of voicing is less noticeable. Uprights also tend to be less expensive to maintain, mainly because expensive repairs are not worthwhile and are therefore not performed. Of course, there are quality uprights that are competitive with grands in feel and sound quality, but they cost as much as grands.

Among uprights, spinets are the smallest and generally the least expensive pianos; most do not produce satisfactory sound, even for students. The small height of spinets limits the string length, which is the main limitation on sound output. In theory, the treble should produce satisfactory sound (there is no limitation on string length even for spinets), but most spinets are weak in the treble because of poor quality of construction; therefore, be sure to test the higher notes if you are evaluating a spinet – simply compare it with a larger piano. Console or larger size uprights can be good student pianos. Old uprights with poor sound are generally not salvageable, no matter what their size. At such an age, the value of the piano is less than the cost of restoring them; it is cheaper to buy a newer upright with satisfactory sound. *Most uprights have been "obsoleted" by the electronics. Therefore, there is no reason to buy a new upright, although some piano teachers and most piano stores might suggest otherwise.* Many piano teachers have not had enough experience with electronics and are more accustomed to the feel and sound of the acoustic uprights and tend to recommend acoustics as "real pianos", which is generally a mistake. The difficulty of purchasing a quality upright, the problems frequently encountered with having it properly "prepped" before and after delivery, and the need to keep it regulated and in tune, are not worth the slight difference in "tone", if any.

d. Grands. The advantages of most grands are: greater dynamic range (loud/soft), open structure allowing the sound to escape freely (which provides more control and expression), richer sound, faster repetition, smoother action (use of gravity instead of springs), a "true" soft pedal (see section II.24), clearer sound (easier to tune accurately) and more impressive appearance. An exception is the class of "baby" grands (less than about 5'-2") whose sound output is usually unsatisfactory and should be considered mainly as decorative furniture. A few companies (Yamaha,

Kawai) are beginning to produce baby grands with acceptable sound, so for these very new pianos, don't write them off without testing them. Larger grands can be classified into two main classes, the "student grands" (those below about 6 to 7 ft), and the concert grands. The concert grands provide more dynamic range, better sound quality, and more tonal control.

As an example of this "quality versus size" issue, consider the Steinway pianos. The baby model, model S (5'-2"), is essentially a decorative furniture and very few produce sufficient quality sound to be considered playable and are inferior to many uprights. The next larger size group consists of models M, O, and L (5'-7" to 5'-11"). These models are quite similar and are excellent student pianos. However, advanced pianists would not consider them to be true grands because of poorer sustain, too much percussive sound, and notes with too much harmonic content. The next model, A (6'-2"), is borderline, and B(6'-10"), C(7'-5"), and D(9') are true grands. One problem with evaluating Steinways is that the quality within each model is extremely variable; however, on average, there is a significant improvement in sound quality and output with each increase in size.

Grands require hammer voicing more frequently than uprights; otherwise, they become too "brilliant" or "harsh", at which point most owners will end up playing the grand with the lid closed. Many homeowners ignore voicing entirely. The result is that such grands produce too much and too harsh sound, and are therefore played with the lid down. There is nothing technically wrong with playing a grand with the lid closed. However, some purists will express dismay at such practice, and you are certainly throwing away something wonderful for which you made a significant investment. Performances at recitals almost always require the lid to be open, resulting in a more sensitive piano. Therefore you should always practice with the lid open before a performance even if you normally practice with it closed. In a large room, or in a recital hall, there is much less multiple reflection of the sound so that you do not hear the deafening roar that can result in a small room. A concert hall will absorb the sound from the piano so that, if you are accustomed to practicing in a small room, you will have difficulty hearing your own playing in a concert hall.

One of the biggest advantages of grand pianos is the use of gravity as the return force of the hammer. In uprights the restoring force for the hammer is supplied by springs. Gravity is always constant and uniform across the entire keyboard whereas non-uniformities in the springs and friction can create non-uniformities in the feel of the keys of an upright. Uniformity of feel is one of the most important properties of well-regulated, quality pianos. Many students are intimidated by the appearance of huge grands at recitals and competitions, but these grands are actually easier to play than uprights. One fear that these students have concerning these grands is that their actions may be heavier. However, touch weight is something that is adjusted by the technician regulating the piano and can be adjusted to any number regardless of whether the piano is an upright or a grand. Advanced students will of course find it easier to play demanding pieces on grands than uprights, mainly because of the faster action and uniformity. Consequently, *good grands can save you a lot of time when you try to acquire advanced skills*. The main reason for this is that it is easy to develop bad habits when struggling with difficult material on uprights. Challenging material is even more difficult on electronic pianos (and impossible on models without proper touch weight) because they do not have the robustness and response to touch that are required at high speeds.

Some people with small rooms agonize over whether a large grand would be too loud in such a space. Loudness is usually not the most important issue, and you always have the option of closing the lid to different degrees. The maximum loudness of the medium and large grands is not that different, and *you can play softer with the larger grands*. It is the multiple sound reflections that are most bothersome. Multiple reflections can be easily eliminated by a carpet on the floor and sound-insulation on one or two walls. Thus if the piano physically fits into a room with no obvious difficulties, then it may be acceptable from the sound point of view.

e. Purchasing an Acoustic Piano. Buying an acoustic piano can be a trying experience for the uninitiated, whether they buy new or used. If a reputable dealer can be found, it is certainly safer to buy new but even then the cost of the initial depreciation is large. Many piano stores will rent you the piano with an agreement that the rental will be applied to the purchase price in case you decide to keep it. In that case, make sure that you negotiate for the best purchase price *before* you even discuss rental; after you agree to a rental, you will have very little negotiating power. You will end up with a higher initial price so that, even after subtracting the rental, the final price is not a bargain. Even with expensive pianos, many dealers find it too costly to keep them prepped and in tune. At such dealers, it is difficult to test the piano by playing it. ***Thus buying an acoustic piano is usually a hit-or-miss proposition and is usually a stressful and time-consuming experience.*** For mass produced pianos such as Yamaha or Kawai, the quality of their new pianos tends to be uniform, so that you know pretty much what you will get. The sound quality of the more expensive "hand made" pianos can vary considerably so that buying these pianos is more difficult if you want to pick a good one.

Good used acoustic pianos are difficult to find in piano stores because playable pianos sell first and most stores are left with an excess inventory of unplayable ones. ***Obviously, the best bargains are to be found among the private sales. For the uninitiated, you will need to hire a piano tuner/technician to evaluate the used pianos in the private market.*** You will also need a lot of patience because good private sales are not always there when you need them. However, the wait can be worthwhile because the same piano will cost only half as much (or less) at a private sale compared to the store. There is a steady demand for good, reasonably priced pianos. This means that it is not easy to find bargains at widely accessible sites, such as the internet piano markets, because good pianos sell quickly. Conversely, such sites are excellent places to sell, especially if you have a good piano. The best place to find bargains is the classified section of newspapers at large metropolitan areas. Most such advertisements are placed on Friday, Saturday, or Sunday.

Only a few name brand pianos "hold their value" when kept for many years. The rest quickly lose their value so that trying to sell them years after purchase (new) is not worthwhile. "Hold value" means that their resale value will keep up with inflation; it does not mean that you can sell them for a profit. Thus if you bought a piano for $1,000 and sold it 30 years later for $10,000, you have made no profit if inflation is 10X during those 30 years. In addition, you will incur the cost of tuning and maintenance of at least $2000 for this example. It is cheaper to buy a brand new 7 ft Yamaha grand every 30-40 years than to buy a new Steinway M and completely restore it every 30-40 years; therefore, the choice of which piano to buy does not depend on economics but on what type of piano you need. With very few exceptions, pianos are not good investments; you have to be an experienced piano technician in order to find bargains in the used piano market that can be resold for a profit. Even if you find such a bargain, selling pianos is a time consuming, labor-intensive task. For more details on how to buy a piano, consult Larry Fine's book. Even with the most famous brands, a newly purchased piano will immediately lose 20% to 30% of its purchase price upon delivery, and will in general depreciate to half of the price of an equivalent new piano in about 5 years. As a very rough "rule of thumb" a used piano will cost about half the price of the new one of the same model in a piano store and almost 1/4 at a private sale.

The price of pianos can be roughly classified according to whether they are worth rebuilding. Those worth rebuilding tend to cost at least twice as much when new. Practically all uprights and all mass produced grands (Yamaha, Kawai, etc), are not rebuilt because the rebuilding cost is about as high as the price of a new piano of the same model. Rebuilding such pianos is often impossible because the rebuilding trade and necessary parts are non-existent. Pianos worth rebuilding are Steinway, Bosendorfer, Bechstein, Mason and Hamlin, some Knabe, and a few others. Roughly speaking, it costs about 1/4 of the price of a new piano to rebuild and the resale value is about 1/2 of new; this is why rebuilding such pianos can be cost effective, for both the rebuilder and the buyer.

f. Piano Care. All new pianos need at least a year of special care and tuning after purchase, in order for the strings to stop stretching and the action and hammers to equilibrate. Most piano dealers will try to minimize the cost of servicing the new pianos after delivery. This is assuming that the piano was properly prepped prior to delivery. Many dealers postpone a lot of the prep work until after delivery, and if the customer does not know about it, may omit some steps entirely. In this regard, among the less expensive models, Yamaha, Kawai, Petroff, and a few others may be easier to buy because most of the prep work is completed at the factory. A new piano will need at least 4 tunings the first year in order to stabilize the stretching of the strings.

All pianos require maintenance in addition to regular tuning. In general, the better the quality of the piano, the easier it is to notice the deterioration caused by normal wear and tear, and therefore the more maintenance it should receive. That is, more expensive pianos are more expensive to maintain. Typical maintenance chores are: leveling the keys, reducing friction (such as polishing the capstans), eliminating extraneous sounds, re-shaping the hammers and voicing them (needling), checking the innumerable bushings, etc. Voicing the hammer is probably the most neglected maintenance procedure. Worn, hard, hammers can cause string breakage, loss of musical control, and difficulty in playing softly (the last two are bad for technical development). It also ruins the tonal quality of the piano, making it harsh and unpleasant to the ear. If the action is sufficiently worn, it may need a general regulation job, which means restoring all parts of the action to their original specifications.

If the bass wire-wound strings are rusted, this can deaden those notes. Replacing these strings is worthwhile if those notes are weak and have no sustain. The upper, non-wound strings generally do not need replacing even if they appear rusted. However, for extremely old pianos, these strings can be so stretched out that they have lost all elasticity. Such strings are prone to breakage and cannot vibrate properly, produce a tinny sound, and should be replaced.

Pianists should familiarize themselves with some of the basic knowledge about tuning, such as the parts of a piano, temperaments, stability of tuning, and effects of temperature and humidity changes, in order to be able to communicate with the tuner and to understand what s/he needs to do. Too many piano owners are ignorant of these basics; consequently, they frustrate the tuner and in fact work against her/im, with the result that the piano is not properly maintained. Some owners get so accustomed to their deteriorated piano that, when the tuner does a good job of restoring it to its original glory, the owner is unhappy about the strange new sound and feel of the piano. Worn hammers tend to produce overly bright and loud sounds; this has the unexpected effect of making the action feel light. Therefore, properly voiced hammers may initially give the impression that the action is now heavier and less responsive. Of course, the tuner did not change the force required to depress the keys. Once the owners become accustomed to the newly voiced hammers, they will find that they have much better control of expression and tone, and they can now play very softly.

Pianos need to be tuned at least once a year and preferably twice, during the fall and spring, when the temperature and humidity are midway between their yearly extremes. Many advanced pianists have them tuned more frequently. In addition to the obvious advantages of being able to create better music and to sharpen your musicality, there are many compelling reasons for keeping the piano tuned. One of the most important is that it can affect your technical development. *Compared to an out-of-tune piano, a well-tuned piano practically plays itself -- you will find it surprisingly easier to play. Thus a well maintained piano can accelerate technical development. An out-of-tune piano can lead to flubs and the stuttering habit of pausing at every mistake.* Many important aspects of expression can be brought out only on well-tuned pianos. Since we must always pay attention to practicing musically, it does not make sense to practice on a piano that cannot produce proper music. This is one of the reasons why I prefer Well Temperaments (with their crystal clear chords) to the Equal Temperament, in which only the octaves are clear. See Chapter Two for more discussions on the merits of various temperaments. Higher quality pianos have a distinct edge because they not only hold the tuning better, but can also be tuned more accurately. Lower quality pianos often have extraneous beats and sounds that make accurate tuning impossible.

Those who have absolute pitch (AP) are very much bothered by pianos that are out of tune. If you have AP, severely out of tune pianos can accelerate the gradual loss of AP with age. *Babies and very young children can automatically acquire AP if they hear the piano sound sufficiently frequently, even if they have no idea what AP is. In order for them to acquire the correct AP, the piano must be in tune.*

If you always practice on a tuned piano, you will have a difficult time playing on one that is out of tune. The music doesn't come out, you make unexpected mistakes, and have memory blackouts. This holds true even if you know nothing about tuning and can't even tell if a particular note is out of tune. For a pianist unfamiliar with tuning, the best way to test the tuning is to play a piece of music. Good tuning is like magic to any pianist. By playing a piece of music, most pianists can readily hear the difference between a poor tuning and an excellent one, even if they cannot tell the difference by playing single notes or test intervals (assuming they are not also piano tuners). Therefore, along with technical development, every pianist must learn to hear the benefits of good tuning. It may be a good idea to play an out-of-tune piano once in a while in order to know what to expect in case you are asked to perform on one with questionable tuning. For recitals, it is a good idea to tune the recital piano just before the recital, so that the recital piano is in better tune than the practice piano. Try to avoid the reverse case in which the practice piano is in better tune than the recital piano. This is another reason why students who practice on inexpensive uprights have little problem with playing recitals on large, unfamiliar grands, as long as the grands are in tune.

In summary, grands are not necessary for technical development up to about the intermediate level, although they will be beneficial at any level. Above intermediate level, the arguments in favor of grands over uprights become compelling. Grands are better because their actions are faster, they can be tuned more accurately, have a larger dynamic range, have a true soft pedal, can enable more control over expression and tone (you can open the lid), and can be regulated to provide more uniformity from note to note (by use of gravity instead of springs). These advantages, however, are initially minor compared to the student's love for music, diligence, and correct practice methods. Grands become more desirable for advanced students because technically demanding material is easier to execute on a grand. For such advanced pianists, proper tuning, regulation, and hammer voicing become essential because if the piano maintenance is neglected, practically all of the advantages will be lost.

18. How to Start Learning Piano: Youngest Children to Old Adults

a. Do You Need a Teacher? Many beginners would like to start learning piano on their own, and there are valid reasons for this. There are very few good teachers and the poor teachers can teach you more bad habits than you can acquire on our own. However, there is no question that, for the first 6 months (and probably longer), there is no faster way to start than taking lessons from a qualified teacher. The only teachers to avoid completely are those who cannot teach what you want (you may want pop, jazz, and blues while the teacher teaches only classical), or those who teach strict, inflexible methods not appropriate for the student (one method might be designed for very young children but you may be an older beginner). Why are teachers so helpful in the beginning? Firstly, the most fundamental things that you do every time you play, such as hand position, sitting position, hand movements, etc., are difficult to explain in a textbook, whereas a teacher can show you instantly, what is right and what is wrong. You don't want to pick up these wrong habits and have to live with them all your life. Secondly, a beginner sitting down at the piano and playing for the first time is usually making at least 20 mistakes at the same time (left-right coordination, volume control, rhythm, arm and body movements, speed, timing, fingering, trying to learn the wrong things first, total neglect of musicality, etc., etc.). It is the teacher's job to identify all the mistakes and make a priority list of which ones must be corrected first; for example, can you look at your hands while playing? (yes!). Most teachers know which basic skills you need. Teachers are also helpful in finding the appropriate teaching material. Teachers provide a structured learning environment, without which the student can end up doing the wrong things and not realize that they are not making any progress. In short, teachers are definitely cost effective for beginners.

b. Starter Books and Keyboards. The first order of business is to decide which lesson books to use. For general technique (not specialties such as jazz or gospel), you can use any of a number of beginner books such as Michael Aaron, Alfred, Bastien, Faber and Faber, Schaum, or Thompson; most have books for children or adults. . Of these, many people prefer Faber and Faber; also some older classics: Bach, First Lessons, Book I & II, Selections from Anna Magdalena's NB, Bartok's Mikrokosmos. There is an excellent piano site at:

http://www.amsinternational.org/piano_pedagogy.htm

which lists most of these teaching books and reviews many of them. Pick one book and skip through it quickly by skipping material you already know. These starter books will teach you the fundamentals: reading music, common fingerings such as scales, arpeggios, accompaniments, time signature, etc.

As soon as you are familiar with most of the fundamentals, you can start learning pieces that you want to play. Here again, teachers are invaluable because they know most of the pieces that you might want to play and can tell you whether they are at the level that you can handle. They can point out the difficult sections and show you how to overcome those difficulties. They can play the lesson pieces to demonstrate what you are trying to achieve; obviously, avoid teachers who cannot or refuse to play for you. After a few months of such study, you will be ready to continue by following the material of this book. In order to avoid the numerous pitfalls that await you, it is a good idea to read this book, at least quickly once through, before you begin your first lesson.

At the very beginning, perhaps up to a year, it is possible to start learning using keyboards, even the smaller ones with less than the 88 keys of the standard piano. If you plan to play electronic keyboards all your life, it is certainly permissible to practice only on keyboards. However, practically all keyboards have actions that are too light to truly simulate an acoustic piano. As soon as possible, you will want to transition to a 88-key digital piano with weighted keys (or an acoustic), see section 17 above.

c. Beginners: Age 0 to 65+. Many parents ask: "At what age can our children start piano?", while older beginners ask: "Am I too old to learn piano? How proficient can I expect to be? How long will it take?" We are increasingly beginning to recognize that what we had attributed to "talent" was in reality a result of our education. This relatively recent "discovery" is radically changing the landscape of piano pedagogy. ***Therefore, we can legitimately question whether talent is such an important factor in how quickly you can learn to play.*** So then, what IS an important factor? Age is one, because learning piano is a process of developing nerve cells, especially in the brain. The process of nerve growth slows down with age. So let's examine categories of beginners according to their ages, and the consequences of slowing cell growth with age.

Ages 0-6. Babies can hear as soon as they are born, and most maternity wards test babies for hearing immediately after birth. Brains of deaf babies develop slowly because of a lack of auditory stimuli, and such babies need to have their auditory stimuli restored (if possible) or have other procedures instituted, in order to encourage normal brain development. Thus early musical stimuli will accelerate brain development in normal babies, not only for music but also generally. By the age of 6-10 months, most babies have heard enough sounds and languages to stimulate sufficient brain development to start talking. They can cry and communicate to us within minutes after birth. Music can provide additional stimulation to give babies a tremendous head start in brain development by one year after birth. All parents should have a good collection of piano music, orchestral music, piano and violin concertos, operas, etc., and play them in the baby room, or somewhere in the house where the baby can still hear the music. Many parents whisper and walk softly while the baby is asleep, but this is bad training. Babies can be trained to sleep in a (normal) noisy environment, and this is the healthy alternative.

Up to about age 6, they acquire new skills in stepwise fashion; that is, they suddenly acquire a new skill such as walking and rapidly become good at it. But each individual acquires these skills at different times and in a different order. Most parents make the mistake of giving the baby only baby music. *Remember: no babies ever composed baby music; adults did – baby music only slows down brain development.* It is not a good idea to expose them to loud trumpets and drum rolls that can startle the baby, but babies can understand Bach, Beethoven, Chopin, etc. Music is an acquired taste; therefore, how the babies' brains develop musically will depend on the type of music they hear. Older classical music contain more basic chord structures and harmonies that are naturally recognized by the brain. Then more complex chords and dissonances were added later on as we became accustomed to them over the ages. Therefore, the older classical music is more appropriate for babies because they contain more stimulative logic and less dissonances and stresses introduced later to reflect on "modern civilization". Piano music is especially appropriate because, if they eventually take piano lessons, they will have a higher level of understanding of music they heard as a baby.

Ages 3-12. Below age 3, most children's hands are too small to play the piano, the fingers cannot bend or move independently, and the brain and body (vocal chords, muscles, etc.) may not be sufficiently developed to deal with concepts in music. Above age 4 (2 for those with early training), most children are ready to receive music education, especially if they had been exposed to music since birth; thus *they should be constantly tested for their sense of pitch (relative and absolute pitch; can they "carry a tune?"), rhythm, loud-soft, fast-slow, and reading music, which is easier than any alphabet*. This group can take advantage of the enormous brain growth that takes place during this age interval; learning is effortless and limited more by the ability of the teacher to provide the appropriate material than by the student's ability to absorb it. One remarkable aspect of this age group (there are many!) is their "malleability"; their "talents" can be molded. Thus, even if they would not have become musicians if left alone, they can be made into musicians by proper training. This is the ideal age group for starting piano. Mental play is nothing special – it comes naturally to this age group. Many adults consider mental play a rare skill because, like absolute pitch, they lost it during their teen ages from a lack of use. Therefore, make sure that they are taught mental play, in all its many forms. *They can also quickly forget what they learn.*

Ages 13-19, the "teen" ages. This group still has an excellent chance of becoming concert level pianists. However, they may have lost the chance to become those super stars that the younger beginners can become. Although brain development has slowed down, the body is still growing rapidly until about age 16, and at a slower rate thereafter. This age group can achieve practically anything they want to, as long as they have an intense interest in music or piano. However, they are not malleable any more; encouraging them to learn piano does not work if they are more interested in cello or soccer, and the parents' role changes from giving direction to giving support for whatever the teens want to do. This is the age interval in which the teens learn what it means to take responsibility and what it means to become an adult -- all lessons that can be learned from the piano experience. In order to influence them, you need to use more advanced methods, such as logic, knowledge, and psychology. *They will probably never forget anything they memorized at these ages or slightly younger, unlike the 3-12 group.* Above this age group, age classifications become difficult because there is so much variation among individuals.

Ages 20-35. Some individuals in this age group still have a chance of becoming concert level pianists. They can use the experience they learned in life to acquire piano skills more efficiently than younger students. Those who decide to learn piano in this age group generally have greater motivation and a clearer understanding of what they want. But they will have to work very hard, because progress will come only after a sufficient amount of work. At this age group, nervousness can start to become a major problem for some. Although younger students can become nervous, nervousness seems to increase with age. This happens because severe nervousness arises from fear of failure, and fear arises from mental associations with memories of terrible events, whether imagined or real. These terrifying memories/ideas tend to accumulate with age. ***Therefore, if you want to perform, you should do some research into controlling nervousness, by becoming more confident, or by practicing public performance at every opportunity, acquiring mental play, etc.*** Nervousness can arise from both the conscious and subconscious brain; therefore, you will need to deal with both in order to learn to control it. For those who just want to become sufficiently technically proficient to enjoy playing major piano compositions, starting in this age group should not present any problems. Although some maintenance will be required, you can keep anything you memorized in this age group, for life.

Ages 35-45. This age group cannot develop into concert level pianists, but can still perform adequately for simpler material such as easy classics and cocktail music (fake books, jazz). They can acquire enough skill to play most famous compositions for personal enjoyment and informal performances. The most demanding material will probably be out of reach. Nervousness reaches a maximum somewhere between the ages of 40 and 60 and then often declines slowly. This might explain why many famous pianists stopped performing somewhere in this age interval. Memorizing starts to become a problem in the sense that, although it is possible to memorize practically anything, you will tend to forget it, almost completely, if not properly maintained. Reading the music can start to become a problem for some who require strong corrective lenses. This is because the distance from the eyes to the keyboard or music stand is intermediate between reading and distant vision. Thus you may want a set of eye glasses for intermediate vision. Progressive lenses might solve this problem, but some find them bothersome because of their small field of focus.

Ages 45-65. This is the age range in which, depending on the person, there will be increasing limitations on what you can learn to play. You can probably get up to the level of the Beethoven Sonatas, although the most difficult ones will be a huge challenge that will take many years to learn. Acquiring a sufficiently large repertoire will be difficult, and at any time, you will be able to perform only a few pieces. But for personal enjoyment, there is still a limitless number of compositions that you can play. Because there are more wonderful compositions to learn than you have time to learn them, you may not necessarily feel a limit to what you can play. There is still no major problems in learning new pieces, but they will require constant maintenance if you want to keep them in your repertoire. This will greatly limit your playable repertoire, because as you learn new pieces, you will completely forget the old ones, unless you had learned them at much younger ages. In addition, your learning rate will definitely start to slow down. By re-memorizing and re-forgetting several times, you can still memorize a significant amount of material. It is best to concentrate on a few pieces and learn to play them well. There is little time for beginner's books and exercises – these are not harmful, but you should start learning pieces you want to play within a few months after starting lessons.

Ages 65+. There is no reason why you can't start learning piano at any age. Those who start at these ages are realistic about what they can learn to play and generally do not have unattainable expectations. There are plenty of simple but wonderful music to play and the joy of playing remains as high as at younger ages. As long as you are not terribly handicapped, you can learn piano and make satisfactory progress at any age. Memorizing a composition is not a problem for most. The greatest difficulty in memorizing will come from the fact that it will take you a long time to get up to speed for difficult material, and memorizing slow play is the most difficult memory work. Therefore, if you choose easy pieces that can be brought up to speed quickly, you will memorize those more quickly. Stretching the hands to reach wide chords or arpeggios, and fast runs will become more difficult, and relaxation will also be more difficult. If you concentrate on one composition at a time, you can always have one or two compositions that can be performed. There is no reason to modify your practice methods -- they are the same as those used for the youngsters. And you may not feel as much nervousness as you might have in the middle ages when stage fright reaches is maximum. Learning piano, especially memory work, is one of the best exercises for the brain; therefore, serious efforts at learning piano should delay the aging process, just as proper exercise is necessary to maintain physical health. Don't get a teacher that treats you like a young beginner and give you only exercises and drills – you don't have time for that. Start playing music right away.

19. The "Ideal" Practice Routine (Bach's Teachings and Invention #4)

Is there an ideal, universal practice routine? No, because each person must design her/is own practice routine at each practice session. In other words, *this book is all about designing your own practice routines.* Some differences between a well designed routine and the intuitive routine of section II.1 are discussed in the last paragraph of this section. A good piano teacher will discuss the appropriate practice routines for the lesson pieces during the lesson. Those who already know how to create practice routines might still find this section interesting, as we will discuss many useful points (such as Bach's teachings and specifics on how to practice his Invention #4) in addition to practice routines.

a. Learning the Rules. Therefore, the first "practice routine" you should use is to follow Chapter One, starting from the beginning and applying the concepts to a composition you want to play. The objective is to become familiar with all the available practice methods. Once you have some familiarity with most of the practice methods, we are ready to design practice routines. In order to design generally useful routines, we assume that you have had at least one year of serious piano practice. Our objective is to learn Bach's Invention #4.

b. Routine for Learning a New Piece. "Learning a new piece" means memorizing it. Therefore, without any warm-ups, etc., immediately start memorizing Bach's Invention #4, RH first, starting with segments of one to three bars that make up a distinct phrase, then the LH; for more details on specifics of each step of the routine, see III.6.l. Continue this process until you have memorized the entire piece, HS only. Those already good at using the methods of this book should be able to memorize the entire Invention (not perfectly), HS, on the first day, after one or two hours of practice (for an average person with an IQ of about 100). Concentrate only on memorizing, and don't worry about anything that you "cannot play satisfactorily" (such as the 1,3 trill in the LH), and play at any speed that is comfortable for you. If you want to memorize this piece as quickly as possible, it is best to concentrate only on this piece and not play other pieces. Instead of one long session of 2 hrs, you might practice 1 hr, twice during the day. On the second day, start HT slowly, still in segments of a few bars, and then connecting them. If you want to memorize as quickly as possible, don't practice anything else; even playing finger exercises to warm up will cause you to forget some of what you just memorized.

c. "Normal" Practice Routines and Bach's Teachings. After 3 or 4 days, you can return to your "normal" practice routine. For the "memorizing" routine, we basically did nothing but memorize because mixing memorizing with other practice will slow down the memorizing process. In the "normal" routine, we can take advantage of the beginning, when the hands are still "cold" and play some finished pieces cold. Of course, you cannot play difficult, fast pieces cold. Either play easier pieces, or play the difficult ones slowly. A good procedure is to start with easier ones and gradually play the harder ones. Once you become a strong enough performer so that you have no trouble playing cold (this may take a year), this step becomes optional, especially if you play the piano every day. If you do not play every day, you may lose the ability to play cold if you stop practicing it. Another thing that can be practiced during this warming-up period is scales and arpeggios; see sections III.4.b and III.5 for details on how to practice them. You might also try the finger independence and lifting exercises of III.7.d; some pianists who want to develop finger independence have a routine of practicing these exercises once or twice every day. Start practicing other compositions in addition to the Bach.

By this time, you should be able to play the entire Bach Invention in your mind, HS, with no trouble. This is a good time to conduct maintenance on pieces you had memorized previously, because learning a new piece will often result in forgetting portions of previously learned pieces. Alternate practice between the Bach Invention and your old pieces. You should practice the Bach HS most of the time until you have acquired all the necessary technique. Increase speed as quickly as you can, to speeds faster than the final speed, in short segments. Practice mostly those sections that give you difficulty; there is no need to practice sections that are easy for you. Once you get to a certain speed HS, start practicing HT at a slower speed. As soon as you feel comfortable HT at a slow speed, bring it up to a faster speed, again, in short segments. *To increase speed (HS or HT), do not use the metronome or force your fingers to play faster. Wait until you get the feeling that the fingers WANT to go faster, and then increase the speed by a comfortable amount.* This will allow you to practice relaxed and avoid speed walls.

In order to transition successfully from HS to HT practice, cultivate the feeling that the two hands need each other in order to play. This will help you to find those motions that help HT play. HS play is useful even during HT play; for example, if you make a mistake in one hand while playing HT, you can keep playing with the other hand and then pick up the error hand whenever you can. Without extensive HS practice, such a feat would be impossible. You can practice such a maneuver as part of the memorizing process – don't wait until recital time to try to execute it!

In order to acquire the specific techniques that Bach had in mind, we must analyze this Invention in some detail. Bach's Inventions were composed as practice pieces for technique and each Invention teaches you specific techniques. Therefore, we must know what skills this Invention is intended to teach. *Bach teaches us not only specific skills, but also HOW TO PRACTICE THEM! That is, by analyzing the Inventions, we can learn many of the practice methods of this book!!* First, play the entire piece using TO. Note that Bach inserted a maximum number of thumb crossings so that we have plenty of chances to practice them – obviously an intentional construct. In the 212345 of the RH in bar 1, practice pivoting around the first 2 with the hand in the glissando position to facilitate TO.

The main theme of this Invention is given by the first 4 bars of the RH. This is then repeated by the LH. *Bach is telling us to practice HS!* Both hands play basically the same things, giving us the opportunity to balance the technical levels of the two hands; this can only be achieved by HS practice and giving the weaker hand more work. There is no better way to practice hand independence, the principal lesson of the Inventions, than by practicing HS. The section where one hand is trilling would be devilishly difficult to practice HT from the beginning, whereas it is quite easy, HS. Some students who do not know HS practice will try to "match" the two hands by figuring out the trill notes ahead of time and then slowing it down for HT practice. This may be appropriate for beginners or youngsters who have not yet learned to trill. Most students should trill (HS) from the beginning, and work on accelerating the trill as soon as possible. *There is no need to mathematically match the two hands; this is art, not mechanics! Bach wants you to trill one hand independently of the other.* This will allow you to play this Invention at any speed without having to change the trill speed significantly. The reason why you should not match the notes is that these trills are a device to sustain the notes for a long time, and the individual notes have no rhythmic value. What do you do, then, if you happen to end up with the wrong trill note at the end? You should be able to compensate for that by either waiting briefly or changing the speed of the trill near the end -- that is the type of skill that this Invention teaches. Therefore, matching the trill to the other hand for practice defeats the lessons of this Invention. The staccato in bars 3 and 4 of the RH is another device for practicing hand independence; staccato in one hand versus legato in the other requires more control than both legato. The staccato in all similar passages should be used throughout the piece although, in many editions, they are indicated only at the beginning.

Most Bach lesson pieces teach not only independence between the hands but also independence of the fingers within one hand, and especially the 4th finger. Thus in bars 11 and 13, there are 6 notes in the RH that can be played as two triplets but are actually three doublets because of the 3/8 time signature. These bars can be difficult for beginners because they require the coordination of three difficult motions: (i) the RH fingering symmetry is that of 2 triplets (345345 rhythm), but it must be played as 3 doublets (345345), (ii) at the same time, the LH must play something completely different, and (iii) all this must be accomplished using mostly the three weakest fingers, 3, 4, and 5. Bach frequently used this device of forcing you to play a rhythm that is different from the fingering symmetry in order to cultivate finger independence. He also tries to give the 4th finger as much work as possible, as in the final **45**.

The triplets are easier to play using 234 fingering instead of 345, especially for larger hands, and most editions suggest the 234 fingering because most editors did not know the concept of parallel sets (PSs). Knowledge of PS exercises indicates that Bach's original intent was 345 (for maximum technical development value), and it is a "musical license" to change it to 234 in order to facilitate musicality. That is, in any composition other than this Invention, 234 would be the correct fingering. Use of 234 can be justified here because it teaches the student the principle of choosing the fingering with the greatest control. Therefore, the student can choose either fingering. A similar situation arises in bar 38 where Bach's original intention for the LH was probably 154321 (a more complete PS) whereas musical license would indicate 143212 which is technically less demanding. Without help from PS exercises, the obvious choice is the musical license. By using PS exercises, the student can learn to use either fingering with equal ease and follow Bach's original intentions.

The "triplets in 3/8 signature" is a good example of how reading the music incorrectly makes it difficult to get up to speed and how speed walls form. When playing HT, you will encounter problems if you play the RH triplets in two beats (wrong way) and the LH in three (correct). Even if you made a second mistake of playing the LH in two beats in order to match the RH, there will be a problem with the rhythmic change from adjacent bars. You might manage to play through these mistakes at slow speed, but when speeded up, they become impossible to play and you begin to build a speed wall. This is an example of the importance of rhythm and how the wrong rhythm can make it impossible to play at speed. It is amazing how many lessons Bach can cram into something that looks so simple, and these complexities partly explain why, *without proper practice methods or guidance from knowledgeable teachers, many students find it impossible to memorize Bach or to play his compositions beyond a certain speed. The lack of proper practice methods is the main reason why so many students end up playing so few Bach pieces.*

The Inventions are excellent technical lesson pieces. Hanon, Czerny, etc., tried to achieve the same ends using what they thought were simpler, more systematic approaches but failed because they lacked critical knowledge and tried to simplify something that is extremely complex. Bach squeezed as many lessons as he could into every bar, as demonstrated above. Hanon, Czerny, etc., must have been aware of the difficulties of learning Bach but were unaware of good practice methods, and tried to find simpler methods of acquiring technique by following their intuitive instincts (see III.7.h). This is one of the best examples of the pitfalls of the intuitive approach.

Because the Inventions were composed for teaching specific skills, they can sound somewhat constrained. In spite of this constraint, all of Bach's lesson pieces contain more music than practically anything ever composed and there are enough of them to satisfy the needs of students at any level, including beginners. If the inventions are too difficult, consider studying the large number of delightful (and eminently performable) simpler lesson pieces Bach composed. Most of them can be found in the "Clavier Book of Anna Magdalena Bach" (his second wife). Because there are so many, most books contain only a small number of selections. *Because the Inventions are lesson pieces, almost every edition has the critical fingerings indicated.* Therefore, figuring out the fingerings, which is extremely important, should not be a problem. "J. S. Bach, Inventions and Sinfonias" by Willard A. Palmer, Alfred, CA, (www.alfredpub.com) has all the non-obvious fingerings indicated, and also has a section on how to play the ornaments.

The Inventions were composed by assembling well defined segments that are usually only a few bars long. This makes them ideal for using HS segmental practice, a key element of the methods of this book. This, and many other properties of Bach's compositions make them ideal music for learning the methods of this book, and it is quite probable that they were composed with these practice methods in mind. Bach may have been aware of most of the practice methods of this book!

Another important lesson of Bach's Inventions is PSs. The main technical lesson of this Invention #4 is the PS 12345, the basic set needed to play the scale and runs. However, Bach knew that a single PS is too dangerous from a technical point of view because you can cheat by phase locking without acquiring technique. In order to prevent phase locking, he added one or two notes to the PS. Now if you tried to cheat, you will be caught immediately because the run will not come out even: Bach has given you no choice but to acquire the required technique if you want to play this musically! Here is another example of Bach teaching us why music and technique are inseparable (by using music as a criterion for technique acquisition). Therefore, the quickest way to learn to play this Invention is to practice the 12345 and 54321 PSs, and learn TO. ***As soon as you test your fingers using these PSs, you will understand why Bach composed this Invention.*** If you can do these PS exercises satisfactorily, this piece will be quite easy, but you will find that the PSs are not easy at all, and will probably require lots of work even if you are at an intermediate level. First work on these PSs using only white keys; then work on others that include black keys, as suggested by Bach. A good example is the LH 12345 PS of bars 39-40, with the difficult 4th finger on a white key following 3 on black. Bach extracts the most difficult part of this PS, 2345, and repeats it in bar 49.

Bach clearly saw the value of playing a small number of notes very quickly, such as ornaments and trills, for developing technique (velocity). Thus his ornaments are another key device for acquiring technique, and they are essentially a small assemblage of PSs. There are numerous discussions on how to play Bach's ornaments (see Palmer, 3 paragraphs above); these discussions are important from the point of view of correct musical expression, but ***we must not miss the point that technically, ornaments in lesson pieces are an essential device for practicing velocity, and are not just musical ornaments***. Play both the RH and LH trills with fingers 1 and 3, which will make the LH trill easier to learn. Most students will be able to play the RH trill better than the LH trill in the beginning; in that case, use the RH to teach the LH. This "technique transfer" from one hand to the other is easier if both hands use similar fingering. Because the purpose of the trill is simply to sustain the notes, there is no specific trill speed that is required; however, try to trill the two hands at the same speed. If you want to trill very fast, use the PSs to practice them as described in section III.3.a. It is important to start the first two notes rapidly if you want to trill fast. Watch the positions of fingers 2, 4, and 5 while trilling. They should be stationary, close to the keys, and slightly curved.

Most students find it difficult to play these Inventions beyond a certain speed, so let's visit a practice routine for increasing speed. Using this type of routine, you should be able to eventually play at practically any reasonable speed, including speeds at least as fast as those of Glen Gould and other famous pianists. We will learn to play bars 1 and 2 fast, and after that, you should be able to figure out how to accelerate the rest. Note that these two bars are self-cycling (see section III.2). Try cycling it rapidly. Chances are, you will fail because stress develops rapidly with speed. Then practice 212345 of bar 1 until it is smooth and fast. Then practice 154, then 54321 of the 2nd bar. Then connect them, and finally, cycle the two bars. You may not be able to complete everything the first day, but the post practice improvement will make it easier on the second day. Using similar methods, solve all your technical difficulties in the entire piece. The key difficulty in the LH is the 521 of bar 4, so practice 521 PS until you can play it at any speed, completely relaxed. Note that the 212345 of the RH and the 543212 of the LH are thumb-passing exercises. Clearly, Bach recognized that thumb over and thumb under are critical technical elements at high speed and created numerous ingenious opportunities for you to practice them. Before you can play HT fast, you must get up to HS speeds that are much faster than the HT speed you want. "Getting up to speed" doesn't mean just being able to attain the speed, but you must be able to feel the quiet hands and have complete control of each individual finger. Beginners may need months of HS practice for the higher speeds. Many students tend to extract more speed from their fingers by playing loud; this is not true speed, so play everything softly for these practice sessions. When starting to play HT fast, exaggerate the rhythm -- this might make it easier. Although most Bach compositions can be played at different speeds, the minimum speed for the Inventions is the speed at which you can feel the quiet hands when you acquire the necessary technique, because if you don't get up to that speed, you have missed one of his most important lessons (quiet hands).

An intermediate level player should be able to conquer the technical difficulties of this Invention in about a week. ***Now we are ready to practice playing it as a piece of music!*** Listen to several recordings in order to get an idea of what can be done and what you want to do. Try different speeds and decide on your own final speed. Video record your own playing and see if the result is visually and musically satisfactory; usually, it is not, and you will find many improvements you will want to make. You may never be completely satisfied even if you practiced this piece all your life.

In order to play musically, you must feel each note with the fingers before playing it, even if it is for a split second. This will not only give you more control and eliminate errors, but also allow you to accelerate continuously through the keydrop so that the hammer shank is flexed by the right amount when the hammer strikes the strings. Pretend that there is no bottom to the keydrop and let the bottom of the keydrop stop your finger. You can do this and still play softly. This is called "playing deeply into the piano". You cannot "raise your finger high and plonk it down" as Hanon recommended and expect to make music. Such a motion can cause the hammer shank to oscillate instead of flexing and produce an unpredictable and harsh sound. Therefore, as you practice HS, practice for musicality, using the "flat finger positions" of section III.4.b. Combine these with a supple wrist. Play as much as possible with the fleshy front pad of the finger (opposite the fingernail), not the bony fingertip. If you video record your playing, the curled finger position will look childish and amateurish. You cannot play relaxed until you can completely relax the extensor muscles of the first 2 or 3 phalanges of fingers 2 to 5. This relaxation is the essence of the flat finger positions. At first, you will be able to include all these considerations only at slow speed. However, as soon as you develop quiet hands, you will gain the ability to include them at higher speeds. In fact, because these finger positions allow complete relaxation and control, you will be able to play at much faster speed. This is one of the (many) reasons why quiet hands is so important.

Tone and color: Improved tonality will be most clearly evident when playing softly; the softer play also helps relaxation and control. The flat finger position is what enables softer play with control. How soft is soft? This depends on the music, speed, etc., but for practice purposes one useful criterion is to play softer and softer until you start to miss some notes; this level (or slightly louder) is usually the best for practicing softly. Once you have control over tonality (sound of each individual note), try to add color to your music (effect of groups of notes). Color for each composer is different. Chopin requires legato, special staccato, rubato, etc. Mozart requires the utmost attention to the expression markings. Beethoven requires uninterrupted rhythms that run continuously over many, many bars; therefore, you need to develop the skill for "connecting" consecutive bars in Beethoven's music. Bach's Inventions are somewhat contrived and "boxed in" because they are mostly confined to simple parallel sets. You can easily overcome this handicap by emphasizing the multitude of musical concepts that give his music almost infinite depth. The most obvious musicality comes from the harmony/conversation between the two hands. The ending of every piece must be special, and Bach's endings are always convincing. Therefore, don't just let the ending catch up to you; make sure that the ending is purposeful. In this Invention, pay special attention to bar 50, in which the two hands move in opposite directions as you enter the authoritative ending. When you bring the music up to speed and develop quiet hands, the 6-note runs (e.g., 212345, etc.) should sound like rising and falling waves. The RH trill is bell-like because it is a full note, while the LH trill is more sinister because it is a semitone. When practicing HS, note that the RH trill is not a simple trill but it comes crashing down at the end. Similarly, the LH trill is an introduction to the ensuing counterpoint to the RH. *You cannot bring out color unless you lift each finger at precisely the right moment.* Most of Bach's lesson pieces contain lessons in lifting the fingers accurately. Of course, the coloration should initially be investigated HS. Quiet hands is also most easily acquired HS; therefore adequate HS preparation before HT practice is of critical importance for tone and color. Once the preparation work is done, you can start HT and bring out the incredible richness of Bach's music!

Tone and color have no limits in the sense that once you succeed, it becomes easier to add more, and the music actually becomes easier to play. All of a sudden, you may discover that you can play the entire composition without a single audible mistake. This is probably the clearest illustration of the statement that you cannot separate music from technique. The act of producing good music makes you a better pianist. This provides one of the explanations of why you have good days and bad days -- when your mental mood and finger conditioning are just right so that you can control the tone and color, you will have a good day. This teaches us that on bad days, you may be able to "recover" by trying to remember the fundamentals of how you control tone and color. This ends the discussions on Invention #4. We now return to the practice routine.

You have been practicing for over one hour by now, and the fingers are flying. This is the time when you can really make music! You must make every effort to practice making music during at least half of the total practice time. Once you have built up a sufficiently large repertoire, you should try to increase this "music time" from 50% to 90%. Therefore, you must consciously set aside this portion of your practice routine for music. Play your heart out, with all the emotion and expression you can muster. *Finding musical expression is very exhausting; therefore, initially, it will require much more conditioning and effort than anything you can do with Hanon.* If you don't have a teacher, the only known ways to learn musicality are to listen to recordings and to attend concerts. If you are scheduled to perform a particular composition in the near future, play it slowly, or at least at a comfortable and fully controllable speed once, before going on to something different. *Expression is not important when playing slowly. In fact, it may be beneficial to purposely play with little expression when playing slowly before moving on to something else.*

Learning Bach is strongly emphasized in this book. Why? *Because Bach's music written for technical development is unique in piano pedagogy in its healthy, complete, efficient, and correct approach to technique acquisition -- there is nothing else like it.* Every experienced teacher will assign some Bach pieces for study. As mentioned above, the only reason why students do not learn more Bach pieces is because, without the proper practice methods, they seem so impossibly difficult. You can demonstrate to yourself the benefits of the Bach lessons by learning five of his technical compositions and practicing them for half a year or more. Then go back and play the most difficult pieces that you had learned previously, and you will be amazed at the greater ease and control that you have gained. Bach's compositions were designed to create concert pianists with sound fundamental technique. Chopin's etudes were not designed for gradual, complete technical development and many of Beethoven's compositions can cause hand injury and ear damage if you don't get proper guidance (they probably damaged Beethoven's hearing). Neither of them teaches you how to practice. Therefore, Bach's compositions stand out above all others for technical development. With the practice methods of this book, we can now take full advantage of Bach's resources for technical development that has been sadly under-utilized in the past.

Of course, Hanon, etc. (there are many others, such as Cramer-Bulow) are not even worth discussing here because they missed the most important point: that without music, technique is not possible. But scales and arpeggios are necessary because they form the foundation of practically anything we play. The requirement of musicality means that you must practice them in such a way that when others hear you playing scales, they will say "Wow!". Then why not practice Hanon the same way? You can, but they aren't necessary; there is so much better material with which to practice the art of the musician.

In summary, there is no such thing as a standard practice routine. The concept of a fixed practice routine arose because practitioners of intuitive methods who did not know how to teach practice methods used it because they did not know what else to teach. To those who know the practice methods, the concept of a standard practice routine becomes a somewhat silly idea. For example, a standard intuitive routine might start with Hanon exercises; however, you can quickly bring the Hanon exercises up to ridiculous speeds by applying the methods of this book. And once you accomplish that, you begin to wonder why you need to keep repeating this. What will you gain by playing these ridiculously fast Hanon pieces every day?? Instead of a standard practice routine, you must define what your objective for the practice session is, and select the practice methods needed to achieve that goal. In fact, your practice routine will constantly evolve during each practice session. Thus the key for designing a good practice routine is an intimate knowledge of all the practice methods. How different this is, from the intuitive routine described in section II.1!

20. Bach: the Greatest Composer and Teacher (15 Inventions and their Parallel Sets)

We briefly analyze Bach's fifteen 2-part Inventions from simple structural points of view in order to explore how and why he composed them. The objective is to better understand how to practice and benefit from Bach's compositions. As a by-product, we can use these results to speculate on what music is and how Bach produced such incredible music out of what (we will demonstrate) is basic "teaching material" that should be no different from Czerny or Dohnanyi. Clearly, Bach used advanced musical concepts in harmony, counterpoint, etc., that music theoreticians are still debating to this day, while others wrote "lesson music" mainly for their finger training value. Here, we only examine the Inventions at the simplest structural level. Even at this basic level, there are some educational and intriguing ideas that we can explore and arrive at the realization that music and technique are inseparable.

There is a nice essay on Bach's Inventions and their history, etc., by Dr. Yo Tomita of Queen's University in Belfast, Ireland. *Each Invention uses a different scale that was important in the Well Temperaments favored during Bach's time.* They were initially written for his oldest son Wilhelm Friedemann Bach when Friedemann was 9 years old, around 1720. They were subsequently upgraded and taught to other students.

One striking feature common to all the Inventions is that each one concentrates on a small number of parallel sets (PSs). Now, you might say, "That's not fair -- since practically every composition can be decomposed into PSs, of course, the Inventions must be all PSs, so what's new?" The new element is that each Invention is based on only one to three specific PSs that Bach chose for practice. To demonstrate this, we list these PSs below for each Invention. In order to concentrate entirely on simple PSs, Bach completely avoids the use of thirds and more complex chords (in one hand), that Hanon uses in his highest numbered exercises. Thus Bach wanted his students to master PSs before chords.

Simple PSs are almost trivial from a technical point of view. That is why they are so useful -- they are easy to learn. Anyone with some piano experience can learn to play them pretty fast. The real technical challenges arise when you have to join two of them with a conjunction in between. Bach obviously knew this and therefore used only combinations of PSs as his building blocks. *Thus the Inventions teach how to play PSs and conjunctions -- learning PSs is of no use if you can't connect them.* Below, I use the term "linear" PS to denote sets in which the fingers play sequentially (e.g., 12345), and "alternating" sets when alternate fingers play (132435). These joined PSs form what is normally called "motifs" in these Inventions. However, the fact that they are created using the most basic PSs suggests that the "motifs" were not chosen because of their musical content, but were chosen for their pedagogical value and the music was then added with the genius of Bach. Thus only Bach could have achieved such a feat; this explains why Hanon failed. Of course, the main reason why Hanon failed was that he did not know good practice methods while Bach did. Only one representative combination of PSs is listed below for each Invention; Bach used them in many variations, such as reversed, inverted, etc. Note that Hanon based his exercises on essentially the same PSs, although he probably accomplished this by accident, by extracting these motifs from Bach's works. ***Perhaps the most convincing evidence that Bach knew about PSs is the progressively complex PSs he chose with increasing Invention number.***

List of the PSs in each Invention (listed for the RH; LH is similar):

#1: 1234 and 4231 (linear followed by alternating); this was a mistake because the first Invention should deal with only the simplest (linear) sets. Accordingly, in a later modification of this Invention, Bach replaced the 4231 alternating set with two linear sets, 432,321. This modification provides supporting evidence for my thesis that Bach used PSs as the basic structural study units. However, the order of difficulty of each Invention may not follow the same order as PS complexity for most people, because the structural simplicity of the PSs does not always equate to easier playing.

#2: Linear sets as in #1, but with a wider variety of conjunctions. An added complexity is that the same motif, appearing at different times, requires a different fingering. Thus the first two inventions deal mainly with linear sets, but the second one is more complex.

#3: 324 and 321 (alternating followed by linear). A short alternating set is introduced.

#4: 12345 and 54321 with an unusual conjunction. These longer linear sets with the unusual conjunction increase the difficulty.

#5: 4534231; full blown alternating sets.

#6: 545, 434, 323, etc., the simplest example of the most basic 2-note PSs joined by one conjunction; these are difficult when the weak fingers are involved. Although they are simple, they are an extremely important basic technical element, and alternating them between the two hands is a great way to learn how to control them (using one hand to teach the other, section II.20). It also introduces the arpegic sets.

#7: 543231; this is like a combination of #3 and #4 and is therefore more complex than either one.

#8: 14321 and first introduction of the "Alberti" type combination 2434. Here, the progression in difficulty is created by the fact that the initial 14 is only one or two semitones which makes it difficult for combinations involving the weaker fingers. It is amazing how Bach not only knew all the weak finger combinations, but was able to weave them into real music. Moreover, he chose situations in which we had to use the difficult fingering.

#9: The lessons here are similar to those in #2 (linear sets), but are more difficult.

#10: This piece consists almost entirely of arpegic sets. Because arpegic sets involve larger finger travel distances between notes, they represent another progression in difficulty.

#11: Similar to #2 and #9; again, difficulty is increased, by making the motif longer than for the preceding pieces. Note that in all the other pieces, there is only a short motif followed by a simple counterpoint section which makes it easier to concentrate on the PSs.

#12: This one combines linear and arpegic sets, and is played faster than previous pieces.

#13: Arpegic sets, played faster than #10.

#14: 12321, 43234; a more difficult version of #3 (5 notes instead of 3, and faster).

#15: 3431, 4541, difficult combinations involving finger 4. These finger combinations become especially difficult to play when many of them are strung together.

The above list shows that:

(i) There is a systematic introduction of increasingly complex PSs.

(ii) There tends to be a progressive increase in difficulty, with emphasis on developing the weaker fingers.

(iii) The "motifs" are, in reality, carefully chosen PSs and conjunctions, selected for their technical value.

The fact that motifs, chosen simply for their technical usefulness, can be used to create some of the greatest music ever composed is intriguing. This fact is nothing new to composers. To the average music aficionado who has fallen in love with Bach's music, these motifs seem to take on special significance with seemingly deep musical value because of the familiarity created by repeated listening. In reality, it is not the motifs themselves, but how they are used in the composition that produces the magic. If you look simply at the barest, basic motifs, you can hardly see any difference between Hanon and Bach, yet no one would consider the Hanon exercises as music. The complete motif actually consists of the PSs and the attached counterpoint section, so-called because it acts as the counterpoint to what is being played by the other hand. Bach's clever use of the counterpoint obviously serves many purposes, one of which is to create the music. The counterpoint (which is missing in the Hanon exercises) might appear to add no technical lessons (the reason why Hanon ignored it), but Bach uses it for practicing skills such as trills, ornaments, staccato, hand independence, etc., and the counterpoint certainly makes it much easier to compose the music and adjust its level of difficulty.

Thus music is created by some "logical" sequence of notes or sets of notes that is recognized by the brain, just as ballet, beautiful flowers, or magnificent scenery is recognized visually. What is this "logic"? A large part of it is automatic, almost hard-wired brain data processing, as in the visual case; it starts with an inborn component (newborn babies will fall asleep when they hear a lullaby), but a large component can be cultivated (e.g., Bach versus Rock and Roll). But even the cultivated component is mostly automatic. In other words, when any sound enters the ears, the brain instantaneously begins to process and interpret the sounds whether we consciously try to process the information or not. An enormous amount of this automatic processing goes on without our even noticing it, such as depth perception, eye focusing, direction of origin of sounds, walking/balancing motions, scary or soothing sounds, etc. Most of that processing is inborn and/or cultivated but is basically out of our conscious control. The result of that mental processing is what we call music appreciation. Chord progressions and other elements of music theory give us some idea of what that logic is. But most of that "theory" today is a simple compilation of various properties of existing music. They do not provide a sufficiently basic theory to allow us to create new music, though they allow us to avoid pitfalls and extend/complete a composition once you have somehow generated a motif. Thus it appears that music theory today is still incomplete. Hopefully, by further analyzing music from the great masters, we can approach that goal of developing a deeper understanding of music.

21. The Psychology of Piano

We are all aware that psychology plays a major role not only in music, but also in piano learning. There are numerous ways for taking advantage of our understanding of psychology and we will discuss some of these methods in this section. However, the more important immediate task is to uncover the psychological pitfalls that have created almost insurmountable obstacles to learning piano, such as "lack of talent", or "nervousness" when performing. Another example is the phenomenon of the great artists' inability to teach discussed in section 16.e above. This phenomenon was explained in terms of the artists' psychological approach to teaching which mirrored their approach to music. Since the psychology of music is only minimally understood, composers simply create music in their minds "out of nothing" -- there is no such thing as a formula for creating music. They similarly acquired technique by imagining the musical output and letting the hands find a way to accomplish it. It is a terrific shortcut to a complex result, when it works. However, for most students, it is a most inefficient way for acquiring technique and we now know that there are much better approaches. Obviously, psychology is important in everything from learning, practicing and performing to music composition.

Psychology is mostly controlled by knowledge and it is often difficult to distinguish between psychology and knowledge. In most cases, it is knowledge that controls how we approach a subject. But it is psychology that determines how we use that knowledge. It is now time to examine some specific items.

Perhaps the most important one is how we view piano learning, or our general attitude towards the process of learning to play. The methods of this book are diametrically opposite to the "intuitive" methods. For example, when a student fails to learn, it was because of a lack of talent according to the old system, so failure was the student's fault. In the system of this book, failure is the teacher's fault because the teacher's job is to provide all the information necessary for success. There is no blind faith that practicing Hanon for one hour every day will transform you into a virtuoso. In fact, nothing should be taken on faith and it is the teacher's responsibility to explain each method so that the student understands it. This will require the teacher to be knowledgeable in a wide variety of disciplines, from art to zoology. We have come to a point in history when art teachers cannot ignore reality (education) any more. Therefore, the psychology of piano learning requires profound changes in the attitudes of both the student and the teacher.

For the students, especially those trained in the old system with rules, the transition from the old to the new ranges from "very easy" to complete confusion. Some students will instantly enjoy the new empowerment and freedom and, within a week, are enjoying the full benefits of the methods. On the other extreme are those students who realize that the old rules are not valid anymore, and so they start looking for "new rules" to follow. They are full of questions: When I cycle one hand, is 10 times enough, or do I need 10,000 times? Do I cycle as fast as I can, or at a slower, more accurate speed? Is HS practice necessary, even if I can already play HT? For simple music, HS practice can be awfully boring -- why do I need it? Such questions reveal the extent to which the student has adapted to the new psychology, or failed to adapt. To illustrate, let us psycho-analyze the last question (why HS?). In order to ask such a question, that person must have been practicing blindly because s/he read that it was necessary to practice HS. In other words, s/he was blindly following a rule. That is not the method of this book. Here, we first define an objective, and then use HS practice to achieve it. This objective might be more secure memory in order to avoid blackouts during performances, or technical development so that when you play HT, you can hear that the playing is based on superior technical skills. When these objectives are achieved, the practice is not boring at all!

For the teacher, there is no question that everything in modern society is based on a broad education. There is no need to become a scientist or to study advanced concepts in psychology. Success in the real world is not tied to academic achievements; most successful business entrepreneurs don't have MBAs. Perhaps the most important advance of modern society is that all these concepts that used to be considered specialized knowledge are becoming easier to understand, not because they have changed, but because a better understanding always simplifies and the teaching methods are always improving. Moreover, we are becoming more familiar with them because we need them more and more in our daily lives. The information is certainly becoming easier to access. *Thus a teacher only needs to be curious and willing to communicate, and the results will follow automatically.*

Many students need a psychological device to overcome the unfounded fear of the inability to memorize. In this book, we are not talking about memorizing Fur Elise only. We are talking about a repertoire of over 5 hours of real music, most of which you can sit down and play at a moment's notice. The only requirement for maintaining such a repertoire is that you must play the piano every day. Some people have no difficulty memorizing, but most have preconceived notions that memorizing significant repertoires is only for the "gifted" few. The main reason for this unfounded fear is the past experience in which students are first taught to play a piece well, then taught to memorize which, as explained in section III.6, is one of the most difficult ways to memorize. For students who were taught correctly from the beginning, memorizing is like second nature; it is an integral part of learning any new composition. Adopting this approach will automatically make you a good memorizer, although for older folks, this may take many years.

Nervousness is a particularly difficult psychological problem to overcome. In order to succeed, you must understand that nervousness is a purely psychological process. The present system of railroading young students into recitals without proper preparation is counter productive, and generally produces students that are more prone to nervousness problems than when they started their lessons. Once a student experiences intense nervousness from their piano experience, it can negatively influence anything else that they do that is similar, such as appearing in plays or any other type of public performance. Therefore, the present system is bad for psychological health in general. As discussed in section 15 above, nervousness is an eminently solvable problem for most people and a good program for overcoming nervousness will contribute to mental health because of the pride, joy, and sense of accomplishment that you will feel.

Psychology permeates everything we do in piano, from motivating students to the fundamental basis of music and music composition. The best way to motivate students is to teach practice methods that are so rewarding that the students do not want to quit. Competitions and recitals are great motivators, but they must be conducted with care and with proper understanding of psychology. Most exciting are the psychological aspects of the fundamental basis of music. Bach used the simplest thematic material, parallel sets, and showed that they can be used to compose the deepest music ever written and at the same time teach us how to practice. Mozart used a formula to mass produce music; we now understand how he wrote so much in such a short lifetime. Beethoven used group theoretical type concepts to provide a backbone for his music. He showed how you can hold the audience's attention with a catchy melody in the RH while controlling the emotions with the LH, just as the television industry does today, by showing you an exciting video while controlling your emotions with sound effects. Chopin, known for romanticism and unique musicality like no other, used mathematical devices in his Fantaisie Impromptu to write music straddling the "sound threshold" (III.2), producing special effects on the brain that can mesmerize the audience. The chromatic scale was derived from chords and music follows chord progressions because these frequency relationships simplify the memory and information processing procedures in the brain. Technique cannot be separated from music, and music cannot be separated from psychology; therefore, piano practice is not building finger muscles or repeating exercises: technique is ultimately all about the human brain. Art and artists take us there, long before we can explain analytically why they work.

22. Summary of Method

This method is based on 7 major concepts: Hands Separate Practice (HS, II.7), Segmental Practice (II.6), Relaxation (II.10 & 14), Parallel Sets (II.11, III.7.b, IV.2.a), Memorization (III.6), Mental Playing (III.6 & 12), and Making Music (throughout book).

1. Learn only musical compositions, no Hanon, Czerny, etc., but Scales, Arpeggios, Chromatic Scale (III.5) are necessary. Your first piano should be a weighted key digital; then obtain a quality grand as soon as possible; don't purchase an upright unless you already have one.
2. Listen to performances and recordings for ideas to practice musically. Imitation cannot decrease your creativity because it is impossible to imitate others exactly, and ideas are priceless.
3. Practice old finished pieces cold (without warm-ups, III.6.g), to strengthen your performance skills.

4. When starting a new piece, sight read to identify difficult sections, and practice the most difficult sections first; then

> **a.** Practice HS, in overlapping Segments (Continuity Rule, II.8); switch hands frequently, every 5 seconds if necessary. All technical development should be done HS.
>
> **b.** Memorize first, HS, THEN start practice for technique; get up to speed as quickly as you can. Memorizing after you have learned to play the piece well does not work. Learn Mental Playing as soon as you start to memorize, and use it to acquire Relative/Absolute Pitch (III.12).
>
> **c.** Use Parallel Sets to diagnose your weaknesses; cycle (III.2) parallel sets to overcome those weaknesses and for getting up to speed quickly.
>
> **d.** Divide difficult passages into small segments that are easy to play and use these segments to practice for relaxation and speed.

5. Play the last repetition of any repeated practice slowly before switching hands or moving to a new segment, or before quitting practice.

6. Practice Relaxation at all times, especially HS; this includes the entire body, including Breathing and Swallowing (II.21).

7. Play through mistakes; do not stop to correct them because you will develop stuttering habits. Correct the mistakes later using segmental practice around each mistake.

8. Use the metronome to check the rhythm or speed briefly (typically, a few seconds); do not use it for "slowly ramping up speed", or for long periods of time (more than several minutes).

9. Use pedal only where indicated; practice without pedal until satisfactory HT, THEN add pedal.

10. To learn Hands Together (II.25): practice HS until faster than final HT speed before starting HT practice. For practicing difficult passages HT, pick a short segment, play the more difficult hand, and progressively add notes of the other hand.

11. Practice musically, without forte but with firmness, authority, and expression. Piano practice is not finger strength exercise; it is the development of brain power and nerve connections for control and speed. For FF passages, learn relaxation, technique, and speed first, then add FF. The power for FF comes from the body and shoulders, not the arms.

12. Before quitting practice, play everything you just practiced slowly for ensuring correct Post Practice Improvement (PPI, II.15), which occurs mainly during sleep. The last thing you want for PPI is to include your mistakes (especially from Fast Play Degradation [II.25]).

IV. MUSIC, MATHEMATICS, AND RESEARCH

1. Can We All Be Mozarts?

The answer is a surprising, "Probably yes!". In order to find the answers, we need to examine what Mozart did and how he did them. He had technique, great memory, absolute pitch, and could compose. This book covers the first three, and the last item is partly covered by Mental Play. In fact, most pianists would agree that there are many pianists today whose technique exceeds that of Mozart and we now know how to teach memory to anyone. In today's digital world, at least half of youngsters, who listen to music frequently, have absolute pitch (though most may not know it) because digital recordings are generally on pitch. Therefore, the only remaining uncertainty is whether we can learn to compose as Mozart did. Almost everyone who has successfully navigated the rough waters of learning piano to become a concert level pianist has been able to compose. Also, every great composer and performer had developed strong mental play skills. Therefore, if a person were taught mental play and had developed great technique while very young, and dedicated his entire life to piano as Mozart did, it would not be difficult for him to become a composer. In fact, Mozart was handicapped in that he did not have all the knowledge that was developed since his time, he could not learn from the great composers that followed him, and quality pianos were not yet invented; therefore, it should be easier now than during his time. If it is that easy, why were there so few Mozarts in the world? The only answer I can find is that the piano was a critical instrument for composing music, but the intuitive teaching methods that became almost universally accepted hindered technical development so much that most pianists became too preoccupied with technical difficulties and there was no time left for anything else. These difficulties created an aura around the great composers as being super geniuses whose achievements few people could hope to emulate, thus discouraging most students from even trying such feats. Why try something that is unattainable? ***Therefore, there is ample reason to believe that historical circumstances conspired to suppress creativity.***

Thus far, we considered what Mozart did. There is less information on how he did them. For technique, memory, and absolute pitch, this may not matter much because we understand how to learn them. From all the historical accounts, it was mental play that put him above almost everyone else. Mental play has not traditionally been taught as a specific subject of study, although this subject had to be discussed among the great artists because of its importance. Therefore, with the teaching of mental play at an early age, there is hope that future students will be able to develop their creativity to the fullest. Because technique, memory, and mental play are mainly capabilities of the brain, it is obviously important to teach them at the youngest possible age, when the brain is developing rapidly.

2. Scientific Approach to Piano Practice

a. The Scientific Method. This book was written using the scientific skills learned during my 9-year undergraduate-graduate education and 31-year career as a scientist. I worked in fundamental research (I have been granted six patents), materials science (mathematics, physics, chemistry, biology, mechanical engineering, electronics, optics, acoustics, metals, semiconductors, insulators), industrial problem solving (failure mechanisms, reliability, manufacturing), and scientific reporting (published over 100 peer-reviewed articles in most of the major scientific journals). Even after obtaining my Doctorate in Physics from Cornell University, my employers spent over a million dollars to further my education during my employment. This scientific training was indispensable for writing this book, and most pianists would not be able to duplicate my efforts. I explain below why the results of scientific efforts are useful to everybody, not only scientists.

A common misunderstanding is that science is too difficult for artists. This really boggles the mind. The mental processes that artists go through in producing the highest levels of music or other arts are at least as complex as those of scientists contemplating the origin of the universe. There may be some validity to the argument that people are born with different interests in art or science; however, I do not subscribe even to that view. The vast majority of people can be artists or scientists depending on their exposure to each field, especially in early childhood.

Science is a field that specializes in advancing and using knowledge; but this formal definition does not help non-scientists in their daily decisions on how to deal with science. I have had endless discussions with scientists and non-scientists about how to define science and have concluded that the formal definition is too easily misinterpreted. ***The most useful definition of the scientific method is that it is any method that works.*** Science is empowerment. Although smart scientists are needed to advance science, anyone can benefit from science. Thus ***another way of defining science is that it makes previously impossible tasks possible and simplifies difficult tasks.*** Example: if an illiterate person were asked to add two 6-digit numbers, he would have no way of doing it by himself. However, nowadays, any 3rd grader who has learned arithmetic can perform that task, given a pen and paper. Today, you can teach that illiterate person to add those numbers on a calculator in minutes. Demonstrably, science has made a previously impossible task easy for everyone.

Experience has shown that the scientific method works best if certain guidelines are followed. The first is the use of **Definitions:** Without the precise definitions presented throughout this book, most of the discussions in this book would become cumbersome or ambiguous. **Research:** In scientific research, you perform experiments, get the data, and document the results in such a way that others can understand what you did and can reproduce the results. Unfortunately, that is *not* what has been happening in piano teaching. Liszt never wrote down his practice methods. Nonetheless, a tremendous amount of research has been conducted by all the great pianists. Very little of that had been documented, until I wrote this book.

Documentation and Communication: It is an incalculable loss that Bach, Chopin, Liszt, etc., did not write down their practice methods. They probably did not have sufficient resources or training to undertake such a task. An important function of documentation is the elimination of errors. Once an idea is written down, we can check for its accuracy and remove any errors and add new findings. Documentation is used to create a one-way street in which the material can only improve with time. *One finding that surprised even scientists is that about half of all new discoveries are made, not when performing the experiments, but when the results were being written up.* It was during the writing of this book, that I discovered the explanation for speed walls. I was faced with writing something about speed walls and naturally started asking what they are, how many there are, and what creates them. It is important to communicate with all other specialists doing similar work and to openly discuss any new research results. In this respect, the piano world has been woefully inadequate. Most books on piano playing don't even have references and they rarely build upon previous works of others. In writing my first edition book, I learned the importance of properly documenting and organizing the ideas from the fact that, although I knew most of the ideas in my book for about 10 years, I did not fully benefit from them until I finished that book. I then re-read it and tried it out systematically. That's when I discovered how effective the method was! Apparently, although I knew most of the ingredients of the method, there were some gaps that weren't filled until I was faced with putting all the ideas in some useful, organized structure. It is as if I had all the components of a car, but they were useless for transportation until a mechanic assembled them and tuned up the car.

Basic theory: Scientific results must always be based on some theory or principle that can be verified by others. Very few concepts stand alone, independently of anything else. Explanations like "it worked for me," or "I've taught this for 30 years" or even "this is how Liszt did it" aren't good enough. If a teacher had been teaching the procedure for 30 years, s/he should have had plenty of time to figure out why it works. The *explanations* are often more important than the procedures they explain. For example HS practice works because it simplifies a difficult task. Once this principle of simplification is established, you can start looking for more things like that, such as shortening difficult passages or outlining. The nicest property of basic theory is that we don't need to be told every detail about how to execute the procedure -- we can often fill in the details ourselves from our understanding of the method.

b. Principles of Learning. Isn't it strange that although elementary schools, colleges, and universities are centers of learning, none of them teach you how to learn? Our discovery in this book that piano teaching has historically not taught practice methods is duplicated in learning centers where learning has not been formally taught. In the course of writing this book, it became clear that the basic principles for learning piano have universal applicability to any learning and project execution, such as sports, warfare, or weeding your yard. So let's examine these principles.

Learning versus Age. We now recognize the importance of the learning processes that occur between the ages of 0 and 8. Because the brain is developing at this stage, it has an almost limitless ability to learn, when nurtured properly. Conversely, there are examples of below average intelligence resulting from childhood neglect. Initial brain development is influenced by sensory inputs. The main human senses are touch, temperature, hearing, sight, taste, and smell. A newborn first uses the sense of touch: the baby's cheeks are sensitive to the touch of the mother's breast and rubbing the cheek elicits the reaction to search for the mother's breast and to curl the tongue around the nipple to suckle. This ability to curl the tongue is interesting because many adults are unable to curl their tongues although they were obviously able to do it as a baby. This situation is similar to the case of youngsters acquiring absolute pitch effortlessly, but then losing it after their teen years.

The next sense to develop is hearing. Babies can hear at birth and are now routinely tested immediately after birth in order to detect hearing defects as early as possible. Early detection can prevent mental and developmental retardation caused by lack of hearing input because there are methods of replacing hearing by other inputs to stimulate the brain. Hearing at birth is important for recognizing the mother's voice; in animals, this is a critical survival tool for finding their mothers in large colonies. This is why babies can learn absolute pitch and any other properties of sound instantly with great accuracy. As the baby grows, the hearing related developments change from memory to logic in order to facilitate language learning. In both the memory and logic stages, music plays an important role in brain and emotional development. Thus music precedes language – unlike language, music is a natural built-in brain function that does not need to be taught. Music can create emotions and utilize logic that cannot be expressed in any language; therefore babies can benefit from musical inputs long before they can say "mama" or "dada".

Babies apparently have more brain cells than adults although the brain mass is much smaller. Brain growth occurs by growth of stimulated cells and elimination of unstimulated ones. Greater stimulation causes more cells to be retained, thus increasing memory and intelligence. Although children between the ages of 2 to 8 can learn many things quickly, they can forget them just as quickly because the brain is changing rapidly. In an adult, the brain is much less adaptable because its wiring system has been finalized. Thus any baby can learn to speak any language well, but adults learning a new language often never learn to pronounce words correctly. Language, musical and athletic developments follow similar paths, indicating that the brain plays the major role. It is now generally accepted that geniuses are not born but made – that Mozart was a genius because he was a musician from early childhood. The implications of this conclusion are enormous, because it applies to any of us. Clearly, brain research is going to be one of the greatest revolutions yet to come.

Learning Physical skills. Learning physical skills, such as playing the piano, is a type of *project management*. Project management consists of: defining the objective of the project, estimating how much time and effort will be required, determining whether such resources are available, knowing exactly how the project will end, and then creating a plan of action.

Estimating the time it takes to finish the project is often the most difficult part. It is useful to classify projects as short term or long term: skills that can be learned in a few days, or those that require a good fraction of a lifetime to learn. By knowing that a certain project can be finished in couple days, you know that something is wrong if it takes longer – this can prevent you from wasting time because you must immediately look for a better way. Likewise, knowing that a project is going to take a good fraction of a lifetime can ease the frustration if you work hard for a long time and still can not finish it. All successful projects are knowledge based; theory is not enough. *There is one class of skills that is especially easy to learn; these are skills that have "learning tricks".* In piano practice we saw that HS and parallel set methods are powerful learning tricks. The plan of action involves *simplifying difficult tasks into sub-tasks and executing each sub-task separately*. The basic principles are not enough by themselves because project management is knowledge based. For learning piano, the basic principles will teach you HS and segmental practice, but they will not provide the continuity rule, parallel sets, or TO. Clearly, these general principles of project management have universal applicability, but the success of the project still depends on knowledge.

Other principles: don't start new sections until the previous is completed, know the maintenance procedures for finished sections, and have a clear definition of project completion.

3. Why Is Intuition So Often Wrong?

We saw that intuitive methods are frequently wrong. This happens in most fields, not only piano practice. The reason for this is purely statistical. There are almost an infinite number of ways to perform any task; yet, there is only one best way. That is, our chances of guessing the correct way is basically zero. Nature has endowed us with "intuition" which quickly gives us a workable solution – one which is usually better than most solutions. However, among all possible solutions, there is only one best method. Since the intuitive solutions are generally arrived at quickly with insufficient information, they are seldom optimum. Therefore, your chances of hitting the optimum method using intuition are very low.

4. Mozart's Formula, Beethoven and Group Theory

There is an intimate, if not absolutely essential, relationship between mathematics and music. At the very least, they share a large number of the most fundamental properties in common, starting with the fact that the chromatic scale is a simple logarithmic equation (see Chapt. Two, Section 2) and that the basic chords are ratios of the smallest integers. Now few musicians are interested in mathematics for mathematics' sake. However, practically everyone is curious and has wondered at one time or other whether mathematics is somehow involved in the creation of music. Is there some deep, underlying principle that governs both math and music? In addition, there is the established fact that every time we succeeded in applying mathematics to a field, we have made tremendous strides in advancing that field. One way to start investigating this relationship is to study the works of the greatest composers from a mathematical point of view. Here are a few examples:

Mozart (Eine Kleine Nachtmusik, Sonata K300)

I first learned of Mozart's formula at a lecture given by a music professor. I have since lost the reference -- if anyone knows of a reference (professor's name, his institution), please let me know. When I heard of this formula, I felt a great excitement, because it might shed light on music theory and on music itself. You may at first be disappointed, as I was, because Mozart's formula appears to be strictly structural. Structural analyses have not yet provided information on how to come up with famous melodies; but then, music theory doesn't either. Today's music theory only helps to compose "correct" music or expand on it once you have come up with a musical idea. Music theory is a classification of families of notes and their arrangements in certain patterns. We can not rule out the possibility that music is ultimately based on certain identifiable types of structural patterns.

It is now known that Mozart composed practically all of his music, from when he was very young, according to a single formula that expanded his music by over a factor of ten. That is, whenever he concocted a new melody that lasted one minute, he knew that his final composition would be at least ten minutes long. Sometimes, it was a *lot* longer. The first part of his formula was to repeat every theme. These themes were generally very short -- only 4 to 10 notes, much shorter than you would think of a musical theme. These themes, that are much shorter than the over-all melody, simply disappear into the melody because they are too short to be recognized. This is why we do not normally notice them, and is almost certainly a conscious construct by the composer. The theme would then be modified two or three times and repeated again to produce what the audience perceives as a continuous melody. These modifications consisted of the use of various mathematical and musical symmetries such as inversions, reversals, harmonic changes, clever positioning of ornaments, etc. These repetitions would be assembled to form a section and the whole section would be repeated. The first repetition provides a factor of two, the various modifications provide another factor of two to six (or more), and the final repetition of the entire section provides another factor of

206

two, or 2x2x2 = 8 at a minimum. In this way, he was able to write huge compositions with a minimum of thematic material. In addition, his modifications of the original theme followed a particular order so that certain moods or colors of music were arranged in the same order in each composition.

Because of this pre-ordained structure, he was able to write down his compositions from anywhere in the middle, or one voice at a time, since he knew ahead of time where each part belonged. And he did not have to write down the whole thing until the last piece of the puzzle was in place. He could also compose several pieces simultaneously, because they all had the same structure. This formula made him look like more of a genius than he really was. This naturally leads to the question: how much of his reputed "genius" was simply an illusion of such machinations? This is not to question his genius -- the music takes care of that! However, many of the wonderful things that these geniuses did were the result of relatively simple devices and we can all take advantage of that by finding out the details of these devices. For example, knowing Mozart's formula makes it easier to dissect and memorize his compositions. The first step towards understanding his formula is to be able to analyze his repetitions. They are not simple repetitions; Mozart used his genius to modify and disguise the repetitions so that they produced music and so that the repetitions will not be recognized.

As an example of repetitions, let's examine the famous melody in the Allegro of his Eine Kleine Nachtmusik. This is the melody that Salieri played and the pastor recognized in the beginning of the movie, "Amadeus". That melody is a repetition posed as a question and an answer. The question is a male voice asking, "Hey, are you coming?" And the reply is a female voice, "Yes, I'm coming!" The male statement is made using only two notes, a commanding fourth apart, repeated three times (six notes, plus the starting single note representing the "Hey"), and the question is created by adding two rising notes at the end (this appears to be universal among most languages -- questions are posed by raising the voice at the end). Thus the first part consists of 9 notes (since everyone knows this melody, you can try this out in your mind). The repetition is an answer in a female voice because the pitch is higher, and is again two notes, this time a sweeter minor third apart, repeated (you guessed it!) three times (six notes, the first note representing "Yes"). It is an answer because the last three notes wiggle down. Again, the total is 9 notes. The efficiency with which he created this construct is amazing. What is even more incredible is how he disguises the repetition so that when you listen to the whole thing, you would not think of it as a repetition. Practically all of his music can be analyzed in this way; needless to say, the rest of the Nachtmusik (and practically all of his compositions) follows the same pattern.

Let's look at another example, the Sonata #16 in A, K300 (or KV331 - the one with the Alla Turca ending). The basic unit of the beginning theme is a quarter note followed by an eighth note. The first introduction of this unit in bar 1 is disguised by the addition of the 16th note. This introduction is followed by the basic unit, completing bar 1. Thus in the first bar, the unit is repeated twice. He then translates the whole double unit of the 1st bar down in pitch and creates bar 2. The 3rd bar is the basic unit repeated twice. In the 4th bar, he again disguises the first unit by use of 16th notes. Bars 1 to 4 are then repeated with minor modifications in bars 5-8. From a structural viewpoint, every one of the first 8 bars is patterned after the 1st bar. From a melodic point of view, these 8 bars produce two long melodies with similar beginnings but different endings. Since the whole 8 bars is repeated, he has basically multiplied his initial idea embodied in the 1st bar by 16! If you think in terms of the basic unit, he has multiplied it by 32. But then he goes on to take this basic unit and creates incredible variations to produce the first part of the sonata, so the final multiplication factor is even larger. He uses repetitions of repetitions. By stringing the repetitions of modified units, he creates music that sounds like a long melody, until it is broken up into its components.

In the 2nd half of this exposition, he introduces new modifications to the basic unit. In bar

10, he first adds an ornament with melodic value to disguise the repetition and then introduces another modification by playing the basic unit as a triplet. Once the triplet is introduced, it is repeated twice in bar 11. Bar 12 is similar to bar 4; it is a repetition of the basic unit, but structured in such a way as to act as a conjunction between the preceding 3 related bars and the following 3 related bars. Thus bars 9 to 16 are similar to bars 1 to 8, but with a different musical idea. The final 2 bars (17 and 18) provide the ending to the exposition. With these analyses as examples, you should now be able to dissect the remainder of this piece. You will find that the same pattern of repetitions is found throughout the entire piece. As you analyze more of his music you will need to include more complexities; he may repeat 3 or even 4 times, and mix in other modifications to hide the repetitions. He is a master of disguise; the repetitions and other structures are not obvious when you listen to the music without knowing how to analyze it.

Mozart's formula certainly increased his productivity. Yet he may have found certain magical (hypnotic? addictive?) powers to repetitions of repetitions and he probably had his own musical reasons for arranging the moods of his themes in the sequence that he used. That is, if you further classify his melodies according to the moods they evoke, it is found that he always arranged the moods in the same order. The question here is, if we dig deeper and deeper, will we find more of these simple structural/mathematical devices, stacked one on top of each other, or is there more to music? Almost certainly, there must be more, but no one has yet put a finger on it, not even the great composers themselves -- at least, as far as they have told us. Thus it appears that the only thing we mortals can do is to keep digging.

The music professor mentioned above who lectured on Mozart's formula also stated that the formula is followed so strictly that it can be used to identify Mozart's compositions. However, elements of this formula were well known among composers. Thus Mozart is not the inventor of this formula and similar formulas were used widely by composers of his time. Some of Salieri's compositions follow a very similar formula; perhaps this was an attempt by Salieri so emulate Mozart. Thus you will need to know details of Mozart's specific formula in order to use it to identify his compositions. In fact a large fraction of *all* compositions is based on repetitions. The beginning of Beethoven's 5th symphony, discussed below is a good example, and the familiar "chopsticks" tune uses "Mozart's formula" exactly as Mozart would have used it. Therefore, Mozart simply exploited a fairly universal property of music.

There is little doubt that a strong interplay exists between music and genius. We don't even know if Mozart was a composer because he was a genius or if his extensive exposure to music from birth created the genius. The music doubtless contributed to his brain development. It may very well be that the best example of the "Mozart effect" was Wolfgang Amadeus himself, even though he did not have the benefit of his own masterpieces. Today, we are just beginning to understand some of the secrets of how the brain works. For example, until recently, we had it partly wrong when we thought that certain populations of mentally handicapped people had unusual musical talent. It turns out that music has a powerful effect on the actual functioning of the brain and its motor control. This is one of the reasons why we always use music when dancing or exercising. The best evidence for this comes from Alzheimer's patients who have lost their ability to dress themselves because they cannot recognize each different type of clothing. It was discovered that when this procedure is set to the proper music, these patients can often dress themselves! "Proper music" is usually music that they heard in early youth or their favorite music. Thus mentally handicapped people who are extremely clumsy when performing daily chores can suddenly sit down and play the piano if the music is the right type that stimulates their brain. Therefore, they may not be musically talented; instead, it is the music that is giving them new capabilities. It is not only music that has these magical effects on the brain, as evidenced by savants who can memorize incredible amounts of information or carry out mathematical feats normal folks cannot perform. There is a more basic internal rhythm in the brain that music happens to excite. Therefore, these savants may not be talented but are using some of the methods of this book, such as mental play. Just as good memorizers have brains that are automatically memorizing everything they encounter, some savants may be repeating music or mathematical thoughts in their heads all the time, which would explain why they cannot perform ordinary chores – because their brains are already preoccupied with something else. This would also explain why professors, mathematicians, musicians, etc., are often perceived as absent-minded – their brains are frequently preoccupied with mental play. We already know that savants have a strong tendency towards repetitive acts. Could it be, that their handicap is a result of extreme, repetitive, mental play?

If music can produce such profound effects on the handicapped, imagine what it could do to the brain of a budding genius, especially during the brain's development in early childhood. These effects apply to anyone who plays the piano, not just the handicapped or the genius.

Beethoven (5th Symphony, Appassionata, Waldstein)

The use of mathematical devices is deeply embedded in Beethoven's music. Therefore, this is one of the best places to dig for information on the relationship between mathematics and music. I'm not saying that other composers do not use mathematical devices. Practically every musical composition has mathematical underpinnings. However, Beethoven was able to stretch these mathematical devices to the extreme. It is by analyzing these extreme cases that we can find more convincing evidence on what types of devices he used.

We all know that Beethoven never really studied advanced mathematics. Yet he incorporates a surprising amount of math in his music, at very high levels. The beginning of his Fifth Symphony is a prime case, but examples such as this are legion. He "used" group theory type concepts to compose this famous symphony. In fact, he used what crystallographers call the Space Group of symmetry transformations! This Group governs many advanced technologies, such as quantum mechanics, nuclear physics, and crystallography that are the foundations of today's technological revolution. At this level of abstraction, *a crystal of diamond and Beethoven's 5th symphony are one and the same!* I will explain this remarkable observation below.

The Space Group that Beethoven "used" (he certainly had a different name for it) has been applied to characterize crystals, such as silicon and diamond. It is the properties of the Space Group that allow crystals to grow defect free and therefore, the Space Group is the very basis for the existence of crystals. Since crystals are characterized by the Space Group, an understanding of the Space Group provides a basic understanding of crystals. This was neat for materials scientists working to solve communications problems because the Space Group provided the framework from which to launch their studies. It's like the physicists needed to drive from New York to San Francisco and the mathematicians handed them a map! That is how we perfected the silicon transistor, which led to integrated circuits and the computer revolution. So, what is the Space Group? And why was this Group so useful for composing this symphony?

Groups are defined by a set of properties. Mathematicians found that groups defined in this way can be mathematically manipulated and physicists found them to be useful: that is, these particular groups that interested mathematicians and scientists provide us with a pathway to reality. One of the properties of groups is that they consist of Members and Operations. Another property is that if you perform an Operation on a Member, you get another Member of the same Group. A familiar group is the group of integers: -1, 0, 1, 2, 3, etc. An Operation for this group is addition: $2 + 3 = 5$. Note that the application of the operation + to Members 2 and 3 yields another Member of the group, 5. Since Operations transform one member into another, they are also called Transformations. A Member of the Space Group can be anything in any space: an atom, a frog, or a note in any musical dimension such as pitch, speed, or loudness. The Operations of the Space Group relevant to crystallography are (in order of increasing complexity) Translation, Rotation, Mirror, Inversion, and the Unitary operation. These are almost self explanatory (Translation means you move the Member some distance in that space) except for the Unitary operation which basically leaves the Member unchanged. However, it is subtle because it is not the same as the equality transformation, and is therefore always listed last in textbooks. Unitary operations are generally associated with the most special member of the group, which we might call the Unitary Member. In the integer group noted above, this Member would be 0 for addition and 1 for multiplication ($5+0 = 5x1 = 5$).

Let me demonstrate how you might use this Space Group, in ordinary everyday life. Can you explain why, when you look into a mirror, the left hand goes around to the right (and vice versa), but your head doesn't rotate down to your feet? The Space Group tells us that you can't rotate the right hand and get a left hand because left-right is a mirror operation, not a rotation. Note that this is a strange transformation: your right hand becomes your left hand in the mirror; therefore, the wart on your right hand will be on your left hand image in the mirror. This can become confusing for a symmetric object such as a face because a wart on one side of the face will look strangely out of place in a photograph, compared to your familiar image in a mirror. The mirror operation is why, when you look into a flat mirror, the right hand becomes a left hand; however, a mirror cannot perform a rotation, so your head stays up and the feet stay down. Curved mirrors that play optical tricks (such as reversing the positions of the head and feet) are more complex mirrors that can perform additional Space Group operations, and group theory will be just as helpful in analyzing images in a curved mirror. The solution to the flat mirror image problem appeared to be rather easy because we had a mirror to help us, and we are so familiar with mirrors. The same problem can be restated in a different way, and it immediately becomes much more difficult, so that the need for group theory to help solve the problem becomes more obvious. If you turned a right hand glove inside out, will it stay right hand or will it become a left hand glove? I will leave it to you to figure that one out (hint: use a mirror).

Let's see how Beethoven used his intuitive understanding of spatial symmetry to compose his 5th Symphony. That famous first movement is constructed using a short musical theme consisting of four notes; the first three are repetitions of the same note. Since the fourth note is different, it is called the surprise note and Beethoven's genius was to assign the beat to this note. This theme can be represented by the sequence 5553, where **3** is the surprise note. This is a pitch based space group; Beethoven used a space with 3 dimensions, pitch, time, and volume. I will consider only the pitch and time dimensions in the following discussions. Beethoven starts his Fifth Symphony by first introducing a Member of his Group: 555**3**. After a momentary pause to give us time to recognize his Member, he performs a Translation operation: 444**2**. Every note is translated down. The result is another Member of the same Group. After another pause so that we can recognize his Translation operator, he says, "Isn't this interesting? Let's have fun!" and demonstrates the potential of this Operator with a series of translations that creates music. In order to make sure that we understand his construct, he does not mix other, more complicated, operators at this time. In the ensuing series of bars, he then successively incorporates the Rotation operator, creating 3555, and the Mirror operator, creating 7555. Somewhere near the middle of the 1st movement, he finally introduces what might be interpreted as the Unitary Member: 555**5**. Note that these groups of 5 identical notes are simply repeated, which is the Unitary operation!

In the final fast movements, he returns to the same group, but uses only the Unitary Member, and in a way that is one level more complex. It is always repeated three times. What is curious is that this is followed by a fourth sequence -- a surprise sequence 765**4**, which is not a Member. Together with the thrice repeated Unitary Member, the surprise sequence forms a Supergroup of the original Group. He has generalized his Group concept! The supergroup now consists of three members and a non-member of the initial group, which satisfies the conditions of the initial group (three repeats and a surprise).

Thus, the beginning of Beethoven's Fifth Symphony, when translated into mathematical language, reads like the first chapter of a textbook on group theory, almost sentence for sentence!

Remember, group theory is one of the highest forms of mathematics. The material is even presented in the correct order as they appear in textbooks, from the introduction of the Member to the use of the Operators, starting with the simplest, Translation, and ending with the most subtle, the Unitary operator. He even demonstrates the generality of the concept by creating a supergroup from the original group.

Beethoven was particularly fond of this four-note theme, and used it in many of his compositions, such as the first movement of the Appassionata piano sonata, see bar 10, LH. Being the master that he is, he carefully avoids the pitch based Space Group for the Appassionata and uses different spaces -- he transforms them in time (tempo) space and volume space (bars 234 to 238). This is further support for the idea that he must have had an intuitive grasp of group theory and consciously distinguished between these spaces. It seems to be a mathematical impossibility that this many agreements of his constructs with group theory happened by accident, and is virtual proof that he was experimenting with these concepts.

Why was this construct so useful in this introduction to the Fifth Symphony? It certainly provides a uniform platform on which to hang his music. The simplicity and uniformity allow the audience to concentrate only on the music without distraction. It also has an addictive effect. These subliminal repetitions (the audience is not supposed to know that he used this particular device) can produce a large emotional effect. It is like a magician's trick -- it has a much larger effect if we do not know how the magician does it. It is a way of controlling the audience without their knowledge. Just as Beethoven had an intuitive understanding of this group type concept, we may all feel that some kind of pattern exists, without recognizing it explicitly. Mozart accomplished a similar effect using repetitions.

Knowledge of these group type devices that he uses is very useful for playing his music, because it tells you exactly what you should and should not do. Another example of this can be found in the 3rd movement of his Waldstein sonata, where the entire movement is based on a 3-note theme represented by 155 (the first CGGat the beginning). He does the same thing with the initial arpeggio of the 1st movement of the Appassionata, with a theme represented by 531 (the first CAbF). In both cases, unless you maintain the beat on the last note, the music loses its structure, depth and excitement. This is particularly interesting in the Appassionata, because in an arpeggio, you normally place the beat on the first note, and many students actually make that mistake. As in the Waldstein, this initial theme is repeated throughout the movement and is made increasingly obvious as the movement progresses. But by then, the audience is addicted to it and does not even notice that it is dominating the music. For those interested, you might look near the end of the 1st movement of the Appassionata where he transforms the theme to 315 and raises it to an extreme and almost ridiculous level at bar 240. Yet most in the audience will have no idea what device Beethoven was using, except to enjoy the wild climax, which is obviously ridiculously extreme, but by now carries a mysterious familiarity because the construct is the same, and you have heard it hundreds of times. Note that this climax loses much of its effect if the pianist does not bring out the theme (introduced in the first bar!) and emphasize the beat note.

Beethoven tells us the reason for the inexplicable 531 arpeggio in the beginning of the Appassionata when the arpeggio morphs into the main theme of the movement at bar 35. That is when we discover that the arpeggio at the beginning is an inverted and schematized form of his main theme, and why the beat is where it is. ***Thus the beginning of this piece, up to bar 35, is a psychological preparation for one of the most beautiful themes he composed (bar 35). He wanted to implant the idea of the theme in our brain before we heard it!*** That may be one explanation for why this strange arpeggio is repeated twice at the beginning using an illogical chord progression. With analysis of this type, the structure of the entire 1st movement becomes apparent, which helps us to memorize, interpret, and play the piece correctly.

The use of group theoretical type concepts might be an extra dimension that Beethoven wove into his music, perhaps to let us know how smart he was, in case we still didn't get the message. It may or may not be the mechanism with which he generated the music. Therefore, the above analysis gives us only a small glimpse into the mental processes that inspire music. Simply using these devices does not result in music. Or, are we coming close to something that Beethoven knew but didn't tell anyone?

5. Learning Rate Calculation (1000 Times Faster!)

Here is my attempt to mathematically calculate the piano learning rate of the methods of this book. The result indicates that it is about 1000 times faster than the intuitive method. The huge multiple of 1000 makes it unnecessary to calculate an accurate number in order to show that there is a big difference. This result appears plausible in view of the fact that many students who worked hard all their lives using the intuitive method are not able to perform anything significant, whereas a fortunate student who used the correct learning methods can become a concert pianist in less than 10 years. It is clear that the difference in practice methods can make the difference between a lifetime of frustration and a rewarding career in piano. Now, "1000 times faster" does not mean that you can become a pianist in a millisecond; all it means is that the intuitive methods are 1000 times *slower* than the best methods. The conclusion we should draw here is that, with the proper methods, our learning rates should be pretty close to those of the famous composers such as Mozart, Beethoven, Liszt, and Chopin. Remember that we have certain advantages not enjoyed by those past "geniuses". They did not have those wonderful Beethoven sonatas, Liszt and Chopin etudes, etc., with which to acquire technique, or those Mozart compositions with which to benefit from the "Mozart effect", or books like this one with an organized list of practice methods. Moreover, there are now hundreds of time-proven methods for using those compositions for acquiring technique (Beethoven often had difficulty playing his own compositions because nobody knew the correct or wrong way to practice them). An intriguing historical aside here is that the only common material available for practice for all of these great pianists was Bach's compositions. Thus, we are led to the idea that studying Bach may be sufficient for acquiring most basic keyboard skills.

Mathematics is used to solve problems in the following way: First, you must know the most basic physical law that governs the problem. These laws allow you to set up what are called differential equations; these are mathematical statements of the problem. Once the differential equations are set up, mathematics provides methods for solving them to produce a function which describes the answers to the problems in terms of parameters that determine these answers. The solutions to the problems can then be calculated by inserting the appropriate parameter values into the function.

The physical principle we use to derive our learning equation is the linearity with time. Such an abstract concept may seem to have nothing to do with piano and is certainly non-biological, but it turns out that, that is exactly what we need. So let me explain the concept of "the linearity with time". It simply means proportional to time. Learning is analogous to earning money; the important factor is not the income, but the earnings – how much of the income you retain. Thus, assuming a certain amount of learning, we need to calculate how much of that we retain. Linearity with time means that if we forget a fraction F in a time interval T, we will forget the same fraction F in another time interval T. Of course, we know that learning is highly non-linear. If we practice the same short segment for 4 hours, we are likely to gain a lot more during the first 30 minutes than during the last 30 minutes, and how much we learn or retain depends wildly on how we do it. However, we are talking about an optimized practice session averaged over many practice sessions that are conducted over time intervals of years (in an optimized practice session, we are not going to practice the same 4 notes for 4 hours!). If we average over all of these learning processes, they tend to be quite linear. Certainly within a factor of 2 or 3, linearity is a good approximation, and that amount of accuracy is all we need. Note that linearity does not depend, to first approximation, on whether you are a fast learner or a slow learner; this changes only the proportionality constant. Thus we arrive at the first equation:

L = kT (Eq. 1.1),

where L is an increment of learning in the time interval T and k is the proportionality constant. What we are trying to find is the time dependence of L, or L(t) where t is time (in contrast to T which is an interval of time). Similarly, L is an increment of learning, but L(t) is a function.

Now comes the first interesting new concept. We have control over L; if we want 2L, we simply practice twice. But that is not the L that we retain because we *lose* some L over time after we practice. Unfortunately, the more we know, the more we can forget; that is, the amount we forget is proportional to the original amount of knowledge, L(O). Therefore, assuming that we acquired L(O), the amount of L we lose in T is:

L = -kTL(O) (Eq. 1.2),

where the k's in equations 1.1 and 1.2 are different, but we will not re-label them for simplicity. Note that k has a negative sign because we are losing L. Eq. 1.2 leads to the differential equation

dL(t)/dt = -kL(t) (Eq. 1.3)

where "d" stands for differential (this is all standard calculus), and the solution to this differential equation is

L(t) = Ke(exp.-kt) (Eq. 1.4),

where "e" is a number called the natural logarithm which satisfies Eq. 1.3, and K is a new constant related to k (for simplicity, we have ignored another term in the solution that is unimportant at this stage). Eq. 1.4 tells us that once we learn L, we will immediately start to forget it exponentially with time if the forgetting process is linear with time.

Since the exponent is a number, k in Eq. 1.4 has the units of 1/time. We shall set k = 1/T(k) where T(k) is called the characteristic time. Here, k refers to a specific learning/forgetting process. When we learn piano, we learn via a myriad of processes, most of which are not well understood. Therefore, determining accurate values for T(k) for each process is generally not possible, so in the numerical calculations, we will have to make some "intelligent guesses". In piano practice, we must repeat difficult material many times before we can play them well, and we need to assign a number (say, "i") to each practice repetition. Then Eq. 1.4 becomes

L(i,t,k) = K(i)e(expt.-t[i]/T[k]) (Eq. 1.5),

for each repetition i and learning/forgetting process k. Let's apply this to a relevant example. Suppose that you are practicing 4 *parallel set (PS)* notes in succession, playing rapidly and switching hands, etc., for 10 minutes. We assign i = 0 to one PS execution, which may take only about half a second. You might repeat this 10 or 100 times during the practice session. You have learned L(0) after the first PS. But what we need to calculate is the amount of L(0) that we retain after the 10 minute practice session. In fact, because we repeat many times, we must calculate the cumulative learning from all of them. According to Eq. 1.5, this cumulative effect is given by summing the L's over all the PS repetitions:

$$L(\text{Total}) = \text{Sum(over i)}K(i)e(\text{expt.-}t[i]/T[k]) \quad (\text{Eq.1.6}).$$

Now let's put in some numbers into Eq. 1.6 in order to get some answers. Take a passage that you can play slowly, HT, in about 100 seconds (intuitive method). This passage may contain 2 or 3 PSs that are difficult and that you can play rapidly in less than a second, so that you can repeat them over 100 times in those 100 seconds (method of this book). Typically, these 2 or 3 difficult spots are the only ones holding you back, so if you can play them well, you can play the entire passage at speed. Of course, even with the intuitive method, you will repeat it many times, but let's compare the difference in learning for each 100 second repetition. For this quick learning process, our tendency to "lose it" is also fast, so we can pick a "forgetting time constant" of around 30 seconds; that is, every 30 seconds, you end up forgetting almost 30% of what you learned from one repetition. Note that you never forget everything even after a long time because the forgetting process is exponential -- exponential decays never reach zero. Also, you can make many repetitions in a short time for PSs, so these learning events can pile up quickly. This forgetting time constant of 30 seconds depends on the mechanism of learning/forgetting, and I have chosen a relatively short one for rapid repetitions; we shall examine a much longer one below.

Assuming one PS repetition per second, the learning from the first repetition is e(expt.-100/30) = 0.04 (you have 100 seconds to forget the first repetition), while the last repetition gives e(expt.-1/30) = 0.97, and the average learning is somewhere in between, about 0.4 (we don't have to be exact, as we shall see), and with over 100 repetitions, we have over 40 units of learning for the use of PSs. For the intuitive method, we have a single repetition or e(expt. -100/30) = 0.04. The difference is a factor of 40/0.04 = 1,000! With such a large difference factor, we do not need much accuracy to demonstrate that there is a big difference.

The 30 second time constant used above was for a "fast" learning process, such as that associated with learning *during* a single practice session. There are many others, such as technique acquisition by PPI (post practice improvement). After any rigorous conditioning, your technique will improve by PPI for a week or more. The rate of forgetting, or technique loss, for such slow processes is not 30 seconds, but much longer, probably several weeks. Therefore, in order to calculate the total difference in learning rates, we must calculate the difference for all known methods of technique acquisition using the corresponding time constant, which can vary considerably from method to method. PPI is largely determined by conditioning, and conditioning is similar to the PS repetition calculated above. Thus the difference in PPI should also be about 1,000 times.

Once we calculate the most important rates as described above, we can refine the results by considering other factors that influence the final results. There are factors that make the methods of this book slower and factors that make them faster than the calculated rate. For example, it is not possible to take full advantage of the 1000 times factor, since most "intuitive" students may already be using some of the ideas of this book. On the other hand, there are factors that make the intuitive method slower, so that the above "1000 times faster" result could be an under-estimate. The effects of speed walls are difficult to calculate because speed walls are artificial creations of each pianist. However, it is clear that they slow down the intuitive method significantly. These opposing factors (those that make the intuitive method slower and those that make it faster) probably cancel each other out, so that our result of 1000 times faster should be approximately valid. These calculations show that the use of PSs, practicing difficult sections first, practicing short segments, and getting up to speed quickly, are major factors that accelerate learning.

Of course, we didn't need calculus to tell us that the intuitive method is slower. However, it is gratifying to see that we can numerically calculate a difference in learning rate, and that the difference is so large.

6. Future Research Topics

The scientific approach ensures that errors are corrected as soon as possible, that all known facts are explained, documented, and organized in a useful way, and that we only make forward progress. The past situation of one piano teacher teaching a very useful method and another knowing nothing about it, or two teachers teaching completely opposite methods, should not occur. ***An important part of any scientific research is a discussion of what is still unknown and what still needs to be researched.*** The following is a collection of such topics.

a. Momentum Theory of Piano Playing. Slow play in piano is called "playing in the static limit". This means that when depressing a key, the force of the finger coming down is the main force used in the playing. As we speed up, we transition from the static limit to the momentum limit. This means that the momenta of the hand, arms, fingers, etc., begin to play important roles in depressing the keys. Of course, force is needed to depress the key, but when in the momentum limit, the force and motion can be out of phase, while in the static limit they are always exactly in phase. In the momentum limit, your finger is moving up when your finger muscles are trying to press it down! This happens at high speed because you had earlier lifted the finger so rapidly that you have to start depressing it on its way up so that you can reverse its action for the next strike. The actual motions are complex because you use the hand, arms, and body to impart and absorb the momenta. This is one of the reasons why the entire body gets involved in the playing, especially when playing fast or loud. Examples of situations where momenta are important are fast trills or tremolos, rapid repetitions or staccatos, and quiet hands play. The swing of the pendulum and the dribbling of the basketball are in the momentum limit, so that the momentum limit is a common occurrence. In piano playing, you are generally somewhere between the static and momentum limits with increasing tendency towards momentum limit with increasing speed.

The importance of momentum play is obvious; it involves many new finger/hand motions that are not needed in static play. Thus knowing which motions are of the static or the momentum type will go a long way towards understanding how to execute them and when to use them. Because momentum play has never been discussed in the literature until now, there is a vast area of piano play for which we have little understanding. Beyond mentioning the importance of momentum, I have little to present at this time. The only useful information to the pianist is that there is a transition from static play to momentum play as you speed up, so that in fast play, the technique will require entirely new skills that you didn't need at slow play. In fast trills and the quiet hands play, the hand seems to be motionless, but it is not. It is making rapid adjustments in order to accommodate the momenta of the fast moving fingers, and we must learn to apply forces to the fingers that are not in phase with their motions. This is why practicing slow trills every day will not help you to play fast trills. Parallel sets do a much better job because you can immediately start practicing the momentum mode.

b. The Physiology of Technique. We still lack even a rudimentary understanding of the bio-mechanical processes that underlie technique. It certainly originates in the brain, and is probably associated with how the nerves communicate with the muscles, especially the fast muscles. What are the biological changes that accompany technique, or when the fingers are "warmed up"? What is the mechanism of PPI (II.15)? What muscles are most important for playing the piano: the flexors, interossei, or lumbricals? Research on this type of knowledge applicable to piano practice has been rarely conducted and there is no indication that this situation will improve anytime soon. However, there is little question that this type of research is needed if we are to understand the physiology of technique.

c. Brain Research, Using the Subconscious. Brain research will be one of the most important fields of medical research. Efforts at controlling the growth of mental capabilities, especially in childhood, will surely develop. Music should play an important role in such developments because we can communicate aurally with infants long before any other method, and it is already clear that the earlier you start the control process, the better the results.

We are all familiar with the fact that, even if we can play HS quite well, HT may still be difficult. Why is HT so much more difficult? One of the reasons may be that the two hands are controlled by the different halves of the brain. If so, then learning HT requires the brain to develop ways to coordinate the two halves. This would mean that HS and HT practice use different types of brain functions and supports the contention that these skills should be developed separately as recommended in this book. One intriguing possibility is that we may be able to develop HT parallel sets or better schemes that can solve this problem.

Using the Subconscious: We are only beginning to study the many sub-brains we have within our brain and the different ways to use them. We have at least a conscious and a subconscious part. Most people are unskilled at using the subconscious, but the subconscious is important because (1) it controls the emotions, (2) it functions 24 hrs a day whether you are awake or asleep, and (3) it can do some things that the conscious cannot do, simply because it is a different kind of brain. A pretty good guess is that for half the human population, the subconscious may be smarter than the conscious. Thus, in addition to the fact that you have an extra brain capability, it doesn't make sense not to use this part of the brain that might be smarter than your conscious.

The subconscious controls emotions in at least two ways. The first is a rapid, fight or flight reaction -- generation of instant anger or fear. When such situations arise, you must react faster than you can think, so that the conscious brain must be bypassed by something that is hardwired and preprogrammed for immediate reaction. We might even classify this as another part of the brain – the part that automatically processes incoming information instantly, whether the input it visual, auditory, touch, smell, etc. Clearly, the auditory part is directly relevant to piano.

The second subconscious function is a slow, gradual recognition of a deep or fundamental situation. Feelings of depression during a midlife crisis might be a result of the workings of this type of subconscious: it has had time to figure out all the negative situations that develop as you age and the future begins to look less hopeful. Such a process requires the evaluation of myriads of good and bad possibilities of what the future might bring, including changes in body chemistry. When trying to evaluate such a future situation, the conscious brain would have to list all the possibilities, evaluate each, and try to remember them. The subconscious functions differently. It evaluates various situations in a non-systematic way; how it picks a particular situation for evaluation is not under your control; that is controlled more by every day events. The subconscious also stores its conclusions in what might be called "emotion buckets". For each emotion, there is a bucket, and every time the subconscious comes to a conclusion, say a happy one, it deposits the conclusion in a "happy bucket". The fullness of each bucket determines your emotional state. This explains why people often can sense what is right or wrong or whether a situation is good or bad without knowing exactly what the reasons are ("sixth sense"). Thus the subconscious affects our lives much more than most of us realize. It may control how we feel about piano music or our desire to practice.

Usually, the subconscious goes its own way; you don't normally control which ideas it will consider, because most of us have not learned how to communicate with it. However, the events encountered in daily life usually make it quite clear which are important factors and the subconscious gravitates towards the important ones. When these important ideas lead to important conclusions, it gets more interested. When a sufficient number of such important conclusions piles up, it will contact you. This explains why, all of sudden, an unexpected intuition will flash through your conscious mind. So the question here is, how can you communicate with the subconscious?

Any idea that is important, or any puzzle or problem that you had tried to solve with great effort, is obviously a candidate for consideration by the subconscious. Thus thinking about why an idea is important is one way to present the problem to the subconscious. In order to solve a problem, the subconscious must have all the necessary information. Therefore it is important to do all the research and gather as much information about the problem as you can. In college, this is how I solved many homework problems that my smarter classmates could not solve. They tried to just sit down, do their assignments, and hoped to solve these more difficult problems. Problems in a school environment are such that they are always solvable with the information given in the classroom or textbook. Thus, you only need to assemble the right parts to come up with the answer. What I did, therefore, was not to worry about being able to solve any problem immediately but to think about it intensely and make sure that I have studied all the course material. If I could not solve the problem right away, I knew that the subconscious would go to work on it, so I could forget about the problem and let the subconscious work on it. The most effective procedure was not to wait until the last minute to try to solve such problems – the subconscious needs time. Some time afterwards, the answer would suddenly pop up in my head, often at strange, unexpected times. They most frequently popped up in the early morning, when my mind was rested and fresh; perhaps the subconscious works best at night, when the brain is not preoccupied with conscious work. Thus, you can learn to present material to the subconscious and to receive conclusions from it. In general, the answer would not come if I intentionally asked my subconscious for it, but would come when I was doing something unrelated to the problem. You can also use the subconscious to recall something you had forgotten. First, try to recall it as hard as you can, and then abandon the effort. After some time, the brain will often recall it for you. Try this when you can't recall the name of a composition or composer.

We do not yet know how to talk directly with the subconscious. And these communication channels are very different from person to person, so each person must experiment to see what works best. Clearly, you can improve communications with it as well as block the communication channels. Many of my smarter friends in college became frustrated when they found out that I had found the answer when they couldn't; and they knew they were smarter. That type of frustration can stall the communications within the brain. It is better to maintain a relaxed, positive attitude and to let the brain do its thing. Another important method for making maximum use of the subconscious is to leave the subconscious alone without interference from the conscious brain, once you have presented it with the problem: forget about the problem and engage in sports or go to see a movie or do other things you enjoy, and the subconscious will do a better job because it has its own agenda and schedule. If you practice a difficult passage hard, but get no satisfactory results, and you run out of new hand motions, etc., to try, see if the subconscious can give you new ideas when you practice the next time – part of PPI may be the work of the subconscious!

d. The Future of Piano. The "Testimonials" section gives ample evidence that our new approach to piano practice will enable practically anyone to learn piano to her/is satisfaction. It will certainly increase the number of pianists. Therefore, the following questions become very important: (1) can we calculate the expected increase in pianists? (2) what will this increase do to the economics of the piano: performers, teachers, technicians, and manufacturers, and (3) if piano popularity explodes, what will be the main motivation for such large numbers of people to learn piano?

Piano teachers will agree that 90% of piano students never really learn piano in the sense that they will not be able to play to their satisfaction and basically give up trying to become accomplished pianists. Since this is a well known phenomenon, it discourages youngsters and their parents from deciding to start piano lessons. Since music is generally not a highly paid profession, the economic factor also discourages entry into piano. There are many more negative factors that limit the popularity of the piano (lack of good teachers, high expense of good pianos and their maintenance, etc.), almost all of which are eventually related to the fact that piano has been so difficult to learn. Probably only 10% of those who might have tried piano ever decide to give it a try. Therefore, we can expect the popularity of the piano to increase by 100 times (10X more deciding to study and 10X more successful) if the promise of this book can be fulfilled.

Such an increase would mean that a large fraction of the population in developed countries would learn piano. Since it is a significant fraction, we do not need an accurate number, so let's pick some reasonable number, say 30%. This would require at least a 10 fold increase in the number of piano teachers. This would be great for students because one of the big problems today is finding good teachers. In any one area, there are presently only a few teachers and the students have little choice. Within a few teacher/student generations, the quality of teachers will improve and become uniformly good, and the teaching methods will be standardized. The number of pianos sold would also have to increase, probably well in excess of 100%. Although many homes already have pianos, many of them are not playable. Since most of the new pianists will be at an advanced level, the demand for good grand pianos will increase by an even larger percentage, possibly more than 300%, and the quality and quantity of digital pianos sold will increase dramatically.

Is an increase of 100 times in the population of pianists reasonable? What would they do? They certainly can't all be concert pianists and piano teachers. The very nature of how we view piano playing will change. First of all, the piano will, by then, become a standard second instrument for all musicians (regardless of what instrument they play), because it will be so easy to learn and there will be pianos everywhere. The joy of playing piano will be enough reward for many. The zillions of music lovers who could only listen to recordings can now play their own music -- a much more satisfying experience. As anyone who has become an accomplished pianist will tell you, once you get to that level, you cannot help but compose music. Thus a piano revolution should ignite an explosion in composition, and new compositions will be in great demand because many pianists will not be satisfied with playing "the same old things". Pianists will be composing music for every instrument because of the development of keyboards with powerful software and every pianist will have an acoustic piano and an electronic keyboard, or a dual instrument (see below). The large supply of good keyboardists would mean that entire orchestras will be created using keyboard players. Another reason why the piano would become universally popular is that it will be used by parents as a method for increasing the IQ of growing infants.

With such huge forces at work, the piano itself will evolve rapidly. First, the electronic keyboard will increasingly intrude into the piano sector, quickly obsolescing acoustic uprights. The shortcomings of the electronic pianos will continue to decrease until the electronics become musically indistinguishable from the acoustics, and possibly much better. Regardless of which instrument is used, the technical requirements will be the same. By then, the acoustic pianos will have many of the features of the electronics: they will be in tune all the time (instead of being out of tune 99% of the time, as they are now – see Gilmore), you will be able to change temperaments by flicking a switch, and midi capabilities will be easily interfaced with the acoustics. The acoustics will never completely disappear because the art of making music using mechanical devices is so fascinating. In order to thrive in this new environment, piano manufacturers will need to be much more flexible and innovative – future piano manufacturers will look nothing like those we have today.

Piano tuners will also need to adapt to these changes. All pianos will be self-tuning, so income from tuning will decrease slowly, over several generations. However, pianos in tune 100% of the time will need to be voiced more frequently, and how hammers are made and voiced will need to change. It is not that today's pianos do not need as much voicing, but when the strings are in perfect tune, any deterioration of the hammer becomes the limiting factor to sound quality and becomes readily noticeable. Piano tuners will finally be able to properly regulate and voice pianos instead of just tuning them; they can concentrate on the quality of the piano sound, instead of simply getting rid of dissonances. Since the new generation of more accomplished pianists will be aurally more sophisticated, they will demand better sound and keyboard touch. The greatly increased number of pianos and their constant use will require an army of new piano technicians to regulate and repair them. Even the electronics will need repair, maintenance, and upgrading. Piano tuners will also be much more involved in adding and maintaining electronic (midi, etc.) capabilities to

218

acoustics. Thus most people will either have a hybrid or both an acoustic and electronic piano.

e. The Future of Education. The Internet is obviously changing the nature education. One of my objectives in writing this book on the WWW is to make education more cost effective. Looking back to my primary education and college days, I marvel at the efficiency of the educational processes that I had gone through. Yet the promise of much greater efficiency via the internet is staggering by comparison. Here are some of the advantages of internet based education:

(i) No more waiting for school buses, or running from class to class; in fact no more cost of school buildings and associated facilities.

(ii) No costly textbooks. All books are up-to-date, compared to many textbooks used in universities that are over 10 years old. Cross referencing, indexing, topic searches, etc., can be done electronically. Any book is available anywhere.

(iii) Many people can collaborate on a single book, and the job of translating into other languages becomes very efficient, especially if a good translation software is used to assist the translators.

(iv) Questions and suggestions can be emailed and the teacher has ample time to consider a detailed answer and these interactions can be emailed to anyone who is interested; these interactions can be stored for future use.

(v) The teaching profession will change drastically. On the one hand, there will be more one-on-one interactions by email, video-conferencing, and exchange of data (such as audio from a piano student to the teacher). Any teacher can interact with the "master text book center" to propose improvements that can be incorporated into the system. And students can access many different teachers, even for the same topic.

(vi) Such a system would imply that an expert in the field cannot get rich writing the best textbook in the world. However, this is as it should be -- education must be available to everyone at the lowest cost. Thus when educational costs decrease, institutions that made money the old way must change and adopt the new efficiencies. Wouldn't this discourage experts from writing textbooks? Yes, but you need only one such "volunteer" for the entire world; in addition, the internet has already spawned enough such free systems as Linux, browsers, Adobe Reader, etc., that this trend is not only irreversible but well established.

(vii) This new paradigm of contributing to society may bring about even more profound changes to society. One way of looking at business as conducted today is that it is highway robbery. You charge as much as you can regardless of how much or how little good your product does to the buyer. In an accurate accounting paradigm, the buyer should always get his money's worth. That is the only situation in which that business can be justified in the long run. This works both ways; well-run businesses should not be allowed to go bankrupt simply because of excessive competition. In an open society in which all relevant information is immediately available, we can have financial accounting that can make pricing appropriate to the service. The philosophy here is that a society consisting of members committed to helping each other succeed will function much better than one consisting of robbers stealing from each other. In particular, practically all basic education should be essentially free. This does not mean that teachers will lose their jobs because teachers can greatly accelerate the learning rate and should be paid accordingly.

It is clear from the above considerations that free exchange of information will transform the educational (as well as practically every other) field. This book is one of the attempts at taking advantage of these Utopian dreams, together with Connexions, Curriki, Qoolsqool, and others with similar objectives.

V. JAZZ, FAKE BOOKS, AND IMPROVISATION

It is important to learn contemporary music because it is educational (music theory, freer expression of music, compositional skills), transforms you into a better performer, widens your audience, creates many performance and income opportunities, makes you a more complete musician, gives you a greater sense of empowerment, and is a lot of fun because, compared to classical music, you get quicker rewards for a given investment of time.

Although there is a general feeling that this genre is easier than classical, it still takes considerable work to master. ***What is the most important skill you need to learn? CHORDS!*** Basic chords (3-note), inversions, major/minor, dominant 7th, diminished, augmented, larger chords, and how to use them – combining hands, arpeggios, fast broken chords, rhythmic jumps, etc., and there is a different set for every note (tonic) on the piano! This is a huge number of chords; fortunately, you can start by learning just a few of them. You also need to learn all the scales, their proper fingering, and to coordinate the RH melody with the LH accompaniment (these are the reasons why learning classical gives you a big edge). You will also have to know all about the circle of fifths and chord progressions. Therefore, you may be playing the simplest things in a matter of weeks; but it will take a year for most students to feel comfortable with this genre. For example, there is no such thing as true improvisation for at least a few years because true improvisation is as difficult in this genre as composing is, in classical. What is generally referred to as improvisation is "practiced improvisation" in which you have practiced a set of optional changes to pick from, and these changes usually follow a set of rules.

I review some literature in the "Jazz, Fake Books, and Improvisation" book review section of the Reference section; these will give you a good idea of how to get started. You might begin with ***Blake's "How to Play from a Fake Book"***. Fake books are simplified sheet music in which only the RH melody and the associated chords are indicated. It is up to you to decide how to play these chords – this is why you need to learn all about chords; not only are there so many of them, but each can be played in many different ways. Therefore, learning all about chords is where you will initially spend most of your time. Fake books are the easiest to start with because you don't have to know chord progressions – they are given to you on the sheet music. See the book review in the Reference for more information on Blake's book.

The next reviewed book to use is ***"How to play the piano despite years of lessons" by Cannel and Marx***, which is not a book about technique; instead, it teaches how to play jazz, popular songs, or from fake books. Again, we learn all about chords but, in addition, we learn about the circle of fifths and chord progressions, so that you can "play by ear" – remembering a melody, you should be able to figure out the melody with your RH and add your own LH without a fake book. Gets you started immediately by playing simple stuff – read the review for more details. This is the only book of the 3 discussed here that treats rhythm, which is very important in jazz.

A third book you may want to read is ***Sabatella's "A Whole Approach to Jazz Improvisation"*** which is basically a detailed definition of all the chords and scales, as well as discussions of jazz history and what music you should listen to, as examples of how they are played. This book can be browsed free (see review), but there are no songs or music to play – just theory and discussions.

Perhaps the happiest finding in all this is how restrictive the chord progressions are, in terms of the circle of fifths (see Cannel & Marx, Sabatella). This makes it easy to get started, and to advance progressively into more complex music. ***We must all learn the circle of fifths because it is needed for tuning the violin, learning how to tune the piano in the temperaments, understanding those temperaments, figuring out all the scales, their chords, and the key signatures, as well as understanding music theory.*** But why does the human brain respond in this way to the circle of fifths? Is it because we have become accustomed to the chromatic scale which is a direct byproduct of the circle of fifths, or is there an underlying biological origin? As alluded to by Mathieu, there is an instinctive mental affinity to the small primes (1, 2, 3, 5, 7, etc.) in terms of harmony; the prime 1 is the unison which is one note and does not produce much music, although Phillip Glass uses it a lot (repetitions) in his compositions. 2 is the octave and is used only as small parts in larger compositions (Fur Elise). 3 is the circle of fifths and gives birth to the chromatic scale, all the music we play, and the chord progressions. There is nothing "natural" about the chromatic scale. It does not exist in nature and is a purely human construct that is useful because the notes are sufficiently closely spaced, and span a sufficiently wide frequency range, so that we can represent practically any music with it; it also approximates the principal intervals (which exist in nature) that the brain recognizes. In the absence of research results, my personal opinion is that chords and chord progressions are recognized by the brain because of the logarithmic response of the ear to frequencies. The reason for the logarithmic response is that it covers a wide range of frequencies. This response makes frequency ratios particularly easy to track in the brain because all frequencies of a ratio are equidistant from each other in logarithmic space (possibly, right in the cochlea). Chord progressions are not only ratios but any single change along the circle of fifths leaves at least one note common to both chords, making it especially easy for the brain to calculate the frequencies of the new chord. Therefore, chords and chord progressions along the circle of fifths represent the simplest sets of frequencies for the brain to process. Introduction of any other frequency will create horrendous problems for the brain in terms of memory and processing. Thus harmony and chord progressions have some biological basis in addition to our tendency to become "addicted" to any music scale that we hear frequently. This addiction may be related to a biological need to recognize each other; for example, how does a mother penguin recognize her chick just from its chirp among thousands of other chicks, after returning from a long feeding trip? It is a built-in biological addiction to a familiar sound. However, this biological explanation still leaves open the question of why almost every music ever composed has a tonal key, and why the music must return to this tonal key in order for it to be resolved (end satisfactorily). The brain somehow recognizes a certain key as "home" and must return to it.

In summary, the process of learning this genre consists of practicing the chords and scales sufficiently so that, given a melody, you can "feel" the right and wrong chords that go along with it. This takes a lot of playing and experimentation. Alternatively, you can learn to recognize the chord progressions, which is not easy either, and develop a sounder approach using theory. Therefore, if you take a long term approach, and start with a few simple pieces and gradually add more complexity, you should be quite successful. It is important that you perform these pieces as soon as possible, and to critically assess your strong/weak points and work to improve your performances. Because this genre is still young, the instruction books are not all consistent; for example, the circle of fifths in Sabatella goes clockwise with respect to the sharps, but goes counter clockwise in Cannel and Marx, and exactly how you should use the 7th chords depends on which book you read. It is clear that this genre is here to stay, has great educational and practical value, is relatively easy to learn, and can be a lot of fun.

CHAPTER TWO: TUNING YOUR PIANO

1. Introduction

This chapter is for those who had never tuned a piano and who would like to see if they are up to the task. Piano Servicing, Tuning, and Rebuilding, by Arthur Reblitz, will be a helpful reference. The hardest part of learning to tune is getting started. For those fortunate enough to have someone teach them, that is obviously the best route. Unfortunately, piano tuning teachers aren't readily available. Try the suggestions in this chapter and see how far you can get. After you are familiar with what gives you trouble, you might negotiate with your tuner for 30 minute lessons for some agreed-upon fee, or ask him to explain what he is doing as he tunes. Be careful not to impose too much on your tuner; tuning and teaching can take more than four times longer than simply tuning it up. Each tuner has her/is own methods of solving problems; these solutions can't really be taught because what you do depends on how the piano "behaves". Also, be forewarned that piano tuners are not trained teachers and some may harbor unfounded fears that they might lose a customer. These fears are unfounded because the actual number of people who succeed in displacing professional tuners is negligibly small. What you will most likely end up doing is getting a better understanding of what it takes to tune a piano, develop a sensitivity to the tuning, and end up hiring tuners more often.

For pianists, familiarity with the art of tuning provides an education that is directly relevant to their ability to produce music and to maintain their instruments. It will also enable them to communicate intelligently with their tuners. For example, the majority of piano teachers to whom I posed the question did not even know the difference between Equal temperament and historical temperaments (P. 227). The main reason why most people try to learn tuning is out of curiosity -- for the majority, piano tuning is a baffling mystery. Once people are educated to the advantages of tuned (maintained) pianos, they are more likely to call their tuners regularly. Piano tuners can hear certain sounds coming from the piano that most people, even pianists, don't notice. Those who practice tuning will become sensitized to the sounds of out-of-tune pianos. It will probably take about one year to start feeling comfortable with tuning, assuming that you have the time to practice for several hours at least once every one or two months.

Let me digress here to discuss the importance of understanding the plight of tuners and proper communications with them, from the point of view of getting your money's worth from the tuner so that your piano can be properly maintained. These considerations directly impact your ability to acquire piano technique as well as your decisions on what or how to perform, given a particular piano to play. For example, one of the most common difficulties I have noted with students is their inability to play pianissimo. From my understanding of piano tuning, there is a very simple answer to this -- most of these students' pianos are under-maintained. The hammers are too worn/compacted and the action so out of regulation that playing pianissimo is impossible. These students will never even be able to practice pianissimo! This applies also to musical expression and tone control. These under-maintained pianos are probably one of the causes of the view that piano practice is ear torture, but it should not be. *An out-of-tune piano is one of the major causes of flubs and bad habits.*

Another factor is that you generally have no choice of a piano when asked to perform. You might encounter anything from a wonderful concert grand, to spinets, to (horrors!) a cheap baby grand that was totally neglected since it was purchased 40 years ago. Your understanding of what you can/cannot do with each of these pianos should be the first input into deciding what and how to play.

Once you start practicing tuning, you will quickly understand why your spouse vacuuming the floor, kids running around, the TV or HiFi blaring away, or pots clanging in the kitchen is not conducive to accurate, quality tuning. Why a quick, $70 tuning is no bargain compared to a $150 tuning in which the tuner reshapes and needles the hammers. Yet when you query owners what the tuner did to their pianos, they generally have *no idea*. A complaint I frequently hear from owners is that, after a tuning, the piano sounds dead or terrible. This often happens when the owner does not have a fixed reference from which to judge the piano sound -- the judgment is based on whether the owner likes the sound or not. Such perceptions are too often incorrectly influenced by the owner's past history. The owner can actually become accustomed to the sound of a detuned piano with compacted hammers so that when the tuner restores the sound, the owner doesn't like it because it is now too different from the sound or feel to which he had become accustomed. The tuner could certainly be at fault; however, the owner will need to know a minimum of tuning technicalities in order to make a correct judgment. The benefits of understanding tuning and properly maintaining the piano are under-appreciated by the general public. The most important objective of this chapter is to increase that awareness.

Piano tuning does not require good ears, such as absolute pitch, because all tuning is accomplished by comparison with a reference using beats, starting with the reference frequency of a tuning fork. In fact an absolute pitch ability may interfere with the tuning for some people. Therefore, the "only" hearing skill you will need is the ability to hear and differentiate between the various beats when two strings are struck. This ability develops with practice and is not related to knowledge of music theory or to musicality. Larger grands are easier to tune than uprights; however, most baby grands are harder to tune than good uprights. Therefore, although you should logically begin your practice with a lower quality piano (in case you damage it), it will be more difficult to tune.

2. Chromatic Scale and Temperament

Most of us have some familiarity with the *chromatic scale* and know that it must be *tempered*, but what are their precise definitions? *Why is the chromatic scale so special and why is temperament needed?* We first explore the mathematical basis for the chromatic scale and tempering because the mathematical approach is the most concise, clear, and precise treatment. We then discuss the historical/musical considerations for a better understanding of the relative merits of the different temperaments. A basic mathematical foundation for these concepts is essential for a good understanding of how pianos are tuned. For information on tuning, see White, Howell, Fischer, Jorgensen, or Reblitz in the Reference section at the end of this book.

a. Mathematics of the Chromatic Scale and Intervals. Three octaves of the chromatic scale are shown in Table 2.2a using the A, B, C, . . . notation. Black keys on the piano are shown as sharps, e.g. the # on the right of C represents C#, etc., and are shown only for the highest octave. *Each successive frequency change in the chromatic scale is called a semitone and an octave has 12 semitones.* The major intervals and the integers representing the frequency ratios for those intervals are shown above and below the chromatic scale, respectively. Except for multiples of these basic intervals, integers larger than about 10 produce intervals not readily recognizable to the ear. In reference to Table 2.2a, the most fundamental interval is the octave, in which the frequency of the higher note is twice that of the lower one. The interval between C and G is called a 5th, and the frequencies of C and G are in the ratio of 2 to 3. The major third has four semitones and the minor third has three. The number associated with each interval, e.g. four in the 4th, is the number of white keys, inclusive of the two end keys, for the C-major scale and has no further mathematical significance.

TABLE 2.2a: Frequency Ratios of Intervals in the Chromatic Scale

|--Octave--	|--5th--	|--4th--	|-Maj.3rd-	|-Min.3rd-	|	|
CDEFGAB	**C D E F**	**G A B**	**C # D #**	**E F #**	**G # A # B**	**C**
1	**2**	**3**	**4**	**5**	**6**	**8**

We can see from the above that a 4th and a 5th "add up" to an octave and a major 3rd and a minor 3rd "add up" to a 5th. Note that this is an addition in logarithmic space, as explained below. The missing integer 7 is also explained below. These are the "ideal" intervals with perfect harmony.

The "equal tempered" (ET) chromatic scale consists of "equal" half-tone or semitone rises for each successive note. They are equal in the sense that the ratio of the frequencies of any two adjacent notes is always the same. This property ensures that every note is the same as any other note (except for pitch). This uniformity of the notes allows the composer or performer to use any key without hitting bad dissonances, as further explained below. There are 12 equal semitones in an octave of an ET scale and each octave is an exact factor of two in frequency. Therefore, the frequency change for each semitone is given by

$$\text{semitone}^{12} = 2, \text{ or}$$

$$\text{semitone} = 2^{1/12} = 1.05946. \dotfill \text{Eq. (2.1)}$$

Eq. (2.1) defines the ET chromatic scale and allows the calculation of the frequency ratios of "intervals" in this scale. How do the "intervals" in ET compare with the frequency ratios of the ideal intervals? ***The comparisons are shown in Table 2.2b and demonstrate that the intervals from the ET scale are extremely close to the ideal intervals.***

The errors for the 3rds are the worst, over five times the errors in the other intervals, but are still only about 1%. Nonetheless, these errors are readily audible, and some piano aficionados have generously dubbed them "the rolling thirds" while in reality, they are unacceptable dissonances. It is a defect that we must learn to live with, if we are to adopt the ET scale. The errors in the 4ths and 5ths produce beats of about 1 Hz near middle C, which is barely audible in most pieces of music; however, this beat frequency doubles for every higher octave.

The integer 7, if it were included in Table 2.2a, would have represented an interval with the ratio 7/6 and would correspond to a semitone squared. The error between 7/6 and a semitone squared is over 4% and is too large to make a musically acceptable interval and was therefore excluded from Table 2.2a.

TABLE 2.2b: Ideal versus Equal Tempered Intervals

Interval	Freq. Ratio	Eq. Tempered Scale	Difference
Min.3rd:	$6/5 = 1.2000$	$\text{semitone}^3 = 1.1892$	$+0.0108$
Maj.3rd:	$5/4 = 1.2500$	$\text{semitone}^4 = 1.2599$	-0.0099
Fourth:	$4/3 = 1.3333$	$\text{semitone}^5 = 1.3348$	-0.0015
Fifth:	$3/2 = 1.5000$	$\text{semitone}^7 = 1.4983$	$+0.0017$
Octave:	$2/1 = 2.0000$	$\text{semitone}^{12} = 2.0000$	0.0000

It is a mathematical accident that the 12-note ET chromatic scale produces so many ratios close to the ideal intervals. ***Only the number 7, out of the smallest 8 integers (Table 2.2a), results in a totally unacceptable interval. The chromatic scale is based on a lucky mathematical accident in nature! It is constructed by using the smallest number of notes that gives the maximum number of intervals.*** No wonder early civilizations believed that there was something mystical about this scale. Increasing the number of keys in an octave does not result in much improvement of the intervals until the numbers become quite large, making that approach impractical for most musical instruments. Mathematically speaking, the unacceptable number 7 is a victim of the incompleteness (P. 225) of the chromatic scale and is therefore, not a mystery.

Note that the frequency ratios of the 4th and 5th do not add up to that of the octave (1.5000 + 1.3333 = 2.8333 vs. 2.0000). Instead, they add up in logarithmic space because (3/2)x(4/3) = 2. In logarithmic space, multiplication becomes addition. Why might this be significant? The answer is because the geometry of the cochlea of the ear seems to have a logarithmic component. Detecting acoustic frequencies on a logarithmic scale accomplishes two things: you can hear a wider frequency range for a given size of cochlea, and analyzing ratios of frequencies becomes simple because instead of multiplying or dividing two frequencies, you only need to add or subtract their logarithms. For example, if C3 is detected by the cochlea at one position and C4 at another position 2mm away, then C5 will be detected at a distance of 4 mm, exactly as in the slide rule calculator. To show you how useful this is, given F5, the brain knows that F4 will be found 2mm back! Therefore, intervals (remember, intervals are frequency divisions) and harmonies are particularly simple to analyze in a logarithmically constructed cochlea. When we play intervals, we are performing mathematical operations in logarithmic space on a mechanical computer called the piano, as was done in the 1950's using the slide rule. ***Thus the logarithmic nature of the chromatic scale has many more consequences than just providing a wider frequency range than a linear scale.*** The logarithmic scale

224

assures that the two notes of every interval are separated by the same distance no matter where you are on the piano. By adopting a logarithmic chromatic scale, the piano keyboard is mathematically matched to the human ear in a mechanical way! This is probably one reason for why harmonies are pleasant to the ear - harmonies are most easily deciphered and remembered by the human hearing mechanism.

Suppose that we did not know Eq. 2.1; can we generate the ET chromatic scale from the interval relationships? If the answer is yes, a piano tuner can tune a piano without having to make any calculations. These interval relationships, it turns out, completely determine the frequencies of all the notes of the 12 note chromatic scale. *A temperament is a set of interval relationships that defines a specific chromatic scale; tempering generally involves detuning from perfect intervals.* From a musical point of view, there is no single "chromatic scale" that is best above all else although ET has the unique property that it allows free transpositions. Needless to say, *ET is not the only musically useful temperament, and we will discuss other temperaments below.* Temperament is not an option but a necessity; we *must* choose a temperament in order to accommodate the mathematical difficulties discussed below and in following sections b & c. *Most musical instruments based on the chromatic scale must be tempered.* For example, the holes in wind instruments and the frets of the guitar must be spaced for a specific tempered scale. The violin is a devilishly clever instrument because it avoids all temperament problems by spacing the open strings in fifths. If you tune the A(440) string correctly and tune all the others in 5ths, these others will be close, but not tempered. You can still avoid temperament problems by fingering all notes except one (the correctly tuned A-440). In addition, the vibrato is larger than the temperament corrections, making temperament differences inaudible.

The requirement of tempering arises because a chromatic scale tuned to one scale (e.g., C-major with perfect intervals) does not produce acceptable intervals in other scales. If you wrote a composition in C-major having many perfect intervals and then transposed it, terrible dissonances can result. There is an even more fundamental problem. Perfect intervals in one scale also produce dissonances in other scales needed in the same piece of music. Tempering schemes were therefore devised to minimize these dissonances by minimizing the de-tuning from perfect intervals in the most important intervals and shifting most of the dissonances into the less used intervals. The dissonance associated with the worst interval came to be known as **"the wolf"**.

The main problem is, of course, interval purity; the above discussion makes it clear that no matter what you do, there is going to be a dissonance somewhere. *It might come as a shock to some that the piano is a fundamentally imperfect instrument!* The piano gives us every note, but locks us into one temperament; on the other hand, we must finger every note on the violin, but it is free of temperament restrictions.

The name "chromatic scale" applies to any 12-note scale with any temperament. *For the piano, the chromatic scale does not allow the use of frequencies between the notes (as you can with the violin), so that there is an infinite number of missing notes. In this sense, the chromatic scale is (mathematically) <u>incomplete.</u>* Nonetheless, the 12-note scale is sufficiently complete for a majority of musical applications. The situation is analogous to digital photography. When the resolution is sufficient, you cannot see the difference between a digital photo and an analog one with much higher information density. Similarly, *the 12-note scale has sufficient pitch resolution for a sufficiently large number of musical applications.* This 12-note scale is a good compromise between having more notes per octave for greater completeness and having enough frequency range to span the range of the human ear, for a given instrument or musical notation system with a limited number of notes.

There is healthy debate about which temperament is best musically. ET was known from the earliest history of tuning. There are definite advantages to standardizing to one temperament, but that is probably not possible or even desirable in view of the diversity of opinions on music and the fact that much music now exist, that were written with specific temperaments in mind. Therefore we shall now explore the various temperaments.

b. Temperament, Music, and the Circle of Fifths. The above mathematical approach is not the way in which the chromatic scale was historically developed. Musicians first started with intervals and tried to find a music scale with the minimum number of notes that would produce those intervals. The requirement of a minimum number of notes is obviously desirable since it determines the number of keys, strings, holes, etc. needed to construct a musical instrument. Intervals are necessary because if you want to play more than one note at a time, those notes will create dissonances that are unpleasant to the ear unless they form harmonious intervals. The reason why dissonances are so unpleasant to the ear may have something to do with the difficulty of processing dissonant information through the brain. It is certainly easier, in terms of memory and comprehension, to deal with harmonious intervals than dissonances. Some dissonances are nearly impossible for most brains to figure out if two dissonant notes are played simultaneously. Therefore, if the brain is overloaded with the task of trying to figure out complex dissonances, it becomes impossible to relax and enjoy the music, or follow the musical idea. Clearly, any scale must produce good intervals if we are to compose advanced, complex music requiring more than one note at a time.

We saw in Tables 2.2a and b that the optimum number of notes in a scale turned out to be 12. Unfortunately, there isn't any 12-note scale that can produce exact intervals everywhere. Music would sound better if a scale with perfect intervals everywhere could be found. Many such attempts have been made, mainly by increasing the number of notes per octave, especially using guitars and organs, but none of these scales have gained acceptance. It is relatively easy to increase the number of notes per octave with a guitar-like instrument because all you need to do is to add strings and frets. The latest schemes being devised today involve computer generated scales in which the computer adjusts the frequencies with every transposition; this scheme is called adaptive tuning (Sethares).

The most basic concept needed to understand temperaments is the concept of the circle of fifths. To describe a circle of fifths, take any octave. Start with the lowest note and go up in 5ths. After two 5ths, you will go outside of this octave. When this happens, go down one octave so that you can keep going up in 5ths and still stay within the original octave. Do this for twelve 5ths, and you will end up at the highest note of the octave! That is, if you start at C4, you will end up with C5 and this is why it is called a circle. Not only that, but every note you hit when playing the 5ths is a different note. This means that the circle of fifths hits every note once and only once, a key property useful for tuning the scale and for studying it mathematically.

c. Pythagorean, Equal, Meantone, and "Well" Temperaments. *Historical developments are central to discussions of temperament because mathematics was no help; practical tuning algorithms could only be invented by the tuners of the time. Pythagoras is credited with inventing the Pythagorean Temperament at around 550 BC, in which the chromatic scale is generated by tuning in perfect 5ths, using the circle of fifths.* Unfortunately, the twelve perfect 5ths in the circle of fifths do not make an exact factor of two. Therefore, the final note you get is not exactly the octave note but is too high in frequency by what is called the **"Pythagorean comma"**, about 23 cents (a cent is one hundredths of a semitone). Since a 4th plus a 5th make up an octave, the Pythagorean temperament results in a scale with perfect 4ths and 5ths, but the octave is dissonant. It turns out that tuning in perfect 5ths leaves the 3rds in bad shape, another disadvantage of the Pythagorean temperament. Now if we were to tune by contracting each 5th by 23/12 cents, we would end up with exactly one octave and that is one way of tuning an **Equal Temperament (ET)** scale. In fact, we shall use this method in the section on tuning (6c). The ET scale was already known within a hundred years or so after invention of the Pythagorean temperament. Thus ET is not a "modern temperament" (a frequent misconception).

Following the introduction of the Pythagorean temperament, all newer temperaments were efforts at improving on it. The first method was to halve the Pythagorean comma by distributing it among two final 5ths. *One major development was Meantone Temperament, in which the 3rds were made just (exact) instead of the 5ths.* Musically, 3rds play more prominent roles than 5ths, so that meantone made sense, because during its heyday music made greater use of 3rds. Unfortunately, meantone has a wolf worse than Pythagorean.

The next milestone is represented by Bach's Well Tempered Clavier in which music was written with *"key color"* in mind, which was a property of **Well Temperaments (WT)**. These were non-ET temperaments that struck a compromise between meantone and Pythagorean. This concept worked because Pythagorean tuning ended up sharp, while meantone is flat (ET and WT give perfect octaves). In addition, WT presented the possibility of not only good 3rds, but also good 5ths. *The simplest WT (to tune) was devised by Kirnberger, a student of Bach. But it has a terrible wolf. "Better" WTs (all temperaments are compromises and they all have advantages and disadvantages) were devised by Werckmeister and by Young (which is almost the same as Valotti). If we broadly classify tunings as Meantone, WT, or Pythagorean, then ET is a WT because ET is neither sharp nor flat.*

The violin takes advantage of its unique design to circumvent these temperament problems. The open strings make intervals of a 5th with each other, so that the violin naturally tunes Pythagorean (anyone can tune it!). Since the 3rds can always be fingered **just** (meaning exact), it has all the advantages of the Pythagorean, meantone, and WT, with no wolf in sight! In addition, it has a complete set of frequencies (infinite) within its frequency range. Little wonder that the violin is held in such high esteem by musicians.

Since about 1850, ET had been almost universally accepted because of its musical freedom and the trend towards increasing dissonance by composers. All the other temperaments are generically classified as "historical temperaments", which is clearly a misnomer. Most WTs are relatively easy to tune, and most harpsichord owners had to tune their own instruments, which is why they used WT. *This historical use of WT gave rise to the concept of key color in which each key, depending on the temperament, endowed specific colors to the music, mainly through the small de-tunings that create "tension" and other effects. After listening to music played on pianos tuned to WT, ET tends to sound muddy and bland.* Thus key color does matter. On the other hand, there is always some kind of a wolf in the WTs which can be very annoying.

For playing most of the music composed around the times of Bach, Mozart, and Beethoven, WT works best. As an example, Beethoven chose intervals for the dissonant ninths in the first movement of his Moonlight Sonata that are less dissonant in WT. These great composers were acutely aware of temperament. You will see a dramatic demonstration of WT if you listen to the last movement of Beethoven's Waldstein played in ET and WT. This movement is heavily pedaled, making harmony a major issue.

From Bach's time to about Chopin's time, tuners and composers seldom documented their tunings and we have precious little information on those tunings. At one time, in the early 1900s, it was believed that Bach used ET because, how else would he be able to write music in all the keys unless you could freely transpose from one to the other? Some writers even made the preposterous statement that Bach invented ET! Such arguments, and the fact that there was no "standard WT" to choose from, led to the acceptance of ET as the universal tuning used by tuners, to this day. Standardization to ET also assured tuners of a good career because ET was too difficult for anyone but well trained tuners to accurately tune.

As pianists became better informed and investigated the WTs, they re-discovered key color. In 1975, Herbert Anton Kellner concluded that Bach had written his music with key color in mind, and that Bach used a WT, not ET. But which WT? Kellner guessed at a WT which most tuners justifiably rejected as too speculative. Subsequent search concentrated on well known WTs such as Kirnberger, Werckmeister, and Young. They all produced key color but still left open the question of what Bach used. *In 2004, Bradley Lehman proposed that the strange spirals at the top of the cover page of Bach's "Well Tempered Clavier" manuscript represented a tuning diagram (see Larips.com), and used the diagram to produce a WT that is fairly close to Valloti.* Bach's tunings were mainly for harpsichord and organ, since pianos as we know them today didn't exist at that time. One requirement of harpsichord tuning is that it be simple enough so that it can be done in about 10 minutes on a familiar instrument, and Lehman's Bach tuning met that criterion. Thus we now have a pretty good idea of what temperament Bach used.

If we decide to adopt WT instead of ET, which WT should we standardize to? Firstly, the differences between the "good" WTs are not as large as the differences between ET and most WTs, so practically any WT you pick would be an improvement. We do not need to pick a specific WT - we can specify the best WT for each piece we play; this option is practical only for electronic and self-tuning pianos that can switch temperaments easily. In order to intelligently pick the "best" WT, we must know what we are seeking in a WT. We seek: (1) pure harmonies and (2) key color. Unfortunately, we can not have both because they tend to be mutually exclusive. Pure harmony is an improvement over ET, but is not as sophisticated as key color. We will encounter this type of phenomenon in "stretch" (see 5.j below) whereby the music sounds better if the intervals are tuned slightly sharp. Unlike stretch, however, key color is created by dissonances associated with the Pythagorean comma. *With this caveat, therefore, we should pick a WT with the best key color and least dissonance, which is Young. If you want to hear what a clear harmony sounds like, try Kirnberger, which has the largest number of just intervals.*

We now see that picking a WT is not only a matter of solving the Pythagorean comma, but also of gaining key color to enhance music – in a way, we are creating something good from something bad. The price we pay is that composers must learn key color, but they have naturally done so in the past. It is certainly a joy to listen to music played in WT, but it is even more fascinating to *play* music in WT. Chopin is somewhat of an enigma in this regard because he loved the black keys and used keys far from "home" (home means near C major, with few accidentals, as normally tuned). He probably considered the black keys easier to play (once you learn FFP, section III.4.b, Ch. One), so that the fears many students feel when they see all those sharps and flats in Chopin's music is not justified. Chopin used one tuner who later committed suicide, and there is no record of how he tuned. Who knows? Could it be that he tuned Chopin's piano to favor the black keys? Because of the "far out" keys he tended to use, Chopin's music benefits only slightly from

WT, as normally tuned and frequently hits WT wolves. ***Conclusions: We should get away from ET because of the joy of playing on WT; if we must pick one WT, it should be Young; otherwise, it is best to have a choice of WTs (as in electronic pianos); if you want to hear pure harmonies, try Kirnberger. The WTs will teach us key color which not only enhances the music, but also sharpens our sense of musicality.***

3. Tuning Tools

You will need one tuning lever (also called tuning hammer), several rubber wedges, a felt muting strip, and one or two tuning forks and ear plugs or ear muffs. Professional tuners nowadays also use electronic tuning aids, but we will not consider them here because they are not cost effective for the amateur. We shall learn aural tuning -- tuning by ear. All professional tuners must be good aural tuners even if they use electronic tuning aids. Grands use the larger rubber muting wedges and uprights require the smaller ones with wire handles. Four wedges of each type will suffice. You can buy these by mail order or you can ask your tuner to buy them for you. The most popular muting strips are felt, about 4 ft long, 5/8 inch wide. They are used to mute the two side strings of the 3-string notes in the octave used to "set the bearings" (section 6). They also come as ganged rubber wedges but these don't work as well. The strips also come in rubber, but rubber does not mute as well and is not as stable as felt (they can move or pop out while tuning). The disadvantage of the felt strip is that it will leave a layer of felt fiber on the soundboard after you are finished, which will need to be vacuumed out.

A high quality tuning lever consists of an extendable handle, a head that attaches to the tip of the handle, and an interchangeable socket that screws into the head. It is a good idea to have a piano tuning pin which you can insert into the socket using a vise grip so that you can screw the socket into the head firmly. Otherwise, if you grab on the socket with the vise grip, you can scratch it up. If the socket is not firmly in the head, it will come off during tuning. Most pianos require a #2 socket, unless your piano has been re-strung using larger tuning pins. The standard head is a 5 degree head. This "5 degree" is the angle between the socket axis and the handle. Both the heads and sockets come in various lengths, but "standard" or "medium" length will do.

Get two tuning forks, A440 and C523.3 of good quality. Develop a good habit of holding them at the narrow neck of the handle so that your fingers do not interfere with their vibrations. Tap the tip of the fork firmly against a muscular part of your knee and test the sustain. It should be audible for 10 to 20 seconds when placed close to your ear. The best way to hear the fork is to place the tip of the handle against the triangular cartilage (ear lobe) that sticks out towards the middle of the ear hole. You can adjust the loudness of the fork by pressing the ear lobe in or out using the end of the fork. Do not use whistles; they are too inaccurate. Ear muffs are necessary protection devices, since ear damage is a tuner's occupational hazard. It is necessary to hit the keys hard (pound the keys -- to use a tuners' jargon) in order to tune properly as explained below, and the sound intensity from such pounding can damage the ear, resulting in hearing loss and tinnitus.

4. Preparation

Prepare for tuning by removing the music stand so that the tuning pins are accessible (grand piano). For the following section, you need no further preparation. For "setting the bearings", you need to mute all the side strings of the triplet strings within the "bearings octave" using the muting strip so that when you play any note within this octave, only the center string will vibrate. You will probably have to mute close to two octaves depending on the tuning algorithm. Try out the entire algorithm first to determine the highest and lowest notes you need to mute. Then mute all the notes in between. Use the rounded end of the wire handle of the upright mute to press the felt into the spaces between the outer strings of adjacent notes.

5. Getting Started

Without a teacher, you cannot dive right into tuning. You will quickly lose your bearing and have no idea how to get back. Therefore, ***you must first learn/practice certain tuning procedures so that you don't end up with an unplayable piano that you cannot restore.*** This section is an attempt to get you to the level at which you might try a real tuning, without running into those types of difficulties.

The first things to learn are what not to do, in order to avoid destroying the piano, which is not difficult. If you tighten a string too much, it will break. The initial instructions are designed to minimize string breakage from amateurish moves, so read them carefully. Plan ahead so that you know what to do in case you break a string. A broken string per se, even when left for long periods of time, is no disaster to a piano. However, it is probably wise to conduct your first practices just before you intend to call your tuner. Once you know how to tune, string breakage is a rare problem except for very old or abused pianos. The tuning pins are turned by such small amounts during tuning that the strings almost never break. One common mistake beginners make is to place the lever on the wrong tuning pin. Since turning the pin does not cause any audible change, they keep turning it until the string breaks. One way to avoid this is to always start by tuning flat, as recommended below, and to ***never turn the pin without listening to the sound***.

      The most important consideration for a starting tuner is to preserve the condition of the pinblock. The pressure of the pinblock on the pin is enormous. Now you will never have to do this, but if you were to hypothetically turn the pin 180 degrees very rapidly, the heat generated at the interface between pin and pinblock would be sufficient to cook the wood and alter its molecular structure. Clearly, all rotations of the pin must be conducted in slow, small, increments. If you need to remove a pin by turning it, rotate only a quarter turn (counter clock-wise), wait a moment for the heat to dissipate away from the interface, then repeat the procedure, etc.; without such precautions, the wood surrounding the pin will turn to charcoal.

      I will describe everything assuming a grand piano, but the corresponding motion for the upright should be obvious. ***There are two basic motions in tuning. The first is to turn the pin so as to either pull or release the string. The second is to rock the pin back towards you (to pull on the string) or rock it forwards, towards the string, to release it.*** The rocking motion, if done to extreme, will enlarge the hole and damage the pinblock. Note that the hole is somewhat elliptical at the top surface of the pinblock because the string is pulling the pin in the direction of the major axis of the ellipse. Thus a small amount of backwards rocking does not enlarge the ellipse because the pin is always pulled into the front end of the ellipse by the string. Also, the pin is not straight but bent elastically towards the string by the pull of the string. Therefore, the rocking motion can be quite effective in moving the string. Even a small amount of forward rocking, within the elasticity of the wood, is harmless. It is clear from these considerations that ***you must use the rotation whenever possible, and use the rocking motion only when absolutely necessary***. Only very small rocking motions should be used. For the extreme high notes (top two octaves), the motion needed to tune the string is so small that you may not be able to control it adequately by rotating the pin. Rocking provides much finer control, and can be used for that final miniscule motion to bring it into perfect tune.

      Now, what is the easiest way to start practicing? First, let's choose the easiest notes to tune. These lie in the C3-C4 octave. Lower notes are harder to tune because of their high harmonic content, and the higher notes are difficult because the amount of pin rotation needed to tune becomes extremely small. Note that middle C is C4; the B just below it is B3 and the D immediately above middle C is D4. That is, the octave number 1, 2, 3, . . . changes at C, not at A. Let's choose G3 as our practice note and start numbering the strings. Each note in this region has 3 strings. Starting from the left, let's number the strings 123 (for G3), 456 (for G3#), 789 (for A3), etc. Place a wedge between strings 3 and 4 in order to mute string 3 so that when you play G3, only 1 and 2 can vibrate. Place the wedge about midway between the bridge and agraffe.

      There are two basic types of tuning: unison and harmonic. In unison, the two strings are tuned identically. In harmonic tuning, one string is tuned to a harmonic of the other, such as thirds, fourths, fifths, and octaves. The three strings of each note are tuned in unison, which is easier than harmonic tuning, so let's try that first.

      a. Engaging and Manipulating the Tuning Lever. If your tuning lever has adjustable length, pull it out about 3 inches and lock it in place. Hold the handle of the tuning lever in your RH and the socket in your LH and engage the socket over the pin. Orient the handle so that it is approximately perpendicular to the strings and pointing to your right. Lightly jiggle the handle around the pin with your RH and engage the socket with your LH so that the socket is securely engaged, as far down as it will go. From day one, ***develop a habit of jiggling the socket so that it is securely engaged.*** At this point, the handle is probably not perfectly perpendicular to the strings; choose the socket position so that the handle is as close to perpendicular as the socket position will allow. Now find a way to brace your RH so that you can apply firm pressure on the lever. For example, you can grab the tip of the handle with the thumb and one or two fingers, and brace the arm on the wooden piano frame or brace your pinky against the tuning pins directly under the handle. If the handle is closer to the plate (the metal frame) over the strings, you might brace your hand against the plate. You should not grab the handle like you hold a tennis racket and push-pull to turn the pin -- this will not give enough control. You may be able to do that after years of practice, but in the beginning, grabbing the handle and pushing without bracing against something is too difficult to control accurately. So ***develop a habit of***

finding good places to brace your hand against, depending on where the handle is. Practice these positions making sure that you can exert controlled, constant, powerful pressure on the handle, but do not turn any pins yet.

The lever handle must point to the right so that when you turn it towards you (the string goes sharp), you counteract the force of the string and free the pin from the front side of the hole (towards the string). This allows the pin to turn more freely because of the reduction in friction. When you tune flat, both you and the string are trying to turn the pin in the same direction. Then the pin would turn too easily, except for the fact that both your push and the string's pull jam the pin against the front of the hole, increasing the pressure (friction) and preventing the pin from rotating too easily. If you had placed the handle to the left, you run into trouble for both the sharp and flat motions. For the sharp motion, both you and the string jam the pin against the front of the hole, making it doubly difficult to turn the pin, and damaging the hole. For the flat motion, the lever tends to lift the pin off from the front edge of the hole and reduces the friction. In addition, both the lever and string are turning the pin in the same direction. Now the pin now turns too easily. The lever handle must point to the left for uprights. Looking down on the tuning pin, the lever should point to 3 o'clock for grands and to 9 o'clock for uprights. In both cases, the lever is on the side of the last winding of the string.

Professional tuners do not use these lever positions. Most use 1-2 o'clock for grands and 10-11 o'clock for uprights and Reblitz recommends 6 o'clock for grands and 12 o'clock for uprights. In order to understand why, let's first consider positioning the lever at 12 o'clock on a grand (it is similar at 6 o'clock). Now the friction of the pin with the pinblock is the same for both the sharp and flat motions. However, in the sharp motion, you are going against the string tension and in the flat motion, the string is helping you. Therefore, the difference in force needed between sharp and flat motions is much larger than the difference when the lever is at 3 o'clock, which is a disadvantage. However, unlike the 3 o'clock position, the pin does not rock back and forth during tuning so that when you release the pressure on the tuning lever, the pin does not spring back -- it is more stable -- and you can get higher accuracy.

The 1-2 o'clock position is a good compromise that makes use of both of the advantages of the 3 o'clock and 12 o'clock positions. Beginners do not have the accuracy to take full advantage of the 1-2 o'clock position, so my suggestion is to start with the 3 o'clock position, which should be easier at first, and transition to the 1-2 o'clock position as your accuracy increases. When you become good, the higher accuracy of the 1-2 o'clock position can speed up your tuning so that you can tune each string in a few seconds. At the 3 o'clock position, you will need to guess how much the pin will spring back and over-tune by that amount, which takes more time. Clearly, exactly where you place the lever will become more important as you improve.

b. Setting the Pin. *It is important to "set the pin" correctly in order for the tuning to hold.* If you look down on the pin, the string comes around the right side of the pin (grands -- it is on the left for uprights) and twirls around it. Therefore if you rotate the pin cw (clockwise), you will tune sharp and vice versa. The string tension is always trying to rotate the pin ccw (counter clock-wise, or flat). Normally, a piano de-tunes flat as you play it. However, because the grip of the pinblock on the pin is so strong, the pin is never straight but is always twisted.

If you rotate it cw and stop, the top of the pin will be twisted cw with respect to the bottom. In this position, the top of the pin wants to rotate ccw (the pin wants to untwist) but can't because it is held by the pinblock. Remember that the string is also trying to rotate it ccw. The two forces together can be sufficient to quickly de-tune the piano flat when you play something loud.

If the pin is turned ccw, the opposite happens -- the pin will want to untwist cw, which opposes the string force. This reduces the net torque on the pin, making the tuning more stable. In fact, you can twist the pin so far ccw that the untwisting force is much larger than the string force and the piano can then de-tune itself sharp as you play. Clearly, you must properly "set the pin" in order produce a stable tuning. This requirement will be taken into account in the following tuning instructions.

c. Tuning Unisons. Now engage the tuning lever on the pin for string 1. We will tune string 1 to string 2. *The motion you will practice is: (1) flat, (2) sharp, (3) flat, (4) sharp and (5) flat (tune).* Except for (1), each motion must be smaller than the previous one. As you improve, you will add or eliminate steps as you see fit. We are assuming that the two strings are almost in tune. As you tune, you must follow two rules: *(A) never turn the pin unless you are simultaneously listening to the sound, and (B) never release the pressure on the tuning lever handle until that motion is complete.*

For example, let's start with motion (1) flat: keep playing the note every second or two with the LH so that there is a continuous sound, while pushing the end of the lever handle away from you with the

230

thumb and 2nd finger. Play the note in such a way as to maintain a continuous sound. Don't lift the key for any length of time, as this will stop the sound. Keep the key down and play with a quick up-and-down motion so that there is no break in the sound. The pinky and the rest of your RH should be braced against the piano. The required motion of the lever is a few millimeters. First, you will feel an increasing resistance, and then the pin will start to rotate. Before the pin begins to rotate, you should hear a change in the sound. As you turn the pin, listen for string 1 going flat, creating a beat with the center string; the beat frequency increasing as you turn. Stop at a beat frequency of 2 to 3 per second. The tip of the tuning lever should move less than one cm. Remember, never rotate the pin when there is no sound because you will immediately lose track of where you are with respect to how the beats are changing. Always maintain constant pressure on the lever until that motion is completed for the same reason.

What is the rationale behind the above 5 motions? Assuming that the two strings are in reasonable tune, you first tune string 1 flat in step (1) to make sure that in step (2) you will pass the tuning point. This also protects against the possibility that you had placed the lever on the wrong tuning pin; as long as you are turning flat, you will never break a string.

After (1) you are flat for sure, so in step (2) you can listen to the tuning point as you pass through it. Go past it until you hear a beat frequency of about 2 to 3 per second on the sharp side, and stop. Now you know where the tuning point is, and what it sounds like. The reason for going so far past the tuning point is that you want to set the pin, as explained above.

Now go back flat again, step (3), but this time, stop just past the tuning point, as soon as you can hear any incipient beats. The reason why you don't want to go too far past the tuning point is that you don't want to undo the "setting of the pin" in step (2). Again, note exactly what the tuning point sounds like. It should sound perfectly clean and pure. This step assures that you did not set the pin too far.

Now conduct the final tuning by going sharp (step 4), by as little as you can beyond perfect tune, and then bringing it into tune by turning flat (step 5). Note that your final motion must always be flat in order to set the pin. Once you become good, you might be able to do the whole thing in two motions (sharp, flat), or three (flat, sharp, flat).

Ideally, from step (1) to final tune, you should maintain the sound with no stoppage, and you should always be exerting pressure on the handle; never letting go of the lever. Initially, you will probably have to do this motion by motion. When you become proficient, the whole operation will take only a few seconds. But at first, it will take *a lot* longer. Until you develop your "tuning muscles" you will tire quickly and may have to stop from time to time to recover. Not only the hand/arm muscles, but the mental and ear concentration required to focus on the beats can be quite a strain and can quickly cause fatigue. You will need to develop "tuning stamina" gradually. Most people do better by listening through one ear than through both, so turn your head to see which ear is better.

The most common mistake beginners make at this stage is to try to listen for beats by pausing the tuning motion. Beats are difficult to hear when nothing is changing. If the pin is not being turned, it is difficult to decide which of the many things you are hearing is the beat that you need to concentrate on. **What tuners do is to keep moving the lever and then listening to the changes in the beats.** When the beats are changing, it is easier to identify the particular beat that you are using for tuning that string. Therefore, slowing down the tuning motion doesn't make it easier. Thus the beginner is between a rock and a hard place. Turning the pin too quickly will result in all hell breaking loose and losing track of where you are. On the other hand, turning too slowly will make it difficult to identify the beats. Therefore work on determining the range of motion you need to get the beats and the right speed with which you can steadily turn the pin to make the beats come and go. In case you get hopelessly lost, mute strings 2 and 3 by placing a wedge between them, play the note and see if you can find another note on the piano that comes close. If that note is lower than G3, then you need to tune it sharp to bring it back, and vice versa.

Now that you have tuned string 1 to string 2, reposition the wedge so that you mute 1, leaving 2 and 3 free to vibrate. Tune 3 to 2. When you are satisfied, remove the wedge and see if the G is now free of beats. You have tuned one note! If the G was in reasonable tune before you started, you haven't accomplished much, so find a note nearby that is out of tune and see if you can "clean it up". Notice that in this scheme, you are always tuning one single string to another single string. In principle, if you are really good, strings 1 and 2 are in perfect tune after you finish tuning 1, so you don't need the wedge any more. You should be able to tune 3 to 1 and 2 vibrating together. In practice this doesn't work until you become really proficient. This is because of a phenomenon called sympathetic vibration.

d. Sympathetic Vibrations. The accuracy required to bring two strings into perfect tune is so high that it is a nearly impossible job. It turns out that, in practice, this is made easier because *when the frequencies approach within a certain interval called the "sympathetic vibration range", the two strings change their frequencies towards each other so that they vibrate with the same frequency.* This happens because the two strings are not independent, but are coupled to each other at the bridge. When coupled, the string vibrating at the higher frequency will drive the slower string to vibrate at a slightly higher frequency, and vice versa. The net effect is to drive both frequencies towards the average frequency of the two. Thus when you tune 1 and 2 unison, you have no idea whether they are in perfect tune or merely within the sympathetic vibration range (unless you are an experienced tuner). In the beginning, you will most likely not be in perfect tune.

Now if you were to try to tune a third string to the two strings in sympathetic vibration, the third string will bring the string closest to it in frequency into sympathetic vibration. But the other string may be too far off in frequency. It will break off the sympathetic vibration, and will sound dissonant. The result is that no matter where you are, you will always hear beats -- the tuning point disappears! It might appear that if the third string were tuned to the average frequency of the two strings in sympathetic vibration, all three should go into sympathetic vibration. This does not appear to be the case unless all three frequencies are in perfect tune. If the first two strings are sufficiently off, a complex transfer of energy takes place among the three strings. Even when the first two are close, there will be higher harmonics that will prevent all beats from disappearing when a third string is introduced. In addition, there are frequent cases in which you cannot totally eliminate all beats because the two strings are not identical. Therefore, a beginner will become totally lost, if he were to try to tune a third string to a pair of strings. *Until you become proficient at detecting the sympathetic vibration range, always tune one string to one; never one to two.* In addition, just because you tuned 1 to 2 and 3 to 2, it does not mean that the three strings will sound "clean" together. Always check; if it is not completely "clean", you will need to find the offending string and try again.

Note the use of the term "clean". With enough practice, you will soon get away from listening to beats, but instead, you will be looking for a pure sound that results somewhere within the sympathetic vibration range. This point will depend on what types of harmonics each string produces. In principle, when tuning unisons, you are trying to match the fundamentals. In practice, a slight error in the fundamentals is inaudible compared to the same error in a high harmonic. Unfortunately, these high harmonics are generally not exact harmonics but vary from string to string. Thus, when the fundamentals are matched, these high harmonics create high frequency beats that make the note "muddy" or "tinny". When the fundamentals are de-tuned ever so slightly so that the harmonics do not beat, the note "cleans up". *Reality is even more complicated because some strings, especially for the lower quality pianos, will have extraneous resonances of their own, making it impossible to completely eliminate certain beats.* These beats become very troublesome if you need to use this note to tune another one.

e. Making that Final Infinitesimal Motion. We now advance to the next level of difficulty. Find a note near G5 that is slightly out of tune, and repeat the above procedure for G3. The tuning motions are now much smaller for these higher notes, making them more difficult. In fact you may not be able to achieve sufficient accuracy by rotating the pin. We need to learn a new skill. *This skill requires you to pound on the notes, so put on your ear muffs or ear plugs.*

Typically, you would get through motion (4) successfully, but for motion (5) the pin would either not move or jump past the tuning point. *In order to make the string advance in smaller increments, press on the lever at a pressure slightly below the point at which the pin will jump. Now strike hard on the note while maintaining the same pressure on the lever.* The added string tension from the hard hammer blow will advance the string by a small amount. Repeat this until it is in perfect tune. It is important to never release the pressure on the lever and to keep the pressure constant during these repeated small advances, or you will quickly lose track of where you are. When it is in perfect tune, and you release the lever, the pin might spring back, leaving the string slightly flat. You will have to learn from experience, how much it will spring back and compensate for it during the tuning process.

The need to pound on the string to advance it is one reason you often hear tuners pounding on the piano. It is a good idea to get into the habit of pounding on most of the notes because this stabilizes the tuning. The resulting sound can be so loud as to damage the ear, and one of the occupational hazards of tuners is ear damage from pounding. Use of ear plugs is the solution. When pounding, you will still easily hear the beats even with ear plugs. The most common initial symptom of ear damage is tinnitus (ringing in the

232

ear). You can minimize the pounding force by increasing the pressure on the lever. Also, less pounding is required if the lever is parallel to the string instead of perpendicular to it, and even less if you point it to the left. This is another reason why many tuners use their levers more parallel to the strings than perpendicular. Note that there are two ways to point it parallel: towards the strings (12 o'clock) and away from the strings (6 o'clock). As you gain experience, experiment with different lever positions as this will give you many options for solving various problems. For example, with the most popular 5-degree head on your lever, you may not be able to point the lever handle to the right for the highest octave because it may hit the wooden piano frame.

f. Equalizing String Tension. *Pounding is also helpful for distributing the string tension more evenly among all the non-speaking sections of the string, such as the duplex scale section, but especially in the section between the capo bar and the agraffe.* There is controversy as to whether equalizing the tension will improve the sound. There is little question that the even tension will make the tuning more stable. However, whether it makes a *material* difference in stability may be debatable, especially if the pins were correctly set during tuning. In many pianos, the duplex sections are almost completely muted out using felts because they might cause undesirable oscillations. In fact, the over-strung section is muted out in almost every piano. Beginners need not worry about the tension in these "non-speaking" sections of the strings. Thus heavy pounding, though a useful skill to learn, is not necessary for a beginner.

My personal opinion is that the sound from the duplex scale strings does not add to the piano sound. In fact, this sound is inaudible and is muted out when they become audible in the bass. Thus the "art of tuning the duplex scale" is a myth although most piano tuners (including Reblitz!) have been taught to believe it by the manufacturers, because it makes for a good sales pitch. The only reason why you want to tune the duplex scale is that the bridge wants to be at a node of both the speaking and non-speaking lengths; otherwise, tuning becomes difficult, sustain may be shortened, and you lose uniformity. Using mechanical engineering terminology, we can say that tuning the duplex scale optimizes the vibrational impedance of the bridge. In other words, the myth does not detract from the tuners' ability to do their job. Nonetheless, a proper understanding is certainly preferable. The duplex scale is needed to allow the bridge to move more freely, not for producing sound. Obviously, the duplex scale will improve the quality of the sound (from the speaking lengths) because it optimizes the impedance of the bridge, but not because it produces any sound. The facts that the duplex scale is muted out in the bass and is totally inaudible in the treble prove that the sound from the duplex scale is not needed. Even in the inaudible treble, the duplex scale is "tuned" in the sense that the aliquot bar is placed at a location such that the length of the duplex part of the string is a harmonic length of the speaking section of the string in order to optimize the impedance ("aliquot" means fractional or harmonic). If the sound from the duplex scale were audible, the duplex scale would have to be tuned as carefully as the speaking length. However, for impedance matching, the tuning need only be approximate, which is what is done in practice. Some manufacturers have stretched this duplex scale myth to ridiculous lengths by claiming a second duplex scale on the pin side. Since the hammer can only transmit tensile strain to this length of string (because of the rigid Capo bar), this part of the string cannot vibrate to produce sound. Consequently, practically no manufacturer specifies that the non-speaking lengths on the pin side be tuned.

g. Rocking It in the Treble. *The most difficult notes to tune are the highest ones.* Here you need incredible accuracy in moving the strings and the beats are difficult to hear. Beginners can easily lose their bearing and have a hard time finding their way back. One advantage of the need for such small motions is that now, you can use the pin-rocking motion to tune. Since the motion is so small, rocking the pin does not damage the pinblock. *To rock the pin, place the lever parallel to the strings and pointing towards the strings (away from you). To tune sharp, pull up on the lever, and to tune flat, press down.* First, make sure that the tuning point is close to the center of the rocking motion. If it is not, rotate the pin so that it is. Since this rotation is much larger than that needed for the final tuning, it is not difficult, but remember to correctly set the pin. It is better if the tuning point is front of center (towards the string), but bringing it too far forward would risk damaging the pinblock when you try to tune flat. Note that tuning sharp is not as damaging to the pinblock as tuning flat because the pin is already jammed up against the front of the hole.

h. Rumblings in the Bass. *The lowest bass strings are second in difficulty (to the highest notes) to tune.* These strings produce sound composed mostly of higher harmonics. Near the tuning point, the beats are so slow and soft that they are difficult to hear. Sometimes, you can "hear" them better by pressing your knee against the piano to feel for the vibrations than by trying to hear them with your ears, especially in the single string section. You can practice unison tuning only down to the last double string section. *See if you can recognize the high pitched, metallic, ringing beats that are prevalent in this region.* Try eliminating these and see if you need to de-tune slightly in order to eliminate them. If you can hear these high, ringing, beats, it means that you are well on your way. Don't worry if you can't even recognize them at first-- beginners are not expected to.

i. Harmonic Tuning. Once you are satisfied with your ability to tune unisons, start practicing tuning octaves. Take any octave near middle C and mute out the upper two side strings of each note by inserting a wedge between them. Tune the upper note to the one an octave below, and vice versa. As with unisons, start near middle C, then work up to the highest treble, and then practice in the bass. Repeat the same practice with 5ths, 4ths, and major 3rds.

After you can tune perfect harmonics, try de-tuning to see if you can hear the increasing beat frequency as you deviate very slightly from perfect tune. Try to identify various beat frequencies, especially 1bps (beat per second) and 10bps, using 5ths. These skills will come in handy later.

j. What is Stretch? Harmonic tuning is always associated with a phenomenon called stretch. Harmonics in piano strings are never exact because real strings attached to real ends do not behave like ideal mathematical strings. This property of inexact harmonics is called inharmonicity. The difference between the actual and theoretical harmonic frequencies is called stretch. Experimentally, it is found that most harmonics are sharp compared to their ideal theoretical values, although there can be a few that are flat.

According to one research result (Young, 1952), stretch is caused by inharmonicity due to the stiffness of strings. Ideal mathematical strings have zero stiffness. Stiffness is what is called an extrinsic property -- it depends on the dimensions of the wire. If this explanation is correct, then stretch must also be extrinsic. Given the same type of steel, the wire is stiffer if it is fatter or shorter. One consequence of this dependence on stiffness is an increase in the frequency with harmonic mode number; i.e., the wire appears stiffer to harmonics with shorter wavelengths. Stiffer wires vibrate faster because they have an extra restoring force, in addition to the string tension. This inharmonicity from stiffness has been calculated to within several percent accuracy so that the theory appears to be sound, and this single mechanism appears to account for most of the observed stretch.

These calculations show that stretch is about 1.2 cents for the second mode of vibration at C4 and doubles about every 8 semitones at higher frequency (C4 = middle C, the first mode is the lowest, or fundamental frequency, one cent is one hundredth of a semitone, and there are 12 semitones in an octave). The stretch becomes smaller for lower notes, especially below C3, because the wire wound strings are quite flexible. Stretch increases rapidly with mode number and decreases even more rapidly with string length. In principle, stretch is smaller for larger pianos and larger for lower tension pianos if the same diameter strings are used. Stretch presents problems in scale design since abrupt changes in string type, diameter, length, etc., will produce a discontinuous change in stretch. Very high mode harmonics, if they happen to be unusually loud, present problems in tuning because of their large stretch -- tuning out their beats could throw the lower, more important, harmonics audibly out of tune.

Since larger pianos tend to have smaller stretch, but also tend to sound better, one might conclude that smaller stretch is better. However, the difference in stretch is generally small, and the tone quality of a piano is largely controlled by properties other than stretch.

In harmonic tuning you tune, for example, the fundamental or a harmonic of the upper note to a higher harmonic of the lower note. The resulting new note is not an exact multiple of the lower note, but is sharp by the amount of stretch. What is so interesting about stretch is that a scale with stretch produces "livelier" music than one without! This has caused some tuners to tune in double octaves instead of single octaves, which increases the stretch.

The amount of stretch is unique to each piano and, in fact, is unique to each note of each piano. Modern electronic tuning aids are sufficiently powerful to record the stretch for all the desired notes of individual pianos. Tuners with electronic tuning aids can also calculate an average stretch for each piano or stretch function and tune the piano accordingly. In fact, there are anecdotal accounts of pianists requesting stretch in excess of the natural stretch of the piano. In aural tuning, stretch is naturally, and accurately, taken into account. Therefore, although stretch is an important aspect of tuning, the tuner does not have to do anything special to include stretch, if all you want is the natural stretch of the piano.

k. Precision, Precision, Precision. *The name of the game in tuning is precision.* All tuning procedures are arranged in such a way that you tune the first note to the tuning fork, the second to the first, etc., in sequence. Therefore, any errors will quickly add up. In fact, an error at one point will often make some succeeding steps impossible. This happens because you are listening for the smallest hint of beats and if the beats were not totally eliminated in one note, you can't use it to tune another as those beats will be clearly heard. In fact, for beginners, this will happen frequently before you learn how precise you need to be. When this happens, you will hear beats that you can't eliminate. In that case, go back to your reference note and see if you hear the same beat; if you do, there is the source of your problem -- fix it.

The best way to assure precision is by checking the tuning. Errors occur because every string is different and you are never sure that the beat you hear is the one you are looking for, especially for the beginner. Another factor is that you need to count beats per second (bps), and your idea of, say 2bps, will be different on different days or at different times of the same day until you have those "beat speeds" well memorized. Because of the critical importance of precision, it pays to check each tuned note. This is especially true when "setting the bearings" which is explained below. Unfortunately, it is just as difficult to check as it is to tune correctly; that is, a person who cannot tune sufficiently accurately is usually unable to perform a meaningful check. In addition, if the tuning is sufficiently off, the checking doesn't work. Therefore, *I have provided methods of tuning below that use a minimum of checks.* The resulting tuning will not be very good initially, for Equal temperament. The Kirnberger temperament (see below) is easier to tune accurately. On the other hand, beginners can't produce good tunings anyway, no matter what methods they use. At least, the procedures presented below will provide a tuning which should not be a disaster and which will improve as your skills improve. *In fact, the procedure described here is probably the fastest way to learn.* After you have improved sufficiently, you can then investigate the checking procedures, such as those given in Reblitz, or "Tuning" by Jorgensen.

6. Tuning Procedures and Temperament

Tuning consists of "setting the bearings" in an octave near middle C, and then "copying" this octave to all the other keys. You will need various harmonic tunings to set the bearings and only the middle string of each note in the "bearings octave" is initially tuned. The "copying" is performed by tuning in octaves. Once one string of each note is tuned in this way, the remaining string(s) of each note are tuned in unison.

In setting the bearings, we must choose which temperament to use. As explained in section 2 above, most pianos today are tuned to Equal temperament (ET), but the historical temperaments may be showing signs of gaining popularity, especially the Well temperaments (WT). Therefore, I have chosen ET and one WT, Kirnberger II (K-II), for this chapter. K-II is one of the easiest temperaments to tune; therefore, we will visit that first. Most people who are unfamiliar with the different temperaments may not notice any difference at first between ET and K-II; they will both sound terrific compared to a piano out of tune. Most pianists, on the other hand, should hear a distinct difference and be able to form an opinion or preference if certain pieces of music are played and the differences are pointed out to them. The easiest way to listen to the differences for the uninitiated is to use an electronic piano that has all these temperaments built into it, and to play the same piece, using each temperament. For an easy test piece, try Beethoven's Moonlight Sonata, 1st movement; for a more difficult piece, try the 3rd movement of his Waldstein Sonata. Also, try some of your favorite Chopin pieces. My suggestion is for a beginner to learn K-II first so that you can get started without too much difficulty, and then learn ET when you can tackle more difficult stuff. One drawback of this scheme is that you may like K-II so much over ET that you may never decide to learn ET. Once you get used to K-II, ET will sound a little lacking, or "muddy". However, you cannot really be considered a tuner unless you can tune ET. Also, there are many WTs that you may want to look into, that are superior to K-II in several respects (see 2.c).

You can start tuning ET anywhere, but most tuners use the A440 fork to start, because orchestras generally tune to A440. The objective in K-II is to have C major and as many "nearby" scales as possible to be just (have perfect chords), so the tuning is started from middle C (C4 = 261.6, but most tuners will use a C523.3 tuning fork to tune C4 partly because the higher harmonic gives twice the accuracy). Now, the A that results from K-II tuned from the correct C does not result in A440. Therefore, you will need two tuning forks: A for ET and C for K-II. Alternatively, you can just start with only a C fork and start tuning ET from C. Having two tuning forks is an advantage because whether you start from C or from A, you can check your ET when you get to the other note.

a. Tuning the Piano to the Tuning Fork. One of the most difficult steps in the tuning process is tuning the piano to the tuning fork. This difficulty arises from two causes: (1) the tuning fork has a different (usually shorter) sustain than the piano so that the fork dies off before you can make an accurate comparison and (2) the fork puts out a pure sine wave, without the loud harmonics of the piano strings. Therefore, you cannot use beats with higher harmonics to increase the accuracy of the tuning as you can with two piano strings. One advantage of electronic tuners is that they can be programmed to provide square wave reference tones that contain large numbers of high harmonics. These high harmonics (they create those sharp corners of square waves – you will need to know polynomial math or Fourier transforms to understand this) are useful for increasing the tuning accuracy. We must therefore solve these two problems in order to tune the piano accurately to the tuning fork.

Both difficulties can be solved if we can use the piano as the tuning fork and make this transfer from fork to piano using some high piano harmonic. To accomplish such a transfer, find any note within the muted notes that makes loud beats with the fork. If you can't find any, use the note a half tone down or up; for example, for tuning fork A, use Ab or A# on the piano. If these beat frequencies are a bit too high, try these same notes an octave lower. Now tune the A on the piano so it makes the same frequency beats with these reference notes (Ab, A#, or any other note you had picked). The best way to hear the tuning fork is to press it against your ear lobe, as described above, section 3, or to press it against any large, hard, flat surface.

b. Kirnberger II. Mute all side strings from F3 to F4. Tune C4 (middle C) to the fork. Then use

C4 to tune G3 (4th), E4 (3rd), F3 (5th), and F4 (4th), and
G3 to tune D4 (5th) and B3 (3rd). Then use
B3 to tune F#3 (4th),
F#3 to tune Db4 (5th),
F3 to tune Bb3 (4th),
Bb3 to tune Eb4 (4th) and
Eb4 to tune Ab3 (5th). All tunings up to here are just. Now tune A3 such that the F3-A3 and A3-D4 beat frequencies are the same.

You are done with setting the bearings!

Now tune up in just octaves to the highest notes, then tune down to the lowest notes, using the bearings octave as reference. In all these tunings, tune just one new octave string while muting the others, then tune the remaining one or two strings in unison to the newly tuned string.

This is one time you might break the "tune one string against one" rule. If your reference note is a (tuned) 3-string note, use it as it is. This will test the quality of your tuning. If you have a hard time using it to tune a new single string, then your unison tuning of the reference note may not have been sufficiently accurate and you should go back and clean it up. Of course, if after considerable effort, you cannot tune 3 against 1, you will have no choice but to mute two of the three in order to advance. When all the treble and bass notes are done, the only un-tuned strings left are the ones you muted for setting the bearings. Tune these in unison to their center strings, starting with the lowest note, by pulling the felt off one loop at a time.

c. Equal Temperament (ET). I present here the simplest ET tuning scheme. More accurate algorithms can be found in the literature (Reblitz, Jorgensen). No self-respecting professional tuner would use this scheme; however, when you get good at it, you can produce a useable ET. For the beginner, the more complete and precise schemes will not necessarily give better results. With those complex methods, a beginner can quickly get confused without any idea of what he did wrong. With the method shown here, you can quickly develop the ability to find out what you did wrong.

Mute the side strings from G3 to C#5. Tune A4 to the A440 fork. Tune A3 to A4. **Then tune A3-E4 in a contracted 5th; by tuning E4 slightly flat until you hear a beat of about 1 Hz.** The contracted 5th should beat a little under 1 Hz at the bottom of the muted range (A3) and about 1.5 Hz near the top. The beat frequencies of the 5ths should increase smoothly with increasing pitch. Keep tuning up in contracted 5ths until you cannot go up any more without leaving the muted range, then tune one octave down, and repeat this up-in-5ths and down-one-octave procedure until you get to A4. For example, you started with a contracted A3-E4. Then tune a contracted E4-B4. The next 5th will take you above the highest muted note, C#4, so tune one octave down, B4-B3. All octaves are, of course, just. To get the contracted 5th, start from just and tune flat in order to increase the beat frequency to the desired value and set the pin correctly at the same time. If you had done everything perfectly, the last D4-A4 should be a contracted 5th with a beat frequency of slightly over 1 Hz without any tuning. Then, you are done. You have just done a "circle of fifths". The miracle of the circle of fifths is that it tunes every note once, without skipping any within the A3-A4 octave!

If the final D4-A4 is not correct, you made some errors somewhere. In that case, reverse the procedure, starting from A4, going down in contracted 5ths and up in octaves, until you reach A3, where the final A3-E4 should be a contracted 5th with a beat frequency slightly under 1 Hz. For going down in 5ths, you create a contracted 5th by tuning the lower note sharp from just. However, this tuning action will not set the pin. In order to set the pin correctly, you must first go too sharp, and then decrease the beat frequency to the desired value. Therefore, going down in 5ths is more difficult than going up in 5ths.

An alternative method is to start with A and tune to C by going up in 5ths, and checking this C with a tuning fork. If your C is too sharp, your 5ths were not sufficiently contracted, and vice versa. Another variation is to tune up in 5ths from A3 a little over half way, and then tune down from A4 to the last note that you tuned coming up.

Once the bearings are set, continue as described in the Kirnberger section above.

7. Making Minor Repairs (Voicing and Polishing the Capstans)

Once you start tuning, you cannot help but get involved in small repairs and conducting some maintenance.

a. Hammer Voicing. *A common problem seen with many pianos is compacted hammers. The condition of the hammer is much more important to the proper development of piano technique and for cultivating performance skills, than many people realize.* Numerous places in this book refer to the importance of practicing musically in order to acquire technique. But you can't play musically if the hammer can't do its job, a critical point that is overlooked even by many tuners (often because they are afraid that the extra cost will drive customers away). For a grand piano, a sure sign of compacted hammers is that you find the need to close the lid at least partially in order to play soft passages. Another sure sign is that you tend to use the soft pedal to help you play softly. Compacted hammers either give you a loud sound or none at all. Each note tends to start with an annoying percussive bang that is too strong, and the sound is overly bright. It is these percussive bangs that are so damaging to the tuners'/pianist's ear. A properly voiced piano enables control over the entire dynamic range and produces a more pleasing sound.

Let's first see how a compacted hammer can produce such extreme results. How do small, light hammers produce loud sounds by striking with relatively low force on strings under such high tension? If you were to try to push down on the string or try to pluck it, you will need quite a large force just to make a small sound. The answer lies in an incredible phenomenon that occurs when tightly stretched strings are struck at right angles to the string. *It turns out that the force produced by the hammer at the instant of impact is theoretically infinite!* This nearly infinite force is what enables the light hammer to overcome practically any achievable tension on the string and cause it to vibrate.

Here is the calculation for that force. Imagine that the hammer is at its highest point after striking the string (grand piano). The string at this point in time makes a triangle with its original horizontal position (this is just an idealized approximation, see below). The shortest leg of this triangle is the length between the agraffe and the impact point of the hammer. The second shortest leg is from the hammer to the bridge. The longest is the original horizontal configuration of the string, a straight line from bridge to agraffe. Now if we drop a vertical line from the hammer strike point down to the original string position, we get two right triangles back-to-back. These are two extremely skinny right triangles that have very small angles at the agraffe and at the bridge; we will call these small angles "theta"s.

The only thing we know at this time is the force of the hammer, but this is not the force that moves the string, because the hammer must overcome the string tension before the string will yield. That is, the string cannot move up unless it can elongate. This can be understood by considering the two right triangles described above. The string had the length of the long legs of the right triangles before the hammer struck, but after the strike, the string is the hypotenuse, which is longer. That is, if the string were absolutely inelastic and the ends of the string were rigidly fixed, no amount of hammer force will cause the string to move.

A simple analysis shows that the *extra* tension force F (in addition to the original string tension) produced by the hammer strike is given by f = Fsin(theta), where f is the force of the hammer. It does not matter which right triangle we use for this calculation (the one on the bridge side or on the agraffe side). Therefore, the extra string tension F = f/sin(theta). At the initial moment of the strike, theta = 0, and therefore

F = infinity! This happens because sin(0) = 0. Of course, F can get to infinity only if the string cannot stretch and nothing else can move. What happens in reality is that as F increases towards infinity, something gives (the string stretches, the bridge moves, etc.) so that the hammer begins to move the string and theta increases from zero, making F finite (but still many orders of magnitude larger than your finger force).

This force multiplication explains why a small child can produce quite a loud sound on the piano in spite of the hundreds of pounds of tension on the strings. It also explains why an ordinary person can break a string just playing the piano, especially if the string is old and has lost its elasticity. The lack of elasticity causes the F to increase far more than if the string were more elastic, the string cannot stretch, and theta remains close to zero. This situation is greatly exacerbated if the hammer is also compacted so that there is a large, flat, hard groove that contacts the string. In that case, the hammer surface has no give and the instantaneous "f" in the above equation becomes very large. Since all this happens near theta = 0 for a compacted hammer, the force multiplication factor is also increased. The result is a broken string.

The above calculation is a gross over-simplification and is correct only qualitatively. In reality, a hammer strike initially throws out a traveling wave towards the bridge, similarly to what happens when you grab one end of a rope and flick it. The way to calculate such waveforms is to solve certain differential equations that are well known. The computer has made the solution of such differential equations a simple matter and realistic calculations of these waveforms can now be made routinely. Therefore, although the above results are not accurate, they give a qualitative understanding of what is happening, and what the important mechanisms and controlling factors are.

For example, the above calculation shows that it is not the transverse vibration energy of the string, but the tensile force on the string, that is responsible for the piano sound. The energy imparted by the hammer is stored in the entire piano, not just the strings. This is quite analogous to the bow and arrow -- when the string is pulled, all the energy is stored in the bow, not the string. And all of this energy is transferred via the tension in the string. In this example, the mechanical advantage and force multiplication calculated above (near theta = 0) is easy to see. It is the same principle on which the harp is based.

The easiest way to understand why compacted hammers produce higher harmonics is to realize that the impact occurs in a shorter time. When things happen faster, the string generates higher frequency components in response to the faster event.

The above paragraphs make it clear that a compacted hammer will produce a large initial impact on the string whereas a properly voiced hammer will be much gentler on the string thus imparting more of its energy to the lower frequencies than the harmonics. Because the same amount of energy is dissipated in a shorter amount of time for the compacted hammer, the instantaneous sound level can be much higher than for a properly voiced hammer, especially at the higher frequencies. Such short sound spikes can damage the ear without causing any pain. Common symptoms of such damage are tinnitus (ringing in the ear) and hearing loss at high frequencies. Piano tuners, when they must tune a piano with such worn hammers, would be wise to wear ear plugs. It is clear that voicing the hammer is at least as important as tuning the piano, especially because we are talking about potential ear damage. An out-of-tune piano with good hammers does not damage the ear. Yet many piano owners will have their pianos tuned but neglect the voicing.

The two most important procedures in voicing are hammer re-shaping and needling. When the flattened strike point on the hammer exceeds about 1 cm, it is time to re-shape the hammer. Note that you have to distinguish between the string groove length and flattened area; even in hammers with good voicing, the grooves may be over 5 mm long. In the final analysis you will have to judge on the basis of the sound. Shaping is accomplished by shaving the "shoulders" of the hammer so that it regains its previous rounded shape at the strike point. It is usually performed using 1 inch wide strips of sandpaper attached to strips of wood or metal with glue or double sided tape. You might start with 80 grit garnet paper and finish it off with 150 grit garnet paper. The sanding motion must be in the plane of the hammer; never sand across the plane. There is almost never a need to sand off the strike point. Therefore, leave about 2 mm of the center of the strike point untouched.

Needling is not easy because the proper needling location and needling depth depend on the particular hammer (manufacturer) and how it was originally voiced. Especially in the treble, hammers are often voiced at the factory using hardeners such as lacquer, etc. Needling mistakes are generally irreversible. Deep needling is usually required on the shoulders just off the strike point. Very careful and shallow needling of the strike point area may be needed. The tone of the piano is extremely sensitive to shallow needling at the strike point, so that you must know exactly what you are doing. When properly needled, the hammer should

238

allow you to control very soft sounds as well as produce loud sounds without harshness. You get the feeling of complete tonal control. You can now open your grand piano fully and play very softly without the soft pedal! You can also produce those loud, rich, authoritative tones.

   b. Polishing the Capstans. Polishing the capstans can be a rewarding maintenance procedure. They may need polishing if they have not been cleaned in over 10 years, sometimes sooner. Press down on the keys slowly to see if you can feel a friction in the action. A frictionless action will feel like sliding an oily finger along a smooth glassware. When friction is present, it feels like the motion of a clean finger on squeaky clean glass. In order to be able to get to the capstans, you will need to lift the action off from the keys by unscrewing the screws that hold the action down for the grand. For uprights you generally need to unscrew the knobs that hold the action in place; make sure that the pedal rods, etc., are disengaged.

   When the action is removed, the keys can be lifted out after removing the key stop rail. First make sure that all the keys are numbered so that you can replace them in the correct order. This is a good time to remove all the keys and clean any previously inaccessible areas as well as the sides of the keys. You can use a mild cleaning agent such as a cloth dampened with Windex for cleaning the sides of the keys.

   See if the top, spherical contact areas of the capstans are tarnished. If they do not have a shiny polish, they are tarnished. Use any good brass/bronze/copper polish (such as Noxon) to polish and buff up the contact areas. Reassemble, and the action should now be much smoother.

References

Items in **bold** are reviewed below.

Bach Bibliography.
Bertrand, OTT., *Liszt et la Pedagogie du Piano, Collection Psychology et Pedaogie de la Musique*, (1978) E. A. P. France.
Boissier, August., *A Diary of Franz Liszt as Teacher 1831-32*, translated by Elyse Mach.
Bree, Malwine, *The Leschetizky Method*, Dover, Mineola, NY, 1977.
Bruser, Madeline, *The Art of Practicing*, Bell Tower, NY, 1997.
Cannel, Ward, and Marx, Fred, *How to play the piano despite years of lessons*, What music is, and how to make it at home, Crown & Bridge, NY, 1976.
Chan, Angela, *Comparative Study of the Methodologies of Three Distinguished Piano Teachers of the Nineteenth Century: Beethoven, Czerny and Liszt.*
Eigeldinger, Jean-Jacques, *Chopin, pianist and teacher as seen by his pupils*,Cambridge Univ. Press, 1986.
Elson, Margaret, *Passionate Practice*, Regent Press, Oakland, CA, 2002.
Fay, Amy, *Music Study in Germany.*
Fine, Larry, *The Piano Book*, Brookside Press, 4th Ed., Nov. 2000.
Fink, Seymour, *Mastering Piano Technique*, Amadeus Press, 1992.
Fischer, J. C., *Piano Tuning*, Dover, N.Y., 1975.
Five Lectures on the Acoustics of the Piano,, Royal Institute of Technology Seminar, Anders Askenfelt, Ed., Stockholm, May 27, 1988.
Fraser, Alan, *The Craft of Piano Playing*, Scarecrow Press, 2003.
Gieseking, Walter, and Leimer, Karl, *Piano Technique*, 2 books in one, Dover, NY,1972.
Gilmore, Don A., *In Pursuit of the Self-Tuning Piano.*
Howell, W. D., *Professional Piano Tuning*, New Era Printing Co., Conn. 1966.
Green, Barry, and Gallwey, Timothy, *The Inner Game of Music*, Doubleday, 1986.
Hinson, Maurice, *Guide to the Pianist's Repertoire*, 3rd Edition, Indiana Univ. Press, 2000.
Hofman, Josef, *Piano Playing, With Piano Questions Answered*, Dover, NY, 1909.
Jaynes, E. T., *The Physical Basis of Music.*
(Explanation of why Liszt could not teach, best description of Thumb Over method in literature.)
Jorgensen, Owen H, *Tuning*, Michigan St. Univ. Press, 1991.
Lhevine, Josef, *Basic Principles in Piano Playing*, Dover, NY, 1972.

Lister-Sink, Barbara, _Freeing The Caged Bird_, video, 150 min., 1996, Wingsound, Winston-Salem, NC.

Liszt's Teaching Bibliography:

Below is a list containing information on Liszt's teachings; the contents are disappointing. Liszt's father, Adam, did a terrific job of teaching Liszt but, after soaring to fame, Liszt only gave "master classes" to students who were already concert pianists, while complaining about the conservatories that could not teach. The few teachers who knew how to teach were the parents of Mozart, Beethoven, Chopin, Liszt, etc. That tells us something valuable. The anointed teachers: the great Masters and their students were led astray by the grandeur of "talent", dogma, endless practice, etc., (instead of research, knowledge, documentation, empowerment, etc.) and piano pedagogy ended up in a dead end with no way out.

(1) _Life and Liszt_, Arthur Friedheim, Taplinger, NY, 1961.

(2) _The Piano Master Classes of Franz Liszt: 1884-1886, Diary Notes of August Gollerich_, Indiana Univ. Press, 1996.

(3) _Living with Liszt: From the Diary of Carl Lachmund, and American Pupil of Liszt 1882-1884_, Pendragon Press, Stuyvesant, NY, 1995.

(4) _Memories of a Musical Life_, William Mason, Century Co., NY, 1901.

(5) _My Musical Experiences_, Bettina Walker, R. Bently & Son, London, 1892.

(6) There are a diary by Lina Schmalhausen, the other articles already cited (by Amy Fay and August Boissier), and the books by Ronald Taylor and Alan Walker.

Lloyd, Norman, _The Golden Encyclopedia of Music_Golden Press, NY, 1968.

Mark, Thomas, _What Every Pianist Needs To Know About The Body_, GIA Publications, Chicago, 2003.

Mathieu, W. A., _Harmonic Experience_, Inner Tradition International, Rochester, VT, 1997.

Moscheles, _Life of Beethoven_.

Neely, Blake, _How to Play from a Fake Book_, Hal Leonard, Milwaukee, WI, 1999.

Olson, Steve, _COUNT DOWN: The Race for Beautiful Solutions at the International Mathematical Olympiad_, 2004; "Olson explains the creative thinking process of these competitors and defies the assumption that genius is born, not made, as in music."

Prokop, Richard, _Piano Power, a Breakthrough Approach to Improving your Technique_, Greenacres Press, NY., 1999.

Reblitz, Arthur, _Piano Servicing, Tuning, and Rebuilding_, 2nd Ed., 1993.

Richman, Howard, _Super Sight-Reading Secrets_, Sound Feelings Publ., 1986.

Sabatella, Marc, _A Whole Approach to Jazz Improvisation_, ADG Productions, Lawndale, CA, 1996.

Sandor, Gyorgy, _On Piano Playing_, Schirmer Books, NY, 1995.

Sethares, William A., _Adaptive tunings for musical scales_, J. Acoust. Soc. Am. **96**(1), July, 1994, P. 10.

Sherman, Russell, _Piano Pieces_, North Point Press, NY, 1997.

Suzuki, Shinichi (et al), two books (there are more):

The Suzuki Concept: An Introduction to a Successful Method for Early Music Education, Diablo Press, Berkeley, CA, 1973.

HOW TO TEACH SUZUKI PIANO, Summy-Birchard, Miami, FL, 1993.

Taylor, Ronald, _Franz Liszt, the Man and the Musician_, Universe Books, NY, 1986.

Tomita, Yo, _J. S. Bach: Inventions and Sinfonia_, 1999.

Walker, Alan, _Franz Liszt, The Virtuoso Years, 1811-1847_, Cornell Univ. Press, Ithaca, NY, 1983.

Weinreich, G., _The Coupled Motions of Piano Strings_, Scientific American, Jan., 1979, P. 118-127.

Werner, Kenney, _Effortless Mastery_, Jamey Aebersold Jazz, New Albany, IN, 1996, with meditation CD.

White, W. B., _Piano Tuning and Allied Arts_, Tuners' Supply Co., Boston, Mass, 1948.

Whiteside, Abby, _On Piano Playing_, 2 books in one, Amadeus Press, Portland, OR, 1997;

Indispensables of Piano Playing, and _Mastering the Chopin Etudes and Other Essays_.

Young, Robert W., _Inharmonicity of Plain Wire Piano Strings_, J. Acoust. Soc. Am., **24**(3), 1952.

Book/Video Reviews

Reviewed Books: Classical Music

General Conclusions from the Reviewed Books

(i) In the last 100 years, the piano literature evolved from attention to fingers and finger exercises to using the entire body, relaxation, and musical performance. Therefore, the older publications tend to contain concepts that are now discredited. This does not mean that Mozart, Beethoven, Chopin, and Liszt didn't have proper technique; just that the literature recorded mostly the great performances but not what you had to do to become that good. In short, the piano literature has been woefully inadequate, up to modern times.

(ii) One concept that has not changed is that musical considerations, such as rhythm, tone, phrasing, etc., cannot be separated from technique. There is universal agreement among teachers who teach the best practice methods that piano proficiency is not talent but a set of (learned) skills.

(iii) Almost every book deals with a subset of the same subjects; the main differences are in the approach and degree of detail that each presents. Almost all of them are partial treatments and are incomplete. They treat first the human mind and anatomy and their relationships to the piano: mental attitude and preparation, sitting posture, bench height, role of arms, hands and fingers - often with appropriate exercises, and discussions of injury. Then concepts of technique and musicality: touch, tone, thumb, legato, staccato, fingering, scales, arpeggios, octaves, chords, repeated notes, velocity, glissando, pedal, practice time, memorization, etc. There is surprisingly little literature on sight reading.

(iv) With a few older exceptions, most discourage the use of "thumb under" for playing scales; however, thumb under is a valuable movement for some specific applications. Chopin preferred thumb under for its legato, but taught thumb over where it was technically advantageous.

(v) The lack of bibliographies (references) in many books is a reflection of the fact that piano teaching methods have never been adequately or properly documented or even researched. Each author in effect had to re-invent the wheel each time. This is also reflected in the actual teaching methods. Piano teaching methods were basically handed down by word of mouth from teacher to student, reminiscent of the way in which prehistoric humans handed down their folklore and medical practices through generations. This basic flaw almost completely arrested the development of teaching methods and they have remained basically unchanged for hundreds of years. Even "scholarly" works like Fink's has only a list of suggested reading material, and Sandor has no references whatsoever, an inexcusable omission that reflects the primitive nature of the literature on piano pedagogy.

Whiteside's book was widely acclaimed mostly because it was the first real attempt at a scientific approach to discovering the best practice methods. However, according to anecdotal accounts, most of her "discoveries" had been taught by Chopin, although this information was apparently not available to Whiteside. However, it may be more than just a coincidence that she used Chopin's music most extensively in her teachings. Whiteside's book failed miserably because, although she conducted experiments and documented the results, she did not use clear language, organize her results, and make any cause-and-effect analyses, etc., that are needed for good scientific project. Nonetheless, her book was one of the best available at the time of its publication, because of the inferior quality of all the others.

A large number of teachers claim to teach the Liszt method, but there is only fragmentary and preciously little documentation of what that method is. There is abundant literature on where Liszt visited, whom he met and taught, what he played, and what magical feats of piano he performed, but there is practically no record of what a student must do to be able to play like that. Even Liszt was not able to analyze his technique; when asked to teach, he could only demonstrate on the piano.

(vi) Chang's book is the only one that provides practice methods for solving specific technique problems (overcoming speed walls, relaxation, stamina, memorizing, slow vs. fast practice, etc.) that should be taught at the beginner stage, but have been infrequently taught. The other books deal mostly with "higher" levels of piano playing, but seem totally ignorant of practice methods, so that Chang's book fills a gap in the literature on learning piano.

List of MUST READ Books (alphabetically): Eigeldinger, Fink or Sandor, Fraser, Prokop, Richman; & MUST VIEW Videos: Lister-Sink.

Book Review Format: Author, Title, Year of publication, number of Pages in book, and whether References are cited (bibliographies).

The references are an indication of how scholarly the book is. These reviews are not meant to be comprehensive; they are concerned mainly with how relevant these books are to the piano student interested in piano technique. Most "irrelevant" materials have been ignored.

Bree, Malwine, "The Leschetizky Method". 1997 (1913), 92P, no references.

Although this book appeared in 1997, it is a re-publication of 1913 material.

Teaching lineage: Beethoven-Czerny-Leschetizky-Bree.

Book of exercises for developing technique, photos of finger positions. Advocates thumb under method. Hand position, finger independence exercises, scales, chords, touch, glissando, pedal, performance, etc., a relatively complete treatment. Good book to read after reading Chang, shows fingering conventions, hints of HS practice and flat finger positions, and beginnings of TO motion.

Bruser, Madeline, "The Art of Practicing". 1997, 272P, references & suggested readings.

http://artofpracticing.com/ Based on starting with preparing the mind (meditation) and body (stretching exercises), then goes into some useful specifics of piano skills. The amount of piano instruction is unfortunately reduced by the parallel instructions for other instruments (mostly string and wind). Though physical exercise (calisthenics) is good, exercises such as scales are not helpful. Contains a small amount of useful information.

Chang, Chuan C., "Fundamentals of Piano Practice". 2007, over 200P., continuously updated; references, book reviews, links. This book was inspired by Mlle. Yvonne Combe's teachings.

Combe's teaching lineage: Beethoven-Czerny-Liszt-Debussy (also Long, Cortot)-Combe. Combe's mother was a voice teacher and probably gave Yvonne a good start in piano. Yvonne studied under Marguerite Long, and had won most of the piano 1st prizes at the Paris Conservatory during her time there. The teaching methods at that Conservatory were greatly influenced by Liszt, and the "French School of Piano/Music" reflected many of his thoughts. Her main mentors in Paris were Cortot, Debussy, and Saint Saens, and her interpretations of the latter two composers were without peer. She was one of the most promising pianists of her time until she injured her right hand in a bicycle accident (she was quite an athlete), ending her performing career. She subsequently dedicated herself to teaching, organizing schools in Switzerland and later in Plainfield, NJ, USA, where she briefly coached Van Cliburn because her teaching methods were similar to his mother's. Though she was proud of her Beethoven-Liszt lineage (through Saint Saens and Debussy), her interpretations of Beethoven were at times inadequate, and assigned only a few Czerny pieces to her students. She had lost most of her hearing by age 86, but taught till the year of her passing at age 96. -- biographic notes by C. C. Chang, from anecdotal accounts; also, see comments on P. 1.

Chang's book teaches the most basic practice methods for acquiring technique quickly (hands separate practice, chord attack [parallel sets], shortening difficult passages, memorizing, relaxation, eliminating speed walls, etc.). No other book discusses all of these essential elements needed for rapid progress and correct technique. Mental play is the single most important skill for the advanced pianist and should be taught from the first year of lessons. Also treats sight reading, preparing for recitals, controlling nervousness, gravity drop, which exercises are good and which ones are useless or harmful, learning absolute pitch, outlining, etc. Has a chapter on piano tuning, explains the chromatic scale and tempering. Go to the above web site for downloading the book free; it has been translated into several languages. A **MUST READ.**

Eigeldinger, Jean-Jacques, "Chopin, pianist and teacher as seen by his pupils". 1986, 324P, bibliography.

The most scholarly and complete compilation of relevant material on Chopin concerning teaching, technique, interpretation, and history. Because of a lack of direct documentation in Chopin's time, practically all the material is anecdotal. Yet the accuracy seems unquestionable because of the exhaustive documentation, lack of any detectable bias, and the obvious fact that such deep understanding could only have come from Chopin himself - the results are in uncanny agreement with the best material available today. Eigeldinger has arranged the subjects into helpful groupings (technique, interpretation, quotes, annotated scores and fingerings, Chopin's style). I certainly wish that there were more practice methods, but we must all realize that the lack of documentation in Chopin's time has resulted in the loss of a large fraction of what he taught. In the case of F. Liszt, the situation is far worse.

The technical teachings are presented concisely on pages 23-64. These teachings are in almost complete agreement with those of all the best sources, from Liszt and Whiteside to Fink, Sandor, Suzuki, and this book (Chang). The presentation is in stark contrast to Whiteside; here it is authoritative (Whiteside sometimes retracts her own findings), brief (only 41 pages compared to 350 pages for Whiteside!), organized, and clear, while covering a similar range of topics. The second part, pages 65-89, covers interpretation and therefore contains much less information on technique, but is just as informative as the first section. It touches (very!) briefly on how to interpret each of his major compositions. The remaining 200 pages are dedicated to documentation, illustrations, Chopin's annotations on his own compositions and fingerings, and a 10 page "sketch" of basic material to teach beginners.

Notes on technique: Chopin was self-taught; there is little known about how he learned when young except that he was taught by his mother, an accomplished pianist. Chopin didn't believe in drills and exercises (he recommended no more than 3 hr practice/day). Chopin's methods are not as contrary to Liszt's as they might appear at first, although Liszt frequently practiced over 10 hours a day and recommended exercises "to exhaustion". Chopin, like Liszt, wrote etudes; these and Liszt's "exercises" were not mindless repetitions but specific methods of technique acquisition.

Learn to make music *before* learning technique. The whole body must be involved, and use of arm weight (gravity drop) is a key element of technique. He taught thumb over (especially when the passed note is black!!) as well as thumb under, and in fact allowed any finger to roll over any other whenever it was advantageous - the thumb was not unique and had to be "free". However, every finger was different. Thumb over (as well as other fingers) was especially useful in double chromatic scales (thirds, etc.). To Chopin, the piano had to speak and sing; to Liszt, it was an orchestra. Since C major scale is more difficult, he used B major to teach relaxation and legato; ironically it is better to start learning scales staccato, to eliminate the difficult legato problems although, in the end, he always came back to his specialty - legato. Wide arpeggios require a supple hand more than a wide reach. Rubato is one in which the rhythm is strictly held while time is borrowed and returned in the melody. [My opinion is that this definition is often misquoted and misunderstood; just because he said that a few times, it does not mean that he applied it to everything. This definition of rubato applied specifically to the situation in which the RH plays rubato while the LH keeps strict time. Chopin certainly also allowed that rubato was a freedom from strict tempo for the sake of expression.] Chopin preferred the Pleyel, a piano with very light action. His music is definitely harder to play on modern instruments, especially the pianissimo and legato. **A MUST READ.**

Elson, Margaret, "Passionate Practice", 2002, 108P., a few references.

Written from the point of view of a psychologist. Contains precious little analytical advice on technical development and practice methods. Has a nice treatment of mental visualization (see Mental Play in Chang's book). Useful for those who commit psychological mistakes (who doesn't?), and covers the correct/wrong mental approaches and environmental factors from practice to performance. Good for starting students not yet familiar with daily requirements of pianists or those with no performing experience. Art and psychology can be surprisingly close –"artist type" readers may enjoy this short book.

Fink, Seymour, "Mastering Piano Technique", 1992, 187P., excellent list of suggested reading; video also available.

Most scholarly of all books listed here, as befits the work of a university professor. Scientific treatise using correct terminology (in contrast to Whiteside who was frequently unaware of standard terminology), easy to understand, starts with human anatomy and its relation to the piano, followed by a list of movements involved in playing, including pedal. Scale must not be played thumb under, but thumb under is an important movement (P. 115). Illustrates each movement and the corresponding piano exercises. Good description of gravity drop. Strictly mechanical approach, but this book emphasizes production of richer tone and playing with emotion. The motions are difficult to decipher from diagrams, making it desirable to purchase the video. You must read either Fink or Sandor; preferably both since they approach similar subjects from different points of view. Some readers may love one and hate the other. Fink is based on exercises, Sandor is based more on examples from classical compositions.

The first half is a treatment of all the basic motions and exercises for these motions. These include: pronation, supination, abduction, adduction, hand positions (extended, palm, claw), finger strokes, motions of the forearm, upper arm, shoulder (push, pull, cycling), etc. The second section applies these motions to examples from famous classics, from Ravel, Debussy, and Rachmaninoff, to Chopin, Beethoven, Mozart, and many others. **MUST READ** either this or Sandor.

Fraser, Alan, "The Craft of Piano Playing", 2003, 431P., bibliography.

Contains an incredible amount of information, some of which are the most advanced that you can find anywhere; however, the book lacks organization, leaving you to pick up the nuggets as he throws them out. The materials are extremely broad-based, taking teachings from Feldenkrais to awareness training and Tai Chi Chuan to Chi-Gung, but clearly from a well educated concert pianist/composer. The most useful are precise instructions on specific technical material: Chopin's glissando motion (finger "split"), the amount of note over-lap in legato, playing with sides of fingers, interpretation errors in otherwise useful concepts such as arm weight, correct use of thumb, chord attack type exercises, octaves, fortissimo, developing extensor muscles, uses of forearm rotation, musicality: rhythm-phrasing-orchestration, etc., etc. The only weakness I could find was that he comes so awfully close to the ultimate truth, but doesn't quite get there – there is still room for improvement, and the reader should look for these advanced areas where even newer ideas may be hiding. **A MUST READ**; more informative than Fink or Sandor in some respects.

Gieseking, Walter, and Leimer, Karl, "Piano Technique", 2 books in one, 1972, no references. Teaching lineage: Leimer-Gieseking.

First book: Gieseking, 77P. Importance of listening, "whole body" method (a la arm weight school), concentration, precise practice, attention to detail. Excellent treatment of how to analyze a composition for practicing and memorizing. This book is representative of most books written by these great performers. Typical advice on technique is, "Concentration, precise practice, and attention to detail will automatically lead to technique" or "Use your ear" or "All notes of a chord must sound together" without any advice on how to actually acquire such skills.

Takes you through how to practice Bach's Invention in C major (#1), Three Part Invention in C major (#1) and Beethoven's Sonata #1, but more from analysis and interpretation than technical skill points of view. He guides you through the first 3 movements of this Sonata, then dismisses the most technically demanding 4th movement as "presenting no new problems"! Note that this last movement requires a strong, difficult, and very fast 5,2,4 fingering followed by a thumb-over descending arpeggio in the LH and rapid and accurate large chord jumps in the RH. These are where we would have wanted some advice from Gieseking. Chang's book plugs up this hole by providing the missing guidance in Chapt. One, section III.8. Worth reading even just for the specific guidance on the above pieces.

Second book: Leimer, 56P., no references. Importance of rhythm, counting, accurate timing, phrasing. Excellent section on pedaling. Contains some specific information that is difficult to find elsewhere.

Green, Barry, and Gallwey, Timothy, "The Inner Game of Music", 1986, 225P., no references. Mental approach to music; relaxation, awareness, trust. Almost no technical piano playing instruction. Only for those who think that mental attitude is the key to playing piano. Those interested in specific instructions for practice will find little useful information.

Hinson, Maurice, "Guide to the Pianist's Repertoire", 2000, 933P., large bibliography. Very complete compilation of piano compositions, with brief descriptions of important information/characteristics of each, degree of difficulty, availability of music scores, useful references for each composition, etc. Main part is "Composers: solo works in Various Editions", then many useful groupings: Anthologies and Collections (by nationality, contemporary, Bach family, etc), Recital programs by Rubinstein, Busoni, and Gabrilowitsch, and special indexes (Black Composers, Women Composers, under Nationality, etc.).

Hofman, Josef, "Piano Playing, With Piano Questions Answered", 1909, 183P., no references. Teaching lineage: Moszkowki, Rubinstein.
The first half deals with very useful general rules and the second half is in question and answer form. Most of the book discusses general concepts; not much detailed technical instruction. Not an essential book for technique, but makes nice side reading.

Lhevine, Josef, "Basic Principles in Piano Playing", 1972, 48P., no references.
Excellent treatment of how to produce good tone. Brief discussions of: basic knowledge of keys, scales, etc., rhythm, ear training, soft & loud, accuracy, staccato, legato, memorizing, practice time, velocity, pedal. Mostly superficial -- book is too short. Good general summary, but lacks specific details and does not contain material you cannot find elsewhere.

Lloyd, Norman, "The Golden Encyclopedia of Music", Golden Press, NY, 1968,
A handy music encyclopedia where you can find just about everything in one place.

Mark, Thomas, "What Every Pianist Needs To Know About The Body", 2003, 155P., can purchase companion video; no references or index but has 8 suggested reading material.
One of best treatments of human anatomy and its relation to piano playing (actually any keyboard), with section for organists and injury/recovery; scholarly and medically/scientifically/technically accurate. Book is not about technique but about preparing the body/arm/hand for technique and covers discussions on practically every bone/muscle from head to toe. Also has numerous discussions on correct/wrong ways to play, such as proper thumb motions that agree with promoters of "thumb over", dangers of curled fingers (debunks belief that flat fingers cause injury), need for acceleration of key drop (gravity drop), importance of the tactile awareness of the front finger pad, etc.

Mathieu, W. A., "Harmonic Experience", 1997, 563P., bibliography, extensively indexed.
An advanced book on the *experience* of harmony; I don't have the music theory education to truly evaluate this book, but will review it from the point of view of an amateur pianist curious about harmony. It starts with the just intonations: unison, octave, fifths, etc., and their relationships to primes 1,2,3,5,& 7. The harmonies are actually experienced by singing over a drone, such as the Indian tamboura. Then reviews the concept of a lattice of notes for tracking harmony, and then the scales, from Lydian through Phrygian. An interesting observation is how the 7th partial used in blues

music fits into this scheme. Most of the book is devoted to the myriads of ways in which Equal temperament affects harmony which may be great for composers confined to this temperament, but a disappointment for someone seeking simple fundamental principles of harmony and harmonic progressions (which don't strictly exist in reality because of the Pythagorean comma and its consequences). Thus musicians have no choice but to explore what is possible with *the* chromatic scale, and Mathieu does a terrific job of discussing the issues that harmony specialists struggle with. Thus cataloguing the harmonies in this imperfect system becomes an enormous task, even when confined to Equal temperament, where you can base the catalogue on the various commas – remember, he does all this with respect to how you *feel* about these harmonies, not by counting frequencies. To give you some idea of the contents:

"There are many books that this book is not: it is not a book about counterpoint, or figured bass, or melodic or rhythmic structure, or compositional development, although all of those subjects come into play. It is a harmony book that is meant to reconcile and go beyond, but not supplant, traditional texts. . . . . .

REVIEW OF THEORY: We recognize low-prime frequency ratios between tones as more than agreeable – they are affective in various ways. The primes 2, 3, 5, and 7 serve as norms both as given by nature and internalized by experience: inner/internalized norms. The overtone series is only one incarnation of this, not the source. . . . .

Flaws and Limits of the Theory: . . . . Anyone can create a subjective tautology. The notion that affective commas are the driving force behind equal-tempered harmony can never be objectively proved. What is presented in this book is an elaborate, operative system based on what is presumed to be the clear sensibilities of the investigator. . . . . . ."

I certainly agree with that; this is not a conventional textbook on harmony for the beginner; for that, there is more practical information in the "Jazz, Fake Books and Improvisation" review section below.

Prokop, Richard, "Piano Power, a Breakthrough Approach to Improving your Technique", 1999, 108P., a few references.

This book is like a condensed form of Chang. This pianist, piano teacher, and composer has done an excellent job of researching piano technique. He briefly covers HS and segmental practice, specifics on relaxation, need for musical play, memorization, and mental play. Excellent photos of finger/hand positions, and examples of what/how to perform exercises. Importance of extensor muscles (lifting fingers); accurate lifting of fingers (and pedals), exercises for lifting each finger. Gives the best description of the bones, tendons, and muscles of the finger/hand/arm and how/what motions are controlled by each. Detailed analysis of the advantages/disadvantages of small, medium, and large hands. His use of "Theorems and Proofs" is somewhat silly because piano practice is not math, and this compact book is incomplete, missing items such as Thumb Over versus Thumb Under (he treats only TU), chord attack, arpeggios, etc., and there is no space to treat each topic adequately. **A MUST READ**, as you will see the same concepts in Chang, but from a different person.

Richman, Howard, "Super Sight-Reading Secrets", 1986, 48P., no references.

This is the best book on sight reading. It contains all the fundamentals; they are described in complete detail, teaching us all the correct terminology and methodologies. It starts from how to read music, for the beginner, and advances logically all the way to advanced sight reading levels; it is especially helpful for the beginner. It is also concise, so you should read the whole book once before starting any actual drills/exercises. Starts with how to psychologically approach sight reading. Basic components of sight reading are Pitch, Rhythm, and Fingering. After an excellent introduction to music notations, appropriate drills are given. Then the sight reading process is broken down into its component steps of visual, neural, muscular, and aural processes that start with the music score and end up as music. This is followed by drills for learning "keyboard orientation" (finding the notes without looking at the keyboard) and "visual perception" (instantly recognizing what to play).

Depending on the person, it may take from 3 months to 4 years to learn; should practice every day. Finally, about one page of ideas on advanced sight reading. **A MUST READ.**

Sandor, Gyorgy, "On Piano Playing", 1995, 240P, no references!

Teaching lineage: Bartok-Kodaly-Sandor.

A complete and scholarly, but the most expensive, book. Contains most of the material in Fink, stresses arm weight methods. Discusses: free fall, scale (thumb-over method; has most detailed description of scale and arpeggio playing, P. 52-78), rotation, staccato, thrust, pedals, tone, practicing, memorization, performance. Takes you through learning the entire Waldstein Sonata (Beethoven).

Numerous examples on how to apply the principles of the book to compositions from Chopin, Bach, Liszt, Beethoven, Haydn, Brahms, Schumann, many others. This book is very complete; it covers subjects from the effect of music on emotions to discussions of the piano, human anatomy, and basic playing motions, to performing and recording; however, many topics are not treated in sufficient detail. A major defect of this book is the absence of any references, casting doubt on whether there was sufficient research to support the contents of the book. A **MUST READ**, but Fink will give you similar information at lower cost.

Sherman, Russell, "Piano Pieces", 1997, no references.

Consists of five sections dealing with playing, teaching, cultural issues, musical scores, and "everything else". The contents are arranged in no particular order, with no real solutions or conclusions. Discusses the politics of art (music), opinions, judgments, and observations that pianists can relate with; whether non-pianists can understand these musings is questionable but will provide insight. Seating position, thumb serves as momentum balance. Fingers = troops, but body = supply line, support, carrier ship, and manufacturing. Fingers vs. body = sales vs. CEO; thus controlling fingers does not result in music. Easy pieces are valuable for learning to make music. What is the value of learning piano? It is not even a good career, financially. Should you slide the finger? What is involved in beauty or character of piano sound? How important are quality pianos and good tuners? Pros and cons of competitions (mostly cons): preparing for competitions is not making music and often becomes more like an athletic competition; is the stress and effort worth it?; judging is never perfect.

Deals with issues faced by pianists, teachers and parents; describes many of the major problems but presents few solutions. This book touches on numerous issues, but is as aimless as its title. Read it only if you have time to burn.

Suzuki, Shinichi (et al), two books (there are more):

"The Suzuki Concept: An Introduction to a Successful Method for Early Music Education", 1973, 216P., no references, has large, excellent bibliography.

Mostly for violin education starting at an early age. One small chapter (7 pages) on piano teaching methods.

"HOW TO TEACH SUZUKI PIANO", 1993, 21P., no references.

A brief, general outline of the Suzuki Piano methods. The methods described by Chang are in general agreement with the Suzuki methods. Let baby listen; no Beyer, Czerny, Hanon or etudes (even Chopin!); must perform; teachers must have uniform teaching methods and open discussions (research groups); balance memory and reading, but memorizing is more important. Teachers are given a small set of graded music on which to base their lessons. Suzuki is a centrally controlled teaching school; as such, it has many of the advantages of the faculties of established music universities and colleges, but the academic level is, in general, lower. Suzuki teachers are at least one notch above the average private teacher because they must meet certain minimum standards. Describes many general approaches to teaching, but few specifics on how to practice piano for technique. Classic example of how an authoritarian system can eliminate bad teachers by imposing minimum standards, but good "Suzuki piano teachers" must find their own materials beyond what

Suzuki provides.

Taylor, Ronald, "Franz Liszt, the Man and the Musician", Universe Books, NY, 1986, 285P., bibliography, index.

Biography – another endless accounts of his numerous liaisons, none of whom he married (that produced at least 3 offspring). The list of musicians, most of whom he met, is astounding: Wagner, both Schumanns, Paganini, Chopin, Beethoven, Schubert, Berlioz, Brahms, Salieri, etc., not to mention the equally famous writers, artists, etc., as also covered by Walker (no need to read both books – read Walker or this one). Distressingly little information on how Liszt learned to play. He disliked the curled finger position as producing dry sounds (P. 32) and used a flexible system in which the fingers changed to meet each requirement. Other teaching methods mentioned are the well known litany of pedagogical tools such as encouragement versus criticism, too much body or arm motion, etc., that do not address the specifics of technical play.

Walker, Alan, "Franz Liszt, The Virtuoso Years, 1811-1847", 1983, 481P., references.

This is the first of 3 books; it covers the period from Liszt's birth until the time he decided to stop performing at age 36. The second book covers the years 1848-1861, when he mainly devoted himself to composing. The third book covers the years 1861-1886, his final years. I review only the first book here.

Liszt is known as the greatest pianist of all time. Therefore, we would expect to learn the most about how to acquire technique from him. Unfortunately, every book or article written about Liszt is an absolute disappointment from that point of view. Perhaps technique was like a "trade secret" in Liszt's time and his lessons were never documented. Paganini practiced in complete secrecy, and even covertly tuned his violin differently in order attain results no one else could. Chopin, on the other hand, was a composer and professional teacher - those were his sources of income, and there are more accounts of his lessons. Liszt's claim to fame was his performances. His success in this regard is reflected in the fact that practically every book on Liszt is an endless and repetitive chronicle of his incredible performances. This secrecy might explain why so many pianists of the time claim to have been students of Liszt yet they seldom describe Liszt's teaching methods in any useful detail. However, when these details are probed among today's teachers of the "Liszt school", they are found to use similar methods (hands separate, shorten difficult passages, chord attack, etc.). Another possibility is that Liszt's concepts of technique were too deep and complex to be reduced into simple analytical explanations, an idea that conveniently played into the adulation of "prodigies" and "talent" that was a foundation of their commercial success. In reality, Chang's book shows that the fundamental elements are almost childishly simple (once someone explains them to you), almost common sense to someone like Liszt, and too obvious to be bothered with. My guess is that he was simply unable to translate what was in his fingers to a teachable system. Whatever the real reasons, Liszt's teaching methods were never adequately documented. One legacy that Liszt left us is the well-chronicled fact that the kinds of feats he performed are humanly possible. This is important, because it means that we can all do similar things if we can rediscover how he did it. Many pianists have, and I hope that my book is a step in the right direction for producing a written documentation of the best known practice methods.

Walker's book is typical of other books on Liszt that I have read, and is basically a chronicle of Liszt's life, not a textbook on how to learn piano. As such, it is one of the best Liszt biographies and contains numerous discussions on particular compositions with specific pianistic demands and difficulties. Unfortunately, a description of an impossible passage "that was executed with the greatest of ease" does not teach us how to do it. This lack of technical teaching information is surprising in view of the fact that bibliographical accounts of Liszt number well over ten thousand! In fact, any useful technical information we might glean from this book must be deduced from the contents using our own knowledge of the piano (see the "relaxation" example below). The section entitled "Liszt and the Keyboard" (P. 285-318) contains a few pointers on how to play. As in all three books, Liszt is revered as a demi-god who can do no wrong, even endowed with super hands somehow configured ideally for the piano -- he could reach a tenth easily. This bias reduces credibility and the incessant, repetitive accounts of superhuman performances create a boredom that detracts from the vast amount of revealing and fascinating historical details in these books.

From the point of view of "incredible performances" resulting in broken strings, perhaps an interesting observation is that Liszt was a thin, sickly man in early youth. At age three, he was given up for dead after an illness and they even ordered a coffin. He started piano sometime before age six and didn't even have a decent practice piano until seven, because his family was so poor. He was taught by his father, a talented musician, passable pianist and close acquaintance of Haydn, and was steeped in music since birth. Nonetheless, by seven, he was "amazing his parents with piano playing and was already composing". Such reports do not do justice to his father who was probably most influential in Liszt's rapid development. Czerny was his first "real" teacher, at age 11 (when Czerny notes that Franz didn't even know proper fingerings), and Czerny claims to have taught Franz all of his fundamental skills. However, he acknowledges that Franz was already an obvious prodigy when they were first introduced (he could sight read practically anything) -- which seems suspiciously inconsistent. Franz actually rebelled at Czerny's drills, but nevertheless used exercises extensively for his technical developments and expressed the greatest respect for his teacher as well as Beethoven. The things he practiced were the fundamentals: runs, jumps, repeat notes. My interpretation is that these were not mindless repetitions for building muscle but skill exercises with specific objectives in mind, and once the objectives were achieved, he would move on to new ones.

But how does a frail person perform "impossible" exercises to exhaustion? By relaxing! Liszt may have been the world's greatest expert on relaxing, out of necessity. Concerning relaxation, it may not be a coincidence that Paganini was also a sickly man. By the time he became famous, in his thirties, Paganini had syphilis, and his health further deteriorated because of an addiction to gambling and contraction of tuberculosis. Yet, these two men of poor health were the two greatest masters over their instruments (as an adult, Liszt was comparatively healthy for his time). The fact that both were not physically robust indicates that the energy for superhuman performances does not come from athletic muscle power but, rather, from complete mastery over relaxation. Chopin was also on the frail side, and contracted tuberculosis. A sad historical note, in addition to Paganini's poor health and the grotesque consequences of the primitive surgical attempts of that time, is the circumstances of his ghastly death, as there was a delay in his burial and he was left to rot in a concrete cistern.

Another notable teacher of Liszt was Saliery who taught him composition and theory. Saliery also taught Schubert, but Liszt never met him. By then Saliery was over 70 years old and, for years, had been suffering under the suspicion of having poisoned Mozart out of jealousy. Liszt was still improving at age 19. His feats are credited with popularizing the piano. He is credited with inventing the piano recital (by bring it out of the salon and into the concert hall). One of his devices was the use of many pianos, as well as many pianists. He even played multi-piano concerts with Chopin and other luminaries of his time. This climaxed in extravaganzas with up to 6 pianos, advertised as a "concert of 60 fingers". In one stretch of 10 weeks, he played 21 concerts and 80 works, 50 from memory. That he could so enthrall his audiences was the more surprising because adequate pianos (Steinway, Bechstein) were not available until the 1860s, almost 20 years after he stopped concertizing.

Whiteside, Abby, "On Piano Playing", 2 books in one, 1997, no references.
This is a re-publication of "Indispensables of Piano Playing" (1955), and "Mastering Chopin Etudes and Other Essays" (1969).
Teaching lineage: Ganz-Whiteside.

First book: "Indispensables of Piano Playing", 155P.
Uses non-standard English, convoluted logic, biblical phraseology, long winded and repetitive.

Contents are excellent, but the terrible write-up makes learning unproductive. Many of the ideas she describes appear in other books but she may have originated (or rediscovered) most of them. Although I had difficulty reading this book, others have claimed that it is easier to understand if you can read it rapidly. This is because she often takes a paragraph or even a page to describe something that can be written in one sentence.

Almost the entire book is like this (P54): "Q: Can Weight - an inert pressure - help develop facility? A: It is exactly the inert pressure of weight which cannot be used for speed. Words are important in teaching. Words of action are needed to suggest the coordination for speed. Weight does not suggest the muscular activity which moves the weight of the arm. It does suggest an inert pressure." I did not pick this section because it was particularly convoluted -- it was picked at random by opening the book with my eyes closed.

Contents: Must follow her methods religiously; why rhythm is important, the body-arms-hand-finger combination has infinite possibilities of which we are mostly unaware; thumb under scale is reviled; functions of each part of anatomy for playing piano (horizontal, in-out, vertical motions); discussions on creating emotion, memorizing, pedaling, phrasing, trills, scales, octaves, teaching methods. Points out importance of rhythm to music and how to attain this using outlining (P. 141). Czerny and Hanon are useless or worse.

The following is her attack on passing thumb-under for playing scales, excerpted from over two pages; the ( ) are my clarifications:

"*Passing.* Here we are faced with a welter of stress in traditional teaching concerning the exact movements that should take place with finger and thumbs. . . . .If I could blast these concepts right out of existence I would not hesitate to do so. That is how faulty and pernicious I think they are. They can literally cripple a pianist . . . . . If it (playing perfect scales) seems quite hopelessly impossible and you have no glimmer of an idea as to how it can be accomplished, then you are trying with a coordination which actually makes a scale an impossible feat. It means thumb snapping under the palm and reaching for position; and fingers trying to reach over the thumb and seeking a legato key connection. It doesn't matter if the performer achieving the swift and beautiful scales and arpeggios tells you he does just that (thumb under) -- it isn't true. No suggestion is meant that he is lying, but simply that he was successful in discarding the coordination that he was taught when the occasion arose which made it inadequate . . . . They (thumb under players) have to be re-educated physically to a new pattern of coordination; and that re-education can mean a period of wretched misery to them. . . . . . Action (for thumb over passing) can be taken through the shoulder joint in any direction. The top arm can move so that the elbow end of the humerus can describe a segment of a circle, up or down, in and out, back and forth, or around and about . . (etc., an entire page of this type of instruction on how to play thumb over). . . . .With control from center the entire coordination operates to make it easy to have a finger available at the moment it is needed . . . . The best proof of this statement is a beautiful scale or arpeggio played with complete disregard for any conventional fingering. This often happens with a gifted, untaught pianist . . . . For passing (thumb over), the top arm acts as fulcrum for all the "other techniques" involving the forearm and hand; flexion and extension at elbow, rotary action, and lateral hand action at wrist, and last and least, lateral action of fingers and thumb. . . . . Between rotary action and alternating action, passing is made as easy as it looks when the expert does it."

Second book: "Mastering the Chopin Etudes and Other Essays", 206P, no references. Compendium of edited Whiteside manuscripts; much more readable because they were edited by her students, and contains most of the ideas of the first book, based on the playing of the Chopin etudes which were chosen for their unequaled musical content as much as for their technical challenge. This is like a catechism to the above bible; may be a good idea to read this book before reading the first book above. Describes outlining in some detail: P. 54-61 basic description, and P.191-193 basic definition, with more examples on P.105-107 and P. 193-196. Although outlining can be used to overcome technical difficulties, it is more valuable for learning, or learning to play, the musical concept of the composition.

These two books *are* a diamond mine of practical ideas; but like a diamond mine, you must dig deep and you never know where it's buried. The use of the Chopin Etudes here turns out not to be a random pick; most of Whiteside's basic tenets were already taught by Chopin (see Eigeldinger); however, Eigeldinger's book was written long after Whiteside's book and she was probably unaware of many of Chopin's methods.

There is no middle ground -- you will either love Whiteside for the treasure trove of information or hate it because it is unreadable, repetitive, and unorganized.

Weinreich, G., "The Coupled Motions of Piano Strings", Scientific American, Jan., 1979, P. 118-127.

This is a good article on motions of piano strings if you need to learn the very basics. However, the article is not well written and the experiments were not well conducted; but we should be cognizant of the limited resources that the author probably had. Even more advanced research had surely been conducted long before 1979 by piano manufacturers and acoustics scientists. I will discuss below some of the deficiencies that I have found in this article in the hope that the awareness of these deficiencies will enable the reader to glean more helpful information from this publication and avoid being misled.

There is no information at all on the specific frequencies of the notes that were investigated. Since the behavior of piano strings is so frequency dependent, this is a vital piece of information that is missing. Keep this in mind as you read the article, as many of the results will be difficult to interpret without knowing the frequency at which the experiments were conducted and therefore become of questionable value. For example, different experiments might have been performed at different frequencies, in which case we would not know how to compare them.

The center graph in the lower row of figures on P. 121 (there are no figure numbers anywhere in this article!) is not adequately explained. The article, later on, proposes that the vertical modes produce the prompt sound. The figure therefore might be interpreted as showing the sustain of a single string. I know of no note on a grand piano having a single string sustain of less than 5 seconds as suggested by the figure. The left hand figure of the upper row of graphs from a single string shows a sustain of over 15 seconds, in agreement with my cursory measurements on an actual grand. Thus the two plots from single strings appear to be contradictory. The upper plot measured sound pressure whereas the lower one measured string displacement, so that they may not be strictly comparable, but we would have liked the author to at least provide some explanation of this apparent discrepancy. Strings with very different frequencies may have been used for the two plots.

In reference to these figures, there is this sentence: "I used a sensitive electronic probe to separately measure the vertical and horizontal motions of a single string," with no further information. Now any investigator in this field would be very interested in how the author did it. In proper scientific reporting, it is normal (generally *required*) practice to identify the equipment (usually including the manufacturer and model numbers) and even how it was operated. The resultant data are some of the few new information presented in this paper and are therefore of utmost importance in this article. Future investigators will probably have to follow up along this line of study by measuring string displacements in greater detail and will need this information on instrumentation.

The four figures on page 122 are not referenced anywhere in the article. Thus it is left to us to guess about which parts of the article pertain to them. Also, my guess is that the lower two plots showing oscillations are just schematics and do not represent anything close to actual data. Otherwise, the prompt sound would be over in about 1/40th of a second, according to these plots. The curves plotted in these two lower figures are purely imaginary in addition to being schematic. There are no data to back them up. In fact the article presents no other new data and the discussions on the ensuing 5 pages (out of an 8 page article) are basically a review of known acoustical principles. As such, the descriptions of the springy, massive, and resistive terminations, as well as the sympathetic vibrations, should be qualitatively valid.

The major thesis of this article is that the piano is unique because it has an after-sound and that the proper tuning of the after-sound is the essence of good tuning and creates the unique piano music. My difficulty with this thesis is that the prompt sound typically lasts over 5 seconds. Very few piano notes are played for that long. Therefore, essentially all of piano music is played using only the prompt sound. In fact, piano tuners use mainly the prompt sound (as defined here) to tune. In addition, the after-sound is at least 30 db less in power; that is only a few percent of the initial sound. It will be completely drowned out by all the other notes in any piece of music. What is happening in reality is that whatever is controlling the quality of the piano sound controls both the prompt and after-sounds, and what we need is a treatise that sheds light on this mechanism.

Finally, we need a publication with proper references so that we can know what has or has not been previously investigated (In defense of the author, Scientific American does not allow any references except references to previously published articles in Scientific American. This makes it necessary to write articles that are "self-contained", which this article is not. According to Reblitz [P. 14], there is a 1965 Scientific American article on "The Physics of the Piano", but that article is not referenced in this report.).

Five Lectures on the Acoustics of the Piano, Royal Institute of Technology Seminar, Anders Askenfelt, Ed., Stockholm, May 27, 1988.
Some of the most advanced series of lectures on how the piano produces its sound. The Introduction gives the history of the piano and presents the terminology and background information needed to understand the lectures.

The first lecture discusses piano design factors that influence tone and acoustical performance. Hammers, soundboards, case, plate, strings, tuning pins, and how they work together. Tuners tune the transverse vibrational modes of the string, but the longitudinal modes are fixed by the string and scale design and cannot be controlled by the tuner, yet have audible effects.

The second lecture focuses on the piano tone. The hammer has two bending modes, a shank flex mode and a faster vibrational mode. The first is caused by the rapid acceleration of the hammer, much like the flex of the golf club. The second is most pronounced when the hammer bounces back from the strings, but can also be excited on its way towards the strings. Clearly, the backcheck is an important tool the pianist can use to reduce or control these extraneous hammer motions, and thereby control the tone. The actual time dependent string motion is totally unlike the motion of vibrating strings shown in text books with fundamentals and harmonics that are integral fractional wavelengths that fit neatly between the fixed ends of the string. It is actually a set of traveling waves launched by the hammer towards the bridge and towards the agraffe. These travel so fast that the hammer is "stuck" on the strings for quite a few passes of these traveling waves back and forth, and it is the force of one of these waves hitting the hammer that eventually throws it back towards the backcheck. Then, how are the fundamentals and partials created? Simple - they are just the Fourier components of the traveling waves! In non-math terms, what this means is that the only traveling waves possible in this system are waves that have nodes at both ends because the system is constrained by the fixed ends. The sustain and harmonic distribution are extremely sensitive to the exact properties of the hammer, such as size, weight, shape, hardness, etc.

The strings transfer their vibrations to the soundboard (SB) via the bridge and the efficiency of this process can be determined by measuring the acoustical impedance match. This energy transfer is complicated by the resonances in the SB produced by its normal modes of vibration because the resonances produce peaks and valleys in the impedance/frequency curve. The efficiency of sound production is low at low frequency because the air can make an "end run" around the piano so that a compressive wave above the SB can cancel the vacuum underneath it when the SB is vibrating up (and vice versa when moving down). At high frequency, the SB vibrations create numerous small areas moving in opposite directions. Because of their proximity, compressed air in one area can cancel an adjacent vacuum area, resulting in less sound. This explains why a small increase in piano size can greatly increase sound production, especially for the low frequencies. These complications make it clear that matching the acoustical impedances across all the notes of the piano is a monumental task, and explains why good pianos are so expensive.

The above is my attempt at a brief translation of highly technical material, and is probably not 100% correct. My main purpose is to give the reader some idea of the contents of the lectures. Clearly, this web site contains very educational material.

Reviewed Books: Jazz, Fake Books and Improvisation

Cannel, Ward, and Marx, Fred, "How to play the piano despite years of lessons", What music is, and how to make it at home, 239P., 1976, no references.
Starts by bashing misconceptions concerning talent, repeated exercises, superiority of classical music, etc., that discourage us from becoming musicians. Great book for beginners, starting with the most basic information, playing single note melodies, etc. You learn by playing melodies/songs from the very beginning. One major mistake is – no fingering instructions anywhere in entire book! Then basic chords (3 notes), then "skeletal arrangement", a universal scheme of RH melody and LH accompaniment that enables you to play almost anything. Then 4-note chords, rhythm (important!), arpeggios. Bolero (rhumba, beguine, calypso), tango, shuffle. Circle of 5ths and chord progressions: classical, romantic, impressionist, modern – very practical and useful. Playing by ear, improvisation. How to end any piece. A well-designed sequence from very simple to more complex concepts, leading you along the simplest possible route. A supplement with 29 popular songs to practice with and learn from (guitar and organist markings, changing arrangements on the fly, making things more interesting, etc.). Full of easy-to-understand explanations of basic concepts and useful tricks. This book is not for those looking to acquire technique and play difficult material.

Neely, Blake, "How to Play from a Fake Book", 87P., 1999; no references, but has a good list of fake books.
Excellent starter book; fake books are easy because you don't need to learn chord progressions – they are indicated on the music, so you won't learn about the circle of fifths here. However, you must know scales and chords well; fake books are all about the accompaniments – the LH. Starts very easily, playing only one note with the LH (while RH plays single note melodies), then 5ths, and 3-note chords. Then progresses through all the useful chords, chord symbols, how to make things sound better, etc. From the beginning, each concept is illustrated by actually playing a song (60 in all). Inversions, common-tone voicing, arpeggios, major/minor chords, dominant 7th, augmented, diminished, larger chords, etc. Major faults are: no fingering instructions, almost no discussion of rhythm. Has complete list of: chord symbols and their notes, all scales & key signatures.

Sabatella, Marc, "A Whole Approach to Jazz Improvisation", 85P., 1996, no references, but has a bibliography of fake books, jazz instructional books, and jazz history literature. This book can be browsed free at Jazz Primer.
This not a beginner's book. No actual music to play; teaches the language of jazz, understanding how jazz players play, and improvisation. Detailed definitions/discussions of chords, scales, and chord/scale relationships (swing, bebop, fusion, free improvisation, etc.) – these are the heart of jazz theory, performance, and history; they are also where students must spend the majority of their time. Suggests many names of jazz players that you should listen to ("selected discography"), and a list of 92 "jazz standards" (no music score) including blues, swing, rock, latin, ballad, and standard/modal jazz.

Werner, Kenney, "Effortless Mastery", 191P., 1996, with meditation CD, references as footnotes and lots of suggested listening material.

Mental/spiritual approach to making music; almost no descriptions of the mechanics of playing or how to practice. Detailed instructions on meditation. In the same category as Green and Gallwey, but a different approach. Written for jazz players, but applies to all pianists and other instrumentalists. The first half of book consists of discussions of dysfunctional practice, teaching, performances, etc.; the second half provides solutions, but they are the classic exhortations of "practice until you can play without thinking", and controlling playing through mental attitudes – if you want to see a caricature of the "intuitive method" (see Chang), this is it! This book is for those who believe meditation can solve problems without technical knowledge. However, there is little question that controlling the mind/body system is an important factor in successful musicianship.

Reviewed Videos
Lister-Sink, Barbara, "Freeing The Caged Bird", video, 150 min., 1996, Wingsound, Winston-Salem, NC.

Readers of piano books often want to see videos of the actual playing; well, here it is, professionally produced. The teachings are based on the Alexander Method; discusses finger, hand, arm, body, bench positions and motions. Covers relaxation, gravity drop, basic piano stroke, flat finger vs. curled finger, scales, arpeggios, etc. Tension free (effortless) play, avoiding or recovering from injury, kinesthetic awareness and listening to your own music. Training program for relaxation and technique: methods/exercises/tests for stress release, HS/segmental practice, sight reading, etc. List of bad habits: heavy arms, lifting elbows outward, raising shoulders, unnecessary body motions, curled fingers, collapsed wrist, etc. Piano is a set of skills, not talent. Complex tasks consist of simple steps; start from simplest steps, don't advance to next step until previous is completely mastered. Though not explicitly discussed, you can see TO ("thumb over") in fast passages, students practicing TU, and parallel set type practice, flexible fingers, etc. If you just watch this video without preparation, you will miss a lot; however, if you read the books, every clip will teach you many things. **A MUST VIEW.**

Web Sites, Books, Videos
General
http://www.chopin.pl/
http://www.faqs.org/faqs/music/piano/general-faq/
Bie, Oscar, *The History of the Pianoforte and Pianoforte Players*, Da Capo Press, NY (1966)
Gerig, Reginald R., *Famous Pianists and Their Technique*, Robert B. Luce, Inc., NY (1974).
Harvard Dictionary of Music, by Willi Apel.
Mach, Elyse, *The Liszt Studies*, Associated Music Publishers, 1973.
Schonberg, H. C., *The Great Pianists from Mozart to the Present*, Simon & Schuster, Inc. NY (1987).
Sites with Free Sheet Music and Other Goodies
http://www.pianostreet.com/, a piano forum.
http://www.imslp.org, very large!
http://nma.redhost24-001.com/mambo/index.php, a Mozart site.
http://www.geocities.com/Vienna/Strasse/8840/free.html
http://www.kjos.com/
http://www.rainmusic.com/pianomusic/piano.htm
(Pianist Resource Center)
Piano Instruction (Classical), Teachers, Schools
http://alexandertechnique.com/
http://library.thinkquest.org/15060/data/lessons/
http://musicstaff.com/
http://www.taubman-institute.com/
http://www.cco.caltech.edu/~boyk/piano.htm
http://www.cvc-usa.com

http://www.feldenkrais.com/
http://www.KenFoster.com/
http://www.musicplay.com/
http://staff.mwsc.edu/~bhugh/piano-practice.html
http://www.pianoteachers.com/
http://www.serve.com/marbeth/piano.html
http://www.Suzuki-Music.com/
http://pianoeducation.org/
(Piano Education page)
http://www.wannalearn.com/Fine_Arts/Music/Instruments/Piano/

Books Not Referenced Above, by title

A Dozen A Day, by Edna-Mae Burnam.

A History of Pianoforte Pedalling, by David Rowland.

A Music Learning Theory for Newborn and Young Children, Edwin Gordon, 1997.

All-in-One, by Alfred.

Beethoven on Beethoven: Playing his Piano Music his Way, by William S. Newman, 1988.

Chopin Playing, from the Composer to the Present, by James Mathuen-Campbell, 1981.

Chopin: The Pianist's Repertoire – A Graded Practical Guide, by Eleanor Bailie.

Composing Music, by William Russo.

Comprehensive Guide for Piano Teachers and Piano Auditions Syllabus, published by THE MUSIC EDUCATION LEAGUE, INC., 119 West 57th St., New York 19, NY, (1963).

Debussy, by Marguerite Long.

Faber and Faber Piano Adventures, by Nancy and Randall Faber.

Franz Liszt, The Weimar Years, 1848-1861, by Alan Walker, 1993.

Franz Liszt, The Final Years, 1861-1886, by Alan Walker, 1997.

Golden Age of the Piano, video.

Good Music, Brighter Children: Simple and Practical Ideas to Help Transform Your Child's Life Through the Power of Music, by Sharlene Habermeyer.

Great Pianists on Piano Playing, by James Francis Cooke.

Keeping Mozart in Mind, by Gordon Shaw, 1999.

Learning Sequences in Music, Skill, Content and Patterns, A Music Learning Theory, by Edwin Gordon, 1997.

Making Music for the Joy of It, by Stephanie Judy.

Mikrokosmos, by Bartok.

Music for the Older Beginner, by J. Bastien.

Music magazines: *American Music Teacher, Clavier, Classics, Piano and Keyboard*.

Music Notation, by Gardner Read.

Musicianship for the Older Beginner, by J. Bastien.

On the Sensations of Tone, by Hermann Helmholtz.

Ornamentation, by Valery Lloyd-Watt, Carole Bigler, 1995.

Pedaling the Modern Pianoforte, by York Bowen.

Playing the Piano for Pleasure, by Charles Cooke.

Pianists at Play, by Dean Elder.

Pianists' Guide to Progressive Finger Fitness, by Jana S. and Richard L. Bobo.

Piano for Quitters, video, by Mark Almond.

Piano Lessons, by Noah Adams.

Principles of Piano Technique and Interpretation, by Kendall Taylor.

Raising Musical Kids, by Patrick Kavanaugh.

Second Time Around, by J. Bastien.

Sight Reading at the Keyboard, Schirmer.

Studies in technique, also *Daily Technical Studies*, by Oscar Beringer.

Teaching Music in the Twentieth Century, by R. Abramson, L. Choksy, A. E. Gillespie, D. Woods.

The Amateur Pianist's Companion, by James Ching.

The Art of Piano Fingering, by Penelope Roskell.
The Art of Piano Playing, by Heinrich Neuhaus, 1973.
The Art of Piano Playing: a Scientific Approach, by George Kochevitsky.
The Complete Pianoforte Technique Book, by the Royal Conservatory, Toronto, Canada.
The AB Theory Book, by Eric Taylor (basic, comprehensive theory).
The Complete Idiot's Guide to Music Theory, by Michael Miller.
The Listening Book, by W. A. Matthieu.
The Literature of the Piano, by Ernest Hutchison.
The Music Tree, by Frances Clark.
The Musicians' Guide to Reading and Writing Music, by Dave Stewart.
The Pianist's Guide to Pedaling, by Joseph Banowetz.
The Pianist's Problems, by William S. Newman.
The Technique of Piano Playing, by J. F. Gat.
The Visible and Invisible in Pianoforte Technique, by Matthay, Tobias.
The Well-Tempered Keyboard Teacher, by Uszler, Gordon, Mach.
The Wonders of the Piano, by Cathy Bielefeldt.
Tone Deaf and All Thumbs, by Frank R. Wilson.
Understanding Harmony, by Robert L. Jacobs.
With Your Own Two Hands, by Seymour Bernstein.
20 Lessons in Keyboard Choreography, by Seymour Bernstein.

Piano Technology, Tuning, Parts, Manufacturers

http://musicyellowpages.com/
(Links and addresses of practically every piano parts supplier in US and Canada; must do your own search)
http://www.americanpianofactory.net
http://www.balaams-ass.com/piano/piano.htm
http://www.globetrotter.net/gt/usagers/roule/accord.htm
(Examples of temperaments)
http://www.ptg.org/
(Piano Tuners' Gild web site)
Five Lectures on the Acoustics of the Piano, ed. By Anders Askenfelt, 1990.
Piano Servicing, Tuning, and Rebuilding, by Arthur Reblitz, 2nd Ed., 1993.
The Piano Book, by Larry Fine.
The Piano, its Acoustics, by W. V. McFerrin.
Tuning, by Owen H. Jorgensen.

Injury from Piano Practice

http://eeshop.unl.edu/music.html
Musicians' Injuries: A guide to their Understanding and Prevention, by Nicola Culf, 1998.

Jazz, Chords, Theory, Instruction (Popular Music)

http://www.homespuntapes.com/
An Understandable Guide to Music Theory: The Most Useful Aspects of Theory for Rock, Jazz & Blues Musicians, by Chaz Bufe.
Basic Materials in Music Theory: A Programmed Course, by Paul O. Harder, Greg A. Steinke, 1995.
Blues, Jazz & Rock Riffs for Keyboards, by William Eveleth.
Composing at the Keys, by Sue Shannon.
Elementary Harmony, by William J. Mitchell.
Exploring Basic Blues for Keyboards, by Bill Boyd.
Harmony Book for Beginners, Preston Wade Orem, 1907.
How to Play . . . Blues and Boogie Piano Styles, by Aaron Blumenfeld.
How to Play from a Fake Book, by Michael Esterowitz.
How to Use a Fake Book, by Ann Collins.
    Lead Lines and Chord Changes, by Ann Collins.

Keyboard Musician, by Summy-Birchard, Inc.
Keyboard Musician for the Adult Beginner, by Frances Clark.
Music Theory for the Music Professional, by Richard Sorce.
Scales and Arpeggios for the Jazz Pianist, by Graham Williams.
The AB Guide to Music Theory.
The Jazz Piano Book, by Mark Levine.
The 20-minute Chords and Harmony Workout, by Stuart Isacoff.

Sheet Music, Video, CD, Book, Stores
http://www.cdmusic.com/
http://musicbooksplus.com/
http://www.alfredpub.com/
http://www.bookshop.blackwell.co.uk/
http://www.burtnco.com/
http://www.chappellofbondstreet.co.uk/
http://www.jumpmusic.com/
http://www.sheetmusic1.com/
(Also sells piano parts)

Notes for Translators:

Translators should know some HTML, and be able to provide a site for the web page; Yahoo and AOL should work fine. My vision is that this book will eventually move to some permanent site. All translations should be able to move to the same site. The memory requirement of even all potential translations is modest, since each language requires less than 1 MB. Translators are responsible for their own web sites and will need to keep up with the updates. There is plenty of software for comparing updated versions with older versions, so this should not be a problem, but you will need to keep a copy of the older version in your computer, because the older version will disappear from my web site when it is updated.

Translators should preferably be pianists or piano teachers and know something about the piano itself (tuning, regulation, rebuilding). If the translator is deficient in a particular subject, we can always find helpers just for that subject, so a lack of total expertise by any one translator is not a problem.

I am writing this book on a voluntary basis and cannot afford to pay translators until some benefactor shows up. I will of course be happy to help with anything I can do to expedite the translation, and will provide a link to the translation on my web site (HOME page).

We are clearly pioneering a unique type of internet book which is the wave of the future, and is really exciting. This book should evolve into the most complete textbook on learning piano that is free, always up-to-date, in which errors are eliminated as soon as detected, and which will be available in all major languages. There is no reason why schools and students have to pay for fundamental textbooks from Arithmetic to Zoology. In the future, they will all be downloadable free. The world economy will be helped enormously by making all educational material free and accessible to everyone. It is simply mind boggling to contemplate the future of education on the internet. Because all you need is a few of the best experts in the world to write the textbook, and other volunteers to translate them, funding requirements are negligible compared to the economic benefits. Therefore, translators are not only providing benefits to their countrymen, but are also participating in a brave new experiment that will benefit all pianists, piano teachers, tuners, and the piano industry.

ABOUT THE AUTHOR:

I was born in Taiwan in 1938, grew up in Japan (1945-1958), started piano lessons in 1949, and moved to the U.S. in 1958; received a BS degree in Physics from RPI in Troy, NY, and PhD in Physics from Cornell Univ. in 1967. Worked in analytical research (electron spectroscopy) until 1998, mostly at Bell Labs. The writing of this book originated in an incident in 1978 when I took one of our two daughters to her piano lesson with Mlle. Yvonne Combe. Little did I know that it would change my life, a once in a lifetime experience. After a few years of lessons, our daughters were progressing at unbelievable speed, which my wife and I attributed (mistakenly) to their exceptional musical talent. During this lesson, the teacher took out a frayed book with all the lesson pieces arranged according to difficulty, for choosing a new piece to study. Mlle. Combe said, "Choose whatever you want!!!", and my daughter looked all over the book for what she might like. I couldn't help interfering to ask "Shouldn't she stay within her level of difficulty?" The teacher smiled knowingly with our daughter and answered "Difficulty isn't our problem, is it?" I was so impressed by the implications of what she said that I decided to investigate this teaching method. It took me about 15 years of research to realize that most teachers do not teach practice methods and another 10 years to gather the material for this book.

I taught myself to tune the piano by reading books because, as a married student living on a research stipend and my wife's baby-sitting income, I did not have the money to pay a piano tuner to keep my piano always in tune. Since neither my wife nor I had absolute pitch, I must attribute our daughters' accurate absolute pitch to the fact that our piano was in tune since their birth.

List of Tables, Equations, and Videos

Index

Pages in **bold** are most informative; you can save time by using word search in conjunction with this index.

16601622R00142

Made in the USA
Lexington, KY
03 August 2012